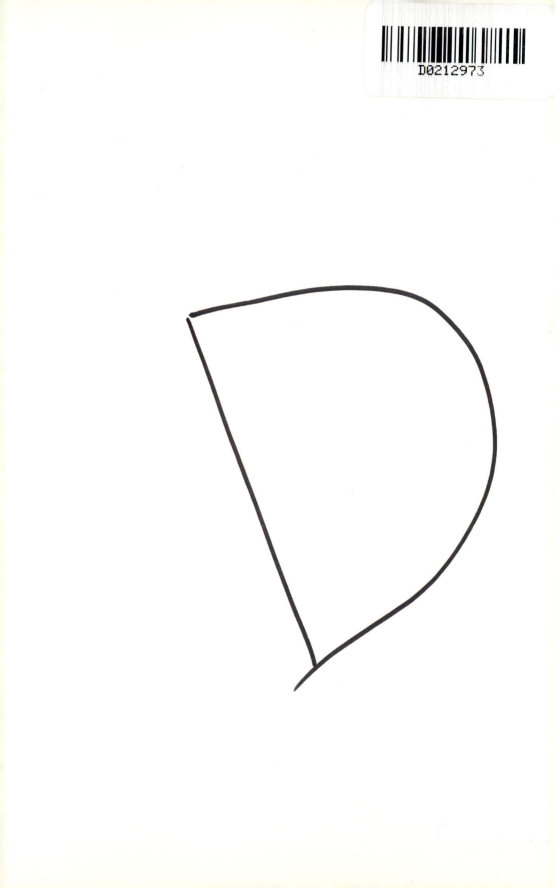

PROTESTANTS ABROAD

Also by David A. Hollinger

After Cloven Tongues of Fire (2013)

Cosmopolitanism and Solidarity (2006)

Postethnic America (1995, 2000, and 2006)

Science, Jews, and Secular Culture (1996)

In the American Province (1985)

Morris R. Cohen and the Scientific Ideal (1975)

The American Intellectual Tradition
  (co-edited with Charles Capper, 7th edition, 2017)

The Humanities and the Dynamics of Inclusion since World War II
  (edited 2006)

Reappraising Oppenheimer: Centennnial Studies and Reflections
  (co-edited with Cathryn Carson, 2005)

Protestants Abroad

HOW MISSIONARIES TRIED TO CHANGE THE WORLD BUT CHANGED AMERICA

{⚊⚊⚊⚊}

David A. Hollinger

ᴠERSITY PRESS

& OXFORD

Copyright © 2017 by Princeton University Press

Published by Princeton University Press,
41 William Street, Princeton, New Jersey 08540
In the United Kingdom: Princeton University Press,
6 Oxford Street, Woodstock, Oxfordshire OX20 1TR

press.princeton.edu

Jacket photograph courtesy of Tiki Davies

ISBN 978-0-691-15843-3

Library of Congress Cataloging-in-Publication Data

Names: Hollinger, David A., author.
Title: Protestants abroad : how missionaries tried to change the world but
    changed America / David A. Hollinger.
Description: Princeton, NJ : Princeton University Press, 2017. | Includes
    bibliographical references and index.
Identifiers: LCCN 2017022440 | ISBN 9780691158433 (hardcover)
Subjects: LCSH: Missions, American—History. | Protestant
    churches—Missions—History. | United States.
Classification: LCC BV2410 .H65 2017 | DDC 266/.02373—dc23 LC record available at
    https://lccn.loc.gov/2017022440

British Library Cataloging-in-Publication Data is available

This book has been composed in Miller

Printed on acid-free paper. ∞

Printed in the United States of America

10 9 8 7 6 5 4 3 2 1

For Joan Heifetz Hollinger

Every valley shall be exalted, and every mountain and hill shall be made low: and the crooked shall be made straight, and the rough places plain.

—ISAIAH 40:4

The first step in the evolution of ethics is a sense of solidarity with other human beings.

—ALBERT SCHWEITZER

CONTENTS

NO, I AM NOT part of a missionary family. It is usually the first question people ask when they learn what I am working on. If this book accomplishes nothing else, I hope it will persuade readers they don't have to be personally connected to missionaries to find them worth understanding.

What most makes missionaries worth understanding is their sustained, intimate engagement with the peoples of the globe beyond the North Atlantic West. Even today, the planet's panorama of societies and cultures remains an enigma to many Americans, inspiring countless prejudices, anxieties, and idealizations. The missionaries were out there early and stayed late. They were transformed by their experience with the peoples of the Middle East, China, India, Japan, and other distant lands. They brought their changed selves and their foreign-influenced children back to the United States. Then they and their children challenged many of the Home Truths dear to the folks who had stayed at home. During the middle decades of the twentieth century, missionary-connected individuals and groups broadened the perspectives of the American public and influenced the operations of many institutions, including federal agencies, universities, churches, foundations, and political advocacy organizations.

I did not realize how important this historical episode was until the 1990s, when I was studying the multiculturalist movement of that era. While writing *Postethnic America: Beyond Multiculturalism* (New York, 1995), I explored earlier affirmations of cultural diversity. I soon recognized Protestant missionaries as precursors of the most defensible aspects of multiculturalism. Although missionaries are often represented as "monocultural," interested only in getting others to adopt their own opinions, I encountered numerous cases of missionaries pushing their fellow Americans to renounce the provinciality of their own society. This sense of the missionaries as diversifiers struck me all the harder because I was just then finishing a book about cosmopolitan Jewish intellectuals, *Science, Jews, and Secular Culture* (Princeton, 1996). The missionaries, I said to myself, are the closest thing to an Anglo-Protestant equivalent of the Jews who dramatically expanded American public life during the same period.

Soon after recognizing these connections, I decided to try to write the book now before you. After a brief start, focusing on interviews that I rushed to do with a number of aging participants in the episode, I put the project aside for several years while completing other research and writing projects. Then I came back to the missionaries and became all the more certain this was the book I must write. Even as I finish *Protestants Abroad*, I remain surprised that such an important aspect of modern American history has not received more sustained scrutiny until now.

Many colleagues with knowledge of particular fields have answered my queries and helped me avoid mistakes. For these ad hoc but in many cases vital collegial favors, I am grateful to Maria Abunnasr, Julia Allen, Joel Alvis, Nancy T. Ammerman, Betty Anderson, Margaret Lavinia Anderson, Kai Bird, Anne Blankenship, Mark A. Bradley, Charlotte Bunch, David Chappell, Jim Cogswell, Robert Cohen, Warren I. Cohen, Peter Conn, Nancy Cott, Philip Dow, R. M. Eaton, Richard Elphick, Kristopher Erskine, Sara Evans, Brian C. Flota, Elizabeth Flowers, Robert Frykenberg, Linda Gesling, Jacqueline Hall, J. E. Heavens, Fred Hoxie, William Hutchison, Donald Keene, David Keightley, Marjorie King, Diane Kunz, Christine Lindner, Thomas Lippman, Laurie Maffly-Kipp, Sarah Miller-Davenport, Jeanne Moskal, Ronald Numbers, George Packard, Kathleen A. Pandora, Elizabeth Perry, Christine Philliou, Mark Pittinger, Laura Premack, Robert Priest, Mark Ramsayer, Barbara Reeves-Ellington, Russell A. Richie, Donald A. Ritchie, Robert Shaffer, Michael H. Shank, Heather J. Sharkey, Winton U. Solberg, David Swartz, Jeremy Treglown, Grant Wacker, Kate Weigand, Hugh Wilford, Lamar Williamson, Alan Willis, Robert Dudley Woodberry, and Peter Zinoman.

Members of families of the men and women I write about in *Protestants Abroad* have been generous in sharing private letters and in answering my questions. Some of these individuals are acknowledged by name in the notes. Talking with them has been one of the most rewarding experiences in the writing of this book.

For comments on an entire draft of this book I am deeply indebted to Joan Heifetz Hollinger, Daniel Immerwahr, James T. Kloppenberg, Bruce Kuklick, Melani McAlister, Yuri Slezkine, and an anonymous reader for Princeton University Press. Others read one or more chapters dealing with parts of my topic on which they had special knowledge. For this invaluable assistance I am grateful to Karen Barkey, Andrew Barshay, Margaret Bendroth, Mary Elizabeth Berry, James T. Campbell, Charles Capper, Ann Cottrell, Nicholas J. Dirks, Maggie Jane Elmore, Joseph Esherick, Ada J. Focer, Charles Hayford, Susan Kupner, Ira Lapidus, Martin E. Marty, James C. McNaughton, Thomas Metcalf, Joanne Meyerowitz, Michael Montesano, Andrew Patrick, E. Bruce Reynolds, Dana L. Robert, Greg Robinson, Thomas J. Sugrue, Matthew Sutton, David Szanton, Wen-hsin Yeh, Marilyn Young, Pauline Yu, and Gene Zubovich.

I am also indebted to the many archivists who helped me identify and access materials essential to this project, including the Bancroft Library at the University of California, Berkeley, the Hoover Institution Library at Stanford University, the Presbyterian Historical Society Library, the Houghton Library at Harvard University, the Schlesinger Library at Harvard University, the Burke Library of Union Theological Seminary, the Seeley Mudd Library of Princeton University, the Methodist Historical Collections at Drew University, the Garrett Library at Northwestern University, the Archives of the University of Pennsylvania, and the Archives of the American University in Beirut. I owe special thanks to Martha Smalley at the Yale Divinity School, Kenneth Call at Wheaton College, and Marcia Tucker at the Institute for Advanced Study.

I have been blessed with a sequence of excellent research assistants, and want here to thank the four who have done the most work on this book: Maggie Jane Elmore, Daniel Immerwahr, Susan Haskell Khan, and Gene Zubovich. I owe these wonderful students to the simple fact of teaching at Berkeley. Another benefit of being at Berkeley, for which I am deeply grateful, is having so many splendid colleagues. Several are named above for their advice. But in addition to those named above, others have listened so often to my talk about missionaries, and have responded so helpfully, that I want to acknowledge here the sustaining friendship of Carol J. Clover, Martin Jay, and Thomas W. Laqueur. To Berkeley I also owe thanks for the generous support of the research fund associated with the Preston Hotchkis Professorship.

This is my third book with Princeton University Press. I am again the beneficiary of this publisher's splendid treatment of its authors. I want especially to acknowledge the wise and steady advice of my editor, Brigitta von Rheinberg, and the excellent work of my copyeditor, Emily Shelton.

While I am not part of a missionary family, I did grow up in a Protestant social setting in which missionaries were important characters. As a child in Idaho and Washington, I remember as house guests a succession of missionaries on furlough from China and India. I did not then fully understand what special cultural beings missionaries were. But every word and gesture of the missionaries, over the dinner table and at church events, alerted me that there was a wider world beyond the small-town America of my experience.

Berkeley, California
November 2016

PROTESTANTS ABROAD

CHAPTER ONE

Introduction

THE PROTESTANT BOOMERANG

THE PROTESTANT FOREIGN missionary project expected to make the world look more like the United States. Instead, it made the United States look more like the world. The missionary encounter with peoples beyond the historically Christian West yielded relatively generous dispositions toward the varieties of humankind, and led the missionaries to question many cherished beliefs of the folks at home. Missionaries, their children, and their closest associates became conspicuous players during the middle decades of the twentieth century in the Foreign Service, universities, foundations, churches, literature, journalism, the military, and several reform movements. Missionary-connected Americans advanced domestic programs that would later be called "multicultural" and foreign policies that prioritized alliances with nonwhite, colonized peoples. More globally conscious than all but a few of their contemporaries, the missionary contingent was the Anglo-Protestant counterpart of the cosmopolitan Jewish intelligentsia whose influence in expanding American public life has been rightly recognized. But while Jewish cosmopolitanism was intensely European, missionary cosmopolitanism was predominantly Asian.

Confidence in the eternal and universal validity of certain values propelled the missionary endeavor. These certainties, including the rudiments of the Christian faith, were expected to achieve a dominant place throughout the globe. But the project had ironic consequences. The "gospel of inclusive brotherhood" preached by the missionaries, observed the Congregationalist leader Buell G. Gallagher in 1946, flew back like a boomerang to the hands of those who had flung it outward, carrying on its return trip an awareness of the provincialism of its original construction.

"The missions boomerang has come back to smite the imperialism of white nations, as well as to confound the churches," wrote Gallagher. Sustained experience with the indigenous peoples abroad gradually led more and more missionaries to appreciate aspects of foreign cultures largely ignored by the classic ideology of missions. Even the pagan religions of Asia turned out to have some redeeming qualities. The "gospel of inclusive brotherhood" changed its meaning: there was a lot more to include than had been discerned at the start. What had been thrown "across Asia, Africa, and the Seven Seas" and supposed to stay there had come back. And when it came back, it was laden with an indictment of "cultural imperialism and arrogant paternalism" and a plea for a more genuinely universal human community.[1]

Gallagher's "boomerang" figure of speech gets across an important reality. Normally we think of a boomerang as returning to its point of origin unchanged. Here, an ideal of universal fraternity became a boomerang when it was immersed in alterity. One could also speak of "blowback."[2] Yet *boomerang* conveys more precisely the essential dynamic: an enterprise formidably driven by ethnocentrism and cultural imperialism—and often linked closely with military, diplomatic, and economic imperialism—generated dialectically a counterreaction that was enabled by the religious ideology of its origin. This counterreaction developed first among missionaries themselves, then spread through a number of religious and secular domains.

The missionary experience cut America and its religious and racial particularities down to size and led missionary-connected Americans to make adjustments. The missionary contingent led the ecumenical movement within Protestantism, joined with their Jewish counterparts in diminishing Christian cultural hegemony in the nation, and facilitated a drift toward post-Protestant secularism. Missionary-connected individuals and groups were prominent in efforts to end the mistreatment of people of non-European ancestry at home and abroad, and they opened the public ear to nonwhite voices within and beyond the United States. Even when missionary-connected individuals were not in the ideological forefront, they supplied the expertise and energy for one endeavor after another that expanded American horizons. They did not all think alike, and they operated in many different arenas, but their efforts often converged. Walter Russell Mead is correct: "A dispassionate study of the American missionary record would probably conclude that the multicultural and relativistic thinking so characteristic of the United States today owes much of its social power to the unexpected consequences of American missions abroad."[3]

The missionary cosmopolitans were not alone in challenging the provinciality of American public life. Other agents and circumstances during the same period posed comparable challenges, from different starting points. These other deprovincializing forces have been extensively studied, and rightly so. They include the popularization of cultural anthropology, the efforts of African Americans to achieve an equitable position in American politics and society, the expansion of secondary and post-secondary education, the federal government's strategic needs during World War II and the Cold War, and the cultural influence of Jewish immigrants from Europe and their offspring. Jews added a distinctly non-Christian element to American public life, especially in politics, the arts, academia, and many professions. Although heavily based on a late nineteenth- and early twentieth-century migration, Jewish cosmopolitanism achieved special prominence with the arrival of intellectuals fleeing Hitler's Europe.

Missionaries brought some public attention to Africa, Latin America, and the South Pacific, but they had the most to say about the regions of the world in which they had been involved in the largest numbers: China, Japan, India, and the Arab societies of western Asia. Missionary cosmopolitanism was more diffuse than Jewish cosmopolitanism. It traded in many fragments of world civilization.[4]

In its heyday the Protestant foreign missionary project was anything but obscure. It was a major feature of the United States from the late nineteenth through the middle of the twentieth century. Thousands of Methodists, Presbyterians, Baptists, Congregationalists, Episcopalians, Dutch Reformed, Quakers, and other kinds of Protestants served abroad. Between 1886 and 1920, more than 10,000 young people were sent out by the Student Volunteer Movement, an aggressive recruiting organization centered on college campuses.[5] In 1925, there were more than 4,000 American missionaries in China, more than 2,400 in India, and more than 1,000 in Japan. Several thousand other American missionaries were widely distributed in smaller fields throughout Asia, Africa, the South Pacific, and Latin America.[6]

But the cultural significance of missionaries was much greater than their numbers. Missionaries were in the vanguard. In 1900 or 1920, a young man or woman thinking of becoming a missionary was contemplating one of the most honorable and widely admired of callings. "Am I a soldier of the cross?" a hymn popular during that era asked. "Must I be carried to the sky on flower beds of ease, while others fight for that prize and sail through bloody seas?"[7] Missionaries were celebrated and revered for the risks they took in advancing abroad truths that their contemporaries at home believed to be universal. For millions who never ventured outside the North Atlantic West, missionaries were not only cultural heroes, but the most intimate and trusted sources of information about the non-European world. Missionaries were the "point persons" of the national community's engagement with peoples beyond the United States and Europe.

The community on whose behalf the missionaries engaged the world was understood as truly national. Missionaries from the major denominations were part of mainstream America. The public life of the United States was then much more heavily Protestant than it is today. Even as late as 1960, anyone in charge of a major enterprise with a substantial opportunity to affect the direction of the society was likely to be at least nominally affiliated with one of the leading Protestant denominations. Despite some exceptions to the rule, all branches of the federal government were chiefly in the hands of people born into Protestant families, whatever their degree of commitment to the doctrines and practices of the faith. The same social demography applied to most other major institutions, including corporations, universities, schools, the service professions, publishing houses, and philanthropic organizations. Protestantism mattered.

Indeed, Protestantism mattered in the United States much more than in any of the other industrialized societies of the North Atlantic West. Some of the Protestant missionaries going abroad from the United Kingdom, the Netherlands, Germany, and the Scandinavian countries also came to believe their own religious and cultural inheritances were too narrow. But except for influencing their own churches, they had little impact. What Anglican missionaries had to say amounted to less because Anglicanism, despite its constitutionally established status, was no longer in 1940 nearly as influential a frame for national life as ecumenical Protestantism remained in the United States. Nor were missionaries the primary source of information about foreign peoples. Colonial empires brought substantial quantities of foreign experience into popular view, and on steeply hierarchical terms. The United States was anomalous. It still possessed an intensely Protestant national culture, and it had fewer civil servants and military personnel going back and forth from colonies to homeland. Americans were accustomed to dealing with the native population of North America, sometimes through missions and often through genocide, but foreign missions brought an otherwise relatively sheltered population into abrupt contact with a great range of peoples who were very different from themselves.

What the missionaries did in the company of those foreign peoples has since been a matter of widespread embarrassment. Missionaries from the United States and Europe often did exactly what their harshest critics claimed. They supported imperialist projects, accepted the white supremacist ideology of the West, imposed narrow moral codes, and infantilized the peoples they imagined they were serving. It is no wonder that many nationalist movements scorned and killed missionaries. The Boxer Rebellion in China had many sources and made few distinctions among those who became its victims, but the rebels had plenty of cause to identify missionaries with the imperialism of the Western powers.[8] All this is true. But it is the only truth about missionary history that is widely understood.

The narrowness of prevailing attitudes toward missionaries is revealed by the speed with which the term "missionary position" caught on and how popular it remained long after it was shown to be based on a factual error. Alfred Kinsey in the 1940s said that South Pacific islanders had used the term to describe face-to-face sexual intercourse with the woman lying on her back. This position had long been known as "matrimonial." Kinsey had simply misread— probably in an honest mistake—Bronislaw Malinowski's *The Sexual Life of Savages in North-Western Melanesia*. That book reports the islanders' comments about "white traders, planters, [and] officials," not missionaries. Following Kinsey, it became standard to display moral superiority to missionaries by invoking "the missionary position" as an emblem for their limited sexual imagination and for the "on top" location they were understood to maintain in their relations with indigenous peoples.[9] In 2001, Robert Priest's discovery of Kinsey's error was not altogether welcome. None of the seventeen anthropologists invited by the editors of *Current Anthropology* to comment found fault with Priest's research, but most were reluctant to grant its significance. Some justified ignoring Priest's discovery altogether. We may have "an ethical and political obligation" to continue to speak of the missionary position exactly as we have been doing, concluded one scholar. The usage expressed a large truth, and we should not be sidetracked by the particulars of this case. Another quoted several missionary manifestos about the need to convert the peoples of the world to Christianity and argued, therefore, that "missionaries have made their own bed" and are to blame if anthropologists and others continue to use the phrase. A third counseled recognition of the "rational kernel" contained by traditional usage of "the missionary position."[10]

A colonial, exploitative image of the missionary project was kept alive by Barbara Kingsolver's bestselling novel of 1998, *The Poisonwood Bible*. In her telling of the missionary story in the Belgian Congo, missionaries arrogantly refused to engage with indigenous cultures and were oblivious to the humanity of the people to whom they ostensibly ministered.[11] Nadine Gordimer had little patience for this narrative. "The facts disprove" the old tale of missionaries as the inevitable agents of empire, the great South African writer railed in 2003, reminding readers that the church's gospel produced many anticolonial activists who were "inspired by the rebel Jesus' example" and remained "unreconciled" to colonialism. Missionaries were prominent in that important "minority of colonizers, mainly of the Left," Gordimer continued, "who identified themselves with the position that colonialism was unjust, racist, and anti-human."[12]

Recent scholarship has emphasized the aspects of missionary history to which Gordimer referred, and even when missionaries behaved in ways now considered reprehensible, they often lost control of Christianity to indigenous peoples who made their own uses of tools left to them by missionaries.[13] Missionaries established schools, colleges, medical schools, and other technical infrastructures that survived into the postcolonial era. Missionaries were especially active in advancing literacy. They translated countless books into indigenous languages, produced dictionaries, and created written versions of languages that had been exclusively oral. Some missionary institutions became vital incubators of anti-imperialist nationalisms, as in the case of the American University in Beirut, founded in 1866, and the alma mater of several generations of Arab nationalist leaders. Christianity itself has assumed shapes in the Global South quite different from the contours designed by European and American evangelists. Religious voices purporting to speak on behalf of indigenous peoples have occasionally claimed that the missionary impact was beneficial for endowing local populations with Christian resources that proved to be invaluable.[14] Feminist scholars have called attention to the ways in which African women were able to use Christianity—for all the patriarchal elements in its scriptures— as a tool for increasing their autonomy, especially in choosing their own spouses.[15]

Scholars continue to inquire just where and how the actions of missionaries affected the subsequent histories of the societies they influenced.[16] That inquiry is an important and contested aspect of today's discussions of colonialism and the postcolonial order that is largely beyond the scope of *Protestants Abroad*. But not altogether. As scholars come to recognize the interactive dimensions of the missionary project, we can comprehend that project itself as a genuinely global, dialectical event. Missions were part of the world-historical process by which the world we call modern was created.[17]

This book's cast of characters was involved with missions in three different capacities. The first of these was service abroad as a missionary. People routinely classified as missionaries included not only evangelists, but teachers, doctors, nurses, YMCA leaders, university professors, and social service workers affiliated in any way with institutions and programs sponsored by missionary societies, churches, and missionary-friendly foundations. All were understood to be part of the greater missionary enterprise, even though some would say, "I wasn't really a missionary," by way of explaining they were not directly involved in evangelism. A second order of involvement was to grow up as the child of missionaries, often spending many years in the field. The third capacity was the least direct: to be closely associated with missionaries, typically through missionary support organizations.

Although there were persons of both sexes in all three of these categories, the gender ratio was different in each case. In the field, about two-thirds of missionary personnel were women, either unwed or married to male missionaries. Missions afforded women opportunities to perform social roles often denied to them in the United States. Glass ceilings in the mission field were higher and more subject to exceptions than in most American communities. By the 1950s, nearly half of the missionary physicians in India were female. Women led many colleges in China. These included one of the most famous missionaries of all time, Minnie Vautrin, who turned the campus of Ginling College into a fortress during the Nanking Massacre of 1937 and 1938. She is credited with saving several thousand Chinese women from rape and murder at the hands of marauding Japanese soldiers.[18] Women were sometimes allowed to preach in the mission field, even though Paul the Apostle had told the Christians of Corinth, "Let your women keep silent in the churches: for it is not permitted unto them to speak; but they are commanded to be under obedience."[19] While home on furlough, female preachers were often prohibited from speaking from the pulpits of their own denominations, sometimes even in their home congregations.[20]

Among missionary children, there were of course equal numbers of males and females. In missionary support organizations, women were very prominent. Most denominations had women's missionary boards that exercised strong influence in church affairs and stood among the largest women's organizations in the United States in the late nineteenth and early twentieth centuries. These women's missionary boards were often active on social issues, urging their denominations to take more vigorous stands, especially against racism. A group of 150 women from the various denominational missionary boards picketed a Washington, D.C., hotel in 1945 to protest its refusal to serve black members of the United Council of Church Women.[21]

To understand the lives of these men and women, it is essential to begin with chronology. American churches sent missionaries abroad from early in the nineteenth century, but the numbers increased rapidly in the mid-1880s. From then until World War II, missionaries were the primary source of information for most Americans about the non-European world, especially Asia.[22] Newspaper correspondents, travel writers, *National Geographic Magazine*, world's fairs, and the public representations of diplomats and businessmen all contributed impressions of non-European peoples. Missions were different; they provided a more intimate and enduring connection. Local churches often financed particular missionary families, with whom they regularly corresponded for many years. Religious periodicals kept foreign scenes constantly in front of readers in millions of American homes. The lectures delivered by missionaries on furlough were widely attended events in local communities as well as at regional and national meetings of denominations and cross-denominational organizations. The bravery and heroism of missionaries was the stuff of countless pamphlets and periodicals and memorials. The "Memorial Arch" on the Oberlin College campus, honoring the thirteen Oberlin graduates and their five children killed in the Boxer Rebellion, is a well-known example.[23]

World War II and the decolonization of Asia and Africa catapulted missionary-connected Americans into positions of unprecedented importance because they were so far ahead of the global curve. That is why so much of this book is about the 1940s and 1950s. Knowledge of distant lands suddenly became much more functional. Individuals with experience abroad in business or diplomacy were also in demand, but their numbers were smaller and their language skills rarely as well-developed. After World War II, the public had many more sources of information about foreign countries. Never again would missionaries serve as the leading edge of American society's engagement with the remote regions of the globe. But in the short run, missionary expertise was much in demand.

When former missionary Kenneth Landon was called to Washington in 1941 to advise President Roosevelt on the situation in Southeast Asia, he discovered that the US government's entire intelligence file on Thailand consisted of a handful of published articles that he himself had written. When Edwin Reischauer was installed as the head of a military language training program in 1942, he noticed, upon arriving in Washington to take charge of his unit, that every person in the room was, like him, a child of missionaries or had spent time as a missionary. The China and Arab sections of the Foreign Service included a number of missionary sons. The Office of Strategic Services—predecessor to the Central Intelligence Agency—employed many missionaries and missionary children. The ability of OSS agent Rosamond Frame to speak the nine dialects of Mandarin she learned as a missionary daughter in China opened discursive doors that would otherwise have remained closed.

Chronological distinctions are thus crucial for understanding the timing and character of the role missionary-connected Americans played in public life. These distinctions are important, too, for understanding the shifting priorities of the missionary enterprise itself and the cultural orientation and class position of different missionary cohorts.

The great surge of missionaries going abroad in the 1880s and 1890s included many fervently evangelical men and women who believed that the world might end fairly soon. Quick conversion was necessary. Missionaries of this otherworldly orientation were only marginally interested in establishing long-term institutions. They also saw little reason to immerse themselves in local cultures. By 1900, however, and especially by the 1910s, the proportion of missionaries affected by the worldly priorities of the social gospel had increased.

Missionaries of this more down-to-earth and reformist persuasion were quicker than their apocalyptic colleagues to assess and respond to the immediate needs of indigenous populations by building schools and launching other service programs designed to help people cope with life in the here and now. Missionaries inspired by the social gospel were also more likely to be engaged by global politics. Many admired Woodrow Wilson's vision of the world, according to which the great powers would learn to cooperate with each other and together promote the self-determination of all peoples. These more worldly missionaries were also better educated. They were familiar with the basics of the Higher Criticism of the bible. A sense that even the truest of faiths took form through real people acting in real time made them more sympathetic with the religious and cultural practices they encountered.

These liberal missionaries sometimes allowed that Buddhism, Islam, and Hinduism were early stages of a spiritual development that would eventually lead to a fully Christian world. This had long been a Protestant perspective on Judaism. It proved quite easy to apply the same idea to what came to be called the world's other Great Religions. Missionaries departing for the field after 1900, and the children born to them, were more likely than their predecessors to discard blatantly ethnocentric and colonialist perspectives. Eventually, many of their descendants rejected as condescending even the notion that other religions were stepping-stones toward Christ. But in the meantime, this "stepping-stone" conception of the function of non-Christian religions served as a genuine stepping-stone in its own right, enabling American Protestants traveling away from the parochialism of the original missionary calling to get to some other place. As so often in history, an outlook later generations found lacking in courage and truthfulness had once served as a crucial means of intellectual transformation.

These men and women were almost always shaped by what came to be called the "mainline" or "ecumenical" denominations that controlled the spiritual capital of American Protestantism through the 1960s. This proud company included Methodists, Presbyterians, Congregationalists, Disciples of Christ, Dutch Reformed, Episcopalians, Northern Baptists, Quakers, several Lutheran denominations, and a smattering of smaller Anabaptist and Reformed confessions.[24] Each of these groups had internal divisions. Some were sharply divided during the fundamentalist-modernist disputes of the 1920s and 1930s. All contained strongly historicist and social gospel cadres. These classic American denominations saw themselves as part of a single, if quarrelsome family, institutionalized in the Federal Council of Churches and various issue-specific, transdenominational organizations.

There was another churchly family. This second constellation consisted of the Seventh- day Adventists, the Church of the Nazarene, the Assemblies of God, the Southern Baptist Convention, and other denominations that were actually defined by fundamentalism or extremely aggressive evangelism. The denominations in this second family were hostile to the social gospel and to historical biblical criticism, and less engaged by Wilsonian efforts to reform international politics. The Protestants in this second family had their own missions abroad, and eventually took over most of the American Protestant missionary enterprise when the liberal groups of the first family pulled back from it in the 1950s and 1960s. Evangelicals developed their own network of periodicals, colleges, seminaries, and recreational facilities.

Since this second family of Protestants cooperated among themselves, one might ask why they are not also called "ecumenical"? Part of the answer is that the first family cooperated earlier and more ambitiously, and on the basis of more flexible notions of what was essential to the gospel. For many in the second family, biblical "inerrancy" was essential, requiring a host of particulars, including the virgin birth and physical resurrection of Jesus and a literal reading of the creation story in Genesis. For the Pentecostal groups within this second family, immediate religious experience was central. It would be misleading to apply the term "ecumenical" to this second family, especially after the founding of the National Association of Evangelicals in 1942. From then on, this second family of Protestants successfully claimed for itself a label—*evangelical*—that earlier applied to any Protestant concerned with bringing more souls into the faith.[25] A polemical defense of the evangelical party put the point cogently in a 1956 book title: *Cooperation without Compromise*. The evangelicals "cooperated," while the ecumenists "compromised."[26]

The evangelical family resented the social status of the ecumenical family and generally shunned it for having betrayed the gospel by accommodating too much of modern culture. The ecumenical family largely ignored the evangelicals or patronized them as poor country cousins. This changed when the evangelical family gained political prominence in the Ronald Reagan era. The rise of evangelical Protestantism in public life followed decades of essentially separatist institution building supported by wealthy political conservatives. When the Republican Party developed its no-compromise agenda against the traditions of the New Deal and Great Society, Republican leaders found in evangelical Protestantism a sizable constituency well insulated from the liberal mainstream and eager for a chance to exercise greater influence.[27]

In the midcentury decades, the overwhelming majority of the missionary-connected men and women who became prominent in American public life were products of one or another of the classically liberal denominations and the colleges and seminaries they had founded. This was true no matter where they fell as individuals on the relevant spectra of personal beliefs and practices. They went to Amherst, Bryn Mawr, Mount Holyoke, Oberlin, Princeton, Swarthmore, and Yale, or to colleges more closely affiliated with churches, such as Carleton, Occidental, Pomona, and Wooster. The second family sent its children instead to Bob Jones, Calvin, Mercer, Westmont, Wheaton, or one of a number of scattered bible institutes. The adjective "mainline" caught on to describe the ecumenical family because its members were recognized as players in national life and as stakeholders in its major institutions.

Rarely before the end of the twentieth century did missionary-connected Americans from the second family become leaders in any institutional or discursive domain beyond evangelical Protestantism itself.[28] They simply did not become outspoken Foreign Service officers, civil rights activists, Ivy League professors, or critically acclaimed writers.

Often, this evangelical family resisted the very changes in American public life promoted by the missionary-connected Americans of the ecumenical family. A study of foreign missions as such—rather than a study like this one, of their impact on American public life—would have much more to say about the evangelical family, which has maintained a robust foreign missionary project all the way down to the present.

Where are African Americans in this story? A number of the churches within each of these two Protestant families had African American congregants, some of whom participated in the missionary project. But not many. The most renowned African American missionary was William Henry Sheppard, sent by the Southern Presbyterians to the Congo, where he gained fame for helping to expose King Leopold II's depredations against the Congolese. But Sheppard persistently refused to criticize white Americans and, as James Campbell has shown, "adapted seamlessly to life in the Jim Crow South" when he returned from Africa in 1909.[29] Black missionaries "were sent by white churches only to tropical area of western and central Africa," notes Walter L. Williams, "where disease took a great toll on white missionaries." This toll was exacted from black missionaries, too, of course, which was not always appreciated. Williams adds that by the early twentieth century some of the independent black churches of the United States began to send their own missionaries abroad, mostly to coastal areas in western Africa.

These independent missionary experiences contributed to the development of pan-Africanist ideas within the American black population, but resolutely secular leaders like W.E.B. Du Bois were the most enthusiastic proponents of pan-Africanism. The black missionaries tended to be religiously and culturally conservative. They were even inclined to share "the white stereotypes of African savagery," explains Williams, and they believed that conversion to Christianity would release Africans to the ostensibly fuller humanity of the North Atlantic West.[30] Moreover, the black missionary experience was so largely segregated from the missionary projects of both major Protestant families that the latter paid very little attention to it. [31]

What about Americans of Asian descent? Very few were involved in missions, and only a handful of Asian Americans were in a position to influence the public life of the United States in any arena. Their numbers were small prior to Congress's opening of immigration from Asia in 1965, and even the best-educated during the midcentury decades had trouble gaining respectful attention from empowered Anglo-Protestants. The Japanese American men who fought against the Axis powers during

World War II had a hard time gaining acceptance. *Protestants Abroad* does touch upon the lives and activities of some Asian Americans, but usually in relation to missionary sponsors. As whites, the missionaries could get a hearing for things Asian. Hence missionary cosmopolitanism, like the missionary project itself, was largely a white enterprise, reflecting the color hierarchy of the country as a whole.

Du Bois understood this. In the midst of his vigorous attack on white supremacy as a global phenomenon, Du Bois said that white missionaries did as much good as harm. This in itself made them very different from most white people. "The missionaries," wrote Du Bois in 1945 in his *Color and Democracy*, "represent the oldest invasion of whites, and incur at first the enmity of business and the friendship of natives." The missionaries have included "all sorts of persons: unworldly visionaries, former pastors out of a job, social workers with and without social science, theologians, crackpots, and humanitarians." This motley crew has "influenced hundreds of millions of men with results that literally vary from heaven to hell." The atheist Du Bois reluctantly acknowledged that by 1945, the missionary project was a vital resource for good world politics: "The majority of the best and earnest people of this world are today organized in religious groups," and the defeat of colonialism depended upon their energies instructed by a scientific understanding of the world. "Missionary effort and social reform" must together put an end to the colonialism.[32]

The chronological and cultural distinctions noted above enable us to recognize the difference theology made in how Americans in the mission field reacted to what they found there. The impact of foreign experience was far from unmediated. What people took from the encounter varied to some extent according to the mentalities they brought to it. Missionaries who went abroad with historicist and social gospel perspectives discerned features of local life less visible to missionaries rigidly programmed to see heathens and little else. Overall, the religious orientation of missionaries upon arrival in the field was a good predictor of the speed with which they and their offspring became critics of American provinciality and sympathetic commentators on at least some aspects of the indigenous culture.

In China, by far the largest of the mission fields, personnel recruited to the China Inland Mission were defiantly more conservative than those recruited as YMCA secretaries, or as teachers and professors at missionary-sponsored institutions like Nanking University, Peking Union Medical College, and Yenching University. Theologian Langdon Gilkey, who was teaching English at Yenching when interned by the Japanese after Pearl Harbor, remembered how differently the two groups of

American missionaries behaved during their nearly three years of captivity. Gilkey marveled at the capacity of some of the fundamentalist internees to close their minds to foreign influences, and to feel at home only when they had fled the company of the liberals. The missionaries "whose religion had been graced by liberalism in some form" were "able to meet cooperatively and warmly with others, even with those who had no relation to Christianity at all," while the fundamentalists were often petty, sanctimonious, and scornful of any in the camp, including the ecumenical missionaries, who did not agree with them. Only the service-focused Salvation Army missionaries, Gilkey insisted, broke the pattern he found among fundamentalists.[33] Of the China-reared individuals I discuss in *Protestants Abroad*, Foreign Service officer John Paton Davies Jr. is highly unusual for having grown up in the China Inland Mission, where a critical mass of theological conservatives prevailed in the fundamentalist side in the fundamentalist-modernist debates of the 1920s and early 1930s.

Chronology is also important for distinguishing home missions from foreign missions. What missionary societies continued throughout most of the twentieth century to call "Home Missions" were survivors of early nineteenth-century initiatives to create evangelical outposts serving the entire population beyond the Appalachian Mountains, including both slave and free states. These initiatives proceeded simultaneously with the spread of foreign missions, but eventually they diverged as foreign missions grew in size and as more and more Anglos in the West joined churches. Once the Anglos of the Mississippi Valley had affiliated, mostly with the Methodists, the Baptists, and the Disciples of Christ, Home Missions focused on the "foreign-like" populations of African Americans, Indians, and immigrant Jews, Hispanics, and Japanese. By the middle of the twentieth century, Home Missions had become largely social welfare programs, still bearing the starkly hierarchical implication that some Americans were to be treated like foreigners because of their race or ethnicity.

The experience of working in Home Missions could inspire individuals to social action and liberalized practices in their own communities, but home missionaries remained in much closer contact with the culture of their natal community than was true for missionaries living abroad for whom it was not as easy to "go home." This was the case even for mission outposts on Indian reservations. Some Baptists, Methodists, and others who were active in Home Missions were outspoken antiracist voices within their denominational communities.[34] But Home Missions did not have remotely as much influence as foreign missions in the formation of missionary cosmopolitanism. Gallagher did not mention Home Missions; they were not players in the world-historical drama that impressed him.

As the distinction between foreign and home missions implies, part of the foreign missionary projects' significance was purely instrumental. It got Americans to places where fewer Americans would otherwise have gone, even briefly. It sent them to China, Egypt, India, Japan, Angola and other distant places, and gave them a reason to learn the local languages. Prior to World War II, there were relatively few nonmissionary jobs to be had in countries beyond the North Atlantic West. When historian John K. Fairbank traveled in China in the 1930s, doing research for his doctoral dissertation, his American contacts were primarily missionaries.

The missionary project was a much more powerful instrument than commerce or diplomacy in getting Americans deeply embedded in things foreign. Business executives, military officers, and diplomats rarely remained in one place long enough to become as fluent in the indigenous languages. They and their families were also better protected against the violence that periodically erupted against foreigners, especially in China and Arab lands.[35] "American and Asian merchants found they needed each other," according to one sensitive treatment of the relationship, because "they shared a profit motive." Business people did not want religion or ideology to get in their way, and often eschewed contact with missionaries.[36] Gilkey observed that the many business families interned in the Japanese camp wanted as little as possible to do with missionaries of any theological orientation. The business families Gilkey got to know belonged, he concluded, to an entirely different tribe. They never concerned themselves with "the wider Chinese culture" around them, remained in their "clubs and offices," and attended to the Chinese only as instruments of their commerce.[37] Their children, like the parents, almost never learned local languages.

While some missionary children learned only "kitchen Chinese" and its equivalents in other languages, many others counted the foreign tongue as their first language. It was also common to identify as strongly with the foreign country of their upbringing as with America. Even those with a stronger and more unified sense of American identity almost always felt they had been "born a foreigner," as in the title one of the most sensitive of the autobiographies of missionary children, or "a stranger at home," as in the title of another book about missionary children.[38]

Most of the men and women discussed in this book are missionary children. Therefore, the distinctive features of mission childhoods invite further exploration. Missionary children were in the missionary project from the start; they were its heirs. Some decided to become missionaries themselves, but most did not. The "mish kids" are an identifiable population; some compared themselves to "an ethnic group."[39] To grow up in a missionary community was not simply to live abroad. This experience they shared with nonmissionary children whom sociologists also refer to as "third culture kids" or "global nomads," usually the children of business, diplomatic, or military families.[40] The missionary children were immersed in foreign cultures more deeply than most of the other American children raised abroad. Missionary children, moreover, were surrounded by a highly self-conscious version of their own culture, sharply enough defined to enhance its power to influence the people the mission was designed to serve.

Some of the other "global nomads" interacted with missionary children at missionary-sponsored residential schools. The most important were Kodikanal and Woodstock in South Asia, the Shanghai American School and the North China American School in China, and the American Community School in the Middle East. Not until well after World War II did the Department of Defense develop its own global network of schools designed for the children of military personnel. Whatever the values of the parents, the children were taught by missionary-employed teachers and had as their own classmates and roommates—at least for a brief time— the sons and daughters of missionaries. The missionary-sponsored schools could thus blur the difference between growing up in a missionary family and in a business or diplomatic family, but only temporarily.[41]

The special circumstances of missionary children inspired widespread discussion within the churches beginning about 1930.[42] A study of several hundred Methodist missionary children from India found that the sons and daughters of missionaries were much more likely to attend college and to obtain postgraduate degrees than other Americans, and that they "tend to become cosmopolitan in their interests."[43] More cosmopolitan, but also, it was often said, more traumatized by the cultural shock of adjusting to life in the United States, regardless of their age when they left the foreign mission field.[44] From the 1930s to the present, missionary organizations have offered advice to missionary children on how to cope with the distinctive psychological traumas associated with a missionary upbringing.[45]

It is far from clear that missionary children as adults were disproportionately subject to emotional problems and mental illness, more likely to be depressed or to commit suicide than others in their age cohort. Nor do I find reliable evidence that parental religious beliefs, parenting styles, the mission environment, encounter with "natives," or any other specific set of factors correlate more than others with the psychological stress of missionary children. Yet that such risks were greater for them has been taken for granted. The memoirs of even the most successful of missionary children comment on the psychological challenges they experienced in adjusting to mainstream American life. Princeton University president and ambassador Robert Goheen felt his own experience was relatively easy, in part because he was a younger son and had the experiences of his older siblings to make the entry into American society less traumatic.[46] So firmly established is this pattern in the self-representation of missionary children that John Hersey included the travails of an emotionally disturbed missionary son in *The Call*, a novel of 1986 designed as a panoramic commentary on the American missionary experience in China.[47]

The literature on missionary children identifies a number of sources for this pervasive sense of psychological risk. Separation from parents to attend boarding school or to live with relatives in the United States was one. Another was the culture shock of immersion in American life as a teenager after having spent one's childhood in a different environment. Alternating between one household abroad and another in an American community made some children feel that they lacked a single and stable home. Some missionary parents left the impression that their labors were so important ("I must be about my father's business," Jesus told followers who wanted his attention, according to Luke 2:49) that the needs of children became secondary.

In one searching autobiographical meditation, Mennonite J. D. Stahl describes his own "quest from loneliness toward belonging" as demanding great efforts to assign meaning to experiences much more diverse than those of the nonmissionary families he knew back home in Virginia. Growing up not knowing just where he belonged, he "even envied bigots" because of "the security of their prejudices." Eventually, his experience as a missionary son led him to reject "the cultural assumptions that accompanied much of missions: we are saved, you are lost; we are advanced, you are backward; we have the way of the future, you are shipwrecked in the past." Instead, concludes Stahl, the ultimate message of his own life was expressed in Cromwell's cautionary reminder "I beseech you, in the bowels of Christ, think it possible you may be mistaken." Connecting the old Puritan past with his own appreciation for scientific modernity, Stahl cited Cromwell as "quoted by Jacob Bronowski in *The Ascent of Man* as Bronowski knelt in the mud at Auschwitz."[48]

The first conversation I ever had with a missionary child, many decades before I ever imagined studying missionaries, was about a feeling of having been abandoned. A family friend told me that when she was eleven her missionary parents left her and several younger siblings with an aunt and uncle in Ohio while the parents returned to India after a year's furlough. She never forgave them, and I have never forgotten how affected she was, forty years later, describing her experience. Her parents told the story in different terms, in keeping with the official ideal of stoic, self-effacing children: the girl tearlessly assured her mother, "We'll get along all right," as she bade farewell to her parents. This religiously correct version of the goodbye found its way into the hagiographic biography of the girl's father published by church authorities.[49]

There were plenty of "casualties," one missionary daughter reminded a girlhood friend when they were both middle aged in the 1970s, marveling that they had survived as well as they had.[50] One of the most frequently mentioned casualties was Pearl Buck's brother, Edgar Sydenstricker, who managed a successful career as an epidemiologist before alcoholism seriously disabled him while still in his forties. Another widely noticed casualty was Joan Smythe. In 1963, this China-born daughter of a leading Disciples of Christ missionary couple took her own life at the age of twenty-nine, while a graduate student at Harvard. The death surprised her family and friends, several of whom still remember her as an unusually tough, sophisticated woman and cannot fathom why she ended her life.[51]

Joseph Littell had a sister who killed herself in the family kitchen when she was in her early twenties. Littell eventually had a successful career as a publisher, but "Let's face it—our family statistics are staggering," he wrote of himself and his siblings. All were born in the 1910s and 1920s to Episcopalian missionaries to China. Referring to himself and his siblings as "we mish kids," Littell noted that "of the eight of us, three remained single," and the other five "accumulated a sorry record of fourteen marriages and eight divorces." A brother was diagnosed as schizophrenic.[52]

Missionary children who escaped becoming "casualties" were often high achievers. Of the twelve missionary sons who finished high school at the Kodikanal School in India in 1949, eleven later obtained either MD or PhD degrees.[53] Most made similar career choices. The missionary children who left a mark on American life did so most often in education, scholarship, science, medicine, literature and the arts, or social services. Only a few pursued careers in business, law, or engineering. Those who went into medicine often did so as missionary doctors. Many testified that the most important legacy of the missionary experience for their career choices was a desire to live a life of "service," however defined. "We were supposed to make the world a better place," as Goheen put it.[54] "I had been raised to think that the purpose in life," wrote Edwin O. Reischauer, "was to make one's maximum contribution to society, however humble that might be."[55] Few were comfortable with openly profit-making vocations.

The missionary children who made their away into the *American National Biography* exemplify this pattern decisively. Thirty identifiable missionary children born between 1860 and 1920 to parents stationed outside the North Atlantic West are the subject of biographical articles in the *ANB*.[56] Six of the thirty spent all or a substantial part of their careers in the mission field themselves, several as doctors. These six earned a place in the *ANB* through their contributions in the mission field, and are less pertinent to an inquiry into the role of missionary-connected Americans in the public life of the United States. The remaining twenty-four constitute an ideal sample of high-achieving missionary children who spent their adulthoods in America.

Half of the twenty-four were writers, academics, or scientists who worked largely outside academia. In addition to these dozen intellectually focused individuals, one was a composer and another was an architect. This vocational pattern differs somewhat from that of Jewish counterparts, many of whom had distinguished careers in business and law as well as science, scholarship, and the arts. Only two of the twenty-four *ANB* missionary children went into business and another two into the legal profession. None of those four had typical careers. The publishing magnate Henry Luce got into business through journalism and, for all his moneymaking, was always more interested in changing the world than adding to his fortune. The oil company executive William A. Eddy did not get into business until he was fifty, after substantial careers as a professor of English literature and as a Marine Corps intelligence officer. James Landis was primarily an academic administrator and government official, serving as dean of Harvard Law School and as chair of the Securities and Exchange Commission.[57] The other lawyer, Jerome Greene, was a close adviser to three Harvard presidents and was a senior consultant to the Rockefeller Foundation.

The same vocational pattern is evident in what we know of other missionary sons and daughters, most of whom did not, of course, find their way into the *ANB*. In the 1970s, Sarah R. Mason surveyed two hundred former students of the Shanghai American School. She found that the most common occupations were higher education, Foreign Service or CIA, clergy or other church work, and elementary or secondary education.

Only two of Mason's two hundred were lawyers. Some became doctors or nurses, many of whom then worked in missionary hospitals.[58]

Not all missionary-connected Americans were engaged in the kinds of careers on which I focus in this book. My attention is directed at people who affected the public life of the country. Some missionary-connected individuals simply pursued one profession or another with great distinction. Missionary daughter Anne Tyng (1920–2011) was an influential architect. Missionary son Bentley Glass (1906–2005) was a leading biologist and a president of the American Association of University Professors. Actresses Jayne (1919–2015) and Audrey (1922–1996) Meadows were the daughters of Episcopalian missionaries to China. Brigadier General David "Tex" Hill (1915–2007), born in Korea as the son of Presbyterian missionaries, was a successful fighter pilot during World War II and had a distinguished military career after the war. Labor economist John T. Dunlop (1914–2003), who served briefly as secretary of labor under President Gerald Ford, grew up in the Philippines as the son of Presbyterian missionaries. China-born John Espey (1913–2000) was an accomplished literary critic and memoirist, as well as the celebrated pseudonymous coauthor of what were called the "Monica books," a series he candidly described as "airplane literature for smart people."[59] There are many others.

One missionary son who made a distinctive mark as a novelist in 1941 but was never heard from again invites attention here because he was the first person to use the word "multicultural" in print. So the *Oxford English Dictionary* tells us. The term did not achieve wide use until nearly fifty years later. Edward F. Haskell (1906–1986) was born in a Bulgarian province of the Ottoman Empire as the son and grandson of missionaries. His *Lance: A Novel about Multicultural Men* tells the story of Lanceton Tenorton, a British officer in World War I who had grown up in Germany after having been adopted there as a foreign orphan. Tenorton is accused of treason because of his contacts with the German military. At Tenorton's court-martial, his advocate explains that the accused is "mixed, not only biologically but also culturally and legally." In the dock stood a British citizen who "speaks, reads, and writes six languages" and is an example of a future the court should contemplate: a global future in which all peoples "are rapidly being scrambled."[60] The hero had indeed been in contact with the enemy. Haskell does not resolve his fate, but focuses instead on the meaning of the trial, which was, above all, that multicultural individuals glimpse enough of the world to be worried about their own ignorance about the rest of it.

Tenorton's communist-influenced American wife, along with the couple's closest friend, an American who had grown up in South Africa, try to understand what world-historical transformations have done to them. "We, being children of the great age of transportation and communication," the friend remarks, "have contacts with *many* languages, *many* faiths, and *many* nations. We are *multi*cultural." When facing the globe's vastness, "we and all multicultural people . . . crawl shakily out of the national narrows." We are equipped with "no more than half-evolved world feeling and world knowledge."

> We see things relatively instead of as absolutes. We think multiordinarily instead of in fixed patterns. We find ourselves at odds with strong, sure unicultural people. We feel sure that our vision is much truer than the vision of provincial people. We see their mistakes. We try to save us and them from themselves, and lead everyone to a higher, and we hope, happier way of life.[61]

Read today, the prose in *Lance* comes across as rather wooden, and its tone and substance heavily didactic. Some of Haskell's efforts to create a new vocabulary—"multiordinarily," for example, and "unicultural"—seem clunky now, just as *multicultural* must have seemed in 1941. For all the literary limitations of *Lance*, it stands as a register of the antiprovincial feelings common among missionary-connected Americans of Haskell's generation. It serves also as ideological bridge to the preoccupations of later generations, as exemplified by Nathan Glazer's book of 1997, *We Are All Multiculturalists Now*.[62]

What most connects Haskell with the multiculturalist enthusiasms of the 1990s is his insistence on a balance between challenging and respecting particular cultures. Against the model of "assimilation of ethnic minorities and immigrants," explains literary scholar Werner Sollors, Haskell presents Tenorton's having become German "as a reversible process through which a new identity is added while the old one is not erased." *Lance* espouses a cosmopolitanism that incorporates several identities within a single individual. Haskell encouraged his readers to believe that deep awareness of the particularity of the world's communities could produce "social engineering" that would eventually end war as a means of resolving conflicts. Ultimately, it is the United States, not Soviet Russia, which *Lance* holds out as the best possibility for appreciating the highly idealistic version of multiculturalism that his characters represent.[63]

Lance was well received. The *New York Times* and the *Saturday Review* published appreciative reviews. But it has been given almost no critical attention.[64] Haskell never wrote another novel, or a book of any kind. He was briefly a political activist, serving as executive secretary of the

International Committee for Political Prisoners, an organization close to the American Civil Liberties Union. After a hit-and-miss academic career as a sociologist and philosopher, Haskell lived quietly in New York on an inheritance, working on a polymathic study of "unified science" that remained incomplete when he died in obscurity in 1986.[65] That apparently abortive effort to bringing things together—so typical an aspiration for missionary children—was mentioned as being in progress forty-five years earlier, on the dust jacket of *Lance*, which is one of the few sources of information about this elusive figure in American literary history. The dust jacket also described Haskell as a convert to Quakerism, a religious persuasion obviously compatible with his political and social ideals, and represented Haskell's own life as an embodiment of a multicultural experience and of a multiculturalist ideological stance toward diversity:

> When he was three, his American father, Swiss mother, and Bulgarian neighbors so affected him that he was speaking a conglomeration of English, Swiss-German, and Bulgarian. However, as his primary schooling progressed—in America, Turkey, Greece, Bulgaria, and Switzerland—he was obliged to differentiate sharply not only among languages, but among customs, rules of behavior, and politico-religious views. . . . He was forced either to become a human chameleon, changing his world-view with every change in country . . . or else to develop a world-view that fitted everywhere, a multicultural view.[66]

Three of Haskell's most famous and globally engaged contemporaries are the subjects of the following chapter. Their debates with each other and their self-interrogations blend with the conversations of Haskell's fictional characters. Just what did it mean to try to embrace the whole world in a single cosmopolitan vision? Henry Luce, Pearl Buck, and John Hersey were all missionary children from China who knew each other as adults. Their lives have never been extensively considered in relation to one another. Their differences and similarities highlight the major themes of *Protestants Abroad*, including the strong Asian component in missionary cosmopolitanism.

Before turning to this remarkable threesome, I want to observe that few missionary-connected Americans understood the world as fully as they supposed they did. In this failing, they resembled almost everyone else. Often, missionary cosmopolitans retained hierarchical assumptions and Orientalist attitudes, even if less pronounced than among the people against whom they struggled. From a twenty-first century perspective, the anti-imperialism of many of the people discussed in *Protestants Abroad* looks less complete than they thought it was, and more functional than they realized in the advancing of distinctly American national interests. Some of their formulations come across now as naïvely hopeful about the capacities of different kinds of human beings to work together.

Yet a substantial measure of what these people said and did resists condescension. Insofar as poor comprehension of the world's peoples continues to be a prominent and dangerous feature of American politics and culture, the saga of missionary-connected Americans is all the more instructive. They learned it was hard to be a "citizen of the world," but they put more effort into it than most of their contemporaries. They experienced to a higher degree and within a broader context than most Americans the tension between inclusion and identity, between an impulse to bring everyone together and a need to make a community viable by defining it in some particular set of terms. This tension existed first in the missionary project itself: How could Christianity be configured so it could work for all human souls and still be Christian? Second, it was manifest in the national project of the United States: how could the liberal ideals for which America ostensibly stood become instruments of human progress without either losing their character or being exposed as mere masks for the interests of a single nation? In both cases, the world's prodigious diversity heightened the tension between a drive to include and a drive to define.[67] Understanding how far these proto-multiculturalists and proto-world-citizens got—and where they stopped or were derailed by others—can be part of the ongoing effort of Americans to figure out the boundaries of their community and to decide just what their role in the world can and should be.

CHAPTER TWO

To Make the Crooked Straight

HENRY LUCE, PEARL BUCK, AND JOHN HERSEY

"IT WAS A MAGNIFICENT imperialism of the spirit, incredible and not to be understood except by those who have been reared in it and have grown beyond it."[1] So Pearl Buck (1892–1973) described the missionary project that defined the life of her father and shaped hers. That imperialism of the spirit, with its imperative to change the world, also helped to make Henry Luce (1898–1967) and John Hersey (1914–1993) into the men they became. The moral imperative was intense. It needed to be acted upon without delay. It knew no boundaries. "The Evangelization of the World in This Generation" was, after all, the slogan adopted at the great Edinburgh missionary conference of 1910, the high point of confidence in the missionary project.

The publisher Luce, the novelist Buck, and the multi-genre writer Hersey were all born in China. All inherited the missionary imperative to make things right. All acted upon it in secular modes, but quite differently from each other. Buck was convinced that if the crooked were ever to be made straight, the crookedness of American life was the place to start. Luce had no doubt that what needed to be fixed was the rest of the world, and he thought America offered every bit as good a model as his parents had once thought the Presbyterian Church to be. Hersey represented the missionary tradition at its most reflective and brooding. His choice of causes was more like Buck's than Luce's, but he worried even more than she did that American efforts to lead the world could easily go astray. All three sought to advance a species-wide solidarity instructed in some way by an idealistic vision of American democratic culture. The three careers do not encompass all of the varieties of global vision found among missionary cosmopolitans, but they do provide sharply articulated examples. All were egalitarians of one sort or another. All tried to get their Eurocentric contemporaries to engage Asia.

The three were never friends. But they knew each other and were acutely aware of each other's doings. Hersey was a staff writer for Luce's *Time* and *Life* magazines in the late 1930s and early 1940s, but Luce scorned Hersey as disloyal when his prize foreign correspondent began to write for the *New Yorker*. It was in the pages of that rival magazine in 1946 that Hersey published *Hiroshima*, his account of the human consequences of the atomic bomb, which was instantly recognized as one of the most important pieces of journalism ever written. Hersey and Buck had little contact, but after Buck's death Hersey wrote warmly of Buck's generous love for all of humankind and credited her with anticipating "nearly every single one" of the discoveries about gender made by "the Women's Liberation Movement."[2] Luce and Buck got along well enough until Buck proved to be a vigorous critic of Chiang Kai-shek. Luce then instructed the editors of all his magazines that nothing favorable to Buck should ever appear in any of them. She responded by writing a novel, *God's Men*, the story of a missionary son who became an avaricious and duplicitous publisher.[3]

Buck's bitterness toward Luce reflected personal animosity, but her basic opinion of him was not unusual in missionary circles. Luce was an outlier there, where skepticism about nationalism and American bravado was common. But in American society as a whole, Luce rode the political and cultural waves of the majority of his generation like no other missionary child or former missionary. He had critics, but many more fans. While Buck was invariably associated with her missionary past, and often patronized for it, Luce came across as more fully emancipated from his, even though I argue here that he was more uncritically under its ordinance than Buck or Hersey. Luce was happy to be a representative American, full stop. He was widely recognized as such. To his career I turn first, then to Buck's, and finally to Hersey's.

Luce's publishing enterprise was one of the supreme entrepreneurial achievements of an American generation of great business triumphs. In the media era just prior to the coming of television, no one took shrewder advantage of the potential for magazines to consolidate a national middle-class culture and to make a profit in the process. Luce launched *Time* in 1926, and within a few years *Fortune* (1930) and *Life* (1936), followed two decades later by *Sports Illustrated* (1954). *Time* and *Life* especially were central to American popular culture throughout the midcentury. Being on the cover of *Time* was recognized as a true register of one's importance.

Luce's ideas, which he took very seriously, were not distinctive. Through his magazines his thoughts gained much more public attention than they otherwise would have. One of his biographers, Alan Brinkley, shows that Luce "was almost never able to exercise as much power as he wished and as his adversaries believed he had," but another of his biographers, Robert E. Herzstein, is probably equally correct to insist that Luce was "the most influential private citizen in the America of his day."[4] Luce was given credit for enabling Wendell Willkie to become the Republican presidential candidate in 1940 and for helping tip the balance from Robert Taft to Dwight Eisenhower in 1952. Eisenhower's appointment of Clare Booth Luce to be ambassador to Italy was understood as a response to her husband's support. All presidents and their advisers from Franklin Roosevelt to Lyndon Johnson were highly conscious of what Luce was thinking. Although he tepidly endorsed Richard Nixon for president in 1960, Luce ended up watching the election returns on television with his old friend, Joseph P. Kennedy, in whose son's presidency Luce then took a highly sympathetic interest.

Luce's central driving idea was simply that the United States had an obligation to change the world, and in its own image. One did not have to be a child of missionaries to gravitate to this idea, but in Luce's case the source of its pull would not be in doubt even had he not flagged it. But he did, and never more explicitly than in his most famous utterance, "The American Century." This epochal essay, published in *Life* early in 1941, called upon Americans to openly reorganize the world. "The life of mankind," he declared in a climactic passage, must be raised "from the level of the beasts to what the Psalmist called a little lower than the angels." His reference was to Psalms 8:5: "For thou hast made him a little lower than the angels, and hast crowned him with glory and honor." As an agent of this sacred mission the United States was obliged, Luce explained, to become "the Good Samaritan of the entire world," feeding the hungry anywhere and everywhere.[5]

Readers in that era of high biblical literacy would have recognized Luce's casual scriptural allusions. In the parable of the Good Samaritan (Luke 10:30-37, KJV), a man beaten and robbed and left to die on the roadside was rescued and nurtured by a passing member of the ostensibly inferior Samaritan tribe. The imperative to help other people means helping not just members of your own group, indicated Jesus of Nazareth, but all human beings, and the capacity to live by this principle can be found among all peoples, even the despised (by Jews of Jesus's time) Samaritans. What was understood in the missionary tradition as the "Christian duty" to help the world overcome its suffering became, in Luce, "the manifest duty of this country" to do it. He understood the United States as the one nation-state that had inherited the values of Christianity and possessed the power to act upon those values on behalf of the entire human species.[6]

Luce's social life diverged dramatically from all but a handful of other missionary children. While it was not unusual for missionary sons to attend New England preparatory schools and Ivy League colleges, Luce was caught up in the social hierarchy of those institutions. He was competitive and status-conscious even at the Hotchkiss School, but even more so at Yale. His election to Skull and Bones, Yale's legendary secret society, was one of the great emotional triumphs of his life and he was quick to advance himself through the connections it famously offered.

In the early and mid-1920s, Luce made adroit use of one Yale connection after another to gain money, access, and employment. He was known even within his privileged milieu as unusually preoccupied with wealth, power, and social standing, a feature of his personality that his siblings and his retired missionary parents viewed with some ambivalence. His first marriage to a wealthy Chicago socialite in 1923 was striking enough, but when in 1935 he divorced Lila Holtz to marry the even more glamorous Clare Booth Brokaw—a divorcee and an already-famous author—it was clear to all that Henry Luce was determined to spend his life as a recognized member of the nation's social elite. With the extraordinary professional and financial success Luce achieved, he gloried in his standing and was found by the many talented editors he hired over the years to be an imperious and self-important boss.[7]

"He has such intellectual arrogance that he does not believe anyone can tell him anything," one of his editors complained. Repeatedly, his editors conspired to prevent an issue of a magazine from being twisted out of shape by the boss's latest enthusiasm. One of their most difficult struggles was sidelining the fanatical anti-communist Whittaker Chambers, who joined *Time* in 1939 and quickly became one of Luce's favorites. Hersey, who was still at *Time* during the war years, was typical in charging that Chambers' articles were "written with bias" and "filled with unjustified implications." Hersey was so annoyed at Luce's defense of what Hersey thought unforgivable distortions in Chambers' articles about China, that he later named it as the single most important reason he withdrew from *Time*.[8] The episode was big enough to be named "the Chambers war" within *Time*. Eventually, the other editors persuaded Luce to at least banish Chambers from the office and oblige his protected zealot to write from his home. Luce's editors were glad to be working at the most popular and journalistically dynamic magazines in the country, but frustrated to be dealing with a man who, in the sardonic words of one editor, "fancies he is molding the destiny of the US in the world."[9]

Luce seems always to have believed that he was mobilizing his wealth and high standing in the service of society. But only with the coming of World War II (which *Time* is generally credited with being the first to name[10]) did this feeling propel Luce to articulate just what kind of service he could provide, and in relation to just what vision of the United States and of the globe. The warfare in both Europe and the Pacific "brought out the best of [Luce's] missionary temperament," notes Brinkley, above all "commitment, energy, moral inquiry, and high purpose," but it also "brought out the worst . . . arrogance, impatience, didacticism, and occasional dogmatism."[11] The immediate stimulus for "The American Century" was Luce's annoyance with the isolationist sentiment that stood in the way of greater American support for the war effort against the Axis Powers.

"We are in this war" whether we know it or not, Luce impatiently told Americans. The interests of the United States were at stake, and the aid the US government was supplying to Britain and China reflected this deep truth. The big trouble was that the United States "as the most powerful and vital nation in the world" was so far unwilling to "accept wholeheartedly our duty and our opportunity . . . to exert upon the world the full impact of our influence, for such purposes as we see fit and by such means as we see fit." The United States could have done this back in 1919, Luce complained, but instead withdrew from its responsibilities as a world power. The world was in fact a single entity, "fundamentally indivisible," and Americans should stop supposing that they could isolate themselves from it.[12]

If only the United States could be persuaded to do its duty in the world, the twentieth century would be the "American" century. Above all, that exercise of power would mean "sharing with all peoples our Bill of Rights, our Declaration of Independence, our Constitution, our magnificent industrial products, our technical skills." Already Americans have spread "American jazz, Hollywood movies, American slang, American machines and patented products," and can spread many more of the items in the American inventory because "we have that indefinable, unmistakable sign of leadership: prestige." Luce proclaimed as "American ideals":

> a love of freedom, a feeling for the equality of opportunity, a tradition of self-reliance and independence and also of co-operation. In addition to ideals and notions which are especially American, we are the inheritors of all the great principles of Western civilization—above all Justice, the love of Truth, the ideal of Charity. [13]

So, the American century would be an era in which American power would implant widely treasured, broadly humane ideals in every continent and in every nation? Exactly. Among the reasons the article created such a splash is that its leading ideas were neither new nor foreign. Walter Lippmann and others had advanced this line of thought with increasing fervor during the previous year's interventionist arguments against isolationists. The time was right for a more dramatic statement. Luce, in keeping with his exceptional sensitivity to the emotional temperature of his contemporaries, pulled it all together cogently and in the pages of *Life*, which had at the time a paid circulation of more than three million. Luce's essay was widely reprinted, in *Reader's Digest*, the *Washington Post*, and elsewhere. The manifesto played very well, and continued to do so once the United States entered the war and later began its Cold War rivalry with the Soviet Union.[14]

Not everyone liked it. Reinhold Niebuhr, who in 1941 was just as interventionist as Luce, was appalled. In an article entitled "Imperialism and Responsibility," Niebuhr warned that "Luce is to be distrusted," because he "revels" in "the white man's new burden." The *Christian Century* agreed, blasting Luce's essay as an insidious charter for an "American imperialism." The *Nation*, too, was contemptuous. From its secular perspective, this progressive magazine agreed with the proudly Protestant *Christian Century* and denounced Luce's essay as merely "a new brand of imperialism." The most widely publicized response was Vice President Henry Wallace's address of the following year, "The Century of the Common Man." Wallace took rather narrow issue with Luce, complaining that he had not pushed hard enough for egalitarian goals within an evangelical nationalism that Wallace actually endorsed. Wallace's vision for America and for the common people of the world was more explicitly Christian than Luce's essay, and considerably more florid in style.[15] Many missionary-connected ecumenical Protestants, however, were reluctant to take public issue with Luce's "American Century" because Luce was so vigorously advocating assistance to China in the face of Japanese aggression. Anyone preoccupied with the fate of the Chinese people welcomed Luce's assistance, even if he was generally a problem child for ecumenical Protestants.

In "The American Century" and throughout his career Luce voiced the conviction that "a moral order," as he put it in 1951, "is universal in time and space." He resisted any suggestion that the classical political ideals of the United States were anything but a manifestation of that universal moral order. "A nation that is formed out of a belief in liberty under law—for others as well as for itself—need not be timorous about asserting its

Authority," Luce said in a widely noted speech of 1961 that fit the attitudes he had been displaying for several decades. Such a nation "need not be laggard in backing its Authority, as necessary, with power."[16]

Luce's unabashed civil-religious talk was a basis for his easy rapport with the American public. It was also a basis for the discomfort felt by theologians like Niebuhr, who had civil-religious ideas of their own but balked at Luce's simplemindedness and his refusal to accept the plurality and contingency of the world. Luce, in turn, had little patience for Protestantism's "eggheads," as he called people like Niebuhr. While he thought of himself as a great man of ideas, Luce enjoyed the company of the deeply anti-intellectual Billy Graham. Luce often invited Graham to write for *Life*, corresponded with him cordially, and spoke warmly to others about Graham's "old fashioned religion."[17] Luce had no interest in Graham's personally confining, socially provincial style of evangelicalism. Nor did Luce seriously contemplate emulating his wife, Clare Booth Luce, who converted to Catholicism in 1946. While remaining institutionally committed to a Presbyterianism for which he rarely displayed any deep feeling, Luce bounced from one spiritual confidant to another. He became friendly with the old missionary theorist and philosopher William Ernest Hocking, who figures largely in several chapters of this book, and with the Jesuit leader John Courtney Murray. Luce's real church was the United States.

However often Luce shifted his spiritual affiliations, he was consistent about China. His affection for the country of his birth was Americo-centric: he ascribed to China the features of the United States that he most liked. He viewed the China of Chiang Kai-shek as a welcome instantiation of what the world could look like under American guidance. His fixation with China appeared suddenly and with great force in 1932, when he visited China for the first time since his departure at the age of twelve. He had paid virtually no attention to China during his years at Hotchkiss and Yale, nor later on, when developing *Time* and *Fortune*. Yet he visited China just when he was beginning to take seriously his own aspirations to redirect the world. China was a big part of that world, and Generalissimo and Madame Chiang Kai-shek made sure Luce understood just how important China was.

The Chiangs were effusive and generous hosts, and made an indelible impression on the thirty-four-year-old Luce. In addition to being Protestant, the Chiangs also conveyed a magnitude and grandeur that appealed to Luce's inclination to assign great historical agency to individual, heroic figures. Luce's susceptibility to the charms of the Chiangs may owe something to his not having an independent take on China. Unlike

Buck and Hersey and many other missionary children, Luce learned very little Chinese. He lived in a missionary compound sharply separated from the local population. Thus the China of the Chiangs was virtually the only China he actually knew. Luce felt a primal connection to China, but when developing this emotion at a pivotal time in his life he was in the thrall of the Chiangs. Once he grabbed on to their cause, he never let go. He put Chiang on the cover of *Time* no fewer than eleven times.[18]

Hence, when it came to American politics, China was different from the other causes Luce espoused. Luce was only mildly right of center. He was on the liberal side of the Republican Party, and regularly collided with Robert Taft, Joseph McCarthy, Barry Goldwater, and other conservative Republicans. But he was with them on China. Luce would not listen when his chief reporter in China during World War II, Theodore White, exposed the corruption and systemic failings of Chiang's government. Editors despaired of the boss's pig-headedness but were obliged to go along. They scored an occasional triumph, as in 1943, publishing in *Life* Pearl Buck's article criticizing Chiang—of which more below. Perhaps the most dramatic indicator of Luce's China-centrism was the specific reason he gave for lamenting the bombing of Hiroshima: by forcing an early Japanese surrender, the American military had prevented Chiang's armies from contributing significantly to the defeat of the Japanese, ensuring that, Luce believed, the Kuomintang would dominate postwar East Asia.[19]

After the Communist Revolution of 1949, Luce joined in the attack on the State Department for having "lost" China. He was less fanatical than Alfred Kohlberg, William F. Knowland, and other leaders of the "China Lobby," but his public standing endowed that informal coalition with more legitimacy than it might otherwise have attained.[20] In that political stance Luce was joined by former Congregationalist missionary Walter Judd, a member of Congress for twenty years, beginning in 1943. Judd was an important figure, but, like Luce, he was far from typical of missionary-connected individuals in this context. Most kept their distance from the postwar attacks on those who "lost" China. Luce's fellow Presbyterian John A. Mackay, the president of Princeton Theological Seminary and himself a former missionary, was among the churchmen who favored American recognition of the People's Republic of China shortly after the Communist Revolution and was vilified for it by evangelical Protestants and right-wing politicians.[21]

Luce's far-right tilt on China-related issues contrasts with his perspective on race, which was more in line with that of missionary children from all foreign fields. *Life* in the 1930s ran stories on the injustices suffered by black Americans. The willingness of Luce's magazines to confront the evils of white racism was anomalous in the context of the affirmative, indeed cheerful perspective on American life that dominated these magazines throughout the years of their greatest popularity. Luce was no radical, even as an advocate of civil rights, but in regard to racial bias, at least, Luce's standard narrative of American society as a consumer's paradise was periodically interrupted. And here Luce's liberal editors suffered no negative micromanaging from the boss, even when residents of the Old Confederacy cancelled subscriptions in droves.

There is no reason to doubt that Luce's views on race owed something to the same missionary-encouraged egalitarianism that propelled many of his contemporaries to yet stronger opposition to Jim Crow and other racial injustices. Luce's egalitarianism was facilitated by the liberal Republican company he kept. There, the political demands of white southerners were more easily ignored than within the contemporary Democratic Party. Still, civil rights was the chief point of disagreement between Luce and Eisenhower, whose commitment Luce thought too weak. Luce strongly supported the US Supreme Court's 1954 *Brown v. School Board* decision to outlaw racial segregation in schools, and he gave extensive attention in *Life* to the use of federal troops to enforce that decision in Little Rock, Arkansas, in 1957. In the next five years Luce's magazines provided sympathetic coverage to the civil rights movement, and commissioned contributions from African American leaders including W.E.B. Du Bois and Stokely Carmichael for *Life*. Luce confronted these Eisenhower-era events in the context of his earlier history of supporting civil rights for African Americans. As early as 1943, Luce told the staff of *Time* that the magazine was "unshakably committed to a pro-Civil Rights policy and a square-deal policy for Negroes as for every kind of American."[22]

Hence Luce's nationalism did not operate in tandem with the white racism common to so many of his nationalist contemporaries. His imperialism was never as overtly racial as that of the European powers. Indeed, Luce's opposition to explicit racism within the United States was part of his global aspirations: the less racist the United States became, the more it deserved to be the world's greatest power. Luce idealized the United States, but white supremacy was a flaw that he recognized and against which he mobilized his magazine's energies.

Luce's career was, among other things, an enactment of the old missionary feeling that one had a responsibility to make things right. In Luce's variation on this theme, the United States replaced Christ as the symbolic and substantive center of the enterprise. This substitution has often been ascribed to many American leaders who proclaim an American "mission" in the world, but neither William McKinley nor Woodrow Wilson or any of the others commonly spoken of in that idiom made this switch as literally as did Henry Luce.

Given that orientation, Luce was right to be suspicious of Buck, and to try to contain her influence. Her sense of what a righted world would look like was not at all like his. Buck had little patience with Chiang Kai-shek and even less for Luce's other great hero, Winston Churchill. Buck was not at all persuaded that the world needed an American empire. Many powerful people were afraid of the great publisher. Buck was not. She was just as famous as Luce, and more revered by her admirers than Luce was by his.

Pearl Sydenstricker Buck was an extraordinary woman whose significance in the histories of the United States, of women, and of feminism remains to be fully registered.[23] Luce's importance has been clear for some time, even if rarely analyzed in relation to his missionary background. Buck is most often remembered as an overrated novelist and as a major influence on American images of China. She was both. But she was also more than that.

Buck was, as James C. Thomson Jr. has observed, the most influential interpreter of China to the West since Marco Polo.[24] *The Good Earth*, published in 1931, was the first and foremost vehicle for her most widely disseminated message, which was that Chinese people were as fully human and endowed with dignity as the average American, and equally worthy of respect. Buck wrote more than seventy other books, fifteen of which were Book-of-the-Month-Club selections and many of which have been published in hundreds of editions. Her writings have been translated into at least thirty-six languages. She is one of the most famous American writers of any generation, and by far the most widely translated female author in American history.[25]

Buck's anti-imperialist, antiracist, and even feminist credentials are impeccable. She advocated independence for India well before it was achieved, opposed the confinement of Japanese Americans, campaigned for the repeal of the Chinese Exclusion Act, and criticized the Kuomintang without romanticizing the Chinese Communists. She demanded that women have access to birth control technologies and as early as 1941 had articulated most of the ideas about women later popularized by Betty Friedan's 1963 volume *The Feminine Mystique*. Buck founded and financed the first adoption agency specializing in transracial adoption, and designed a program to rescue the mixed-race offspring of American soldiers—especially African Americans who fought in the Korean

War—from neglect and rejection in Asian societies. She was a major figure in the reconsideration of the American missionary project itself. In these and other activities, Buck was "an evangelist for equality," in the words of biographer Peter Conn.[26] Buck was, for "three decades," affirms another biographer, Hilary Spurling, a campaigner "for peace, tolerance, and liberal democracy, for the rights of children and minorities, for an end to discrimination on grounds of race and gender."[27]

Buck especially touched American women of her generation, above all those who read magazines like *Reader's Digest* and *Saturday Evening Post*. As late as 1966 readers of *Good Housekeeping* voted her as one of the most admired women in America, surpassed only by Rose Kennedy, mother of the recently martyred president. In 2004, Oprah Winfrey renewed *The Good Earth*'s status as a best-seller by choosing a new edition for her own highly influential Book Club. In a typical reflection of 2010, the young writer Deborah Friedell observed that Buck was the favorite novelist of both of her grandmothers.[28]

It all began with *The Good Earth*. The China depicted in this story of the daily life of a Chinese peasant farmer and his wife is not the China Americans were accustomed to reading about, nor is it the one that China's own intelligentsia wanted broadcast in the United States. In Buck's pages there are no faceless supplicants for assistance, waiting for the American Christians to endow their lives with meaning. Nor are there any cosmopolitan progressives inspired by Sun Yat-sen, bravely propelling a new national community to its rightful, respected place in the company of modern nations. Instead, Buck narrated the tale of a stoic couple, the husband for a while reduced to supporting his family by carrying people on a rickshaw, the wife smothering one baby at birth and selling another into sexual slavery as an adolescent. Wang Lung and Olan are surrounded by, and sometimes participants in, sexual relationships represented in nonromantic but explicitly physical terms. In his old age the male protagonist buys a twelve-year old girl as a concubine.

Buck wrote on the basis of her experience, especially after 1918, when she and her husband moved to the countryside to work among farm families. Lossing Buck was an agricultural economist, studying Chinese farming practices and designing means by which to improve farm productivity. In this rural setting, Pearl Buck dealt regularly with a group of women who told her they had killed female babies of their own, some more than one. These women, and others she met in later years, also spoke to her matter-of-factly about their sexual experiences in a way none of her American friends did. Buck witnessed firsthand throughout the first four decades of her life—even in the more urban environments to which she had been exposed as a child—poverty of the sort described in *The Good Earth*. Her closest missionary friends in China understood what Buck had written, and praised her for telling the truth about what life was like for Chinese peasants.[29]

Some Chinese reviewers were offended. The dreadful conditions experienced by Wang Lung and Olan did not constitute what the Chinese intellectuals of the early 1930s thought was a positive and hopeful view of their society. But in the United States the mundane struggles of this humble pair came across as both stereotype-smashing and appealing. The virtues that Buck ascribed to those suffering from poverty resonated almost magically with American readers, perhaps because the Depression intensified the ability of Americans to see in the Chinese peasant the essential features of the humanity they saw in themselves. Charles Hayford points out that the word *peasant* never appears in the book. Instead, Buck talked about *farmers*.[30] This choice in vocabulary made it much easier for American readers to identify with the Chinese people.

The *Christian Century*'s reviewer marveled that Wang Lung would have been no different "spiritually" had he "toiled on the Nebraska prairie rather than China."[31] The characters in *The Good Earth* were multi-dimensional, striving individuals, each with a distinctive personality, profoundly different from the abstract candidates for conversion and benevolence featured in missionary publications and Sunday night lectures at the local church by furloughed missionaries. Will Rogers, the Oklahoma savant, said it was "not only the greatest book about a people ever written, but the best book of our generation."[32] Few were surprised when *The Good Earth* received the Pulitzer Prize in 1932.

But was China really so much like Nebraska? Of course not. Although *The Good Earth* enabled millions of Americans to see the Chinese people more fraternally than ever before, Buck "in effect created a new stereotype," journalist Harold Isaacs concluded in 1958. "Nobody remembered the evil and wickedness and cruelty" that was abundant in the pages of *The Good Earth*. "What they had retained was an image of the Noble Chinese Peasant, solid, wonderful, virtuous, admirable." Isaacs based these conclusions on interviews with 181 leading academics, public officials, foundation officers, journalists, and other Americans then influential in discussions of China and India. No fewer than sixty-nine "spontaneously mentioned Pearl Buck as a major source of their impressions of the Chinese."[33]

Buck, in fact, presents a more complicated picture than most people remembered. Most of the characters in *The Good Earth* do not display the virtues of Olan and Wang Lung. Other family members, including the couple's own children and their spouses, are shown to be as capable of deceit and dishonorable acts as are human beings elsewhere. Wang Lung's sons conspire to defy his deathbed wishes. Buck is not entirely responsible for the new, somewhat romantic view of the Chinese peasant that is often said to be her chief legacy. Yet *The Good Earth* did not address many complexities of Chinese society, especially the political conflicts implied by Mao Zedong's revolutionary organization of what he called "peasants," a movement that began a hundred miles or so from where Buck was writing.[34]

Buck returned to the same themes in many of her later novels, but in 1936 she published two additional, substantial books that were not about the Chinese, but about American missionaries to China. *The Exile* was a heavily fictionalized biography of her mother, Caroline Stulting Sydenstricker, a missionary wife. *Fighting Angel* was written in the same ambiguous genre, but about her father, Absalom Sydenstricker. Buck herself described both books as biographies, and they have usually been so classified, even though the names are changed, and provide no documentation. The reader is left to wonder, throughout both books, when Buck is recounting an event or a conversation that actually happened or is taking poetic license to an unmeasurable extreme.[35]

Both books are severely negative toward the entire missionary project, and indeed toward Christianity. In Buck's account of her mother's death, the old woman instructed her family to stop playing hymns on the Victrola her daughter had brought home from Shanghai. "O rest in the Lord, Wait patiently for Him," counseled one hymn that the family played. "Take that away. I have waited and patiently—for nothing," Buck has her mother say "with a quiet and profound bitterness."[36] The dying missionary wife lamented that she had not lived her whole life in America. She asked to listen to a foxtrot.

Buck had actually written *The Exile* in 1920, immediately after her mother's death. It was composed rapidly, in anger, first at what she considered to be her mother's largely wasted life and, second, at her father's responsibility for this waste. Buck had not thought to publish it, but reconsidered after *The Good Earth* established her reputation. Her father died, enabling her suddenly to feel comfortable putting the story of her mother before the public, including what the daughter depicted as a disastrous marriage. In addition, Buck's publisher, Richard Walsh, who was also her new husband (she and Lossing Buck divorced in 1934) saw the commercial promise of the manuscript as soon as he read it.

The Exile was such a critical as well as commercial success that Buck was emboldened to write about her father in the same mode. *Fighting Angel* flew out of Buck's typewriter in the spring of 1936 with the same speed and emotional intensity as *The Exile*, and was ready for publication by the fall. *Fighting Angel* mixed resentment at Absalom Sydenstricker with grudging but powerfully expressed appreciation for many aspects of his character. The father had never had much regard for his talented daughter and, if Buck's own testimony is to be believed, handed back the copy of *The Good Earth* she presented to him as a gift, explaining that he did not have time to read it.[37] It was in *Fighting Angel* that Buck stood with almost reverent awe in the face of the "magnificent imperialism of the spirit" quoted at the beginning of this chapter.

The most remarkable feature of *Fighting Angel* is Buck's denial that religious faith defined what really mattered about Absalom Sydenstricker. She would not "tolerate for a moment any mawkish notion" that it was this that gave him strength of character. "Religion had nothing to do with it." Then, registering her own confident stride into post-Protestant secularism, she wrote a passage perhaps unmatched in its intensity in any critical writing about American Protestant missionaries until half a century later, in Hersey's *The Call*: "Had he been of a lesser mind," Buck said about her missionary father,

> he would have chosen a lesser god, had he been born for today he would have chosen another god but whatever he chose would have been as much a god to him. Whatever he did he would have done with that sword-like singleness of heart. As it was, born of the times and of that fighting blood, he chose the finest god he knew and set forth into the universe to make men acknowledge his god to be the one true God before whom all must bow. [38]

Thus did the free-thinking daughter emancipate what she admired in her father from the historically particular Protestant faith in which it was instantiated.

Fighting Angel is all but forgotten today, but it is Buck's most powerful piece of writing. While *The Good Earth* came just at the time American readers were ready to hear about a different China, and made an enduring mark on public attitudes, the constituency for *The Exile* and *Fighting Angel* was limited to the smaller population who cared about missionaries.[39] To secular literary critics of the late 1930s and early 1940s, these books made it easier to classify Buck as "that missionary lady." There was much grousing along this line when Buck was awarded the Nobel Prize in 1938. Robert Frost was widely quoted as saying, "If she can get it, anybody can."[40]

At the time, Sinclair Lewis and Eugene O'Neill were the only Americans to have won the prize. Neither Ernest Hemingway nor John Dos Passos had been so honored, nor Willa Cather, Sherwood Anderson, Thomas Wolfe, James T. Farrell, F. Scott Fitzgerald, or William Faulkner. All of these authors received respectful treatment in Alfred Kazin's *On Native Grounds*, a book of 1942 still appreciated as a comprehensive study of what was then recent American literature. The author of *The Good Earth, The Exile*, and *Fighting Angel* did not make the cut.[41] Michael Gold, Granville Hicks, and Paul Elmer More did. They were in Kazin's view significant enough authors of the 1930s to oblige him to address their work in relation to the work of contemporaries. Kazin was one of a number of critics who simply ignored Buck, even before her fiction deteriorated in the 1940s and after. It was in this spirit that Faulkner in 1949 said he would not want to get a prize from any outfit that would recognize "Mrs. Chinahand Buck."[42]

This disparaging view of Buck continued to be a feature of the American literary scene down through the 1950s and beyond. It became harder to think of Buck as a major writer, in part because her later writings got in the way. Buck imported "the alien conventions of Western pulp fiction into an Eastern setting," notes Spurling, making one novel after another exciting to readers who responded to "the tremulous beating hearts of virgin lovers, the stolen kisses, secret trysts, and sacred pacts, the bloodless stereotypes of true romance." Many millions of her sales followed "not in spite but because of their bland, trite, ingratiating mass-market techniques."[43] Hersey, while apparently trying to be nice, said Buck wrote sixty books too many. Buck was frequently described as a woman who wrote for women and was thus a less serious writer than her male contemporaries. A scholarly study of the history of best sellers egregiously compared *The Good Earth* to the works of Gene Stratton-Porter, the author of the notoriously saccharine *Pollyanna* of 1913 and a series of other books that made Stratton-Porter a favorite foil for the toughness-admiring mid-twentieth-century American literary intelligentsia.[44] There is no doubt, from a twenty-first-century perspective, that sexist prejudice damaged Buck's literary reputation.

But Pearl Buck was not only a novelist and memoirist. By the end of the 1930s she was one of the most vocal feminists in the United States and one of the most active of the white Americans supporting the antiracist struggles of black American leaders.

When Buck talked about women and their place in society, she was, as Hersey noted, forceful and blunt. Buck praised Margaret Sanger's championing of women's reproductive freedom as "the most important movement of the twentieth century." She used her own fame to support Sanger, who in turn hailed Buck as one of the birth control campaign's most effective agents.[45] Buck supported the Equal Rights Amendment as a feminist priority, disagreeing with many friends in the American Association of University Women and elsewhere who thought it a political mistake. In a 1941 symposium on "Woman's Next Step," Buck was "the most uncompromising" voice, concludes Peter Conn. Even in the company of Margaret Mead, Eleanor Roosevelt, Ethel Barrymore, and the eighty-two-year-old relic of an earlier feminist wave, Carrie Chapman Catt, Buck was way out in front. Sexually, according to Buck, the United States was trapped in the Middle Ages. Equality, moreover, was constantly downplayed under the guise of giving women "privileges."[46] In a *New York Times* symposium and in other writings of the late 1930s and 1940s, Buck exhorted American women to abandon their alleged "privileges," In her strident book of 1941, *Of Men and Women*, she asked women to renounce

> the privilege of remaining ignorant in spite of education, the privilege of mental laziness, of not having to think thoroughly through anything because she knows the ultimate decision will not rest on her, the privilege of being willful and capricious and irresponsible, the privilege of idleness and of having time to spend lavishly on self-adornment and amusement, and the privilege of escape from the problems of the world, which are now the real problems of life, by retreating from them into her home and considering that her whole duty is there.[47]

Instead, the American woman should "become an adult creature ready for the responsibilities of liberty." In keeping with these sentiments, Buck emulated Elizabeth Cady Stanton and lamented that Stanton's radicalism had been forgotten. A generation earlier Stanton "was called the greatest woman in the United States, and by some the greatest in the world," she remarked ruefully. "The truth has never been told about women in history," she observed in 1941. She railed against the idea that women's place was in the home, and advocated equal pay for men and women doing equal work. She complained that the constraints of American life had made too many women into "social idiots," unaware of their own potential. Unless women are made free, Buck prophesied in the same agitator's voice she directed against the traditional missionary project, "someday men are going to find that it is cheaper just to keep women in cells and cages or barracks or harems whence they can be summoned when service is wanted."[48] In 1958, Buck stood down television journalist Mike Wallace in an interview in which Wallace tried to depict Buck as an enemy of men and as someone who had no sympathy for women who choose to focus on their families.[49]

Buck's own personal life scandalized the more conservative segment of her old missionary community. Before divorcing her first husband in 1934, she travelled openly and with undisguised pleasure in China, France, and the United States with her publisher, Richard Walsh. She was rumored to have had an affair even earlier with a dashing Chinese man-about-town in Nanking, but Buck seems to have enjoyed the notoriety whether or not the affair actually took place. Buck soon married Walsh, but when this second husband, to whom she was undoubtedly devoted, died in 1960, Buck soon took up with a young man whom she had hired as a dancing instructor for her daughters. Theodore Harris was a handsome high school dropout nearly forty years Buck's junior. She lived with Harris in her final years and, against the advice of friends and family, left him with full authority over her affairs following her death at the age of eighty-two.[50] It is unclear how many of her millions of female fans knew or cared about these behaviors, which were, of course, not unusual among males of her generation. Henry Luce, to take an example close to Buck, had extramarital affairs, several of which were not very secret even at the time. In many ways, then, professionally and politically and sexually, Pearl Buck lived "like a man."

In this respect, as in others, Buck's feminism is very much like that voiced by Betty Friedan in 1963. Consider Friedan's petulant complaint in *The Feminine Mystique* that Margaret Mead betrayed in her writings about gender the lessons that Mead was simultaneously and compellingly teaching in her actual life. Mead's celebration of stereotyped femininity "cut down" women, while her actions in the world proved women could be everything that Mead in her writings suggested they should not be. "Margaret Mead has lived a life of open challenge, and lived it proudly," Friedan proclaimed, making her way "in what was still very much a 'man's world' without denying that she was a woman."[51] Friedan never mentions Mead's contemporary, Buck, who by Friedan's standards was a much better feminist. Friedan's publisher sent the manuscript of *The Feminine Mystique* to Buck, who endorsed it with great enthusiasm.[52]

Buck's vibrant feminism is too easily missed even today because of the relative absence, during her generation, of organizations devoted to the radical view of women's rights she espoused. By contrast, Buck's endeavors on behalf of African Americans were allied with a number of institutions, affiliations, and initiatives. Upon returning from China in 1932, she became a regular contributor to *The Crisis*, the magazine of the National Association for the Advancement of Colored People (NAACP), on the board of which she then served. She also joined the board of the National Urban League, and wrote for its magazine, *Opportunity*. For several decades she was a trustee of the historically black Howard University. During World War II, especially, African American leaders Channing Tobias and Walter White could count on Buck to take part in antiracist symposia and rallies. In a Madison Square Garden meeting of 1942, White, as president of the NAACP, named Buck and Eleanor Roosevelt as two white Americans who, unlike just about all other whites, had a deep understanding of the situation of American blacks.[53]

Buck supported the argument of the African American intelligentsia that the war against fascism abroad must also be a struggle against racism at home. She vehemently criticized the racism of Winston Churchill and the British Empire, and liked to remind people that America's great ally Churchill was doggedly defending a racist operation from top to bottom. The *New York Times* reported Buck saying, in a speech of September 1943, that America's alliance with the British Empire sent a signal to "three-quarters of the people of the world that we are fascist-minded, that we believe in a dominant race, a dominant State, the domination of color, of empire." Buck was friendly with Paul Robeson, while finding him too uncritical of the Soviet Union, and in 1949 coauthored a book about racism with Robeson's wife, Eslanda. Such doings caught the attention of J. Edgar Hoover's FBI, which eventually compiled a dossier of more than three hundred pages on Buck's political activities and affiliations. At a time when the perspective of W.E.B. Du Bois was ignored or considered too radical by most white liberals, Buck in 1945 wrote a resoundingly positive review of Du Bois's *Color and Democracy: Colonies and Peace* in the *New York Herald Tribune.*[54]

Buck was driven in part by impatience with the empowered white males with whom she dealt and to whose enlightenment she felt a duty to contribute, given the remarkable opportunities with which she found herself. She acted in the spirit of the old missionary feeling that one had to make the world right. "In the night, or a dozen times a day," Buck once confessed to her sister, Grace, "I find myself thinking furiously about the peoples of the world, as if they were my personal responsibility."[55]

The confluence of opportunity and duty also resulted in Buck's distinctive role in the development of both transracial and international adoption. In 1949, she established Welcome House, which became a leading agency for placing mixed-race and foreign-born children with American adoptive parents. There was a prior, personal context for Buck's interest in adoption. Buck gave birth to a daughter, Carol, in 1920, but soon thereafter had to undergo a hysterectomy. She and her then husband, Lossing Buck, decided to adopt a child, and were all the more eager to do so when it became clear that Carol suffered from severe mental retardation. The Bucks adopted a girl, Janet, in Ithaca, New York, in 1928. Buck later adopted four more children with her second husband, Walsh.

Because Buck was widely known to be an adoptive parent, as well as an anti racist and humanitarian, she was asked late in 1948 to help place a fifteen-month-old, mixed-race boy. His two extended families rejected him: both the white missionary family whose daughter had given birth to him, and the South Asian family of the boy's father. A social worker at her wit's end literally dropped off the little boy at Buck's door. Buck took up the cause with her characteristic determination, only to discover that none of the agencies she approached would help because of the child's racial mixture. Infuriated by the racism of the adoption system, the radical universalist-integrationist Buck founded her own agency. Welcome House survived Buck, and by the 1990s had placed more than five thousand children.[56]

Buck developed the specialty of dealing with the offspring of American soldiers and Asian women, especially in Korea, but other countries, too, where mixed-race babies were routinely mistreated.[57] Buck knew that racism was not peculiar to the United States, and she was no less vitriolic in condemning it abroad than at home. Having always considered herself as much Asian as American, both causes of transracial and international adoption were natural for her. Buck's feeling that she had both a duty and an opportunity to do something in this domain intensified when she found that American magazines, normally eager to print anything Buck sent them, refused an article she had written about mixed-race babies in Korea. Neither the *Ladies Home Journal* nor *Look* wanted to call readers' attention to the frequency with which American soldiers impregnated Korean women.[58] Might the sons and husbands of the women reading these magazines be guilty of such conduct? It was a thought not even to be considered, and certainly could not be prompted by anything American women might read in a popular magazine.

During the 1950s the causes of transracial and intercountry adoption became the primary focus of Buck's philanthropic energy. She and Richard Walsh adopted two more children, both mixed-race, as their earlier adopted children had not been. Adoption and child protection remained a major interest for the rest of Buck's life. When she died in 1973, a different movement was emerging in adoption circles, arguing that children should always be placed with parents of the same race, and that mixed-race children should always be classified as nonwhite. Buck did not live to contest this movement, but the institutions she founded continued to flourish, including the Pearl S. Buck Foundation, which focuses on the welfare of children of mixed Asian and non-Asian (black or white) descent. Theodore Harris's alleged mismanagement of the affairs of this foundation led to great tensions between Harris on the one side and Buck's children on the other.

In these later years Buck was a less active discussant of American policy toward China than previously, but what she said in the 1940s about Nationalist and Communist China was not forgotten, especially by those who disagreed with her. Her major concern at first was the defense of the Chinese people from Japanese aggression and she was, by 1940, a leading figure in organizations lobbying for American support for Chiang Kai-shek in the war against the Japanese imperial army. She also produced fiction with the same message, most notably in *Dragon Seed*, a novel of 1941 based on the 1937 Nanking Massacre.[59] But Buck was never enthusiastic about Chiang, whose doings even before she departed China in 1932 had dismayed most of the missionary community there. Her public statements about the generalissimo and his regime were increasingly skeptical. She did not claim to know much about the Communists but let it be known that she would not be surprised if eventually they controlled China. Buck had been reserved in her complaints about the Kuomintang, but in the spring of 1943 came out swinging.

Eleanor Roosevelt asked Buck's opinion of the Chiangs in the wake of a well-organized propaganda visit Madame Chiang made to Washington that year, where she received a standing ovation from a joint session of Congress and was a guest at the White House.[60] Further, the First Lady asked Buck's advice concerning a good will visit that Mrs. Roosevelt had suggested to the president that she, as the president's wife, make to China. Eleanor Roosevelt knew Buck reasonably well and trusted her judgment. Buck responded that the Kuomintang would never be a democratic force in China and that Henry Luce's increasingly florid celebration of the Chiangs in *Time* partook of a Churchill-like imperialism. In response to Mrs. Roosevelt's request for a more detailed briefing, Buck wrote a confidential twelve-page memorandum. In it, Buck compared Chiang's purges to Stalin's, predicted that the masses of Chinese would not support Chiang in the struggle against the Communists expected to follow the defeat of the Japanese, and admitted that much as she despised Communism, its Chinese leaders appeared to be confronting the needs of the people more effectively than the Nationalist government. Buck suggested that her friend try to meet personally with Zhou Enlai to learn more for herself about the Communist movement in China. [61]

The president and his advisers decided against sending Mrs. Roosevelt to China, at least at that time. But Buck knew that her ideas, once discussed in high Washington circles where Chiang had many friends, would soon be bandied about. So Buck determined to go public and asked Luce himself if he would be willing to publish her opinions in *Life* magazine. He agreed. Just this once. Luce went ahead despite his worry that, once published, "President Roosevelt can take the Buck analysis as an excuse" to reduce American aid to Chiang. Buck's article in *Life* of May 10, 1943—"A Warning about China"—actually argued for more aid to Nationalist China, and it is not clear what impact the article had on Roosevelt and his circle of advisers. But the article cut significantly into what had been the American press's uncritical treatment of the Kuomintang. "American disillusionment as to Free China came with a bang," wrote John K. Fairbank forty years later. Buck's article and two others that followed quickly by journalists Hanson Baldwin and T. A. Bisson changed the conversation about Chiang.[62] Buck's brief essay warned that Chiang's corrupt government, however obliged the United States may be to work with it during the war against Japan, was not a reliable ally in the long run. The Kuomintang had failed to institute the reforms that would benefit the masses of Chinese people.

Buck's intervention was important because of her unique prominence as a popular authority on China and also because it came so early in the development of doubts about the Kuomintang. Her *Life* article appeared well over a year before Foreign Service officers John Paton Davies, Jr. and John S. Service pressed privately upon the State Department their strongly negative assessments of Chiang and their evidence that the Communists were winning the struggle to control the future of China. Since the "China Hands" were government officials rather than private citizens expressing an opinion, it was they, more than Buck, whom the China Lobby and conservative Republicans later blamed for "losing China." But Buck was part of the problem, and Luce personally was unforgiving. It was following this article of 1943 that Luce told his editors that "we must never say anything favorable about Pearl Buck."[63]

Buck's participation in the policy debates about China contains a paradox important to understanding her career. She was recognized as an authority on China, but her pronouncements about it were rarely as specific as her ideas about race, gender, and empire, domains where she had no more expertise than countless other intellectuals of her time and place. Buck was always more of a position-taker than an analyst. She was the most comfortable with clear-cut, black-and-white contentions, where she could speak confidently on the basis of general principles.[64] This worked well enough for her on many of the issues on which she held forth, but it proved difficult on the matter of policy toward China. On that vexing issue, complexities refused to dissolve into clear-cut rules for action. Buck never engaged the Chinese Communist movement closely enough to get beyond general suspicions matched with general impressions of its successful appeal to the impoverished and exploited Chinese masses. What she said about Chiang Kai-shek and his government was more substantive, but Buck had not been in China since 1932 and she never developed the more detailed political analysis that distinguished the books and articles of Edgar Snow, T. A. Bisson, Hanson Baldwin, and other journalists of the period.[65]

Buck's commentaries on China were always village-centered. She continued, year after year, to imply that the Chinese "farmer" was apolitical or could somehow be analyzed without taking into account the actual political conflicts of the period. "Buck was at her best," diplomatic historian Michael H. Hunt explains, in reshaping "American attitudes toward Asia," in advancing perspectives on China in particular that were more "realistic" than had been the norm, and in offering "prescient" visions of the future of China and Asia in world history.[66] But Buck did not have much to say about the most important event in modern Chinese history, the Chinese Revolution of 1949.

When the American public was bombarded with poorly informed and ideologically driven analyses of the revolution, Buck did not produce the book or article on this world-historical event that everyone would have eagerly read. Instead, in 1951 she published her novel excoriating Luce, which got little attention and was, in any event, a peculiar investment of her energy at the time. She shifted her attention to transracial and inter-country adoption. She became a more authoritative voice on many issues other than the one on which she had earned the most authority: China.

But late in life, long after she had withdrawn from the China debates, Buck still identified strongly with that land. She was eager to be part of the delegation led by President Richard Nixon and Secretary of State Henry Kissinger that reopened American relations with China in 1972. Sadly for her, she was refused, despite the intervention made on her behalf by missionary son John S. Service. By then Service was restored to grace within the circles of the American government and had reestablished contact with some of the Chinese Communist leaders he came to know during the war. But Zhou En-lai himself was said to have made the decision to refuse Buck entry. She received a letter from a low-ranking official in the Canadian embassy of the People's Republic explaining that "in view of the fact that for a long time you have in your works taken an attitude of distortion, smear, and vilification towards the people of China and its leaders, I am authorized to inform you that we cannot accept your request for a visit to China."[67] Buck died the next year, too late for the great reversal in her standing in China. Buck was rehabilitated and widely celebrated as one of China's best friends in the West.[68]

Buck's personal identification with China deepened during the last few years of her life. At odds with her children, including Janice, the oldest, who told interviewers that Buck had scarcely gotten to know them, the elderly author withdrew even more than before into the company of Theodore Harris. She also kept around her a group of women who struck some visitors as "ladies in waiting," with Buck herself affecting the manners of a Chinese empress. This impression was left on the highly sympathetic James Claude Thomson Jr., who grew up knowing her as "Aunt Pearl." Thomson's mother, Margaret Thomson, had been one of Buck's closest friends in China.[69]

The tombstone of the author of *The Good Earth* bears, at her request, only Chinese characters.

Buck died at a time when second-wave feminism was changing the United States. Buck herself was no longer paying attention. Few who wrote about her on the occasion of her death in 1973 linked her to that contemporary movement. John Hersey did just that. He insisted that Buck had anticipated "nearly every single one" of the discoveries about gender that were commanding unprecedented attention.[70] Hersey's own work never focused on gender, but he was sensitive to a dimension of Buck's career that really mattered, and at a time when it was not recognized by others as it surely could have been. This sensitivity reflected a deep continuity in basic values between the younger Hersey—he was born twenty-two years after she was—and the older author whom he wished ruefully had written fewer, better books.

The most striking continuity between Hersey and Buck, almost never noticed, was in the character and cultural impact of their two greatest achievements. *Hiroshima* of 1946, like *The Good Earth* of 1932, offered a stark, realistic picture of Asian peoples. Both rendered a distant population more fully human than American readers had previously been encouraged to see. Hersey's target population was of course the Japanese, as represented by the victims of the atomic bomb dropped on the city of Hiroshima on August 6, 1945. Hersey's book was reportage, not fiction, and the basic humanity of its cast of characters gained significance in the wholly different context of savage warfare. Hersey was primarily addressing a particular weapon and the effects of its use, not the character of

Japanese life. But the book's humanization of an alien people followed all the more compellingly from the fact that it was the hated "Japs" who experienced the bomb's effects as detailed by Hersey. Moreover, it was the absence of any theoretical apparatus or hortatory and didactic framing that enabled *Hiroshima*, no less than *The Good Earth*, to seize the moral sensitivities of American readers at a specific historical moment. The two books are of different genres and emerged from different matrices, but their methods and their consequences have much in common.

In addition to *Hiroshima*, of which I have more to say below, Hersey wrote many other books. His novel of 1944, *A Bell for Adano*, won a Pulitzer Prize and became the model for a host of later books that address the good and bad roles Americans play abroad, including the novel of 1958 by Eugene Burdick and William Lederer, *The Ugly American*.[71] Another of Hersey's novels, *The Wall*, published in 1950, was widely acclaimed at the time of its publication. Hersey was also known for two books of wartime reportage, *Men on Bataan* (1942) and *Into the Valley* (1943), written while he was on assignment for Luce's *Time* and *Life* magazines. In his later career he taught at Yale University and published several volumes of short stories and many other novels—*A Single Pebble* (1956), *The War Lover* (1959) and *The Child Buyer* (1960) were the best received—culminating in his most distinguished work of fiction, *The Call* (1985), a 767-page meditation on the missionary impulse to make things right.

Hersey was so important a writer by 1953 that he was, at the age of thirty-nine, elected to the American Academy of Arts and Letters, the youngest person ever to be so honored. During his lifetime Hersey was also highly visible in his civic engagements. He was active in the presidential campaigns of Adlai Stevenson, in opposing the Vietnam War, in defending black civil rights activists, and in lobbying for progressive educational policies and practices. He was an officer in several organizations of professional writers, and was a close friend of James Agee, Ralph Ellison, and a number of other leading writers of his time. His *The Algiers Motel Incident* (1971), a book about a police killing of black men in Detroit, helped establish him, along with Norman Mailer, as one of the most politically active writers of his generation. He wrote an introduction to a volume of Ansel Adams's photographs of the Manzanar internment camp for Japanese Americans that was influential in the later creation of the Manzanar memorial.[72] He was a committed internationalist, and a longtime member of the United World Federalists. "My prevailing interest has been in the world as a whole," he declared near the end of his life, "and in the place of a person in a larger setting than one defined by national boundaries."[73]

Hersey spent his early years in the coastal city of Tientsin, where his Congregationalist father worked as a YMCA secretary. Although residing in the British concession, Hersey's family encouraged him to get to know local Chinese. He learned to speak their language before he mastered English. In the urban environment of his father's YMCA station, Hersey was surrounded by the most liberal and reformist style of missionary activity then found in China. Hersey's path into American life, like Luce's, proceeded through the Hotchkiss School and Yale University. But Hersey, even though also elected to Skull and Bones, was less in the thrall of the prep-and-Ivy social hierarchies than Luce had been a few years earlier. After finishing college in 1936, Hersey studied for a year in England at the University of Cambridge. He then took a job at *Time* in 1937, although apparently with little connection to Luce. "I wrote a piece that was as far from *Time*'s style as I could make it be," he enjoyed telling people in later years. "I wrote a twenty-four-page essay on how rotten *Time* was."[74] The staff person who hired him liked its brass and literary zing, so Hersey's life as a journalist began. Hersey interacted occasionally with Luce, who in 1939 sent him to Chungking to cover the Japanese-Chinese War.

Hersey's assignments for *Time* and *Life* took him all over the Pacific, including Guadalcanal, where he was embedded with Marine combat troops. The secretary of the navy later commended him for volunteering to go under fire to assist in hauling wounded soldiers to a field hospital. While working from China, he hired the later-to-be-famous journalist Theodore White as a "stringer" for *Time*. Both Hersey and White became more and more at odds with Luce.[75] Still, Luce understood that Hersey was a crack journalist and asked him to help run his magazines. Hersey pondered the offer but decided to stay in the field. He was also posted to Europe, where he was among the journalists who followed Gen. Patton's Third Army into Italy.

Hersey's revulsion at Patton's crypto-fascist style led to *A Bell for Adano*. In that novel, which he wrote in a three-week period of reclusion upon his return home from Europe, Hersey contrasted the moral qualities of two imaginary American army officers. One is a conscientious major who tries mightily to serve the interests of the occupied community of Sicilians in his charge; the other is the general in command of the entire operation, "a bad man, something worse than what our troops were trying to throw out." Hersey's pointed prose quickly dispelled any doubt that Patton was the model for General Marvin. "Probably you just know what has been in the Sunday supplements," a great hero, "the man who still wears spurs even though he rides everywhere in an armored car; the man who fires twelve rounds from his captured Luger pistol every morning before breakfast . . . the beloved deliverer of Italian soil."[76]

To discredit the general's comic bravado, gratuitous cruelties, and vulgar characterizations of the local population, Hersey invented Major Joppolo, an American son of Florentine immigrants who was deeply sensitive to the loss—amid warfare—of the fictional town of Adano's seven-hundred-year-old bell. The townspeople had measured their daily lives by its hourly ringing. Joppolo's efforts to replace the bell are an emblem for his constant and even-handed administration of local affairs. Joppolo was obviously the kind of American the world needed—not only generous and fair, but appreciative of local conditions and culture— while Marvin was the kind of American that should embarrass the folks at home: imperious, self-aggrandizing, and oblivious to the actual needs and aspirations of the people around him. The American army was there to free the Italians, but the residents of Adano "would not feel truly free," the major explained to some naval officers he knew, "until they heard a bell ringing from the clock tower in the Palazzo."[77] Joppolo was based on the best qualities Hersey had seen in among the American troops. These qualities were exactly what many American readers were eager to ascribe to their soldiers.

Hersey's Joppolo functioned,more concretely as an image of what the American military occupation of a defeated country should look like. Historian Susan L. Carruthers suggests that *A Bell for Adano*'s "most consequential ideological achievement was perhaps its least self-conscious," the popularization of the sense that the American military's "untrammeled authority over a defeated population" was natural and, given proper leadership (Jappolo instead of Patton!), benevolent and suitably respectful of local interests. For all of Hersey's critique of the wrong kind of Americans, *A Bell for Adano* depicts Sicilians "as people without either ideas or initiative," lacking "political convictions" about the postwar order "beyond simple gratitude" for the American liberation.[78] Carruthers calls attention to features of the 1944 novel that are all the more striking when considered in relation to *Hiroshima*, where Hersey attends carefully to the distinctive personhood of individual Japanese victims of the atomic bomb. Hersey's rapidly written *A Bell for Adano* was perhaps all the more popular on account of the simplicity of a good vs. bad framing that was much less characteristic of his later work. As an artifact of the historical moment, *A Bell for Adano* has much in common with another best-seller of 1944, *Anna and the King of Siam*, written by former missionary Margaret Landon, which I take up in a later chapter.

Neither *A Bell for Adano*'s enthusiastic readers, nor its author—stunned as he was by its success—had any notion at the time of the book's long-term significance as the pioneer work in a literary tradition of similar accounts of how Americans behaved in non-Western countries. Vern Sneider's 1951 novel, *Teahouse of the August Moon*, told the story of an American army captain trying to establish democratic institutions on Okinawa immediately after the war. Sneider himself had been a soldier in the occupation of Okinawa, and was inspired by Hersey's novel about the occupation of Italy. Playwright John Patrick turned Sneider's novel into a long-running Broadway production in 1951, and Sneider's story was further etched in American popular consciousness by a 1956 Hollywood film starring Glenn Ford and Marlon Brando. *The Ugly American* developed the theme with characters from the US diplomatic corps and within a fictional country in Southeast Asia. For these reasons, in part, this novel became a classic of the Vietnam and post-Vietnam eras.[79]

The success of *A Bell for Adano* consolidated Hersey's transformation from journalist to novelist. Yet when he received the Pulitzer Prize in 1945, Hersey was still a foreign correspondent, too. By this time he was married to Frances Ann Cannon, a textile heiress from North Carolina whose Protestant family had discouraged her from marrying her previous boyfriend, the Catholic youth John F. Kennedy. Hersey and Frances had begun a family but Hersey was off again, this time to Moscow during the final stages of the European war. Soviet authorities allowed him to travel behind the Red Army, where he saw the ruins of the Warsaw ghetto after its destruction by the Nazis. This experience was the foundation for *The Wall*, his Holocaust-centered novel of 1950. Shortly after returning from Europe, Hersey received the journalistic assignment that resulted in *Hiroshima*. Still writing for Luce's magazines but not bound exclusively to them, Hersey accepted the joint invitation of Luce and *New Yorker* editor William Shawn to spend the winter of 1945–46 in Japan, writing about the aftermath of the war.[80]

Hersey decided to focus on the city of Hiroshima and the survivors of the atomic bomb attack. He interviewed more than forty local inhabitants, and selected the stories of six to recount in a single article. The idea of telling six stories was inspired, Hersey later explained, by his reading of Thornton Wilder's *The Bridge at San Luis Rey*, a novel about six people killed when a suspension bridge in the Andes collapsed early in the eighteenth century.[81] None of Hersey's six were soldiers, which meant that the victims of the bomb could be distinguished from those who may well have tortured American POWs or raped Chinese women in Nanking.

Once they read it, the *New Yorker*'s editors took the extraordinary decision to devote one entire issue to Hersey's text, dated August 31, 1946, just over a year after the dropping of the bombs on Hiroshima and Nagasaki. It was an instant sensation. Albert Einstein reportedly ordered a thousand copies to distribute to people he wanted to read it. Countless readers reported that they stopped everything to finish the article in silence. The piece was widely reprinted and was published as a book. There were a few negative reviews, mostly from New York intellectuals associated with the *Partisan Review*. Dwight Macdonald wished for the moral outrage that was so obviously lacking. Mary McCarthy complained that Hersey had filled his book with "busy little Methodists."[82] But *Hiroshima* played just as well over the long run as it did when it first came into print. In 1999, a thirty-six-expert panel named *Hiroshima* the finest piece of journalism written in the twentieth century.[83] In 2015, the seventieth anniversary of the dropping of the bomb and the Japanese surrender, *Hiroshima* received another round of appreciation.

Hiroshima is a materially dense, highly naturalistic, and meticulously detailed account of the experience of each of the six survivors, told without any reflection. Hersey does not even suggest that the significance of the stories is that nuclear arms should be banned, or that their use on the Japanese was a moral error. Nor does he hint that it was all a matter of collateral damage, something that had to be done to end the war and save the lives of American soldiers and many more Japanese than were killed or injured by the atomic bombs. Those issues were very much on the minds of readers, and the ensuing discussion of the work shows that appreciation for what Hersey wrote bridged virtually all gaps between people with differing opinions on those issues.

"The power of his text is not just a matter of its raw material," the British writer Jeremy Treglown has observed. "There is his startling intimacy with the people he writes about: with poor, maddened Mr. Fukai, determined to break free of his rescuers and run back into the flames to die; with Dr. Sasaki, wearing the spectacles he has borrowed from a nurse, applying first aid to surviving patients." Hersey was "a war poet as much as a journalist," adds Treglown, because of the "combination of subdued, empirical fact-telling and unobtrusive fantasy."[84] It was Hersey's exact word choice that made the big difference.

He did not publish the transcripts of what his interviewees said; rather, he rendered the details of their experience in his own carefully selected words. Two examples:

> Just as she turned her head away from the window, the room was filled with a blinding light. She was paralyzed by fear, fixed still in her chair for a long moment. Everything fell and she lost consciousness . . . bookcases right of her swooped forward and the contents threw her down with her left leg horribly twisted and breaking beneath her. There, in the tin factory, in the first moment of the atomic age, a human being was crushed by books.[85]

> Mr. Tanimoto . . . met hundreds and hundreds who were fleeing, and every one of them seemed to be hurt in some way. The eyebrows of some were burned off and skin hung from their faces and hands. Others, because of pain, held their arms up as if carrying something in both hands. Some were vomiting as they walked. Many were naked or in shreds of clothing. On some undressed bodies, the burns had made patterns—of undershirt straps and suspenders, and on the skin of some women (since white repelled the heat from the bomb and dark clothes absorbed it and conducted it to the skin), the shapes of flowers they had had on their kimonos.[86]

Treglown is the latest in what is now a seventy-year procession of commentators trying to find the right vocabulary to describe such novelistic but fact-driven passages. Hersey's prose seems neither fish nor fowl, but whatever is, it is vividly so. Literary scholars have come to classify *Hiroshima* as a "non-fiction novel." This is the designation chosen by *The Cambridge History of the American Novel* of 2011.[87] Hersey hated to hear this work described as virtually a novel. He cared deeply about its verisimilitude, and always distinguished sharply between journalism and fiction. Historian Michael Yavenditti accurately summarized much of the discussion:

> Hersey's work aroused many readers but incited few of them. It enabled American readers to reaffirm their humane sentiments and to examine their consciences, but "Hiroshima" did not require Americans to question the legitimacy of the bomb's use. Hersey did not write a call to action or a polemic against American decision-makers. Had he done so, his appeal might well have been reduced. Hersey struck precisely the right note by inviting readers to view the bomb victims as objectively and sympathetically as he had.[88]

Hersey himself told Yavenditti in 1971 of his own enduring belief that his "deliberate suppression of horror" was vital to the work's impact, creating "an effect far more morally disturbing" than if "I shouted or screamed my outrage."[89]

It is this nonhortatory quality that most renders *Hiroshima* akin to *The Good Earth*. And, like Buck's novel, Hersey's poetic reportage enables readers to experience a great variety of emotions while recognizing the basic humanity of the people whose lives are being displayed on the page. Ruth Benedict's *The Chrysanthemum and the Sword* also enabled Americans of 1946 to recognize more humanity in "the Japs" than they had before, but Benedict wrote sweepingly about national traits, while Hersey, like, Buck, wrote about specific individuals. Unlike Benedict's book, which sold only twenty-eight thousand copies in twenty-five years,[90] *Hiroshima* was a runaway bestseller and Hersey received personal letters from readers for decades, right up until his death in 1993. Just as Edgar Snow addressed many more issues about the China of the 1930s than Buck, Benedict presented a broad picture of Japanese culture as a matrix for contemporary politics and society. But neither Snow nor Benedict reached the audiences Buck and Hersey did, conveying the humanity of the most distant and foreign peoples.

The writing of *Hiroshima*, Hersey later declared, made him all the more determined to act on the inspiration he had in 1944 when he visited the Warsaw ghetto and several Red Army- controlled sites where Germans had slaughtered Jews. (In one case, in Estonia, he saw the bodies still on the ground, left by the rapidly retreating Germans.) *The Wall*, like *Hiroshima*, is about survivors. Composing *The Wall* was a process antithetical to the quick effusion that produced *A Bell for Adano*. Hersey spent three years collecting information, working with translators, and struggling with the deep question of how he as a non-Jew could find an appropriate voice to write about Jews in the Third Reich. When the 632-page novel finally appeared, it was told in the persona of a Jewish historian experiencing the Warsaw ghetto and escaping from it. Noach Levinson recorded what he saw in a diary and cited documents from the earlier history of Polish Jewry. Although entirely fictional, the text Hersey wrote in Levinson's voice was dominated by details plausible to anyone who had studied the history of the Warsaw ghetto and its destruction. Hersey's Levinson put before the reader the debates within Levinson's circle, including those over what it meant to be Jewish. Hersey feared that even the device of Levinson did not give him the standing to talk about what he referred to in *The Wall* as "the holocaust."[91] *The Wall* was well received, including by Jewish readers, about whose reaction Hersey had been the most concerned.

The magazine *Commentary*, then at the peak of its influence as a forum for and about American Jews of secular as well as religious orientation, published a highly appreciative review. "It is amazing that someone with no trace of a Jewish background should have been able to write convincingly about the Warsaw ghetto using throughout the words of an imaginary Jewish character," wrote David Daiches. "Earlier reviewers of *The Wall* have not, it seems to me, sufficiently recognized the magnitude of Mr. Hersey's achievement here, or the degree of human warmth which prompted it." Daiches proposed that the book be read as

> the record of its author's passionate endeavor to discover what these people were who aroused the sadistic furies of the Nazis, how they lived, what they thought and felt, and what it was like to be caught in a ghetto and doomed to extinction. One can see that anxiety to find out what it must have been like in the book's form: Levinson the archivist, always listening, always observing, always interrogating, always writing down what people said or did in particular circumstances, is surely a projection of Mr. Hersey himself.[92]

Part of the novel's significance is its forthright confrontation of a monumental feature of recent history much less discussed in 1950 than in later decades.[93] *The Wall's* critical standing declined in later decades, but in its historical moment the book was a literary event of real consequence. Literary scholar Werner Sollors describes it as "perhaps the first American novel to confront the Holocaust fully and centrally."[94] *The Wall* was also another exercise in empathic identification carried out by a missionary-connected author, demanding that readers very distant geographically and ethnically from the Jewish victims of Nazism achieve at least some understanding of what that Jewish experience had been. Hersey's version of the old responsibility to make things right was above all to overcome the barriers and prejudices between different kinds of human beings.

In the setting of precisely that imperative, *The Wall* was important also for its development, through the character of Levinson, of what Hersey himself described—in a rare interview, when he was seventy-two years old—as a "missionary figure" that had been repeatedly "displaced" by a sequence of his fictional protagonists. "There are repetitions of the same figure throughout my books," Hersey suggested to Jonathan Dee in his *Paris Review* interview of 1986. "Major Joppolo in *A Bell for Adano*, I suppose, displaced" the missionary committed to making things right. These characters in Hersey's novels often operate in confined circumstances, as with Levinson, but they are driven by a commitment to diminish suffering and put things in the best possible order. They are morally intense figures in whatever social domain surrounds them. Hersey also named Noach Levinson in *The Wall* as such a character. "I don't think that any of this is conscious—I've not thought of this sort of connection until now," Hersey told Dee. The exchange was prompted by Dee's remark that Hersey had not written about his native China at any length until his novel of 1956, *A Single Pebble*.[95]

"Yes, and there the missionary figure is displaced by the figure of the engineer," Hersey immediately responded to Dee's observation. *A Single Pebble* tells of an American engineer who expected modern technology and Western social ideals to transform China. The engineer gradually realizes that this is not so easy. China is complicated and in many ways contradictory. *A Single Pebble* is a story, as David Sanders notes, of "the failures of both Western technology and Western meliorism." Hersey's displaced missionaries reflect a highly idealistic version of the missionary impulse, but they do not always succeed, as the case of the naïve engineer illustrates. *A Single Pebble* did not generate much interest, but it prefigures the theme of *The Call*. There, in the career-climaxing novel to which I will turn in a moment, a technologically engaged but religiously devout missionary spends a lifetime of experiencing failure while denying that he failed. There is no displacement in *The Call*. Hersey directly confronted something that he told Dee was his long-term preoccupation: the "deep impulse . . . of wanting to be useful and helpful in the world."[96]

Between writing *A Single Pebble* and publishing *The Call* twenty-nine years later, Hersey produced more than a dozen books, many while teaching at Yale from 1965 until his retirement in 1984. He was an active participant in campus affairs and served as master of Pierson College. In keeping with the gregarious and tolerant persona he developed on campus, he invited back to Yale his own quasi-enemy, Henry Luce, who delivered a disappointingly dull lecture. Hersey and Frances divorced in 1958, and Hersey married Barbara Addams Kauffman (the former wife of the *New Yorker* cartoonist Charles Addams). Hersey and his second wife lived in Key West, Florida, and Martha's Vineyard, Massachusetts, alternately with New Haven for the rest of their lives. Hersey's civic engagement was at its height in the late 1960s and 1970s, when Hersey wrote what is perhaps his most troubled and unsteady book, *The Algiers Motel Incident* (1968).

This is another piece of contemporary journalism, but unlike in *Hiroshima* Hersey inserts himself into the narrative and speaks candidly to the reader about the challenges of writing fairly about black people victimized by empowered whites. Hersey explains that the urgency of the historical moment led him to drop the detached voice he had deployed with such legendary skill in *Hiroshima*, but most readers found Hersey's voice too florid and his narrative hard to follow.[97] *The Algiers Motel Incident* and Hersey's other political engagements no doubt reflected that "deep impulse" to be "useful and helpful in the world" that he identified as the chief theme of his labors, but Hersey gradually found his way back to the original terrain for that impulse. There Hersey's voice was again steady.

The embodiment of the missionary impulse in *The Call* is David Treadup, a composite figure inspired by the characteristics of half a dozen missionaries Hersey knew, including his own father, Roscoe Hersey, to whom the book is dedicated. Treadup's life story is a remarkably complete rendition of all the classic elements in the saga of American Protestant missions in China. It proceeds from the "evangelization of the world in one generation" through the debates over the relative roles of social service and evangelism and then to the eventual and increasingly unforgiving critiques of the whole enterprise as ethnocentric and imperialist. The story is driven in part by zealotries that often blind the Lord's servants to the needs of their own children. Intrusions of scientific learning challenge the viability of even the most liberal versions of Christianity. *The Call* stands today, more than thirty years after it appeared, as the most penetrating piece of missionary fiction ever written in the English language.

An irreligious but resiliently virtuous British physician reminds Treadup, over the course of their many years of friendship, of the power of secular ideas to make sense of the world, and the limitations of faith to explain much of anything. As Treadup gains sophistication in the realities of China, he finds more and more compelling the books by Montaigne, Kant, Gogol, Nietzsche, Cervantes, Weber, and Melville pushed upon him Dr. Phinneas Cunningham.[98] Treadup becomes increasingly secular and technological in his understanding of what he can offer to China, and in the end, like his engineer predecessor in *A Single Pebble*, finds all his hopes dashed. His labors produce little of lasting value that he can hold on to, and his efforts at prayer begin to spur the feeling that "the line had gone dead."[99]

Along the way to final disillusion with the missionary project and its God, Treadup encounters a number of people accurately named as the real people they were, including Edgar Snow, the parents of John S. Service, and Roscoe Hersey himself.[100] Other characters are based on real, specific individuals, a number of whom I discuss in later chapters of *Protestants Abroad*. A titan of the missionary movement who inspires Treadup and eventually turns against him as too liberal, "James Todd," is without question John R. Mott. William Ernest Hocking is easily recognizable as

"Roland J. Farkus, Ph.D." The Chinese-American agricultural reformer Y. C. James Yen is represented as Johnny Wu.

Hersey narrates Treadup's strivings, and his quarrels with other missionaries, against a backdrop of contemporary events: the Manchus are overthrown, the Kuomintang and the Communists gain strength and fight against each other, the Japanese invade (and imprison Treadup), and the Communists make their revolution in 1949 (resulting in Treadup's exile from China). As his life draws to an end in the 1950s, Treadup muses on the paradox that he was too American for the Chinese Communists while his friends in the State Department were not American enough. The "China hands, so many of whom are sons of missionaries," Treadup reflects, are being hounded out of government by "Senator McCarthy" while "the Communists hound me, a neo-missionary, out of China."[101]

Hersey's punctilious attention to the Chinese environment and the culture of the Protestant missionary community no doubt limited the ability of this book to appeal to potential readers beyond that community. Moreover, *The Call* decisively separates itself from the more affirmative meditations on the missionary experience that many readers of missionary-focused fiction hope to find. The novel is bleaker, in the end, than most memoirs of missionary children as well as other missionary fiction. Margaret Landon's 1949 missionary novel *Never Dies the Dream* is also the story of a virtuous missionary's defeat, but Landon concludes her novel with her protagonist's renewal of faith expressed in conventional god-talk.[102] *The Call* can be a depressing book for anyone who wants to find value in the missionary project, or who feels nostalgia for a missionary childhood.

Treadup's long neglected and brokenhearted wife is reduced in her final years to pathetic silence. His children are scattered and of dubious capacity to make much of themselves. Treadup himself, still a man of great character, struggles to find small ways to make himself useful and finds most opportunities closed off to him. At the heart of *The Call* is the progressive recognition that however admirable the desire to help others—to make the world right, to be a Good Samaritan—that desire is too often encased within too narrow a sense of what kind of help was most needed. That desire was fueled, *The Call* makes clear, by a naïve expectation of how much could be accomplished by even the most talented and devoted of missionaries. "It was not all error," Treadup tries to assure himself at the end. "I really think I gave what I could with a whole heart."[103]

If anyone ever wrote with a "whole heart," it was John Hersey, whose books about so many different social settings pushed his own version of the old responsibility to make things right, in his case always directed at egalitarian goals and tempered by a sense of limits. Many of Hersey's characters were "displaced missionaries" and his most fully developed character was the original. Through these characters he carried out his meditation on the moral imperative that drove Luce and Buck, and so many others he knew. Hersey recognized and emulated the generic fellow-feeling for which the Protestant missionary project was an imperfect vehicle. He tried to chart paths toward species-wide solidarity that took account of the world as it was actually discovered to be, including its multitudinous particulars—above all, its powers of resistance to change engineered by Americans. In *A Bell for Adorno* Hersey had given little thought to the interests of Sicilians as distinct from the democratic ideals espoused by the best of Americans, but by the time he wrote *The Call* Hersey was much less sure that Americans of good will knew what was right for the rest of the world.

If we accept Buck's assertion that the missionary project's "imperialism of the spirit" could be understood only by someone who had been inside it and then "grown beyond it," I believe it fair to see Luce as someone who never outgrew it, even as it propelled his creativity. Buck and Hersey also felt its demonic force, but managed to channel it in directions very different from Luce's, and even from each other's. Buck is the most representative of the cultural outlook of the missionary cosmopolitans who made a mark anywhere in American life. Yet Hersey articulated the sacred responsibility to make the world right even more deliberately and critically than Buck ever did, and he explored a greater range of peoples to be brought into the commodious humanity affirmed by all missionary cosmopolitans. Luce is the supreme example of the transferal of the unreconstructed missionary impulse from a church-related vehicle to a national one. Buck's avoidance of moral complexity may owe something to the old missionary project's sense of righteousness. But up to a point, she, like Hersey, flew in the missionary dusk with the wings of Minerva.

When Luce, Buck, and Hersey struggled in secular modes against provincial constraints, they engaged challenges that the Protestant boomerang was simultaneously forcing upon the American Protestant community of faith. The next two chapters analyze that impact at two levels. How was the missionary project itself challenged and changed by experience in the field? And how, in turn, were the churches themselves challenged and changed as a result of the cascading self-interrogations inspired by the experience of missions?

CHAPTER THREE

To Save the Plan

CAN MISSIONS BE REVISED?

WHAT WAS THE missionary project supposed to accomplish? What methods were appropriate? What was the theological basis for foreign missions? How should missionaries comport themselves in relation to non-Christian faiths?

These questions were easy to answer when the parents of Henry Luce, Pearl Buck, and John Hersey went to China. Experience in the field proved otherwise. That experience generated one challenge after another, and produced a long series of efforts to save the missionary project from apparent flaws in its original design. Eventually, the central character in John Hersey's *The Call* reassured himself, against mounting doubts, that "it had not been all error."

Jesus had told his followers plainly enough, according to Matthew 28:19, to evangelize the world: "Go and make disciples of all nations." Soldiers of the cross would act rapidly and decisively on the instructions of the Lord. In 1910, the World Missionary Conference at Edinburgh adopted as its so-called "watchword" the slogan "the evangelization of the world in this generation."[1] The world outside the North Atlantic West was backward and heathen. Some of the European and American church leaders who gathered at Edinburgh resisted blatantly racist and ethnocentric conceptions of the task. But at that time, a typical voice was Arthur H. Smith. He praised the mental powers of the Chinese but found them foolish and almost universally devoid of "Character and Conscience."[2] Smith left no doubt about the superiority of Western culture in every respect. Foreign peoples, even when viewed less invidiously, were understood to be in desperate need of the uplifting that came with the gospel. The prosperous, educated West was willing to do the job. In 1893, Presbyterian missionary James S. Dennis explained to the World Parliament of Religions in Chicago that Christian missionaries offered other religions the "steel hand of truth encased in the velvet glove of love." This phrase captured, as historian Grant Wacker has remarked, "a thousand pages of missionary apologetics."[3]

Just how fully the gospel could be separated from Western culture was not always clear. "Nothing but Christ" had been a motto of many nineteenth-century missionaries.[4] Most discussants were confident that they had a viable perspective on this issue, and that the culture of their own societies embodied a good bit of Christian teachings to begin with. There were disagreements, but also enough missionary societies with different priorities to make room for just about anyone who joined up. Disagreements often concerned what was colloquially called "the second coming of Christ." The premillennialist outlook popular among many of the American missionaries recruited from the mid-1880s through about 1910 held that Christ was coming soon and the world as then known would simply come to an end. The conversion of souls was too imperative to allow much energy to be devoted to mission work of any other kind. From this perspective, the Christ-culture question could be downplayed because a bare salvation narrative was enough. Some of the "nothing but Christ" sloganeers actually resisted educational programs for indigenous peoples for fear their converts would absorb the sinful, as opposed to the virtuous, features of Western civilization. Those whose English was the best, it was often observed, were the least likely to convert.

Other missionaries and their sponsors believed, instead, that schools, hospitals, and other institutions were part and parcel of the evangelization process. Some who believed this were called postmillenialists, based on the idea that the scripture-prophesied reign of Christ on earth would follow, not inaugurate, a thousand years of godly conduct in the world. Whether or not they embraced this label, or regarded the timing of the Apocalypse to be of any special significance, these liberals took the view that if the world was going to be around for a while, converts should be equipped to lead gospel-informed lives and to transfer Christian ways of life to their descendants.

But just what ways of living *were* Christian? Could one see as fully Christian a set of practices that differed all too obviously from what counted back in Rochester or Richmond? Such uncertainties remained in the background at Edinburgh, but they could not be contained for long. The Edinburgh meeting was the high point of missionary self-confidence and consensus. In the years immediately following, a number of mission-aries themselves questioned the character of the project, often pointedly.

World War I was a highly important context for these discussions. The war and its diplomatic and economic aftermath generated less complacent perspectives on the culture of the North Atlantic West. Were "we" in such a strong position to tell the rest of the world how to think and feel? Leaders of the missionary societies and of the Federal Council of Churches (FCC) did their best to promote an upbeat view, displayed in a twenty-three-essay volume of 1920, *The Missionary Outlook in the Light of the War*. For all their efforts at self-reassurance, however, the contributors registered a deeply chastened mood. Edinburgh's priority of converting individuals was clearly inadequate because it failed to deal with the magnitude and complexity of the world as revealed by the recent war. The revised task of missions, wrote the FCC's Samuel McCrea Cavert, was "the creation of a Christian society throughout the world," by trying to move national governments in more Christian directions and promoting the interna-tionalism promised by the League of Nations. Groups, nations, and whole societies should be the targets of missionary endeavor. The "conversion of individuals" was not enough.[5]

Most of the debates were closer to the ground, tied to the actual ex-perience of missions. Historians of the 1920s have often focused on the issue of evolution, flagged by the Scopes trial. Debates over missions were more vexing for church leaders, and had much greater consequences for the character of American Protestantism and for the ways in which Americans engaged the world. A series of reflections and exhortations voiced in 1925, the very year of the Scopes Trial, take us to the heart of these controversies.[6]

All were written by men and women who had served as missionar-ies. This body of literature demonstrates how the impulse to reconsider the missionary project came directly out of experience in the field. These writings were immediately relevant to missionary theory and practice, but they demand close attention here for an additional reason: they shaped the terms in which other issues came to be discussed. What, for exam-ple, did shifting ideas about the missionary project mean for how one should understand churches? The Christian religion itself? The peoples the missionaries were trying to serve? The home society, including its own ethnoracial, gender, and religious hierarchies? American foreign policy? Educational priorities? The Protestant boomerang eventually struck these wider domains, but it reached them after passing through the missionary soul of the American Protestant community.

How would the average American feel, Frank Rawlinson wondered, "if 8,000 Buddhist missionaries backed up by hundreds of societies" were to mount in Christian America a missionary enterprise "equal in economic and propagandic strength to that carried out by us in China?" As a twenty-three-year veteran of missions in China and as the longtime editor of *The Chinese Recorder*—the chief periodical of the missionary community in China—Rawlinson had a voice that could not be ignored. Indeed, the Southern Baptists who had sent him to China did anything but ignore him: in 1921 they had lost patience and dismissed him for his accelerating provocations. The determined Rawlinson sought sponsorship from the more liberal Congregationalists of the New England-based American Board of Commissioners of Foreign Missions, which promptly made him one of its own. Rawlinson spent most of 1925 writing *The Naturalization of Christianity in China*, a book that recounts his own transformation in the circumstances of the mission field from a "naïve and biased" outlook to one of deep respect for the Chinese people and their inherited culture.[7]

Two experiences appear to have done the most to change Rawlinson's mind. One was the incredulity with which Chinese converts confronted the denominational distinctions that Baptist, Presbyterian, and other missionaries defended; looking at American religion from a Chinese perspective was liberating. Another was the intellectual and spiritual depth of classical Chinese literature as he read in it more and more extensively. Advocating an idea heretical to all but the most liberal elements in the missionary community, Rawlinson endorsed a syncretism by which Christianity as understood in the West would be gradually revised in a "synthesis" with the religious experience of the Chinese. Missions needed to be reconfigured, Rawlinson was convinced, so they would facilitate rather than resist this syncretizing process. Americans had as much to learn from the Chinese as the Chinese did from the Americans. The more he understood about the civilization of China, the more embarrassing he found the notions of cultural superiority built into the missionary project as he had been inducted into it.

At the same moment, the nation's leading missionary theorist, Daniel J. Fleming, published *Whither Bound in Missions*. In this probing treatise, distributed throughout the world by the YMCA, Fleming railed against the attitudes of superiority he believed all too common among missionaries and their supporters. Fleming, too, had been changed by his own missionary experience, in his case twelve years in India before becoming a professor at Union Theological Seminary. Missionaries have been "interpreters *of* the West" to the East, but now are "becoming interpreters *to* the

West" of the cultures of the East. Missionaries are not so much instructors but "helpers," said Fleming, reversing the direction of a term long applied to indigenous people who assisted the missionaries. We, not they, are doing the helping, Fleming said on behalf of missionaries. Drawing not only on his own experience, but also extensive discussions with "missionaries on furlough," Fleming allowed that an unpleasant lesson learned abroad is that the United States is actually not very Christian. We "have been startled into the realization that the West is part of the non-Christian world," especially in its "racial and industrial life." White supremacy and unequal distribution of the world's resources are more easily recognized when you see how the rest of the world lives. Looking at the United States through newly acquired foreign eyes enables one to see its evils.[8]

Essential to an improved, more viable missionary project, Fleming insisted, was deep immersion in things foreign. American Christians should study the cultures of the world in order to rid the missionary endeavor of its American parochialism. Fleming later published in *Christian Century* what was destined to become a famous article that tracked Rawlinson's deeply relativistic provocation. In the 1928 piece "If Buddhists Came to Our Town," Fleming took Americans to task for their provincial conceits no less vigorously than anthropologists of the cultural relativist school did at the same time. Imagine, the veteran missionary asked the American faithful, what it would be like to have someone come into your community and tell you to abandon Christianity and become a Buddhist or a Muslim or a Hindu?[9]

A more widely circulated and enduring artifact of this mid-1920s reassessment of missions was *The Christ of the Indian Road* by E. Stanley Jones (1884–1973). A Methodist missionary in India since 1907, Jones was an early and outspoken advocate of "indigenization," the transferal of the center of gravity of missions from the "sending" countries to the "receiving" countries. This 1925 volume was the first and most influential of the twenty-eight books that made Jones— designated the world's greatest missionary by *Time* magazine in 1938—one of the most popular Protestant intellectuals of his generation. In 1929, *Time* reported that *The Christ of the Indian Road* had sold four hundred thousand copies in its first four years, and been translated into fourteen languages.[10] Jones advanced a program similar to Fleming's and Rawlinson's, and using much the same language. Christ is becoming "naturalized" in India, Jones proclaimed in his opening paragraph. Sounding like the multiculturalists of the 1990s, Jones endorsed the world's cultural diversity and insisted that Christ traveled many "roads" quite different from those on which

Americans had made their own spiritual journeys. "We want the East to keep its own soul," he said. The Indians and the Chinese and the Africans everywhere should be actively discouraged from copying the ways of life that Americans often assumed were Christian.[11]

The Christ of the Indian Road was a heavily confessional treatise in which Jones offered his own immediate, searing experience in the mission field as validation for his revisionist outlook. Part of the book's appeal was its direct testimony. Spending a lot of time with Hindus had led him to conclude that American Protestants were more of an obstacle to a genuinely Christian world than Hinduism. He ascribed to Hindus the discovery that Jesus "was colour blind." In recognizing this point, so often lost on Americans with their own comfortable racial hierarchy, the Hindus were working against the ancient caste system of their own society, which Jones invoked as a mirror for American inequalities: the "white caste which we are building up" in the United States shares with the Hindu caste system indefensible inequalities. But "our white-caste idea" is worse because it is "opposed to our faith" rather than connected to it. "Jesus is ideal and wonderful," Jones quoted the Indian savant Rabindranath Tagore, "but you Christians are not like him." Imploring his American co-religionists to give ground to the East, Jones concluded with a vision of India as a bride of Christ. We of the West must "trust India with the Christ and trust Christ with India."[12]

No less radical was yet another volume of 1925, Frank C. Laubach's *The People of the Philippines: Their Religious Progress and Preparation for Spiritual Leadership of the Far East.* Laubach lamented that traditional missions had done little to help indigenous peoples, which had enormous potential if given a chance to flourish. A Congregationalist missionary who eventually left missionary work to become a promoter of literacy in all languages, Laubach was moved by his experience in the field to proclaim that Filipinos and other Asians were ready to perfect Christianity by "Orientalizing" it. Filipinos were developing for East Asia "a simplified, beautified conception of the spirit of Jesus Christ—they will help the Kingdom of God to throw off its European garb," and return it to its origins which were, after all, Asian.[13] Laubach attacked American imperialist prejudices against the Filipino people and advocated Philippine independence. Just as Jones had many good things to say about Hindus, Laubach saw much to appreciate in the Muslims he worked with. What most changed Laubach was the experience of living and working with the Filipinos. When he went abroad, he did not expect to be arguing a decade later that the future of Christianity rested more with Filipinos and other Asians than with Westerners.

The same respect for the people abroad defined yet another effusion of 1925, a series of lectures delivered at Princeton Theological Seminary by A. K. Reischauer, a leading missionary to Japan. Reischauer's Princeton lectures, published the following year as a book, *The Task in Japan: A Study in Modern Missionary Imperatives*, took direct aim at white supremacy. There was no way to justify the continuation of a system, Reischauer declared, in which almost all of the power in the world was vested in white people alone.[14] His son, Edwin Reischauer, the great academic entrepreneur and eventually ambassador to Japan, would strike similar themes. The missionary father's work illustrated how the concerns of progressive missionaries to Japan were identical to those issuing from counterparts in the Philippines, China, and India. The part of missionary experience that most affected A. K. Reischauer was his discovery of the complexity and beauty of traditional Japanese culture.

Simultaneously, a highly respected missionary from Persia, Mary Schauffler Platt (1869–1954) was writing her own treatise from yet another major mission field to the same general effect. Platt's parents and grandparents had been missionaries before her, and she was the widow of a missionary murdered in 1906 by an anti-Christian Muslim. Platt was appreciated for her many works on missionary families and for her "war diary," describing the killings she witnessed in 1915 during the Turkish occupation of the western section of Persia. In *A Straight Way Toward Tomorrow*, Platt relentlessly argued that missionary work should be reconceived as a form of "friendship." Missionaries and their friends among the indigenous peoples of the world were to work together to diminish suffering and injustice wherever it appeared. We must cut back on our influence over indigenous peoples, Platt insisted; it is they who must lead their own societies.[15]

These reflections and exhortations by six high-profile missionaries were not the first to push the missionary project in these directions, but they did bring together and register more loudly and clearly than ever before the discomforts with traditional missionary thinking that had bothered scattered missionaries during the previous decade. These discomforts had been voiced episodically in magazine articles and in the debates of the several missionary societies, denominational governance bodies, and youth assemblies. Occasionally, the reformers outlined their opinions in the secular press. A widely discussed example was "The Modern Missionary," contributed to *The Atlantic* in 1920 by Howard Bliss, the president of the American University in Beirut. Bliss explained that he and his faculty did not believe "that Christianity is the sole channel through which divine and saving truth has been conveyed." All persons seeking God can be the modern missionary's "companions and co-workers." In the most widely quoted passage, Bliss explained how his campus bore witness to the faith while performing secular functions:

> The College is for all conditions and classes of men, without reference to color, nationality, race, or religion. A man, white, black, or yellow, Christian, Jew, Mohammedan, or Heathen, may enter and enjoy all the advantages of the institution for three, four, or eight years and go out believing in one God or many gods or no God; but it will be impossible for anyone to continue with us long without knowing what we believe to be the truth and our reasons for that belief.[16]

Had Bliss, the revered leader of one of the most deeply admired of all American missionary projects, been able to carry the day, all this turmoil visible in the documents just quoted from five years later would not have been necessary. But Bliss's views were still radical. Two multi-year conflicts that came to head in 1925 further illustrate the character and intensity of these debates, and show their origins in the circumstances missionaries encountered while trying to perform their prescribed duties in the mission field.

One conflict involved missionary physician Edward Hume, who headed the Yale-in-China facility in Changsha. Yale in China was a nonprofit organization independent of Yale University itself, but founded and operated by Yale alumni, faculty, and students. It began as the Yale Foreign Missionary Society in 1901, and was reincorporated in 1934 as a secular organization committed to a range of education and philanthropic enterprises in China. It included a hospital and a medical school in Changsha. Hume spent twenty years training and encouraging Chinese doctors, nurses, and associated staff. By 1925 these steps were especially important in view of the sharp increase of nationalism among Chinese students, leading to many acts of violence against foreigners. The trustees back in New Haven and New York were slow to appreciate how rapidly Chinese society and politics were changing; they did not like the speed and extent to which Hume turned responsibilities over the Chinese. He asked that the people sent to him would have learned at least something about China and be of a mind to work closely with Chinese, but he found precious little of these traits in the personnel favored by the trustees. When Hume, as president of Yale-in-China, made cooperative agreements with Chinese institutions, the trustees repudiated them. Hume wrote many letters and memoranda trying to explain the necessity of "grafting ourselves in the living tree of China." If Yale fails to do that, Hume warned, the enterprise was doomed. According to Jonathan Spence, Hume was in despair when he realized that for all his efforts to explain things, "the men in New Haven just did not understand" the situation in China.[17] Hume resigned his presidency and returned to the United States but remained a major liberal voice in the American missionary community until his death in 1957.

Hume's experience took place in the most academic of missionary settings. The second conflict that came to a head in 1925 was located in the quite different atmosphere of the agricultural sector. Sam Higginbotham, a Presbyterian missionary to India since 1903, was at the center of this imbroglio. Higginbotham had developed a program of agricultural reform that won the respect of Mohandas Gandhi and a number of other indigenous leaders. Higginbotham was one of the most famous missionaries in India. What made him controversial was the unambiguous priority he placed on the diminution of economic inequality as a necessary foundation for a genuinely Christian society. Other missionaries in the North India Presbyterian Mission, still oriented to the goal of conversion, complained that Higginbotham had gone too far in the direction of simply offering social services needed by the local population. Higginbotham was attracting money to his endeavors that could be better spent in evangelistic work designed to bring in more converts.

Higginbotham's early years in India transformed his sense of what missions should be doing. "There was now seething in our minds," Higginbotham later wrote about a turning point he and his wife faced, the lesson taught by their "experience and efforts" in the field: that "there would be no Kingdom of God in India without an amelioration of poverty and that this must be founded on a more productive agriculture."[18] By 1925 the complaints about Higginbotham's Agricultural Institute reached the point that the Presbyterian Missionary Board in New York severed it from its North India Presbyterian Mission. But the board was liberal enough to continue to support Higginbotham's Agricultural Institute as an independent project, and trusted—accurately, as it happened—that an increasing number of the missionaries in the field would come to appreciate Higginbotham's endeavor. By the early 1930s the other Presbyterian missionaries in India welcomed Higginbotham back into their diversifying community. Higginbotham was a pioneer not only in agricultural education, but in diplomacy: he made the missionary community more accepting of essentially secular projects which could be seen as advancing the larger enterprise of bringing the Kingdom of God to indigenous peoples around the globe.[19]

Missionary boards had different educational prerequisites for missionary personnel, especially ordained ministers, but the largely

Congregationalist American Board of Commissions of Foreign Missions (ABCFM) was known for its high demands. The educational level of missionaries to the Middle East was consistently higher than the others because that field was developed earlier, before the mission boards were flooded by young people driven by the premillennialist enthusiasms of the 1880s and 1890s.[20] The Presbyterians and Congregationalists who established the American University in Beirut in 1866 (and, later, Robert College in Istanbul and the American University in Cairo) often recruited graduates of Deerfield Academy and other New England preparatory schools, who then obtained their college degrees at Yale, Princeton, Amherst, or Oberlin. The confidence with which Howard Bliss could speak in 1920 was a sign of how firmly ABCFM people like himself were in control of missions in the Near East. In China, by contrast, the average missionary had much less education.[21]

These differences in education and basic theological outlook exploded in the 1920s to play into the modernist-fundamentalist conflict that was especially fierce within the Northern Baptist and Northern Presbyterian churches, but also divided the Methodists and several other denominations. In these struggles, there was no question where Hume, Higginbotham, Laubach, Jones, Fleming, Rawlinson, Reischauer, and Platt were located. The fundamentalists were angered by the growing focus on social service instead of preaching. They also "fretted," as one historian has accurately summarized their concerns, "over the erosion of confessional distinctives [sic] in ecumenical contexts."[22] Popular impressions of the modernist-fundamentalist conflict have continued through the decades to focus on evolution, but many of the earliest and most volatile episodes even in that conflict involved liberal missionaries and had nothing to do with Darwin. Yenching University President John Leighton Stuart's dissents from Presbyterian orthodoxy led to heresy charges.[23] A major consequence of the modernist-fundamentalist fight was the fundamentalists' increased self-isolation. For several decades they managed to avoid public reflection about the challenges to the missionary project that consumed the ecumenists. Joel Carpenter has put it well, explaining that fundamentalists ignored

> the ethical and theological issues about which other Protestants earnestly contended. Left to their own unreflective, activist proclivities, fundamentalist missions and their leaders exhibited the epitome of what European missions leaders thought was the great fault of the American missionary enterprise: its anti-intellectual, impatient, and technique-driven outlook.[24]

But what Carpenter rightly calls the earnest contentions of the ecumenical Protestants soon intensified even further. The writings and episodes of 1925 discussed above were prolegomena to a book of 1932 that commanded the attention of ecumenical Protestants like no other critique of missions.

Re-Thinking Missions: A Laymen's Inquiry After One Hundred Years mattered greatly for several reasons. It was commissioned, carried out, and publicized by the most empowered groups within American Protestantism's informal establishment, and with rare deliberation. It was conceived by John R. Mott, then the undisputed spiritual and organizational leader of the Protestant missionary project.[25] It was funded by John D. Rockefeller, Jr. Fifteen ecumenical leaders spent nearly nine months in India, Burma, China, and Japan examining missionary practices and interviewing missionary personnel at every level. Mott explained to Rockefeller that missions were caught between indigenous nationalist movements inclined to suspect Christianity as an imperialist tool, and fundamentalists determined to present Christianity in just the ways anti-imperialist critics insisted was its essence. The fundamentalist attack on modernists had targeted Rockefeller himself for his sponsorship of liberals within the Baptist church and at the University of Chicago. Rockefeller was close to the great liberal preacher Harry Emerson Fosdick, and since 1921 had employed Fosdick's brother, Raymond, to head the Rockefeller Foundation.[26]

Harvard philosopher William Ernest Hocking (1873–1966) drafted the results of the inquiry. Hocking was then a figure of national stature, known especially for his book of 1912, *The Meaning of God in Personal Experience*.[27] Rockefeller personally persuaded Hocking to accept the assignment. This quest for an "objective view" of the entire missionary enterprise and its "presuppositions" proceeded independently of any and all mission boards.[28] The leadership of six major denominations—the Congregational, Episcopal, Dutch Reformed, Northern Baptist, Northern Methodist, and Northern Presbyterian churches—formally supported it. Many smaller confessions did so informally.

But for all the prestige surrounding it, the "Hocking Report," as it came to be called, might still have found its way to the back shelves of church libraries, next to the annual reports of various agencies, had its sponsors found its message less shocking. What really mattered about missions was not preaching, but "educational and other philanthropic" activities. Trying to persuade people to give up their own religion to become Christians was no longer a good idea. We must be willing to provide services to indigenous people in need, the Report declared, "without any preaching." We must "cooperate with non-Christian agencies for social improvement," the text continued, and we must respond to "the initiative of the Orient in defining the ways in which we shall be invited to help." The missionary should be "a learner and a co-worker," not a preacher. The task of evangelism, in this view, was to be done by exemplifying "the Christian way of life and its spirit" and "by quiet personal contact and by contagion." Any evangelizing done at all was to be done "not by word but by deed," and, as the Report insisted in its own italics, *by living and by human service.* There was no dodging the responsibility to engage the social evils found in many societies. "Missions should recognize and teach that a well ordered community cannot exist when there are too great inequalities," the Report proclaimed. In a characteristic equivocation when it came to actual politics, Hocking and his colleagues explained that they were not advocating "meddling in politics," especially those of foreign countries, yet Christians "can wisely attempt to modify any social order which unduly accentuates economic inequality and privilege." Pushing the social reform envelope as far as its signers thought they could, *Re-Thinking Missions* allowed that "if one man by the honest study of Christ's teaching becomes a communist, another a labor union leader, another a socialist and another a capitalist, none should find himself excluded from the fellowship or prevented from trying to win other Christians to his point of view."[29]

The idea that Communism might be compatible with Christianity was far from the end of it. The top Methodist missionary in India, Bishop Frederick Bohn Fisher, told readers of the *Christian Century* that it was "a book of human rights with a bomb in every chapter."[30] No bomb was bigger than the report's perspective on the religions practiced in the East. These faiths were not such terrible things, according to Hocking and his colleagues. While Christianity could be expected to emerge eventually as the faith of all humankind, for the time being Christians should respect, and in some cases even support, other religions. It may well be that Christ's ultimate triumph will be advanced by "the immediate strengthening of several of the present religions of Asia." The big problem in the world in 1932 was not the power of other religions, as had so often been assumed, but secularism: missions needed to be mobilized in an alliance of all religions against "the same menace, the spread of the secular spirit." In a characteristically generous gesture toward Hinduism, the report described child marriage as an abuse that had "invaded" that religion. When missionaries criticized such abuses, they should see themselves as "joining Hindus" in clarifying and purifying their own faith. "Desiring to be considered a co-worker rather than an enemy," the ideal Christian will "refrain from misrepresentation abroad of the evils he desires to cure," and will make a point of calling attention to "the efforts being made by nationals to correct" those evils.[31]

Just how much trouble the report could make was revealed immediately when Pearl Buck endorsed its most radical aspects with incandescent enthusiasm. The recent winner of the Pulitzer Prize for *The Good Earth* proclaimed that *Re-Thinking Missions* was "the only book" she had ever read "which seems to me literally true in its every observation and right in its every conclusion." Within a few days of her review's publication in *Christian Century*, Buck stunned a New York gathering of Presbyterian women with her blunt "I am weary unto death with this incessant preaching. . . . Let us . . . cut off our talkers and try to express our religion in terms of living service." *Harper's Magazine* rushed the instantly notorious speech into print. Buck's reaction was all the more important because she was a child of missionaries, and was herself formally listed as a missionary of the Southern Presbyterian Church. Hers was yet another voice from the mission field telling people back home things they were not eager to hear. Buck soon left the Presbyterians, but she was still a treasured daughter of the church when she gave even wider visibility to the Hocking Report than it might have otherwise received.[32] The volume went through ten printings in six months.

Commentators less far along on a post-Protestant road than Buck were invariably more cautious. They were especially reserved about the most revolutionary theme in *Re-Thinking Missions*, the diminution of Christianity's uniqueness. Hundreds of pages of the report were devoted to detailed recommendations for the operation of missions, including the better training of mission personnel and the improvement of social services. Some missionary boards felt their work undervalued, but overall these parts of the report played well. However, even the discussants who appreciated the document's practical aspects were often dismayed by its perspective on other religions. Hocking and his colleagues were accused of being insufficiently affirmative about Christian uniqueness.[33] Stop preaching the gospel to the Hindus and Muslims and Buddhists? Acknowledge the spark of divinity within those religions? Even though these ideas had been percolating for some time in the writings of Fleming, Jones, Laubach, Rawlinson, Platt, and others, the Hocking Report forced everyone to drink the brew or refuse it.

The mainstream liberal Protestant leadership waived the drink aside in a collegial spirit, but the fundamentalists did so with scorn. J.

Gresham Machen, the most learned and respected fundamentalist leader of the period, attacked the liberals for failing to condemn *Re-Thinking Missions* with sufficient force and for not having formally expelled the increasingly freethinking Buck instead of allowing her to resign as a missionary, unbloodied. Machen published a fundamentalists' enemies list of individuals whom he accused the liberal Presbyterian missionary board of protecting, including A. K. Reischauer and the eminent YMCA orator Sherwood Eddy. The fundamentalists had no doubt that the gospel had to be preached unapologetically to the multitudes all over the world, no matter what their inherited faith.[34]

The debates over the Hocking Report took place just as the missionary leadership was coming to grips with "secularization" and "indigenization." The first of these portentous developments was located primarily in the North Atlantic West, but was making rapid and deeply disquieting gains in several of the mission fields, especially China. Mott and Eddy discovered that young people were increasingly engaged with Herbert Spencer, Karl Marx, Bertrand Russell, and other European secularists. John Dewey had spent two years in China and won a large following. The second development, the push for greater indigenous control of missions, was peculiar to the mission fields. Indigenization and secularization dominated the two global conferences of the International Missionary Council (IMC) held between the two world wars, one in Jerusalem in 1928 and the other in Madras in 1938. These IMC conclaves, designed as follow-ups to the great Edinburgh meeting of 1910, brought together all the major ecumenical Protestant missionary organizations. The dynamics of these two meetings help explain why the Hocking Report proved to be such a major event.

At Jerusalem the assembled delegates concluded that the most severe threat to Christianity was the growth of secularism in contemporary culture. The Jerusalem conferees recommended a cautious alliance with non-Christian religions in place of the flagrant antagonism that had been the traditional missionary outlook and was still favored by fundamentalists.[35] The authors of the *Laymen's Inquiry* were clearly affected by this understanding of how the challenges of their own time had shifted from those recognized by the voices of 1910. The Hocking Report identified "the philosophies of Marx, Lenin and Russell" as emblematic of world-historical changes since 1910 that now made "the case for any religion at all" more difficult. The alarming popularity of secular views made it imperative for Christianity to become "aligned . . . with the non-Christian faiths of Asia." The Hocking Report's plea that American Protestants "stand upon the common ground of all religion"[36] reflected the ecumenical elite's strikingly more defensive posture two decades after Edinburgh.

While the Jerusalem conferees easily came to an agreement on the evils of secularization, they had more trouble with indigenization. This issue dominated the International Missionary Council's meeting of ten years later, at Madras, India, but when it emerged at Jerusalem it revealed an important division of opinion between British and American delegates. Should the missionaries from the West immerse themselves so fully in communities of indigenous peoples as to renounce the military protection of the Western powers? The Americans allied with the delegates from the churches abroad to pass a resolution urging "all missionary societies" to "make no claim on their governments for the armed defense of their missionaries and their property." The British missionary community, expressing an enduring tension with their American counterparts, opposed the resolution.[37]

Only at the 1938 meeting of the IMC did the relation of Western to indigenous communities come into sharp focus. The "young churches" complained at Madras that they were too often treated as second-class Christians. The Madras conclave was decidedly the most demographically diverse leadership meeting in Protestant history from the Reformation until that time, bringing together 471 delegates from 69 countries, including a number of African nations and colonies. Originally planned for China, the site was changed to India because of the Japanese invasion of China. The organizers had been alerted of the increasing sophistication of the younger churches, and therefore made sure that nearly half of the delegates were from "receiving" countries. The China and India delegations led in questioning the very distinction between "sending" and "receiving" communities, endorsing instead a notion of "world mission" that would treat the churches outside the North Atlantic West as no less involved than the American and European churches in spreading and interpreting Christianity. The Madras meeting featured greater participation by women than any previous major missionary conclave. It was also more oriented to the Social Gospel. E. Stanley Jones joined indigenous Christians in declaring that the basic economic needs of people had to be addressed as part of Christian mission.

European delegates were not happy with the alliance between the Americans and the various delegations of indigenous peoples. The Swedish divine Henrik Kraemer dismissed the reformist, activist mood as all too typically American. A minority of the American missionaries in attendance shared Kraemer's widely discussed objections, and called for a renewal of evangelism. Donald McGavran began at Madras the critique of liberal missionary theory that he would sharpen for the next thirty years, as he moved from ecumenical company into leadership of the evangelical Protestantism that gained greater organizational coherence in the 1940s and after. The point, he said, was to convert people to Christ, not to be diverted by social reform projects. McGavern, who shifted from liberal to conservative missionary theory, was a striking exception to the general pattern of migration in the opposite direction.[38]

The Madras meeting set in motion discussions within the various missionary societies concerning property ownership, administrative authority, the differential treatment of Western and indigenous women, salary scales, and living conditions. These issues consumed enormous amounts of time, energy, and patience during the next several decades. At Madras the American and European missionaries confronted the complexities of what successes they had achieved in making converts: the indigenous churches wanted more control of Christendom, and in pressing for this control posed a challenge very different from the one presented by non-Christian religions. The challenge was not so much how to deal with people who insisted on remaining Hindus, Moslems, and Buddhists, but how to deal with the converts. Were they really—as they supposed themselves to be—as completely Christian as the Americans and Europeans who had taught them the faith? Was the "Christ of the Indian Road" really the equal of the Christ of Indiana Road?

These indigenous Christians made the problem of Christianity's uniqueness more complex. Unlike most of the faithful in Hartford or Harrisburg, these "new" Christians lived every day surrounded by people practicing non-Christian religions. The distinction between Christian and non-Christian really mattered in their own neighborhoods. Hence it was not surprising that the one feature of the Hocking Report that was resisted at Madras was the implication that Christianity was not so very distinctive and indispensable, after all. The clearest conclusion reached at Madras was one of theory and vocabulary: from then on, "foreign missions" would be on the defensive against "world mission." This was consistent with the ecumenical leadership's sponsorship of a number of "reverse missionaries," Christian leaders from abroad who did lecture tours in the United States. The most famous of these, Toyohiko Kagawa, brought to the attention of many churchgoers the growth in authority and eloquence of non-Western Christians that the leadership encountered in Madras.[39] The promotion of Kagawa was an example of the frequency with which missionary-connected Americans introduced nonwhite voices into the public discourse of American life.

The status of non-Christian religions was "the heart of the problem," explained Edmund Davison Soper (1876–1961) in the most ambitious theoretical treatise on missions to follow the Madras meeting. Soper's book of 1943, *The Philosophy of the Christian World Mission*, insisted that "everything hangs on the answer" to the question of Christianity's uniqueness and indispensability.[40] Soper was well qualified to pilot his readership from foreign to world missions. He had grown up in Japan as the son of Methodist missionaries, and by the time he wrote this book had achieved a distinguished career as a missionary board administrator and professor of missions, culminating in his professorship at the Garrett Biblical Institute associated with Northwestern University. He had begun his career as a professor of comparative religions, and was best known for *The Religions of Mankind*, a book of 1921 that he extensively revised in 1938 and would again in 1951.[41] Soper was highly sensitive to issues of diversity, prejudice, and racism; he published this book while coordinating a series of antiracist workshops in Chicago sponsored by the Methodist Missionary Board and while working his way toward his yet more important book of 1947, *Racism: A World Issue*, taken up in chapter 11 of *Protestants Abroad*.

Soper's struggle with the issue of Christian uniqueness brought him to the formulation "uniqueness together with continuity." This justified the continuation of the missionary project, at least, while going forward with indigenization and a strong emphasis on service. "The Christians in each country," rather than "the missionary from outside," must determine the forms of religious life. Eager to have it both ways, Soper followed in the tradition of Fleming, Jones, Rawlinson, Reischauer, Laubach, Platt, and Hocking in recognizing the great value of other religions and their points of convergence with Christianity. Yet in *The Philosophy of the World Christian Mission*, Soper joined the majority of the ecumenical leadership in resisting the Hocking Report's radical diminution of Christian uniqueness. *Re-Thinking Missions* had "burst like a bombshell upon the thinking Christian public," Soper observed, offering "drastic and even revolutionary" ideas about the theoretical basis for missions amid its otherwise "valuable findings and recommendations."[42]

But not to worry. To affirm the uniqueness of Christianity, Soper assured his readers, "does not imply that God has not made himself known in other ways and in other religions." The Hocking Report's strong language had confused people, making it hard for them to hold on to this simple truth. Yet for all of Soper's equanimity, the frequency and intensity with which he invoked the high stakes—"if Christianity is not unique there is no special point in taking it to others"—suggests the depth of the accumulated doubts that this volume of measured assurances was designed to overcome. It is "not contradictory," he said, to believe in both "the uniqueness of Christianity" and in Christianity's "continuity with other religions." We Christians simply have more to offer the world than do the advocates of other faiths: "In the Christian religion we have a recourse not available to others."[43] It is all part of God's plan, yes, and we need to remember that God has not left altogether without any witness those multitudes who await Christianity as we present it. Divine substance was widely distributed. But Christians have more of it.

Soper's striving for a capacious ecumenism in which Christianity remained distinct brought him straight to the question of Roman Catholicism. *The Layman's Report* said nothing of substance about Catholicism. By focusing on Asia, the Hocking group circumvented entirely the vexing question of Protestantism's relation to the Catholic missionary enterprise in Latin America. If Catholics were Christians, why not treat Latin America as Catholic territory? Why should Protestants go there, when there were so many populations elsewhere to which neither Catholic nor Protestant missionaries had ever taken the gospel? So challenging was this question that Soper dealt with it only in an appendix, "Protestant Missions in Latin America."

Yes, Catholics were genuine Christians, Soper argued against the more sectarian of his fellow Protestants. And no doubt many Catholics, Soper continued hopefully, would agree with the basic outlook he outlined in *Philosophy of the Christian World Mission*. But the big problem was that the Catholics, unlike the various kinds of Protestants who managed to cooperate with one another and to recognize one another's value, denied that anyone but a Catholic was part of the true church. Hence it would not do for Protestants to concede the entirety of Latin America to the Catholics. The Christianity that the Catholics had implanted in Latin America for many centuries—and were continuing to practice at that moment—was too sectarian and placed loyalty to one particular church above the welfare of the people while refusing to let them engage Christ the way the Protestants did. The Catholic Church had "not promoted education or fostered a healthy intellectual life," and it actively "opposed the principle of liberty of conscience." Catholicism in Latin America "resisted tolerance for the right of any other church to preach and teach." Protestant missions were justified in Latin America, Soper explained, because Protestants, unlike Catholics, believe in "the rights of man as man," not just as Catholics. Protestantism had a mission in Latin America to advance "liberty of worship and conscience," and to make sure that the faithful could receive "the whole counsel of God as it is found in Jesus Christ and the Holy Scriptures, unfettered and unlimited by any human restraint."[44]

The Catholic question remained awkward for ecumenical Protestants, many of whom preferred to avoid it. But the overall perspective Soper developed in 1943 made good sense to the relevant constituency, at least in the short run. Soper's reassuring arguments inspired widespread agreement, and were long remembered, in the words of a distinguished missiologist more than thirty years later, as "the most complete systematically-constructed exposition of the field of mission studies" ever produced in the United States.[45]

The process of church indigenization went forward, to be sure, and missionary boards became more comfortable with evangelization through what the Hocking Report repeatedly called "contagion" rather than open proselytizing. Real changes occurred, consistent with the recommendations of *Re-Thinking Missions* and its 1920s antecedents, while deeper doubts were kept in abeyance by the growth and general prosperity of mainstream Protestant churches in the late 1940s and the 1950s. Ecumenical leaders succeeded in establishing the World Council of Churches in 1948 and in expanding the old Federal Council of Churches of the United States into a grander National Council of Churches in 1950. Henry P. Van Dusen caught the more confident mood of those years in his book of 1947, *World Christianity*, in which the president of Union Theological Seminary extolled Soper's slogan "uniqueness together with continuity" as an efficacious disposal of what had been a concern of some Christians back in the 1930s, when "men's minds were preoccupied with immediate and practical matters." Van Dusen observed that "the theological position" of the Hocking Report "had made almost no appreciable imprint on missionary philosophy."[46]

Van Dusen was putting a good face on the situation. Kenneth Scott Latourette did the same. The Hocking Report "had a following among some liberal intellectuals," allowed the Yale missiologist at the height of his prestige in 1945. "But the brevity of its career testified to the lack of enthusiasm" felt by others. It was important to focus instead on the ongoing victories of the missionary project.[47] Since Hocking, as the rest of this chapter shows, turned out to be much more prescient than those who tried to minimize the *Layman's Inquiry*, it is worth quoting here the triumphalist summary of the entire missionary project Latourette offered at the conclusion of his seven-volume *History of the Expansion of Christianity*:

> The Church is to be found among almost all tribes and peoples, on all continents, and on the large majority of the islands of the sea, even some of the most lonely and remote. . . . Through it hundreds of millions have been lifted from illiteracy and ignorance and have been placed upon the road of growing intellectual freedom and of control over their physical environment. It has done more to allay the physical ills of disease and famine than any other impulse known to man. It has emancipated millions from chattel slavery and millions of others from thralldom to vice. It has protected tens of millions from exploitation by the fellows. It has been the most fruitful source of movements to lessen the horrors of war. . . . Always the faith seems dying, yet it lives. Culture after culture with which the faith has been intimately associated has passed into history, seemingly to carry it also into oblivion. Yet the faith spreads ever more widely and moulds more and more peoples.[48]

While Van Dusen and Latourette were thinking positively, a number of their colleagues remained worried.[49] In 1950, readers of *Christian Century* were reminded of Hocking's issues when, in an article pointedly entitled "Thinking Again about Missions," a leading British missionary administrator ran through the list of by then standard concerns. Instead of offering reassurance and calling for the energetic support of existing programs, Norman Goodall pled for "more information, more wisdom and more hard thinking." What was most "imperative," declared Goodall, was not action in pursuit of any particular agenda, but "deeper reflection." As editor of the *International Review of Missions*, Goodall was constantly monitoring missionary discourse throughout the world. It was far from clear to him that the Westerners had figured out just what indigenization meant and why missions were still needed at all. Goodall quoted a missionary from Scotland who worried that "what the younger churches mainly require of us is that we shall sit somewhere at the back and give a permanent demonstration of humility." Goodall hastened to explain that this particular individual later found worthy tasks for himself, but "every board secretary can recall numbers of conversations over the last five years with missionaries who have been no less vocationally perplexed." We are dodging the important issues, Goodall warned. "Many of our missionaries have been driven to ask fundamental questions about the whole concept of Christian vocation," and we need to pay closer attention. We are in need of both "front-line data" from the field and renewed inquiry into "the biblical and theological bases" of missions, Goodall declared, because "we stand at the end of an age."[50]

Was the end of the missionary era actually at hand? This was the last thing contemporary fundamentalists were willing to contemplate. In 1950, too, Harold Lindsell published *A Christian Philosophy of Missions*, reaffirming traditional orthodox missiological ideas. A vitriolic attack on ecumenical missionary theory, this book reaffirmed that only an inerrant bible could be the central focus of missionary activity. It was characteristic of Lindsell to describe his book as "a final theology" of missions. He believed he had said it all, and that his ideas were true for all time.[51]

But the explicit question of the possible end of the missionary era opened the study pamphlet for the 1955 meeting of the Student Volunteer Movement for Christian Missions, *Shock and Renewal*. The answer was yes, but with the understanding that a new ecumenical era was one in which the old missionary impulse was reconfigured as the bearing of Christian witness by all churches in their own locales, wherever that might be. This youth conference's doctrinal line centered on, first, a repudiation of the concept of "foreign" even more adamant than the introduction of the concept of "world mission" had entailed, and second, the affirmation that "real frontiers exist wherever the gospel confronts the world." In this view, every church, every congregation, every community of Christians was in effect a collection of missionaries, dealing with whatever conditions invite Christian attention. "The witness of the local congregation," wrote Keith R. Bridston in the introduction to this pamphlet, "in order to be truly indigenous and appropriate, must be *in community* or as a community of commitment." Bridston, a Westerner then serving as a minister and teacher in Indonesia, summarized a pervasive worry: that Westerners would continue to display a patronizing stance toward peoples abroad.[52]

Bridston asserted that all of the excerpts from contemporary Christian writing he had assembled in the pamphlet had essentially the same message: paganism was found in the West, too, and the very idea of defining the responsibilities of Christianity in geographical terms was simply a mistake. Bridston exaggerated the unity of contributions by Jacques Ellul, Lesslie Newbigin, Truman B. Douglass, and other prominent liberal writers. But the essay by Norman Goodall indicates how essentially correct Bridston was about the drift of opinion he identified and hailed. Goodall praised "an increasing flow of Christian laymen and women who go out across the world in business, industry, and government" with a conviction "that God calls them to witness for Him in all of life." Such people are no less part of the Christian mission than "the foreign missionaries sent out by the boards."[53]

That so stalwart a figure in the Protestant missionary establishment as Goodall could speak in this way is a vivid indicator of how far the missionary conversations had moved toward the acceptance and even celebration of secular activities as successors to foreign missions. The end of foreign missions could be "a sign of triumph and vindication" because, Bridston observed correctly, the missionary movement in which the Student Volunteer Movement was so vital a force had always had as its "ultimate aim" making itself "both unnecessary and dispensable." The reality of churches abroad— Bridston hailed the Madras meeting as the great turning point of modern Christian history—showed how irrelevant the old missionary project had become.[54] Only a tiny percentage of the populations of India, China, and other traditional mission fields had converted. Bridston's notion of a task completed is from a historical point of view a naïve self-deception, easily recognized as a version of the "declare victory and get out" strategy so common to enterprises facing a threatening future.

Such rethinking of missions, focusing more and more on America's own sins, did not necessarily mean withdrawing from the needs of the world abroad. Another volume of 1955 popular in the ecumenical Protestant youth conclaves of the period, *Encounter with Revolution*, vigorously argued the contrary. This book, published by the YMCA and written by M. Richard Shaull, who had spent a dozen years as a Presbyterian missionary in South America, would later be recognized as a precursor to the Liberation Theology movement. Shaull's deeply pious, scripture-saturated call for Christians to commit themselves to the social, economic, and political causes of long-disadvantaged populations in Latin America, Africa, and Asia equated "the God of the Bible" with "the God of politics." Shaull made very few references to Catholics, but when he did he was even more dismissive than Soper, and on yet more explicitly political grounds: there were a few priests who understood the need for revolution, but, overall, "Latin American Roman Catholicism has been bound to the most reactionary forces in society." When "the hierarchy speaks," Shaull explained, "it is often to condemn not only Communism, but, it would seem, all liberal forces." Lamenting the merely philanthropic approach to suffering that was traditional to American Protestants, Shaull said that Christian commitment can no longer "rest content with a bread line or a soup kitchen." Rather "it must lead to political action to remove the causes of hunger." Shaull depicted Christianity as an alternative to Communism, which, he testified on the basis of his own extensive experience in Bolivia and Brazil, was addressing injustice head-on while Americans, including Christians, were holding back. American Christians must engage the injustices of the globe through undisguised political action. "I have lived through revolution and persecution," said Shaull, whose *Encounter with Revolution* was yet another missive from the mission field demanding sharp changes. The old missionary approach of trying to steer clear of the politics of foreign lands had simply failed to respond, according to Shaull, to the true imperatives of the gospel.[55]

These two publications of 1955—*Shock and Renewal* and *Encounter with Revolution*— occupied the outer intellectual and political fringe of the period's missionary debates. The center was manifest in a series of conferences organized by the International Missionary Council (IMC) and the World Council of Churches (WCC). These recurring meetings invariably advanced one idea above all others: the de-westernization of Christianity. The conferees accepted "Christian presence," as the successor to conversion, as the goal of Protestant activity abroad, echoing the "contagion" concept of the Hocking Report. The idea of a Christian "presence" was a modified version of the earlier missionary ideology of "nothing but Christ," holding that however the Christ-culture problematic was resolved, there was something intrinsic to the Gospel that enabled it eventually to triumph. Bridston and Shaull and the missionary conclaves of the 1950s and 1960s all stopped short of crossing this line to the post-Protestant secularism that lay so close at hand. The confidence that Christianity embodied truths deep enough to assure that it would have a beneficial effect even if proclaimed through "witnessing" distinguishes even the most liberal of voices from secularists.[56] To the latter, this confidence entailed a mystification of Christianity, ascribing to it powers that made sense only to people who believed that it was a special revelation from a supernatural source.

But those who stayed with the faith struggled mightily to decide just what it was. If the point was to advance Christianity rather than the culture of the West, in what respects were the daily lives of the missionaries— now displaying "Christian presence"—*Christian* rather than simply the most wholesome aspects of the *culture* of the West? By what standard were their exemplary lives of egalitarian tolerance measurably different from the classic humanitarianism espoused by many secularists? Incessant calls for "unity" got little traction. "The precise nature of the unity" being affirmed at the IMC meeting at Whitby, England, in 1947 "was not explored," observes the closest student of this sequence of meetings. Roger C. Bassham finds that at the 1954 WCC meeting in Evanston, Illinois, "little progress" was made in "defining the nature of the unity which the churches were seeking."[57] The ecumenical Protestants, as inspired by the missionary project, were subject to a powerful impulse to include, but struggled to define what it was into which diverse peoples were being included.

The rationale for a separate IMC grew weaker in the 1950s, as the distinction between the missionary project and the more general endeavor of ecumenical churches became blurred. The IMC, the world's premier missionary organization founded in Edinburgh in 1910, had less and less justification if every church was a mission. The IMC merged with the WCC in 1961, a consummation Van Dusen welcomed in another of his upbeat volumes, *One Great Ground of Hope: Christian Missions and Christian Unity*.[58] But the mood of missionary meetings continued to be anxious. The ecumenists were unable to agree on the relation of secular activities to those more traditionally religious. If God is active in the affairs of the world as well as of the churches, as was so often alleged, what are the boundaries of the godly actions that were once focused in missions?

This was the key question in the air at a 1963 Mexico City meeting of the same concerned leaders, but they dodged it. Instead, the Mexico City meeting celebrated the mere fact that Christian witness was being enacted on all six continents, not just the traditional Asia, Africa, and Latin America.[59] While one after another of these meetings took comfort in renouncing yet more vehemently the old distinction between sending and receiving communities, calls for further changes in missionary practice kept coming in from the field. In 1964, Ralph E. Dodge, the Methodist bishop of Angola and one of the most prominent of American missionaries in Africa, climaxed several years of pamphlets and memoranda with a hard-hitting book, *The Unpopular Missionary*, castigating what he saw as the lingering racism of the white missionary establishment. Dodge blamed missionary leaders for failing to train indigenous people to take over the leadership of Christianity in their own societies. Communism was doing better than Christianity in Africa because missionaries had been asleep at the switch and failed to anticipate and advance the revolutionary goals of Africans themselves.[60] No wonder missionaries were so "unpopular"; they had not earned the respect of the African peoples.

In that same year, a leading Lutheran missionary from India published the rhetorically entitled *Missionary Go Home!* James A. Scherer warned that the "very survival" of the missionary enterprise depended upon "repentant self-examination and a genuine willingness to cut the ties with the old order."[61] It was in the context of such accelerating complaints that working papers were prepared for the Uppsala, Sweden, meeting of the

WCC in 1968. In those papers, more voices argued that economic and political reforms were top priorities, and that God was speaking almost everywhere, including, as one American liberal said, "through pagan witnesses."[62]

Christian Century summarized the Uppsala meetings as the historical moment when "the service impulse" was finally liberated "from the missionary project," and ecumenical Protestants were authorized to use other means to serve "the poor, the defenseless, and abused, and the forgotten." The problem to be addressed, the *Century*'s correspondent asserted, is no longer witch doctors in remote areas, but corporate managers in the West, "who erode human dignity" and deny power to anyone they can control.[63] The durable Norman Goodall, put into service as editor of the Uppsala proceedings, described the delegates as preoccupied "with the revolutionary ferment of our time, with questions of social and international responsibility . . . with the plight of the underprivileged, the homeless and starving," and with contemporary radical movements of many kinds.[64]

These emphases outraged the evangelicals and fundamentalists, who, in the tradition of Machen, had never forgiven the ecumenists for taking the ideas of the Hocking Report so seriously. "Uppsala has betrayed the two billion" people who had yet to hear the gospel, complained Donald McGavran.[65] McGavran had long since left the mission field in India and was by then a professor of missiology at Fuller Theological Seminary in Pasadena, California, founded in 1947 to combat the influence of liberal seminaries. McGavran and some of his comrades did welcome, up to a point, the expansion of service activities and a substantial measure of indigenization. Indeed, from the mid-1950s onward, McGavern and Lindsell advanced a service-as-a-form-of-evangelism message, and urged their constituency to attend more closely to the cultures of the target populations of missions.[66]

Still, the evangelicals increased rather than decreased their emphasis on conversion. The crucial step was accepting masses of converts without insisting on doctrinal affirmations except of the most general sort. McGavran's notion of "church growth" eschewed the traditional evangelistic approach of individual conversion experience and welcomed entire communities en masse. The evangelicals thus dealt with the difficulties of gaining converts by lowering the threshold required to join "the Body of Christ." Lindsell explained that "medicine (and education too) is a means to an end," and that the end is "proselytizing." At issue were the souls of men and women, not their bodies. Nor was literacy to be assigned value beyond its instrumental help in advancing the Christian faith: "When men are taught to read via the Laubach literacy program," wrote Lindsell, referring to the literacy program of the former ecumenical missionary Frank Laubach, "it is with an ulterior motive in view: that by learning to read they may read the Word of God."[67] This assertion was inaccurate as a generalization about the Laubach program and many of its supporters, but it neatly encapsulated the conceptual frame in which fundamentalists could embrace crucial service activities.

In order to understand indigenous cultures, several evangelical missionary theorists insisted, it was essential to study and absorb the work of anthropologists. Wheaton College developed an ambitious program in missionary anthropology. Treatises of the 1940s and 1950s quoted copiously from the works of Franz Boas, Alfred Kroeber, Ruth Benedict, and Bronislaw Malinowski. Yet anthropology for the evangelical theorists was a practical tool, not, as for the ecumenists, a trove of reasons to back off from the priority of conversion. It was all a matter of finding a better strategy to achieve traditional goals. This can be seen in two of the most important of these mobilizations of anthropology. Gordon Hedderly Smith's *The Missionary and Anthropology*, published by Moody Press in 1945, explained that detailed empirical knowledge of local customs was essential to bringing "to Christ" peoples he was still willing to call "savages." Eugene A. Nida's *Customs and Cultures: Anthropology for Christian Missions* was more modern in tone, and at one with contemporary ecumenists in condemning the white supremacist tradition that was such an embarrassment to traditional missions. But Nida left no doubt that anthropological knowledge was instrumental in turning indigenous peoples into recognizable Christians.[68] Neither of these bibliographically intensive volumes cited William and Charlotte Wiser, the liberal Presbyterian missionaries to India whose book of 1930, *Behind Mud Walls*—a work of great ethnographic precision—will be discussed in a later chapter. Nor do Smith and Nida cite Donald Johnson Fleming, E. Stanley Jones, William Ernest Hocking, or any of the other ecumenical commentators who had addressed the relation of indigenous cultures to the missionary endeavor.[69]

The evangelical-ecumenical divide in the missionary domain thus remained sharp. Throughout the 1940s, 1950s, 1960s, and beyond, the evangelicals operated their own system of foreign missions and kept their distance from the World Council of Churches and the missionary societies of the mainstream liberal denominations in the United States. Especially galling to the evangelicals was the downplaying of proselytizing and the accommodating of unorthodox theological ideas. "Church Growth" was in part a response to this trend among ecumenists. The Church Growth movement was widely criticized, even by some evangelicals, as an anti-intellectual movement, saving the conversion enterprise at the expense of close attention to what Christianity actually might be. While not always agreeing on everything among themselves, the evangelicals knew who their enemies were. The lines of demarcation were clear at an especially important meeting of 1966 at Wheaton College in Illinois. There, 938 delegates joined in reaffirming the old watchword of 1910: "The evangelization of the world in this generation." There could be no more total rejection of the previous fifty-six years of liberalizing than the restatement of this slogan. Implacably defiant, the Wheaton conferees affirmed "unreservedly the primacy of preaching the gospel to every creature."[70] A year later, during a debate at Fuller Theological Seminary over what to do about the Vietnam War, Fuller's School of Missions welcomed the war as "an opportunity to spread the gospel in Southeast Asia."[71]

Just what *was* the gospel? This question remained a matter of deep disputation, despite repeated calls for unity and cooperation. "Unfortunately," noted a weary, longtime official of the World Council of Churches in 2007, while surveying a half-century of efforts at ecumenical-evangelical cooperation, "attempts at intra-Christian and interreligious dialogue provoked disagreement, since varying traditions could agree neither on basic guidelines nor on theological assumptions."[72]

There were also quarrels in the field, sometimes bitter. Ecumenical missionaries regularly complained that the communities they tried to serve were confused and pushed into destructive conflicts by neighboring evangelical missionaries. When fundamentalist organizations such as the Christian and Missionary Alliance achieved dominance over a region, they sometimes threatened to oust local convents from the church if they cooperated with the Non-Governmental Organizations (NGO) run by ecumenical Protestants, such as Church World Service.[73] Local converts were suddenly informed that they were not real Christians if they had been converted by Presbyterian liberals. In a characteristic lament of 1962, a longtime leader of Presbyterian missions in the South Pacific described "the entrance into the area of . . . Jehovah's Witnesses, the Assemblies of God, the Seventh Day Adventists, and other sects" who had "started work without regard to the churches and missions already established and . . . created division and conflict among the people."[74]

Yet even on the evangelical side of the great divide within American Protestantism, the forces promoting liberalization had some effect. Loath as evangelicals were to admit that they were reacting to experiences in the field by adopting basic ideas of their liberal rivals, they often did exactly that. Their attention to anthropology was an example of this. Further, the evangelicals began to ascribe greater and greater significance to indigenous voices that were not reading from American evangelical scripts, spoke more often about injustice and poverty, and acknowledged with more bite the "heathen" character of American society, treating it, too, as a target for missionary activity. The evangelicals also diminished their hostility to other religions.[75] By the early 1970s the leading evangelicals were emulating the liberals more visibly than ever before.

This became apparent at the most important missionary conclave organized by the evangelicals, at Lausanne, Switzerland, in 1974. Carefully planned by Billy Graham and his formidable network, this conference brought together 2,473 participants, about half of whom were from non-Western countries. Evangelicals, too, had accepted indigenization, and developed churches in the field reflecting their own theological priorities. They now celebrated their domain as "six continents," which became the favored slogan of the period. Several of the delegates from Latin America dominated a discussion of the "service issue," demanding that evangelical missions engage the social needs of poor societies. The respected British Anglican John R. W. Stott acknowledged that he had recently changed his mind. Stott told the assembled evangelicals that Jesus's call to missionary work must "include social as well as evangelistic responsibility." The "Lausanne Covenant" adopted by the conference endorsed service as well as preaching. This was a genuine change in emphasis that would have been anathema to Machen. But the Lausanne evangelicals held the line against the idea that non-Christian religions were significant partners with Christianity.

The extent to which Lausanne represents an accommodation with Uppsala is easily exaggerated. A leading American voice at Lausanne, Harold Lindsell (who, a quarter century before, had answered Soper with his own volume of mission philosophy), criticized his tribe's favorite enemy, the World Council of Churches, for refusing to say, unequivocally, that "some men are lost, that there is a hell, and that those who die without having personally made a profession of faith in Jesus Christ are lost."[76]

The ecumenical-evangelical divide in missions was marked by sheer numbers. In the twenty years after 1960, the personnel of ecumenical agencies decreased by more than two-thirds, from 10,300 to 3,100. This was not simply because fewer ecumenical Protestants volunteered for missions, although that is part of the explanation. The major factor, identified by William R. Hutchison, was the desertion of one missionary society after another to evangelicals. The liberalism of the National Council of

Churches and the World Council of Churches troubled many of the ecumenical Protestants who remained committed to missions. These people, almost always among the most conservative within the ecumenical community, then severed their connections to the ecumenical organizations and signed up with this or that evangelical group.

Exactly while the ecumenical missionary project was declining in numbers and in measures of support, that project's dilemmas and possibilities were displayed in remarkably sharp contours by a small but dynamic initiative begun in 1961. Designed by Margaret Flory (1914-2009), the student affairs coordinator of the Northern Presbyterian Missionary Board, the Frontier Internship in Mission program soon gained Methodist support, too, and attracted volunteers from a number of ecumenical Protestant denominations. The program sent young people abroad for only two years, placed them with Protestant youth organizations already established, and granted them almost unlimited authority to design their style of "Christian presence." Flory thus liberated her "interns"—a name that reflected the brief tenure of the appointment and the fact that they were not full-fledged missionaries—from the supervision of existing missionary societies and from the need to make a long-term commitment. What the interns actually did in Kenya or Peru or the Philippines depended heavily on the arrangements they worked out with their local hosts, who were known to Flory through the international network of the World Student Christian Federation. This ecumenical organization of various national Student Christian Movements was notoriously at odds with its closest evangelical equivalent, the InterVarsity Christian Fellowship. Hence the Frontier Interns fulfilled as completely as any group of missionaries the theme of "helping" rather than "instructing" indigenous populations. College and seminary graduates who would never have been recruited by the standard missionary programs were attracted to Flory's implementation of the critique of classical missions pushed by progressive churchmen from the 1920s onward.[77] It was a creative effort to "save the plan."

Flory herself was commissioned a Presbyterian missionary in 1944 and always referred to herself as a missionary, although she served abroad for only a short time, in Japan, immediately after the war. Perceived as a dynamo of energy with exceptional organizational skills, Flory was embraced by the Presbyterian missionary leadership and held a number of positions until she retired in 1980. "Missionary at large" was one of her official titles. In 1953, she persuaded the Presbyterian Church to develop the first of the American Junior Year Abroad Programs to place American college students outside Europe. She worked simultaneously with the

Student Volunteer Movement (SVM), the quadrennial meetings of which in 1955 and 1959 she chaired. Flory was the full embodiment of the ideal of "presence," downplaying the doctrinal articulation of Christianity in favor of acting out what one took to be its practical meaning in a given social context. Flory herself was "no theologian," as the closest student of her career emphasizes, but she did have a favorite theologian: the radical Richard Shaull. She assigned his *Encounter with Revolution* at the SVM quadrennials, and brought Shaull to each of them as a featured speaker. The 140 Frontier Interns that Flory's office sent from the United States to every continent until the program closed in 1974 were overwhelmingly sympathetic with the most politically engaged of the ecumenical leaders of the period, including Shaull. Another feature of the Frontier Internship in Mission endeavor displayed the historical situation of the ecumenical missionary movement in the 1960s and 1970s: nearly half of the interns eventually left not only their natal churches (primarily Presbyterian and Methodist), but all churches. By their middle age they had no religious affiliations at all, passing, like so many of the career missionaries and their children, into Post-Protestantism.[78]

By the last two decades of the twentieth century, what could be recognized as the Protestant foreign missionary project was overwhelmingly carried out by evangelicals. In 1980, a reliable study found that ninety percent of the "career foreign missionaries" from North America (a figure that thus includes Canada) were employed by the evangelical agencies.[79] Even the tiny Frontier Interns in Mission program was folded into the Geneva office of the World Council of Churches in 1974, and by that time had found its own efforts discredited in many parts of the world by the Vietnam War and other Cold War policies of the US government. Ecumenical Protestants did continue programs abroad, often under the rubric of "global ministries," but their significance to the larger life of the United States had diminished, as had the significance of ecumenical Protestantism itself. In a story often told, the classically liberal Protestant denominations lost numbers in institutionally catastrophic dimensions while the face of Protestantism became increasingly evangelical. The more genuinely cosmopolitan the leadership of ecumenical Protestantism became, the greater the gap between it and the more provincial churchgoing public, especially in regard to ideas about empire, race, gender, and God.[80]

The destiny of ecumenical missions is an important part of that larger saga, some of which is addressed in the next chapter of *Protestants Abroad*. But within the scope of this chapter, it remains to be underscored that the ideas so extensively articulated in 1925 and then consolidated and given greater authority in *Re-Thinking Missions* proved to be much more powerful than commentators of any outlook have acknowledged.[81]

In the 1940s, Soper and Van Dusen still felt obliged to contend with the Hocking Report, but it was rarely mentioned in the missionary debates of the 1950s and 1960s and after. Too toxic to serve as an effective tool for moving the faithful in progressive directions, *Re-Thinking Missions* was left aside. Grant Wacker is correct to observe that "the ideas espoused by liberal missionary theorists" like Hocking and Fleming "may have resonated in the walnut-paneled classrooms of the old-line seminaries, but they played wretchedly in Peoria."[82] Nevertheless, this toxin worked its way through ecumenical minds year after year, especially those paying attention to what was going on abroad. The delegates at Mexico City in 1963 and Uppsala in 1968 often spoke in Hocking's voice without knowing it. The reconstituted "global ministries" of the late twentieth and early twenty-first centuries do not cite *Re-Thinking Missions* as an inspiration, but rarely do they run afoul of its most important ideas. Two scholars argue convincingly that the Presbyterians, over the course of many decades, "adopted the proposals set forth in *Re-Thinking Missions,*" even though it was not cited as an influence.[83] Methodists, too: the perspective on missions found in the leadership of 1960s and after within the United Methodist Church and within the United Church of Christ would have pleased Hocking, Rawlinson, Laubach, Jones, Reischauer, Platt, and Fleming.

Later in their lives, some of these radical reformers of 1925 pulled away from even the liberalized missionary endeavors of their successors that were consistent with what they had advocated in the great debates of the interwar decades. Fleming, Jones, and Reischauer remained fully in the Protestant community until their deaths. Hocking gravitated toward a more comprehensively synthetic outlook. By the mid-1950s he was advancing a notion of a "world civilization" where the great religious traditions and their attendant cultures would merge into a single whole. Although Christianity was a major component of this projected synthesis, Hocking moved considerably farther from orthodoxy than he had in 1932.[84] Laubach, too, found even liberal, ecumenical Protestantism too confining. In a series of devotional books, he espoused an increasingly general mysticism while advancing literacy as a religiously neutral goal. He, like Hocking, became enamored of religious orientations that did not repudiate Christianity but encased it in very general frameworks of spirituality that decisively diminished Christian uniqueness.[85] Pearl Buck went farther: she ceased to be a professing Christian at all. Buck remained friendly with Hocking, appreciated his spiritual searching, and had a brief love affair with him when the two were near the end of their lives. Frank Rawlinson was moving rapidly toward an entirely secular outlook at the time he was killed by a bomb during the Japanese invasion of China in 1937. His letters to his wife indicate that he was close to repudiating the entire missionary enterprise and perhaps the Christian religion itself.[86]

Many factors affected the lives of these major players in the drama of the missionary project's revision, but each life-course testifies to the potentially subversive effect on inherited Protestantism of the ideas pulled together in *Re-Thinking Missions*. It is not so much that this document itself continued to be read and absorbed; rather, their later experience propelled more and more ecumenical Protestants in the specific directions Hocking had outlined so many years before. Even the course of evangelical missionary theory and practice showed the enduring power of the Hocking Report. One prominent evangelical theorist of missions of the 1990s, Wilbert R. Shenk, presented the ideal missionary's relation to indigenous peoples in terms remarkably like Hocking's. In his account of the development of Christianity in the specific regions of Argentina and West Africa, Shenk urged the importance of local conditions and local initiatives no less adamantly than Hocking and Jones. Their names are not in Shenk's index, even though they are mentioned casually in the text.[87]

Inexorably and often imperceptibly, the imperative to recognize the equality of indigenous peoples undercut a foreign missionary project that had been conceived and institutionalized on the basis of assumptions more deeply invidious than the project's designers had themselves understood. The impulse to include everyone—all human souls—into a single community of love had become all the more central to the missionary project as the ecumenical missionaries pulled away from sectarianism, but the imperative to define that community sharply enough to render it a genuine fellowship, endowing its members with a sense of arrival and belonging, remained no less essential to the project. Outsiders to Christianity had to be welcomed into something. What was it?

An obvious way to recognize the moral worth of the foreign was to acknowledge the moral deficit of the domestic, to treat everyone, everywhere, equally, as potential targets of missionary activity. This made good theological sense: the equality of all souls was of course a basic part of the gospel. But the missionary project had been largely propelled by a sense of cultural and social hierarchy. When substantial collections of people on the other side of the implicit social and cultural divide took literally the gospel's claims to transcend it, there was little to do but accept the constructions of the "younger" Christians and redirect the missionary project in ways that renounced the earlier, if often unacknowledged, invidiousness.

Were the constructions of Christianity developed in the Global South, with all their variations drawn on local traditions, really part of a single community of faith with the Protestants of the North Atlantic West? This was a dangerous question for church leaders. "A seismic shift in Christianity occurred in the twentieth century," noted the Scottish missiologist Andrew F. Walls, in trying to save the notion of a unified faith. "Christianity simultaneously entered its most substantial recession and received its most substantial accession." While the West—the historic home of Christianity—was subject to secularization, Walls explained, "the non-Western world, notably sub-Saharan Africa and some parts of Asia," became the great domain for Christianity. In this view, the Old Faith is simply receiving a new instantiation, no longer blinded by the cultural limits of American and European missionaries. "The missionary movement was the great learning experience for Western Christianity," argued Walls; it revealed "huge deficiencies" in its "intellectual equipment" and exposed "the inadequacy of a theology which had made claims to universality but had been formed without reference to substantial areas of humanity." In this transcendent understanding of the faith, the secularization of the West and the increased deployment of the symbolic capital of Christianity in the Global South are parts of a single process whereby the faith moves to a new locale and achieves greater knowledge of itself.[88]

Those American Protestants who accepted this reassuring vision of the direction of world history, and those who did not, could at least share one important conclusion: the less need there was in foreign lands for actual instruction by Americans and Europeans in the ways of western Christianity, the more sharply the critical edge of the whole missionary endeavor could be redirected toward that endeavor's original home. But the force of the endeavor "at home"—make America more Christian!— was blunted because the American population of churchgoers knew full well an awkward truth that church officials and seminary professors preferred to deny: that the point of Protestant missions, for most of its supporters, was to make foreign people as similar as possible to the kinds of Christians already found in the United States. The contrary idea that the point of missions was to change Americans, including their sense of what it meant to be Christian, was a hard sell to the people in the pews, especially when Billy Graham and similar voices from the other family of Protestants were reasserting the Home Truths the liberals found provincial. When ecumenical missionary leaders, espousing the relatively cosmopolitan outlooks consistent with their experiences abroad, ceased to validate the old sense of what the missionary project was about, popular support diminished rapidly.

There is a certain drama in the steps ecumenical Protestants took to save the missionary project, and to affirm that it had not been, as John Hersey's protagonist in *The Call* had feared, "all error." An impulse to establish a moral community extending to all human beings was not the only thing that drove the missions. But it was one very strong imperative. That imperative, that impulse, eventually found missions too confining, and even Christianity, whatever its merits as a particular instantiation, too narrow to accommodate a universalism that claimed empathic engagement with a great range of human cultures. The missionary project, and its ecumenical follow-up endeavors, adopted a thinner and thinner conception of Christianity while using Christianity as a container for a vision of what it meant to be human. But the whole missionary-ecumenical project found itself riding in a vehicle—Christianity—that could not meet the demands placed upon it by the Protestant liberals. They asked Christianity to be open enough to serve as a stand-in for a species-wide "we," and closed enough to distinguish between Christians and non-Christians. The tension between the universal and the particular was crushing.

If you begin with a universalist understanding of human needs which you believe to be better met by the Presbyterians than anyone else, then experience in the field leads you to suppose that what satisfies those needs is less Presbyterianism, as such, than a Christianity that has shown up in a number of Protestant denominations in the United States and Europe, you have moved considerably. If then you come to fear that this historically particular North Atlantic answer to human needs is also too narrowly configured for what you actually see, and you go on to embrace the versions of Christianity developed by Catholics, and by indigenous peoples incorporating elements of various local cultures; and then you go beyond even that and suppose that the original, sound universalist vision of Jesus of Nazareth is best fulfilled by a solidarity of all religious believers, you have moved even farther. By that point in your trajectory you have expanded your ideal community almost all the way to the species itself. Perhaps the species, rather than the community of faith, was the ideal solidarity, and it had been a mistake to suppose that the latter could ever be achieved on the terms of the former? This was the suspicion that missionary cosmopolitans faced as their endeavors reached farther and farther across the globe. Perhaps a notion of human brotherhood should begin with a vision of all humanity, rather than assuming Christianity was the answer for everyone?

It was through this series of doctrinal steps that the liberal, ecumenical Protestant missionary project transformed itself virtually out of existence as it tried to use Christianity as the answer to the question of what a species-wide solidarity would look like. Here at long last was the secularization of the universalism of Galatians 3:28—"you are all one in Christ Jesus"— and of the second chapter of Acts, when all the diverse tribes, endowed with cloven tongues of fire, heard each other as if speaking in each tribe's own language. Humankind as a whole was now fully out from under the canopy of the community of faith.

For some missionary cosmopolitans, the next step, embraced at Uppsala and elsewhere by the most liberal of the Protestants, was to make yet greater common cause with secular agencies and to develop successor projects to missions that were not defined by any form of Christianity or even of religion. Literacy reform, nonsectarian scholarship, community development, human rights, civil rights, antipoverty campaigns, and various sorts of philanthropy served as successor projects for missionary-connected Americans, many of whom migrated out of the faith and became post-Protestants. But there is still more to the institutionally Protestant part of the story: what happened to the churches themselves as this missionary dynamic played out? This is the topic of the next chapter.

CHAPTER FOUR

The Protestant International and the Political Mobilization of Churches

THE CASCADE of self-interrogations generated by the missionary experience just kept flowing, like flood water over the top of a dam. What began as a reconsideration of missions abroad became a reconsideration of churches at home. Missionary experience had two profound consequences for American churches. First, it exposed the parochialism of denominational distinctions, inspiring church leaders to push ecumenical initiatives further and further–even to the point of trying to merge as many denominations as possible into a vast American Protestant church, in frank imitation of the national churches created by Protestant converts in China and India. Second, missionary experience brought world affairs into greater view, inspiring church leaders to recognize it as a domain in which they and Protestants elsewhere might work together as a political force.

The idea of church unification and the idea of a mobilized Protestant witness in world affairs fed each other. The more unified Protestantism could become, the more influence it might wield. The more real the informal Protestant International[1] became, the stronger the impulse for unification. Eventually, each of these closely related endeavors ran up against serious opposition, especially from people in the church pews. But before these movements played themselves out, they stretched the "first family" of ecumenical, mainstream churches into new shapes, sharpened the conflict with the "second family" of evangelical churches, and achieved political alliances with secular constituencies that inadvertently facilitated the later migration of a number of the most educated Protestants to post-Protestant secularism.

These movements attracted the energies of many churchmen and churchwomen who did not have missionary connections. But members of the missionary contingent took the lead. They wrote the most influential theoretical treatises, staffed the major transdenominational organizations, designed and supervised the most important conferences, and presided over many of the mergers that were achieved. They exercised this leadership in distinctive phases. First was the articulation of ecumenical feelings in the mission field. They began this long before World War II, by which time the churches were well into a second phase: the building of networks and organizations capable of influencing world affairs. The third phase was the effort to move from transdenominational organizations to actual church merger. Talk of major mergers had been going on for several decades, but not until the 1940s did it become serious. The merger initiative peaked in the early 1960s and was essentially over by the early 1970s. Thereafter, the ecumenical churches struggled to preserve their leadership with greatly diminished numbers and influence, flanked on the one side by a newly empowered evangelical family and on the other by a rapidly growing population of post-Protestants who had abandoned the churches. This chapter proceeds through each of these phases.

Missionaries in the field understood Christianity to be designed for all human beings. Yet it came in distinctively wrapped packages. Lutheran, Calvinist, Wesleyan, and Anabaptist versions of Protestantism emerged from the circumstances of different European communities, and were transferred to the New World by immigrations of Scottish, English, Dutch, German, and Scandinavian settlers. Denominationalism flourished in the United States, where physical and constitutional space made it easy for churches to go their own way, elaborating and revising doctrines that served as social adhesives for different communities, often ethnic in character. Protestantism was ideally suited to a pluralistic, immigrant-receiving society with a strong church-state separation. The missionaries who went to China, India, Japan, and other countries encountered social conditions no less powerful than those that had shaped and sustained their own denominations. But those conditions were different, and seemed to demand innovation.

In trying to adapt the Christianity they knew to these novel circumstances, the missionary societies realized early on that it was easier for denominations to stay out of each other's way than to decide on a common program. They all depended on the support of churchgoers at home with denominational loyalties. Through what were called "comity agreements," the missionary societies divided geographical space to make it easier for each denomination to maintain itself without having to compete with one another. One of the most sharply defined of these arrangements was implemented in the Middle East in the 1870s. The Congregationalists agreed to handle Turkey, the Dutch Reformed the Persian Gulf, and the Presbyterians Egypt, Syria, and Persia. Within a single country, it was often agreed that the Methodists would work in one region, the Lutherans in another, the Episcopalians in yet another, and so forth. Comity, in the words of a sympathetic historian, enabled missionaries to build "a great Church of Christ in every land through the combined efforts of the separate societies."[2]

By the early twentieth century, converts were increasingly impatient with comity agreements. The new Christians signed up for Christianity, but could not help but notice that the missionaries operated on the basis of parochial Western categories. The converts concluded that what they had in common as Chinese Christians or Indian Christians was in tension with the denomination-specific doctrines and practices of the churches each had joined. At the great Edinburgh meeting of 1910, the Reverend Cheng Jingyi, a twenty-eight-year-old convert from China, sounded a galvanizing plea for "a united Christian church without any denominational distinctions."[3] The idea was endorsed by a group of Western missionaries to China. They had become accustomed to dealing with people like Cheng. They told their colleagues at Edinburgh that there should be "one united church of Christ" in each national mission field, not a series of separate churches tied to the West.[4] A Church of Christ in China was in fact established in 1927.

In China and elsewhere, the phenomenal success of transdenominational organizations offered powerful testimony to the promise of ambitiously ecumenical approaches. The YMCA and the YWCA generally ignored differences in theology, church polity, and sacramental practices. As laymen, YMCA leaders John R. Mott and Sherwood Eddy were freer than ordained ministers to speak for Christianity in general, and had a unifying effect wherever they went. Their less famous Y colleagues—the "secretaries," as directors of local Y institutions were titled—were also ecumenical magnets.[5] Eddy was an especially enterprising proponent of unified, national Protestant churches and was among the first to describe the momentum for national churches abroad as an inspiration for churches in America. As early as 1920, Eddy asked readers of the *Christian Century* to ponder the possibility that the churches in "the mission field" might well "be leading the way toward the church of the future and the reunion of a divided Christendom."[6]

Mott was the charismatic leader of the Edinburgh conference, which was uniquely influential in propelling the ecumenical movement.[7] This conclave brought together missionaries who had been working separately, and encouraged them to see themselves in a single endeavor. The gathering produced, in turn, a set of new institutions through which the missionaries and their supporters at home could cooperate on a regular basis. One was the International Missionary Council, the leading missionary organization in the world until its merger with the World Council of Churches in 1961. But two other follow-ups to Edinburgh enabled Protestant churches to explore ways to bear a unified Christian witness in world affairs with less direct relation to missions: a "Faith and Order" group focused on theology and church organization, and a "Life and Works" group concerned with the practical applications of Christianity. These loose collectivities of American and European church officials, seminary professors, and engaged laymen met periodically during the 1920s and 1930s. In these two networks, the promise of a united Protestantism and the promise of a more politically influential Protestantism grew in tandem.

Many of the participants in Faith and Order and Life and Works continued to keep the Wilsonian flame of global governance. No one was more active in this old cause than Eddy, who was wealthy enough to do things on his own initiative, apart from the church networks at home and abroad.[8] Beginning in 1921, he organized and personally financed what came to be called the "Steamship Seminars." Each of these multi-week excursions across the Atlantic during summers of the 1920s drew more than one hundred participants, including some of the most prominent ministers and laymen from many denominations. They traveled through several European countries, sometimes including Soviet Russia. Although the seminars did not venture beyond the North Atlantic West, they were rife with global talk and often focused on the failures of European leaders to equitably handle not only the affairs of Europeans, but of the peoples abroad over whom the Europeans exercised authority. Eddy's missionary experience and personal contacts with Sun Yat-sen and other Asian leaders gave him credibility as an expert on world affairs. He used these popular cruises to build a constituency for the ideas that then defined *World Tomorrow*, a magazine edited by Kirby Page, Eddy's former assistant in the Student Volunteer Movement.

Page himself was a pacifist, as were a number of the other contributors to *World Tomorrow* and *Christian Century* during the 1920s and 1930s. But the internationalism these journals espoused went beyond pacifism to develop a wide-ranging critique of imperialism, of racism, and of nationalism. While it is accurate to describe the political orientation and sweeping ambition of these Protestant internationalists as "Wilsonian," historian Michael G. Thompson has shown that, for them, Wilsonianism was less an inspiration than a recognizable face for an internationalism to which the Protestant left was already attached. "The origins and character of interwar Christian internationalism," writes Thompson, "in fact owed more to the missionary enterprise than to Wilsonianism, the Social Gospel, or any other factor."[9] Of all the missionary groups, the YMCA, especially, led ecumenical Protestants to see the entire globe as an arena for Christian-directed political action.

These American Protestant internationalists were active in the networks that emerged from the Edinburgh meeting of 1910, but within the United States they also made use of the Federal Council of Churches (FCC). This organization had been founded in 1908, inspired in large part by the domestic concerns of the Social Gospel, but saturated with missionaries. It was an organization of denominational bodies, enabling Protestants to work together in a progressive ethos through their churches, rather than outside them. American Protestants had long been involved in social reform, but through societies organized around slavery, child labor, temperance, and other issues.[10] The FCC was the chief instrument for the ecumenical movement within the United States, and became increasingly important as more and more church leaders sought a cohesive, unified voice in foreign as well as domestic affairs. *The Missionary Outlook in the Light of the War*, a volume of 1920 taken up in the previous chapter, was an FCC project. The FCC had its own network of commissions and its own series of conferences, providing opportunities for cooperation by officers of the more than two dozen denominations that had joined it by the mid-1930s.

The imperative for churches to come together was given great intellectual force in 1929 when the Yale theologian H. Richard Niebuhr published *The Social Sources of Denominationalism*. This brother of the eventually more famous Reinhold Niebuhr was able to show how and why denominations happened. He made church leaders acutely aware of the historical contingency of their own confessions. He condemned denominationalism as an "evil" from a theological point of view—the gospel was one.[11]

Two developments of the late 1930s gave new urgency to the impulses to work together and to act politically. One was the sudden increase of Roman Catholic participation in the public affairs of the United States. The Catholics were, after all, a single presence; Protestant leaders worried about—and in some respects envied—the ability of the

Catholic hierarchy to speak in one voice. Catholic lobbyists persuaded the Connecticut legislature to make it a crime for a physician to inform a patient of the existence of condoms and other birth control technologies. The Catholic Legion of Decency achieved great influence over what could appear in a Hollywood motion picture. The threat of a Catholic "take-over" triggered an unprecedented movement for church unity among ecumenical Protestants. Catholic perspectives on foreign affairs seemed part of the same piece, and sharpened the concern. American Catholic leaders were often openly sympathetic with Franco in Spain and Mussolini in Italy. This concern sharpened in 1940 when the French Catholic church gave its support to the Nazi-collaborationist government of Vichy. In this milieu, "Christian internationalism" was clearly understood to mean "Protestant internationalism."

A second and more important source of concern was the weakness of the Western democracies. The Life and Works network met at Oxford in 1937, only a few days after a Geneva session of the League of Nations revealed the virtual collapse of that organization. The meeting drew more than four hundred delegates, largely from the United States, the United Kingdom, and several British Commonwealth countries, all of whom were concerned about the actions of Nazi Germany in Europe, Fascist Italy in Africa, and imperial Japan in China. No one was more shaken by the Geneva debacle than the keynote speaker at Oxford, John Foster Dulles. The man who later became President Eisenhower's secretary of state was then known primarily as a leading Presbyterian layman and as the Republican Party's chief foreign policy expert.[12] At Oxford, Dulles encountered a global consciousness and resolute attitude he found altogether lacking in the atmosphere at Geneva. He became convinced that ecumenical Protestantism was the most promising foundation for mobilizing the historically Christian democratic nations against the evils of nationalism so apparent in Germany, Italy, and Japan.[13]

Missionary-connected individuals worked closely with Dulles in the next few years to create an informal but highly organized community that spanned the Atlantic. This Protestant International led many American Protestants to think globally just when the United States was in an intensely isolationist phase. In 1938, Faith and Order merged with Life and Works to form the World Council of Churches. The war delayed until 1948 the WCC's official founding meeting in Amsterdam. In the interim, the WCC was located in the United States and was largely run by the missionary contingent. Henry Smith Leiper, a former Congregationalist missionary to China, was the senior American official of the WCC-in-waiting.[14]

During these same years of build-up to the WCC's formal launching, several American denominations joined together in 1946 to establish Church World Service, an international relief and philanthropic organization. This NGO's chief American officer was A. Livingston Warnshuis, a longtime Dutch Reformed missionary to China.[15]

During World War II and its immediate aftermath, the central institution in the Protestant International was the FCC. It worked closely with several other organizations. One of the most enduring and influential was created in 1941 by officers of the denominational women's missionary boards. The United Council of Church Women (UCCW) was founded by women sensitive to the diminution of their role in church affairs by the decision—made by one denomination after another—to fold the long-powerful women's boards into unified missionary boards, reducing the women to a subdivision. The UCCW from the start was more ecumenical than the FCC. The UCCW welcomed Unitarians, who had been spurned by the FCC as insufficiently Christian. Most often known by the name it later adopted, United Church Women (and yet later as Church Women United), this organization carried out its own philanthropic projects and vigorously advocated leadership responsibilities for women inside churches and in church-related institutions. It was never feminist in the ways that Pearl Buck had become by 1941, nor was it as focused on world affairs as were most of the other ecumenical steps taken at the same historical moment. But Church Women United became a substantial partner of the FCC.[16]

In developing the Protestant International, however, the FCC's most important partner was the Foreign Missions Conference of North America. This umbrella organization of American and Canadian missionary boards was founded in 1894 and gained in importance as the ecumenical movement grew in the 1920s and 1930s. Early in 1940, the Foreign Missions Conference sent to the FCC's leadership a letter that might be regarded as a kind of charter for the Protestant International. Since the "Gospel is true for all men," the missionary group pressed the FCC to recognize that "conditions for world government" must be created. Christians themselves must do it. "Twenty years' experience" with such devices as "World Court, League of Nations, treaties, mandates, pacts" had shown that it was not enough to simply try to strengthen these institutions. Rather, missionary-experienced Christians must now achieve and proclaim "a common spirit" to advance the "brotherhood of man under their Father God."[17]

The FCC acted on the Foreign Missions Conference's suggestion by establishing the Commission for a Just and Durable Peace, which was the largest and most widely publicized of the FCC's wartime projects. The

FCC charged the commission with developing a Christian blueprint for the world expected to emerge after the war. It was soon called "the Dulles Commission" because of its high-profile chair. The commission held a series of "study conferences," drawing hundreds of carefully selected representatives from the Methodist, Congregational, Presbyterian, Baptist, Lutheran, and other denominations, small as well as large. These study conferences of the 1940s stopped well short of church merger, but they brought representatives of the various denominations into sustained cooperation at a time when many of them believed they were about to shape history.

At its first major event early in March 1942, the Dulles Commission convened nearly four hundred Protestant leaders in what was arguably the most important ecumenical meeting in American history. This conference, held on the campus of Ohio Wesleyan University in Delaware, Ohio, integrated pacifist and interventionist factions whose disagreements had been sidelined by the Japanese attack on Pearl Harbor only three months before. The delegates passed strongly worded resolutions against colonialism, racism, and economic exploitation, and in favor of a "world government" that would include legislative and judicial authority. *Time* described the conference's radical resolutions as "sensational." The delegates declared that the United States could not "be trusted" to lead the anticipated postwar world "so long as our attitudes and policies deny peoples of other races in our own or other lands the essential position of brothers."[18]

In all its wartime conclaves, no global concern loomed larger than human rights. At the 1942 meeting, the delegates resolved "that the right of all men to pursue work of their own choosing and to enjoy security from want and oppression is not limited by race, color, or creed."[19] The Dulles Commission went on to sponsor a series of other study conferences and workshops, including one the following year at Princeton that issued the "Six Pillars of Peace" manifesto. This widely publicized document— the commission sent it to sixty thousand ministers—sought to boil down to a list of simple principles the outlook developed at the 1942 meeting, and to make sure everyone understood the need for a common ground for Hindus, Muslim Buddhists, and Soviet atheists, as well as Christians and religiously observant Jews. "Autonomy for subject peoples" was a crucial "pillar" for the peace this document outlined for the postwar world.[20]

The Dulles Commission's role in the founding of the United Nations was most evident in a large January 1945 meeting in Cleveland, organized around the proposals for the actual structure of the new organization that the Allied Powers had agreed upon at Dumbarton Oakes the previous fall. Four hundred ecumenical Protestant leaders again assembled. The State Department considered the gathering of such importance in creating support for American involvement in the UN that it waived war-related restrictions on travel costs then in effect. Although the voting delegates at these Dulles Commission meetings were selected by the affiliated denominations, additional representatives from virtually every nonfundamentalist missionary organization were present as invited guests and expressed solidarity with the voting delegates.[21]

The Cleveland delegates complained that the Dumbarton Oakes proposals did not contain a "Human Rights Commission." Pressure for such a commission was led by one of the most missionary-heavy of the FCC's array of committees, the Joint Committee on Religious Liberty, established in 1942 jointly with the Foreign Missions Council. The guiding theorist of the Committee on Religious Liberty was Union Seminary Professor M. Searle Bates, a veteran of more than two decades as a Disciples of Christ missionary in China, and revered for his having remained at his post during the Nanking Massacre of 1937 and written detailed reports of it.[22] Another of the Committee on Religious Liberty's central figures was John S. Badeau, a longtime missionary to Egypt who later became president of the American University in Cairo and, much later, US ambassador to Egypt. At a time when British missionary allies wanted the United Nations to focus "religious liberty" on the right to proselytize, Badeau produced what historian John Stuart calls a "devastating critique" of that idea as too close to a colonialist past, insulting to Muslims and other non-Christian faiths.[23] The view of missionaries Bates and Badeau prevailed at Cleveland. With the support of the Dulles Commission, the Committee on Religious Liberty was able to dominate the FCC's delegation of "consultants," as lobbyists to the San Francisco international conference of that spring were called.

The Protestant International won a great victory in San Francisco. Four of the nine amendments it proposed to the Dumbarton Oakes draft were adopted. The United Nations Charter did affirm the ideal of human rights and establish a Commission on Human Rights. It also established a Trusteeship Council to facilitate the movement of colonized peoples toward independence. Working in close cooperation with several other lobby groups, especially the American Jewish Committee, the FCC's top strategist, Frederick Nolde, got most of what he wanted.[24] Historian Samuel Moyn correctly concludes that American ecumenical Protestants "were by any standard most responsible for the original move to the internationalization of religious freedom and, in fact, for the presence of the entire

notion of human rights in international affairs."[25] It is no wonder that
the American ecumenical leaders in the mid-1940s—before the Cold War
dominated American foreign policy and drastically limited the operations
of the United Nations—allowed themselves to believe that the world was
theirs.[26]

In 1946, Nolde edited a volume of essays that registered the Protestant
International's understanding of itself at its moment of greatest confidence. In *Toward World-Wide Christianity*, Nolde, John A. Mackay, John
C. Bennett, Henry Smith Leiper, and others in this increasingly cohesive
cadre outlined a global future in which enlightened Protestants would
guide governments to establish a secular political order consistent with
Christian principles but in no way unfair to non-Christians. Nolde himself
wrote the most ambitious essay, in which he voiced the Protestant International's understanding that the classic values of an egalitarian, democratic
society constituted the essential meaning of Christianity:

> The Christian gospel relates to all men, regardless of race, language,
> or color ... [T]here is no Christian basis to support a fancied intrinsic
> superiority of any one race. ... The rights and freedoms of all peoples
> in all lands should be recognized and safeguarded. Freedom of reli-
> gion and religious worship, of speech, of assembly, of the press, of cul-
> tural interchange, of scientific inquiry and teaching are fundamental to
> human development and in keeping with the moral law. International
> cooperation is needed to create conditions under which these freedoms
> may become a reality.[27]

Participants in these wartime church conclaves and postwar symposia
were all the more certain about their contributions to world peace because
of the great popularity the missionary project then enjoyed among leading
secular internationalists. Wendell Willkie was at the apex of his fame, enjoying the phenomenal popularity of his book of 1943, *One World*. In speaking tours to promote this fervent affirmation of the potential of diverse
peoples to work together, Willkie praised missionaries for crossing barriers
and helping create the global solidarity the idealistic Willkie hoped would
follow the war. Everywhere he had gone on the goodwill tour narrated in
his book, Willkie professed to have found "universal enthusiasm for what
American missionaries have done." Speaking as an Episcopalian layman,
as well as a politician prominent enough to have been the Republican
presidential candidate in 1940, Willkie praised missionaries for teaching foreign peoples "to provide their own leadership" rather than to copy
Americans.[28] At the same moment, University of Chicago sociologist

Robert Park credited missionaries with having "laid the foundation for a moral order that includes all peoples." Park cited Willkie and shared his feeling that the interests of the United States, of the Christian faith, and of indigenous peoples the world over were the same. Park hailed missionaries as "instruments of a good-neighbor policy."[29] Further, it was at this time that W.E.B. Dubois spoke hopefully about the role that Protestant missionaries could play in making the world a more just place for nonwhites.[30] In 1946, John R. Mott, the single most important American in the missionary project, was awarded the Nobel Peace Prize.

At the same mid-1940s moment, the FCC's agenda of domestic reform was also at its most robust. There, too, missionary-connected individuals and groups were conspicuous. In 1946 the FCC formally called for the end of racial segregation in public accommodations, going well beyond the generalized condemnations of racism that the FCC and several of its denominational affiliates, especially the Congregationalists, had made earlier.[31] The FCC's pivotal resolution was passed at its national meeting in Columbus, Ohio, a location chosen because the hotel owners association of Chicago—the meeting's originally intended site—refused to guarantee that black delegates would be served equally with whites.

A major force behind the FCC resolution was Eugene E. Barnett (1888–1970), a twenty-six-year YMCA missionary in China. Barnett was then serving as the administrative head of the entire YMCA, an organization second in importance only to the FCC in that era's Protestant International.[32] Barnett was the author and chief promoter of the YMCA's own desegregation resolution passed by its National Council, also in 1946, integrating the YMCA's extensive bureaucracy and encouraging local Ys throughout the country to follow suit.[33] The YMCA claimed more than two million members, and operated a local Y in almost every city in the country.

The missionary connection to the FCC resolution and to the integration of the YMCA should not be exaggerated. The people who most moved these organizations to take these steps were the African American leaders within those organizations, especially Channing Tobias, George Haynes, and Benjamin Mays. These black Protestants made more headway because white missionary voices like E. Stanley Jones, Kenneth Scott Latourette, and Edmund Soper had been urging the ecumenical leadership to proceed in their direction. Moreover, in the detailed committee work that led up to the adoption of the FCC resolution, former missionaries Galen Fisher, Harry Kingman, and Edwin Espy, along with Barnett, were brought into the discussion as experts on the global dimensions of racism.[34]

The more the ecumenical leadership committed to this liberal agenda for domestic and foreign affairs, the more they angered the evangelicals.[35] The National Association of Evangelicals (NAE), founded in 1942, was intended to serve as a counterpoint to the FCC. The NAE, like the FCC, was an organization of denominational bodies, not of individuals. In neither case did member denominations relinquish juridical authority. Both were controlled by elites with opinions more extreme than the average church member. The NAE's chief points of irritation were the FCC's theological liberalism, its relative accommodation of non-Christian religions in the mission field, its energetic support of the broadly based WCC, and its direct involvement in politics. The evangelicals had no patience for the United Nations, and were especially put out by the UN Charter's failure to invoke God's name. The fundamentalists and other evangelicals were highly disturbed by the FCC's comfortable ties with the country's governing elite. Congress, the federal courts, and the executive branch were filled with people who were at least nominal members of the denominations affiliated with the FCC.

The FCC and its successor organization, the yet larger National Council of Churches, established in 1950, ignored the evangelicals whenever they thought they could get away with it. The NCC was, like the FCC, a decidedly top-down enterprise. In the 1950s and 1960s, NCC officials tried to continue the political application of Christian universalism that had distinguished the public face of ecumenical Protestantism in the 1940s. Although some voices within the Protestant International worried that it was operating "without a strong theoretical understanding of church-state relations," as one historian has observed, the ecumenical leadership remained remarkably confident that it could identify a Christian approach to world and national politics, and that the secular government of the United States was listening.[36] In 1958, the FCC became the largest national organization of any kind to support the diplomatic recognition of the People's Republic of China. In this case, as in many others, the leadership was confident it could retain the loyalty of its own members, and keep the evangelicals in their place.

Theologian John C. Bennett cogently expressed this perspective in a book of 1958. Then at the peak of his influence, the Union Seminary theologian advances a vision of Christian citizenship within a pluralistic national polity and a multinational global order. In *Christians and the State*, Bennett calls upon "the ecumenical Christian community," as he repeatedly refers to his own tribe, to perfect its witness in domestic and international political arenas. He welcomes collaboration with secularists. In pointed opposition to his evangelical rivals, Bennett insists that "Christians should not desire either our courts or other public bodies to affirm" we Americans to be "a Christian people." T. S. Eliot's *The Idea of a Christian Society*, then fashionable in religious circles, "could not have been written for this country" because American Christians "cannot participate in either the advantages or the illusions" that attend this idea. Going well beyond the "Judeo-Christian" enthusiasms of the 1950s popularized by Will Herberg, Bennett accepted the "atheists or agnostics or Naturalistic Humanists" as citizens of equal standing, and urged Christians to listen to their criticisms of traditional religion. We should "recognize without the least condescension" that these nonbelievers offer criticisms of traditional religion that "are often valid." The secular intellectuals "represent a challenge to obscurantism and clericalism that is needed." Religious people tend toward "stuffiness" if they "never have to face this kind of opposition." Here, as throughout *Christians and the State*, Bennett was sure that ecumenical Protestantism was so strong that it could survive any challenge. In the late 1950s, Bennett wrote at the chronological high point of the ecumenical leadership's corporate belief in itself. Atheists are not to be feared; they can even be functional. They keep the faithful on their toes.[37]

Bennett credited missions with helping American Protestants appreciate how their own churches had to drop their traditional provinciality and engage more of the world sympathetically. "The missionary movement is one of the most astonishing examples of the capacity of Christians to identify themselves with people in other nations," he wrote. "The missionaries are so identified with the nations to which they go" that they become "the most effective defenders of the interests and the aspirations" of those nations "against both the national selfishness and the moral pretensions of western peoples."[38] The world was diverse and dynamic. Churchmen and churchwomen needed to confront it on its own terms. In this endeavor, secularists could be better allies than evangelicals.

But the cosmopolitan leaders of Bennett's type were traveling farther from the average churchgoer than they realized. Just how out of touch they were was made abundantly clear by what happened when they pushed the idea of church unity to the extreme of church merger.

Not until World War II did church leaders start to take church merger seriously as something they might actually achieve within the United States. The Protestant International was going strong. The more impressive it became, the more parochial denominationalism looked. The problem of how to create a more genuinely ecumenical Christianity, Edmund D. Soper allowed in 1943, was "occupying the attention of the church at the home base as much as abroad."[39] Developments abroad, in the indigenous churches founded by missionaries, provided great inspiration.

"If the Christians in India can manage to unite in a single, national church," proclaimed Union Theological Seminary President Henry P. Van Dusen in 1947, "it will solve in principle" the problem of sectarianism. Even better, he added, the Indian example would "provide precedent" for later mergers that could bring about "the ultimate union of non-Roman Christendom." Van Dusen offered these reflections while the Anglicans, Congregationalists, and Presbyterians of South India were deliberating about forming a single church. "The whole Christian world has waited breathless," exclaimed the almost giddy Van Dusen, reflecting the excitement many American church leaders felt about the Indian merger, which actually took place just as Van Dusen's observations were published.[40] Perhaps denominational distinctions within the North Atlantic West, including the United States, would be overcome at last? Sherwood Eddy had speculated about this a quarter century before. Perhaps the "receiving" churches created by foreign missions could become a model for the "sending" churches?

Some mergers gave Van Dusen and his allies reason for hope. The Northern Methodists and the Southern Methodists joined in 1939 to form the United Methodist Church, but this event was understood as a restoration of an earlier unity interrupted by the issue of slavery. Of greater significance, in 1943 the Congregationalists and the Evangelical and Reformed Church (known colloquially as "German Reformed") signed a "Basis for Union" statement. Exciting as this potential union of ethnically English and ethnically German churches was to officers of the two denominations, they struggled to sell the idea to their members. It took fourteen years. The two did merge in 1957 to form the United Church of Christ, although splinter groups from both confessions held out and set up their own independent churches.[41] The establishing of the United Church of Christ inspired a former president of the National Council of Churches to call for the creation of a "super-church." Eugene Carson Blake, who early in his career had served as a missionary educator in India, issued this call in 1960 in what became a famous sermon at San Francisco's Grace Cathedral.[42]

That is not the way things worked out.[43] There was to be no super-church in the United States. The destiny of the Consultation on Church Union (COCU) made the ecumenical elite aware of how badly it had underestimated the attachment of churchgoers to the traditional denominational habits. COCU was established in 1962 by officials of the United

Church of Christ, the United Methodists, the Episcopalians and the Northern Presbyterians. Several other groups joined in the consultation, including the Disciples of Christ and the Southern Presbyterians. It was just then that Pope John XXIII began Vatican II, enabling Protestants to recognize even in the Roman Catholic Church glimmerings of the kind of Christianity they most wanted. The chief Protestant observer at Vatican II was another missionary-connected figure, George Lindbeck, a Lutheran theologian at the Yale Divinity School who had been born and raised in China as the son of missionary parents. After eight years of earnest labor, COCU presented a "plan of union" to the various denominations. The governing assemblies of every one roundly rejected it in 1970 or shortly thereafter. Other denominations, invited to join, had in the meantime refused to become involved, sometimes when their governing bodies, having gotten wind of what the leadership was trying to do, explicitly prohibited participation. A decade after Blake's militant speech, the church merger movement was virtually dead.[44]

Ethnicity—a foundation for religious communities, the vital importance of which was often underestimated by ecumenical leaders—served as the chief foundation for the major mergers that did take place. One was the Methodist merger of 1939, ending a division dating from 1844. A second was the 1983 merger of the Northern and Southern Presbyterians.[45] In both cases the obstacle to unity had been disagreements about the place of black people in the churches and in American society and politics generally, but these disagreements had always been within a single ancestral tribe. The Methodist merger was made possible as early as 1939, when the northerners agreed to a southern demand that all of the predominantly African American congregations be placed under a separate administrative jurisdiction. This segregated polity was opposed by many missionary-connected Methodists, who were then instrumental in having it eliminated in 1968.[46] The northern and southern Baptists remained divided by the legacy of Civil War issues and have not merged to this day.[47]

Hence the grand visions of Van Dusen and Blake were enacted only modestly. Why could not the Methodists and Presbyterians join together as one? The two groups, despite their common British ancestry, were never close to merging with one another. The gap between Calvinist and Wesleyan emphases on the authority of God and on individual responsibility for one's own salvation proved to be enduring. Methodists and Presbyterians of the United States remained very distinct from one another, while their converts abroad had long since joined together across the Calvinist-Wesleyan divide. National churches might be fine, the churchgoers reluctantly allowed, for the Protestants of Japan, Thailand, Zimbabwe, China, and India—all of which, among a number of other countries, experienced the founding of national Protestant churches— but not for the Protestants of the United States.

The ecumenical leaders had ceased to believe in the theological justifications for diverse denominational practices, but remained committed to the unity of the essential gospel. They were slow to appreciate the function of these theologically indefensible practices as social adhesives. Clinging to a mystical understanding of Christianity, they were inclined to ignore the abundant historical and sociological evidence that churches were above all devices for community formation and maintenance. Some of the most worldly of church leaders recognized that general truths can be made more compelling for the average soul through instantiation in particulars. But this insight, which helps explain the function of unified national Protestant churches abroad as well as denominational divisions at home, did not sit easily with the faith's transcendent claims.

Were the seminarians and officials of the great councils going to pretend that what the average Baptist believed was true even when they knew better? Ecumenical leaders in the tradition of Van Dusen and Blake were caught between their commitment to truth-telling and their continued faith in the unique, mystical power of Christianity. Even the sociologically-focused H. Richard Niebuhr endorsed this faith-centric perspective. He concluded his *Social Sources of Denominationalism* with a celebration of "divine love" as a force that would unify Christians all over the globe if they would but cleave to it patiently, fervently, and with a good measure of wisdom about the world.[48] Troubled that he had not made the point with sufficient vigor, he followed his 1929 book with one of 1937, *The Kingdom of God in America*, which emphasizes divinity rather than social structure. His earlier book, wrote Niebuhr, had dealt only with why "the religious stream flowed in these particular channels," but did not "account for the force of the stream itself."[49] The new book ranked sociology decisively below theology.

The advocates of massive church-merger persisted in believing that churches were ultimately driven by that religious stream, rather than by the social function of particular ideas and practices. Calls for greater integration of Sunday mornings in the United States ran up against the feeling of churchgoers and many of their pastors that the rituals and practices distinctive to their own church were actually very important. Differences between many black and white congregations were widely noticed. It was remarked again and again that Sunday morning at eleven o'clock was the most segregated hour of the week. White ecumenists were slow to appreciate the special role that churches played in creating atmospheres of intimacy and belonging for African Americans. But white congregations sometimes felt almost as different from neighboring whites of different denominations. The church merger movement obliged ecumenical leaders to confront as never before the role of religious affiliations in sustaining particular communities.

Yet the idea of a super-church refused to die. No subset of American Protestants did more to keep it alive than the people who were shaped by the mission field instead of by local congregations in the United States. A striking example is Creighton Lacy. A missionary son born in China in 1919 and raised there, Lacy came to the United States to attend Swarthmore College, and upon graduation in 1941 went back to China as a Methodist missionary himself. He stayed until the final withdrawal of American missionaries in 1951. His post-mission career was at the Duke University Divinity School. As late as 1993, Lacy was still expounding the old ecumenical program with gusto; his article "Toward a Post-Denominational World Church" replayed all of the old themes. Lacy quoted Henry P. Van Dusen, praised Frank Laubach and E. Stanley Jones, cited Kenneth Scott Latourette, hailed the united churches of China and India, and called for unity around the essentials of the faith. "Missionaries on the whole appear to be more conscious" than the "home folks," Lacy claimed, and concluded ruefully that when Jesus called upon his disciples to be his own witnesses ("you will be my witnesses;" Acts 1:8 KJV), he called them to witness for him, not for "denominational culture or identity."[50]

If Lacy gave voice to a road not taken, the career of John Coventry Smith illustrates in helpful detail the road that was. Smith, like Lacy, served as a missionary and was an indefatigable ecumenist. But Smith was content to allow denominations to survive and to constitute, he hoped, a unified social and political witness through the National Council of Churches and other transdenominational organizations. His career shows how the ecumenical leadership perpetuated its global and reform engagements even when not focused on church merger. In Smith's career, the story of church unity and the story of political engagement continue to unfold together, although not as triumphantly as the Protestant International's leaders of the 1940s expected.

Smith began as a Presbyterian missionary to Japan in 1929 but spent most of his career moving up the administrative ladder, first among the Presbyterians and then in the National Council of Churches, finally attaining in 1968 the highest office of all, the presidency of the World Council of

Churches. His trajectory invites attention here as a microcosm of the dynamics of church change and the role of the missionary experience in making it happen as it did. Smith was committed to the political expression of Christian universalism that so distinguished the ecumenical leadership of the 1940s. He also typified the cosmopolitan NCC officialdom that presided over the eventual decline in numbers and national influence of the "mainline" churches as some migrated to post-Protestant secularism while others reaffirmed provincial loyalties. He also presided over a Protestant International that had been decisively marginalized by the Cold War.

Smith went to Japan as an evangelist, not as an educator or as a YMCA secretary, which makes his embrace of anti-imperialism and his respect for the integrity of indigenous versions of the faith all the more striking. Soon after his arrival in Japan he took sides within the Presbyterian missionary community, arguing that more authority be granted to the Japanese themselves. His own Northern Presbyterian colleagues were more sympathetic than those from the Southern Presbyterian churches, who scolded him for his romantic exaggeration of the capacity of the new Japanese churchgoers to fully embrace the faith and lead the church. "You trust the Japanese Christians and we don't," the head of the Southern Presbyterian mission in Japan told Smith. On furlough in 1936, Smith took a course from the great Union Seminary theorist, Daniel J. Fleming, whose lectures strongly reinforced Smith's commitment to a "Japanese road" for Christianity radically separated from white supremacy and Western colonialism. Smith applied this renewed commitment to his work in Japan until the beginning of the war, when he as an American citizen was interned. Upon his release he began his service as a missionary administrator in the United States, traveling frequently to East Asia and other mission fields. By the early 1960s he was the head of the missionary division of the National Council of Churches and a loyal, reliable hand on many ecumenical committees and commissions.[51]

Early in 1964, Smith, as an officer of the NCC and of the Northern Presbyterian Church, visited Hattiesburg, Mississippi, to press local church authorities to work against the Jim Crow system. Missionaries like himself, Smith later remarked in his memoirs, "brought a special dimension" to civil rights because "they had themselves crossed racial and cultural lines before." [52] Smith was among the NCC officials who lobbied against the Vietnam War, including face-to-face meetings with Secretary of State Dean Rusk. Typical of the NCC leadership of his generation, Smith was constantly aware of the agitations of fundamentalists like Carl McIntire and the more moderate evangelicals. He struggled to keep the banner of Christ secure in the ecumenical hands.[53]

Throughout the years, Smith's overriding concern as a church official was to do away with any invidious distinction between American Protestants and the Protestants of the indigenous churches abroad. His autobiography of 1982, *From Colonialism to World Community: The Church's Pilgrimage*, reprinted many of the memoranda he had presented to the seemingly endless sequence of committees and commissions of which he was a mainstay. Chapter after chapter recounts Smith's endeavor to move his co-workers in anti-imperialist, anticolonialist directions. If churchgoers had been quicker to get the message that "colonialism is at an end," and that churches must be constituted as genuinely global entities instead of Western institutions, Smith might have felt less obliged to say precisely this "over and over again."[54] Smith found himself in the same situation confronted by the missionary theorists discussed in the previous chapter: the drive to include became all the more powerful, and the character of just what it was into which a diverse population was being welcomed became more elusive.

Smith's globalism did not express itself as a preoccupation with church mergers, then, but rather as a determination to create, maintain, and effectively deploy ecumenical institutions committed to the equality of all peoples.[55] This was indeed the dominant engagement from the mid-1940s onward of the NCC, the WCC, the *Christian Century*, and the American denominational executives and representatives who directed these core embodiments of the ecumenical movement. Although many of these people lacked direct missionary connections, Edwin Espy, the general secretary of the NCC during its greatest decade of activism, 1963 to 1973, came to the NCC from the executive offices of the Student Volunteer Movement. From 1956 to 1964 the *Christian Century*'s editor in chief was Harold E. Fey, a former missionary teacher in the Philippines. Fey, Espy, Smith, John Mackay, George Lindbeck, and their co-workers kept the NCC "out there" on civil rights, on the recognition of Communist China, and on the iniquity of the Vietnam War—exactly the issues that caused churchgoers increasing concern and uncertainty when evangelicals told them that the ecumenical leadership was substituting radical politics for the faith of the fathers.

The ecumenical Protestant leadership at the time of the Dulles Commission had entertained the idea that they could actually affect the direction of history. John C. Bennett in 1958 was more cautious and deliberate, but he still displayed what from the perspective of the early twenty-first century was remarkable confidence. Bennett took for granted that ecumenical Protestants, in partnership with congenial secular contemporaries, would continue to lead the United States. He was mistaken.

Bennett's successors in the generation of John Coventry Smith found the world and American society considerably more resistant to their overtures than even Bennett had supposed. By the end of the 1960s the ecumenical leadership was struggling to hold on to its constituency. The Presbyterians lost nearly twenty percent of their members in a dozen years. The United Methodists experienced a more gradual decline; by the end of the century they had lost nearly thirty percent of their membership. The Episcopalians, the United Church of Christ, and other mainstream denominations experienced similar declines. In the meantime, the other Protestant family grew in numbers and provided substantial support for the Republican Party from Ronald Reagan's election as president in 1980 on into the twenty-first century. At the heart of this massive demographic transformation of American Protestantism was the ever-widening gap between a missionary-inspired, globally conscious, cosmopolitan elite and a churchgoing rank and file that remained focused on local concerns and that was encouraged by evangelicals to be suspicious of the political engagements of the elite.

The needs of churchgoers had long been satisfied, in part, by the particularistic instantiations of Protestant Christianity offered by denominations. But as church leaders downplayed denominationalism, churchgoers were less able to resist the appeal of evangelical megachurches which offered their own, easily grasped version of the "essential" gospel, uncomplicated by the progressive, diversity-affirming social agenda of the ecumenical leadership. The ecumenical leaders not only pushed for church mergers that proved deeply unpopular; beyond that, they sought to mobilize churches on behalf of an expanding set of political causes which made parishioners uneasy.

The budget of the National Council of Churches was reduced by more than half in the late 1970s and early 1980s because the rank and file in the constituent denominations withdrew financial support. The NCC staff had to be cut by nearly three-quarters between the late 1960s and the mid-1980s.[56] The evangelicals triumphed in the numbers game by espousing, or at least refusing to disavow, several ideas about race, gender, sexuality, nationality, imperialism, and the status of the bible that remained popular with the white public despite being abandoned by cosmopolitan church leaders as no longer defensible. Some of the rank and file Methodists, Presbyterians, and Episcopalians migrated to the evangelical churches. But this church-switching was a relatively small factor. Much more important was a demographic change driven by the shift in ecumenical attitudes toward gender.

The ecumenists supported an expanded role for women, approved nonprocreative sex, and encouraged the use of contraceptives. Here, the liberalism of church leaders had less to do with missionary experience than with their relatively strong class position and high educational levels. The churches were followers rather than leaders in the feminist transformations of the 1960s and 1970s. Meanwhile, the evangelical churches remained much more comfortable with traditional gender roles and with a narrower understanding of sex. The drift away from tradition on the part of the ecumenical Protestants resulted in lower birth rates. Evangelical women gave birth to a great many more children than did ecumenical women. There were then fewer ecumenical females of childbearing age, which reinforced the demographic gap between the two Protestant families from the 1960s onward.[57] Demographic changes are sometimes cited as if they were autonomous forces in history, but they rarely are, and certainly were not in this case. The developing cultures of the two Protestant families made a difference.

Beyond its demographic consequences, the more female-friendly atmosphere of the ecumenical Protestant churches during the second half of the twentieth century cast into bold relief the opportunities evangelical churches provided for male, charismatic leadership. Billy Graham perpetuated a florid, evangelistic style of preaching associated with nineteenth-century revivalism. Aimee Semple McPherson and a handful of other female evangelists preached in this style, but it was overwhelmingly a male preserve. Evangelical churches flattered the traditional male leader long after ecumenical churches moved, however haltingly, toward less gender-defined styles of worship. Ecumenical Protestant women had long been worried that their men would flee the churches if traditional male authority was seriously challenged. The loss of the men would mean the decline of the churches, which women valued in part because churches continued to provide so much more space for women than did most other institutions. Some women's groups of the 1920s actually resisted female ordination for fear that it would diminish the appeal of the ministry for men and that the churches would then decline.[58] These intuitions were not altogether paranoid. Part of the appeal of evangelical churches for some churchgoers was the old-fashioned preacher.

The progressive stances the ecumenical churches took on social and political issues had another crucial consequence. It became more difficult to recruit members from what had traditionally been the chief foundation for their own growth: the more conservative, evangelical communities. In earlier times, upwardly mobile members of the Seventh-day Adventist,

Church of the Nazarene, and other evangelical denominations swelled the "mainline" churches by "moving up" to them. The more the ecumenical leadership stretched to recognize diversity and to address inequalities, the less attractive their churches were to those Americans, especially in the Protestant-intensive South and rural Midwest, who were glad for ways to remain Christian without taking on the social obligations the ecumenical leaders were inclined to impose on the faithful.

While this was going on, many of the children of the ecumenists—even those who agreed with the ecumenical leadership's abandonment of ideas increasingly seen as racist, sexist, imperialist, homophobic, unscientific, and excessively nationalistic—did not affiliate with their ancestral church or with any other church. Instead, these young people found secular outlets for the liberalism they had learned from their elders. These elders, like Bennett, had encouraged ecumenical youth to explore rather than hide from the diversity of a world they knew was not going to disappear.

Simultaneously, the evangelicals warned against the perils of a diverse modernity and preached Home Truths. "Accepting Christ" in the milieu of Billy Graham turned out to be less burdensome than it might first appear. It was a means of remaining within the confines of the inherited culture for which Norman Rockwell's paintings were an emblem while at the same time promising to be better at it—better, that is, at living up to that culture's self-image. Practicing the Golden Rule, being faithful to one's spouse, eschewing pornography and homosexuality, steering clear of alcohol and drugs, being ready to lend a helping hand to those less well-off, and supporting the essentials of the American economic and political order were not reliable marks of God's grace. But these behaviors were expected of those who came to Graham's altar, the overwhelming majority of which were of Protestant social background to begin with. Evangelicals not only had a lot more children; they kept most of the ones they had. Thereby the evangelical communities produced the formidable cultural and social foundation for the Religious Right, while the ecumenical leadership facilitated the migration of many of their young into post-Protestant secularism.[59]

Missionary-connected Americans did not, by themselves, cause the changes in American churches I have described. A multitude of forces eventually fractured American Protestantism into three demographic-cultural formations. One formation was the politically potent evangelicalism that gained control of most of Christianity's spiritual capital. A second formation was the diminished community of ecumenical Protestants endowed with novel humility, exchanging proprietary claims for a role as a "prophetic minority." Third was an expanding post-Protestant population within which many of the ideals of the old Protestant International were taken for granted, even if understood in secular terms. This fracturing cannot be detached from the larger dynamics of the secularization process experienced throughout the North Atlantic West. Yet no identifiable group of Protestants did more than missionary cosmopolitans to promote and execute the ecumenical and political steps that helped to produce this particular fracture.

In several fields of action beyond the churches, missionary cosmopolitanism had no less striking effects. One such arena was American perspectives on the Middle East. There, as the next chapter explains, missionary-connected Americans tried to apply the ideal of Christian universalism to Arab peoples.

CHAPTER FIVE

Anticolonialism vs. Zionism

WHEN PRESIDENT Franklin D. Roosevelt met with King Ibn Saud aboard a US naval vessel in the Red Sea early in 1945, a single translator handled the exchange between the two heads of state. Marine Col. William A. Eddy (1896–1962), often called "the American Lawrence of Arabia," was fluent in both Arabic and English. Eddy, at the time the US envoy to Saudi Arabia, had arranged the meeting at Roosevelt's request. The president and the king did not settle the issue of immediate concern: should Jewish migration to Palestine be allowed to continue? But the meeting, the substance of which I take up below, was a dramatic episode in the forging of the postwar alliance between the United States and the Saudi kingdom. Eddy was the single person most responsible for implanting on Saudi soil the American military base at Dhahran that would serve for many decades as the focal point of American power in the Middle East and a matter of contention within the Arab and Islamic worlds. Eddy "probably knew the Arabs better than any other American of his generation," as his biographer claims.[1]

Eddy, who was born of missionary parents in Lebanon, is the most important of the many Middle-East-focused missionary sons who served in the State Department, the Foreign Service, the Office of Strategic Services, or the Central Intelligence Agency. "Mission work defines the American Arabist, much as imperialism defines the British Arabist," Robert D. Kaplan observes in his popular book *The Arabists*.[2] Britain's missionaries were overshadowed by the vast and well-established apparatus of the British Empire. Officials of the US government paid little attention to the Middle East until World War II, except for a brief flurry of interest in the World War I era. Anything happening in that part of the world was understood to be the business of the British and the French. When American officials did need someone to deal directly with Arabs, however, they usually turned to missionaries, who had been involved in the lands of the bible since the early nineteenth century.[3] When World War II began, the Arab section of the State Department had a preponderance of missionary sons. Others, like Eddy, soon joined. In 1941 Eddy was a professor of English and a college president. He re-enlisted in the US Marine Corps, in which he had served in World War I. Eddy soon found himself in North Africa as an agent of the Office of Strategic Services, and then, three years later, helping the president of the United States connect with the king of Saudi Arabia.

This chapter is primarily about Eddy and other missionary sons during and after World War II. A major challenge for them was how to deal with the concern that led Roosevelt to engage the Saudi king. Where did American interests coincide with Arab resistance to the Zionist movement, and where not? Like missionary-connected Americans involved in relations with the Chinese, the Thais, the Japanese, and other foreign peoples, Eddy and his contemporaries felt strong empathic identification with Arabs. In trying to combat anti-Arab prejudice, however, the missionary contingent encountered a complexity unique to Middle Eastern affairs: the Zionist movement. Sympathizers with this movement often asserted that opposition to the creation of a Jewish state in Palestine was based on anti-Jewish prejudice. Where did anti-Zionism end and anti-Semitism begin? What was a fair resolution of the Jewish-Arab conflict in Palestine, and what position concerning that conflict was right for the United States? Uncertainties about the Arab-Zionist conflict remain politically volatile to this day. On no other issue did missionary-connected Americans differ more sharply from the Jewish intellectuals with whom they otherwise shared a role of expanding the horizons of contemporary Americans. On no other issue is the contrast between Europe-centered cosmopolitanism and Asia-centered cosmopolitanism as stark.

The American missionary community had been brooding about conflicting Jewish and Arab claims in Palestine long before the 1940s, when the Nazi slaughter of European Jews and the enhanced appeal of Zionism made Palestine a widely recognized geopolitical issue. In the era of World War I, when relatively few Americans were exercised about how the territories of the defeated Ottoman Empire were to be governed, missionary support groups were intensely concerned. Hence this chapter, before turning to Eddy and his cohort, explains how an earlier generation of missionary-connected individuals and groups became deeply involved in American relations with the Middle East and developed a suspicion which Eddy inherited: that anti-Arab prejudice would disadvantage the Palestinian population.

The place to start is the Armenian genocide as its dimensions were recognized in 1915. American Protestants began in the mid-1890s to attend closely to reports of the killing of Armenian Christians by Turks.[4] These killings suddenly increased with the outbreak of World War I, and generated great alarm in the missionary community.[5] When the American ambassador to the Ottoman Empire, Henry Morgenthau, wired Washington in 1915 that Turks were systematically massacring Armenians, the State Department referred the message to the American Board of Commissioners of Foreign Missions (ABCFM). The United States was then neutral in the war being waged by the British and French against the Central Powers, of which the Ottoman Empire was one. It made sense for the US government to outsource the matter to a private party it knew to be sympathetic with the Armenians. The ABCFM was the most well-established of all American missionary organizations. Its chief administrator, James L. Barton, had himself been a missionary in Ottoman lands.

Barton took the portfolio and ran with it. He and his associates quickly created the Committee for Armenian and Syrian Relief, which later became Near East Relief and, still later, the Near East Foundation.[6] This important early "NGO"—although the term "non-governmental organization" was not yet in vogue—was the second humanitarian agency (preceded only by the American Red Cross in 1881) to be chartered by Congress. Within a few years, Near East Relief raised the early twenty-first-century equivalent of more than a billion dollars. Near East Relief was the largest humanitarian relief effort in history up until that time. Much of the money at the start came from the Presbyterian layman Cleveland H. Dodge of the Phelps-Dodge Corporation. Dodge was a key patron of the two major missionary institutions in the Middle East, Robert College in Istanbul and the Syrian Protestant College, which would soon be renamed the American University in Beirut, when the creation of the new state of Lebanon meant that the college was no longer in Syria.[7]

Dodge had been a classmate of Woodrow Wilson's at Princeton, and remained the president's close friend. In Wilson's administration, missionary-connected voices had more influence than in any other administration before or since. Ambassador Morgenthau himself was a sincere admirer of the missionaries he had encountered in Ottoman lands, several of whom were Morgenthau's most reliable and trusted informants about the fate of the Armenians. The relief project was driven by a concern for Christian victims of the Ottoman Turks: above all, the Armenians, but also Nestorians, Greeks, and scattered groups of Arab Christians from Egypt to Persia. While Near East Relief was Christianity-centered, it developed a proprietary perspective on the entire region and all of its inhabitants. Near East Relief claimed to minister to "all suffering peoples on the basis of need and not creed, and included the Kurds, the Turks, the Tartars" and others.[8] In that broad framework, Near East Relief functioned as a lobby, even though technically only a humanitarian agency.

At the war's end, Barton formally proposed that the United States establish a mandate over all Ottoman lands. This notion of American supervision was peculiar in a diplomatic context. The United States never went to war with the Ottomans. In April 1917, Wilson declined to declare war on the Ottoman Empire because Dodge and others told him that if he did, American missionaries would be killed. Although this fact is rarely noted, it is a striking instance of a major diplomatic decision being driven by missionary-connected Americans.[9]

The British and the French, having actually made war against the Turks and occupied much of their territory, thought the Americans had precious little standing to influence the future of the once-Ottoman territory. Yet Morgenthau himself, late in the Paris conference of 1919, proposed a version of this idea to Wilson, arguing that the Turkish, Armenian, and Kurdish territories, at least, should be supervised by the United States. Morgenthau's advocacy of an American mandate was a sign of the credibility of the missionary lobbyists who, as historian Joseph L. Grabill concludes, "had a monopoly on American opinions about Turkey."[10]

This was all the more true because the oil industry was still at an early stage of development. There were as yet few American business interests in play in the Middle East. Andrew Preston concludes that the internationalism of the Wilsonian era was deeply grounded in a missionary discourse that was sharply divided between an ethnocentric desire to make the world over in an American Protestant image and a religious commitment, however imperfectly formulated, to help alleviate the impoverishments and injustices of many peoples. The geopolitical circumstances of the period made the Ottoman domains the chief focal point for this more general engagement.[11]

The idea of an American mandate went up in smoke amid the incineration of Wilson's vision for American participation in a League-centered international order. Before that denouement, however, the King-Crane Commission of 1919 advanced an ambitious version of this idea. The Inter-Allied Commission on Mandates in Turkey, as this now largely forgotten diplomatic venture was officially named, was informally known by the names of its co-chairs, Henry Churchill King and Charles R. Crane. The commission grew out of Wilson's frustration in Paris with the British and

French determination to divide up the former Ottoman lands according to a once-secret agreement the two powers had reached in 1916.[12] According to the Sykes-Pico Accord, the French would have control over Lebanon, Syria, and northern Iraq while the British would get Palestine, Jordan, and southern Iraq.

Wilson, in keeping with his guiding principle of self-determination, wanted a systematic registering of the opinions of the affected populations. Hence he was attracted to the suggestion of the Arab leader Ali Faisal that an impartial panel of experts be charged with surveying the relevant populations and recommending mandates or other political arrangements maximally consistent with local desires. The British and French reluctantly agreed to such an inquiry, to be carried out jointly with the Americans. But the British and the French actively subverted the plan from the start, rightly fearing that the results would be at odds with their own intentions. Balfour and several other British leaders were especially concerned that the Arabs living in Palestine would resist a Jewish homeland there, as endorsed by the British government's Balfour Declaration of 1917, which was candidly understood as a device for maintaining British imperial influence in that territory. Wilson gave up on the temporizing allies, who persistently refused to appoint their own members to the commission. The president sent his own appointees to the contested territories, and charged them with reporting directly to him.

The commission did hear testimony by local residents, but by the time Wilson received the commission's report, he was already ill, and his Versailles Treaty well on its way to defeat in the United States Senate. Wilson did not even make the report public until 1922, after he had left office. Yet I attend to the King-Crane Commission here because it shows how extensively Wilson relied on missionaries and, more importantly, it reveals how sharply missionary thinking about American policy in the Middle East after 1919 diverged from the path actually taken by the US government. Moreover, the King-Crane Commission marked the point at which the American missionary community increased its engagement with Arab affairs, beyond its earlier focus on Armenians. The King-Crane Commission would demand much more extensive attention here if it had major consequences for American diplomacy. It did not. Much of its historical significance is as a prolegomenon to the activities of missionary-connected Americans of Eddy's generation.

What were the King-Crane Commission's missionary connections, and what were its recommendations?

King was president of Oberlin College, one of the most missionary-involved of all American institutions of higher education. Crane's missionary connections were less direct, but the wealthy business executive was treasurer of Near Eastern Relief. Three others filled out the group of five. Historian Albert H. Lybyer had been a missionary teacher at Robert College. George Montgomery grew up in the Ottoman Empire as the son of missionary parents, and had written extensively about Turkish history and society. William Yale was then representing the Standard Oil Company in its early explorations near Jerusalem. Yale was the only one of the five without some missionary connection. Three were even ordained Protestant clergymen: King, Lybyer, and Montgomery.

The commission's report recommended that further Jewish migration be discouraged on account of the massive opposition the commission had discovered at every turn in its talks with the current non-Jewish inhabitants of Palestine. The report warned that a substantial Jewish presence in Palestine could be established only by military force. Central to the commission's abortive recommendations was an American mandate under the League of Nations for a single state of Greater Syria, embracing all of Palestine and Lebanon as well as Syria (and what later became Jordan), operating as a constitutional monarchy with Faisal on the throne. The report also recommended an American mandate for three other new states in and around Anatolia: one for an "international" polity in the vicinity of Constantinople, to be under the jurisdiction of the League of Nations rather than any local constituency; a second for a new Armenian state, with a corridor to the Black Sea; and a third for a new Turkish state, for what was left of Anatolia after the creation of the Armenian and International states.[13] The British were to be given a mandate for a "Mesopotamia" (i.e., Iraq). King, Crane, and Lybyer had no doubt that the Americans would be more responsive to the democratic potential of the indigenous populations than the European powers. They were especially suspicious of the French.

Montgomery and Yale did not sign the report, but filed memoranda that functioned as minority reports. Each had a low opinion of Arabs, and believed that only a Jewish population they considered inherently superior would be able to develop a modern society in Palestine. Montgomery and Yale favored a British mandate for Palestine, with the understanding that the British would act on the Balfour Declaration. Montgomery and Yale had slightly different ideas as to how the region should be divided up between the French and the British, but they recommended mandates only for those two powers, in whose judgment they expressed great confidence.

The King-Crane Commission's most enduring legacy in the politics of the United States proved to be the report's dissent from the popular view, expressed by Montgomery and Yale, that aside from the special case of the Christian Armenians, only the Jews of all the peoples living in the former Ottoman lands were capable of responsible nationhood. King, Crane, and Lybyer made their share of patronizing remarks about Arabs and Turks, but their refusal of a special standing for Jews was the basis for later charges that the commission had been anti-Semitic. Some Zionists asserted this as soon as the report was made public in 1922, but they did so more insistently when Nazi Germany created a context very different from that of 1919.

Crane's behavior in the 1930s made the accusation credible. Crane told friends in 1933 that he was glad Adolf Hitler was taking action against the Jews, and he was the first American to have a private meeting with Hitler after he became Chancellor of Germany. Crane also reportedly advised Franklin Roosevelt to avoid appointing Jews to government posts. Crane's most recent biographer, Norman E. Saul, accurately points out that even in 1939, when Crane died, persons who had been talking as he had been were yet to be confronted with what happened in the years thereafter, and many such persons changed their tune.[14] Yet there is no doubt that Crane's strong support of Arab causes in the 1930s was fueled in part by an active prejudice against Jews.

It is far from clear, however, that this antipathy toward Jews as a people was a material factor in the 1919 recommendations of the King-Crane Commission. It might have been. But the closest student of the commission, Andrew J. Patrick, finds "no empirical basis for the argument that the anti-Zionism" of the report "had its roots in antisemitism."[15] Patrick concludes that even Crane, along with King and Lybyer, began their travels with a sympathetic view of the Zionist movement. They were turned by the range and depth of the feelings of non-Jewish Palestinians.

Within the US government during the 1920s and 1930s, there was little engagement with the question of Palestine. The State Department tended to see Zionism as a movement of extremists, supported by special-pleading lobby groups who did not understand the complexities of world politics. The government's Arab experts, whether or not missionary-connected, shared a narrowly Anglo-Protestant social background and a professional ethos that was suspicious of public opinion. This was true of senior officers Alexander Kirk and Loy Henderson, neither of whom had missionary connections. Both had been posted to European and East Asian stations prior to the war, and had no background in Middle Eastern affairs.

The missionary contingent within the State Department's Arabists included Harold B. Hoskins, a cousin of Eddy's who was also a missionary son from Beirut, and George Wadsworth, who had taught at the American University in Beirut before entering the Foreign Service. George Merriam had taught at Robert College. Missionary son Philip Ireland came to Washington in summer of 1942, having been a university professor in England for a number of years, and was the only one of the missionary-connected group to display unmistakable anti-Semitic prejudice. He was reserved in his published writings, but in the State Department's meetings on postwar planning displayed what the cautious Philip Baram described as a "mania" about Zionism as the equivalent of the Nazi push for *lebensraum*.[16]

Ironically, the most bona fide anti-Semite within the US government's Arabists was William Yale, who had preferred Jews to Arabs when on the King-Crane Commission. As a senior officer in the State Department's Near Eastern section during the 1930s and 1940s, Yale defended colonial approaches and worked actively to thwart Zionist ambitions and the creation of an Arab state in Palestine. Baram found many expressions of anti-Jewish prejudice in Yale's papers and was stunned, in interviews with Yale in the early 1970s, at the level of belligerence with which the elderly diplomat denigrated Jews as a people.[17]

Eddy came late to this company of government Arabists. After growing up in Beirut and attending Princeton University, he joined the Marines and was decorated for valor in the Battle of Belleau Wood, where he suffered an injury that caused him to limp for the rest of his life. He returned to Princeton, earned a PhD in English literature, and then taught at Dartmouth College and at the American University in Cairo before becoming president of Hobart and William Smith Colleges. Along the way he switched from the Presbyterian to the Episcopal Church, but maintained a strong commitment to a generic, liberal Protestant faith, as displayed in the devotional pamphlets he wrote. Eddy resigned his college presidency to re-enlist in the Marine Corps.

He was quickly discovered by Gen. William Donovan of the Office of Strategic Services, who desperately needed Middle Eastern expertise. Donovan borrowed Eddy from the Marine Corps and sent him to North Africa under the cover of serving as a naval attaché first in Cairo, and then in Tangier, Spanish Morocco. Eddy spent the war as the OSS's leading agent in North Africa, making effective use of his linguistic facility and the myriad personal connections he had accumulated in his Beirut childhood and from his later experience as a professor in Egypt. Eddy could recite long passages from the Koran in three Arabic dialects. Several accounts of Eddy's exploits in North Africa during and after the presence of the Vichy regime invoke the atmosphere of Rick's Café in the 1942 Humphrey Bogart film *Casablanca*. Fluent in French and German as well as Arabic, deeply learned in the Islamic faith and its history, and a combat veteran, Eddy was an ideal OSS operative. Donovan was so devoted to him that he personally wrote the OSS's letters to Eddy's wife back in the United States to assure her that her husband was alive and well, even though he could not disclose the colonel's exact whereabouts and activities.[18]

Eddy cultivated anti-Vichy sentiments in the French population in North Africa, including among some military officers who risked execution for treason because of their secret dealings with Eddy. He largely succeeded in the tasks assigned to him in preparation for Operation Torch, the landing led by Gen. George Patton beginning November 8, 1942. Sadly for Eddy and Patton, the sudden and unexpected appearance in Algiers of Vichy Admiral Jean-Francois Darlan made the officers expected to side with invading Allied forces hold back. Yet Eddy's network of agents throughout North Africa deceived the Germans, leading them to expect the Americans to land at Dakar. The landings in Morocco and Algeria took the Germans by surprise.[19]

Thus, Eddy was known in Washington as an exceptionally effective interlocutor with Arab leaders. When the military progress of the war diminished the need for him in North Africa, he was posted to Saudi Arabia as the American envoy. Upon his first visit with King Ibd Saud in Riyadh, Eddy and his wife, Mary Garvin Eddy—also a missionary child—impressed the king with their ease in Arabic conversation and their familiarity with the Islamic faith. Eddy was almost too good an American to be believed from the viewpoint of the Saudi king who, a few years later, told Eddy he trusted him like one of his own sons.[20] Eddy persuaded the reclusive king to accept Roosevelt's invitation to talk on board the USS Quincy during Roosevelt's return trip from his Yalta meeting with Winston Churchill and Joseph Stalin. The cultural chasm across which Eddy led Ibn Saud in order to meet the president of the United States is hard to measure. The king was an old-fashioned warrior who, unlike most heads of state in the middle of the twentieth century, had achieved his power in part by slaying rivals with a sword.[21]

So, what happened on the boat?

Roosevelt was quick to raise the issue that had inspired his decision to try to talk with Ibn Saud: the settlement of European refugee Jews in Palestine under the authority of the British mandate. According to the report written by Eddy, who had the only nearby pair of ears that could understand both Arabic and English, Roosevelt asked for advice regarding the problem of migration to Palestine of "the remnant of Jews in Central Europe who had suffered indescribable horrors at the hands of the Nazis." Ibn Saud replied, "Give them and their descendants the choicest lands and homes of the Germans who had oppressed them." Roosevelt explained that the Jews were reluctant to live in Germany and had "sentimental" reasons for wanting to live in Palestine, but the king pressed his point: "Amends should be made by the criminal, not by the innocent bystander. What injury have Arabs done to the Jews of Europe? It is the 'Christian' Germans who stole their homes and lives."[22]

Roosevelt knew that the notion of the eventual Jewish state located in Pomerania or Swabia instead of Palestine was not a real political possibility. But there was a certain logic to the king's insistence that Germans should bear the brunt of the problem of the Jewish refugees. The United States had no intention of welcoming large numbers of "displaced persons," nor did the United Kingdom, whose government had issued the Balfour Declaration during World War I to enable the British Empire to control part of Ottoman territory and to deflect future Jewish migration away from Britain.[23] Moreover, when the US Congress endorsed the Balfour Declaration in 1922, it did so in the midst of the anti-immigration movement that culminated two years later in the passage of the Johnston-Reed Act, ending nearly all immigration from Eastern and Southern Europe. Between the two world wars, European diplomatic opinion was increasingly pro-Zionist, but in the important context of widespread anti-Semitism.[24] Even in the wake of the Holocaust, a Jewish Palestine appealed not only to many European Jews, but to the governments of Europe and North America. Those governments wanted as little as possible to do with Jewish immigrants. It is apparent from Eddy's private and public utterances at the time and in later years that Eddy agreed with Ibn Saud's objections to increased Jewish immigration to Palestine, at least without some larger political authority to prevent the establishing of a sovereign Jewish state. Eddy may even have helped the king to formulate his views in terms most likely to sway Roosevelt.

All who witnessed the remarkable conversation, including Fleet Admiral William D. Leahy, agreed that the president and the king got along very well personally and that Roosevelt was eager to minimize their differences. Roosevelt made a portentous promise that climaxed the meeting: the United States "would make no change in its basic policy in Palestine without full and prior consultation with both Jews and Arabs," and, in the meantime, Roosevelt "would do nothing to assist the Jews against the Arabs and would make no move hostile to the Arab people." Roosevelt was simultaneously signaling some American politicians that he sympathized with the Zionist movement, and no doubt realized that his promise to the king rested on shifting sand. But Eddy and most of the relevant State Department officers took Roosevelt's pledge seriously and reminded his successor, Harry Truman, of its existence.[25]

Roosevelt's promise was attractive to the government's Middle Eastern hands because they believed the interests of the United States required cordial relations with the Arabs. The United States should facilitate the liberation of Arabs from the British and French domination that had persisted under League of Nations mandates following the demise of Ottoman authority. The presence of oil in Arab lands was an important foundation for this view, but so, too, was the assessment of Arab nationalism as a formidable reality that the United States ignored at its peril. Eddy and many of his colleagues appreciated *The Arab Awakening*, a nationalist treatise of 1938 by the Arab Christian writer George Antonius that popularized a vision of a multi-religious flourishing of Arabs in the coming postcolonial epoch.[26] Antonius was representative of an urban, cosmopolitan Arab elite based in Beirut, Cairo, and Baghdad. The hopeful view of the Arab future characteristic of the missionary sons in government service was grounded in part in their familiarity with this segment of the Arab population. Antonius's book, however, was dedicated to the anti-Semite Charles Crane, who had helped to finance its publication.

The State Department and the newly created Central Intelligence Agency—established in 1947 as a successor to the wartime OSS—later tried, without success, to dissuade Truman from recognizing Israel. Eddy himself was a forceful voice in Washington's debate over the Palestinian question. After his triumphant negotiation of the rights to an American airfield at Dhahran, Eddy was called back to serve the State Department and then the CIA. Eddy hammered away at what he saw as Truman's flaccid subservience to domestic politics and his failure to grasp the geopolitical dynamics of the postwar, post-imperial Middle East.[27]

Continued Jewish migration to Palestine without "prior consultation with the Arabs," Eddy wrote in October 1945 to his State Department superiors, would violate Roosevelt's promise. This action would cause great damage to "our prestige" in Arab lands. King Ibn Saud, Eddy continued, believed "that the independence and survival of the Arab state of Palestine is a more legitimate concern of the surrounding Arab countries than it is of Americans 5,000 miles away, whether those Americans are Jew or Gentile." Two weeks after this memorandum, Eddy was one of four State Department officers sent to brief the new president. The group told Truman that each of the Arab countries "wants forthrightly to run its own show, as the countries of the Western Hemisphere run theirs, without imperialistic interference, be it British or French, in their internal affairs."[28] The veteran Arabist George Wadsworth, part of the missionary contingent, led the discussion with Truman. Wadsworth's grand manner annoyed Truman, who felt, no doubt correctly, that the men from State were talking down to him, implying that he was not smart enough or well enough informed to do his job. Eddy himself is the source for the often-repeated quotation from Truman at the end of that meeting: "I'm sorry, gentlemen, but I have to answer to hundreds of thousands who are anxious for the success of Zionism; I do not have hundreds of thousands of Arabs among my constituents."[29]

Whether or not Truman actually said this, Truman's path toward his 1948 decision to recognize Israel was heavily influenced by domestic political concerns. Eddy, Wadsworth, and their fellow Arab specialists were more able to appreciate the imperatives of the domestic politics of the Arab countries than of their own. A less defensive man than Truman might have been capable of forgiving the arrogance of the State Department's Arabists, taking into measured account their well-informed warnings. But the Arabists' confidence in their own expertise seems to have blinded them to the need to proceed diplomatically with the inexperienced and sensitive man who was, after all, the president of the United States and at the time the most powerful man in the world.

When Truman acted to recognize the state of Israel, he did so while brushing aside one of the new CIA's earliest official memoranda to the White House, a seventeen-page document of November 28, 1947, of which Eddy is probably the chief author. "The Consequences of the Partition of Palestine" was entirely wrong in predicting that the Arabs would quickly overwhelm Jewish forces in armed conflict, but it was discerning and prophetic in other important respects. Partition would result in "armed hostilities between Jews and Arabs" of long duration, further destabilize the Arab world, and severely damage the previously high regard in which the Arab peoples previously held the United States. This document was highly unusual for the time in warning against jihad: "The Arabs are capable of a religious fanaticism which when coupled with political aspirations is an extremely powerful force." It is unclear, the CIA continued, if the Arab governments will prove able to guide this force, but "religious organizations" such as the "Muslim Brotherhood" based in Egypt can be expected to "oppose any political encroachment of Zionism on Palestine with religious fanaticism," including the declaring of "a 'Jihad' or Holy War."[30]

By the time this memorandum reached Truman, Eddy had sensed Truman's direction and announced his departure from the CIA and from the Marine Corps to become a senior consultant to the Arabian American Oil Company (ARAMCO). This American-based corporation was largely responsible for the development of the oil industry in Saudi Arabia. But Eddy did anything but disappear from the councils of the US government. In December 1947, before his resignation took effect but when all knew he was leaving, the Joint Chiefs of Staff invited him to assess the Middle Eastern situation.[31] Thereafter, Eddy continued to brief CIA Director Allen Dulles on a regular basis while serving for more than a decade as the key intermediary between ARAMCO and the royal family of Saudi Arabia. Given the increased importance of oil and of the friendly relations of the United States with Saudi Arabia amid the Israel-centered quarrels of those years, Eddy's position at ARAMCO afforded him more autonomy than an official position within the CIA. It also gave him greater ability to influence the Saudi government and ARAMCO itself. That the adamantly anti-Zionist Saudi regime retained its American alliance even after the recognition of a Jewish state may owe something to Eddy's regular, apparently reassuring conversations with the king.[32]

In this private capacity Eddy worked more openly to oppose the Zionist lobby. He corresponded with the leaders of anti-Zionist organizations in the United States, lectured widely, and published occasional essays on Middle Eastern affairs. In that mode he made common cause with a number of other missionary-connected Americans who had not held positions in the State Department, the CIA, or the OSS. Among these was Bayard Dodge. Upon finishing a twenty-five-year term as president of the American University in Beirut in 1948, Dodge visited a number of influential persons he knew in Washington, including Secretary of Defense James V. Forrestal, arguing against the partition of Palestine.[33] Dodge's *Reader's Digest* article of April 1948, "Must There Be War in the Middle East," expressed the opinion—widespread in missionary circles—that diplomatic drift toward a Jewish state in Palestine with full sovereignty placed generations of American-Arab friendship gravely at risk.[34] Dodge's contemporary at the American University in Cairo, the missionary educator John S. Badeau, voiced the same concerns in a long cable to Truman then released to the press. Badeau was especially worried that the creation of an ethno-religiously particular nation-state encouraged the Muslim Brotherhood to push for more sectarian governance among Arabs.

Eddy referred to "the rape of Palestine" in a blistering 1953 address to the Naval War College in Rhode Island. He assailed "Zionist stooges" with allegedly too much influence in the American government, and named names, including Vice President Alben W. Barkley and Truman's chief White House aide David Niles. "Suddenly, as though your best friend inexplicably strikes you in the face," Eddy lamented, the liberals of the Arab world "who were bringing together at the same table and in the same club Muslim and Christian, Druze and Maronite, were struck down by America which forced the establishment in Palestine of a state which, by its own constitution, first-class citizenship is reserved to the adherents of only one religion."[35]

In this address as in his other writings, Eddy represented Jews almost exclusively in religious terms. He displayed little understanding of the sense of Jewish peoplehood that was all more vital after the Holocaust. But recent scholarship confirms that lobbyists for the Zionist cause effectively overpowered the late-1940s voices in American politics that focused on the Palestinian refugees and the strategic value of an American alliance with Arab nationalists.[36] Eddy was slow to grasp the historical and domestic political circumstances that gave the Zionist lobby a credibility it lacked prior to World War II. The cause of the Arab lobby had become much harder to sell. Eddy was often flippant and mean-spirited about Zionist influence. In a characteristic swipe, he wrote his children after the assassination of the Jordanian prime minister in 1960 that, while the heavens might fall, it was "comforting to note that both Kennedy and Nixon have promised to rescue Israel, so that while all Gentiles may perish, the chosen will flourish as the green bay tree." But for all this bitterness, Eddy was not making it up when he referred to a strong Zionist lobby in Washington in the late 1940s and after.[37]

Edmund M. Wright, a Persian-born missionary son who was also a missionary himself before being recruited by the OSS in 1942, was even more preoccupied with the perceived damage to American-Arab friendship. Wright remained in the State Department in Washington for a decade after the war, but was never as prominent a figure as Eddy. Wright illustrates the insistence with which many missionary-connected anti-Zionists distinguished their own opinions from prejudice against Jews as Jews. Wright was furious at the US Congress for not welcoming the hundreds of thousands of Jewish refugees he was willing to see added to the American population. He accurately observed that in 1947, when Senate and House committees were considering a bill that would allow four hundred thousand "displaced persons" to enter the United States, Zionist groups were cool toward the idea out of concern that it would undercut support for a Jewish state in Palestine.[38] Yet the failure of the "Stratton Bill"—named for the Republican Illinois congressman who most pushed the measure—was not primarily a result of Zionist qualms. The bill was opposed by the American Legion and the Veterans of Foreign Wars as a threat to the jobs of returning servicemen. A North Dakota senator managed to get the Senate version of the bill amended to give priority to the ethnic Germans who had been displaced from the Soviet Union, a move that drastically diminished the potential of the enactment to bring more Jewish immigrants into the country. Germans would be favored over Jews.[39] Hostile as he was to Israel, Wright professed to have no objection to the migration of more Jews to the United States.

Eddy's preoccupations were not as extreme as Wright's, but Eddy did complain regularly right up until his death in 1962 about the pro-Israel theme in American policy. He proudly proclaimed his identity as an American (and as a Christian and as a Marine), but he was happier living in Lebanon than anywhere in the United States. Eddy and his wife resided primarily in Beirut while he worked for ARAMCO and its closely related corporation, the Trans Arabian Pipeline Company (Tapline). He died there and was buried, in keeping with his own instructions, in a cemetery in which the only other American graves were those of his missionary parents. All the other surrounding dead were Arab Christians, whose permanent company Eddy chose to keep.[40]

Eddy was always reverent toward his parents and their vocation. He was deeply moved whenever Arabs who had known his parents thanked him for what the senior Eddys had done as missionaries. After attending a memorial event for missionaries held in Beirut, Eddy wrote to his children in America, reporting affectionately on the doings of other descendants of missionaries with whom he conversed that day in the very church where his parents were married in 1885.[41] He liked to visit biblical sites, and peppered his letters with allusions to the history of the Middle East, ancient and modern. Eddy believed that his own labors in the American government and in the Saudi-centered oil industry were consistent with the missionary heritage. This appears to have been true throughout his life, but the letters of his last few years are expansive about these feelings. "A hundred years ago," he wrote his children and grandchildren two months before his death in 1962, "the missionary, Protestant and Catholic, was the lonely apostle of goodwill."

> The heritage of goodwill has been openly acknowledged by their heirs: the Arab nationalists; the modern universities; the oil companies; the private and government agencies who now administer programs of health, and education, and welfare in the Near East. The doors for them were opened by the early doctors, teachers, nurses and preachers, who served without political design or personal reward.[42]

Eddy's affirmative, uncritical construction of the missionary enterprise and its secular legacies did not entail negative views of the Islamic religion. On the contrary, in keeping with the liberal, service-centered conception of missions characteristic of the ecumenical Protestants of his generation, Eddy envisaged a gradual coming together of Christians and Muslims in cooperative living arrangements wherever they mingled. He did not shy away from the explicitly religious components of the two traditions, and was persistently idealistic in his characterization of both the Islamic and the Christian faith. He invariably emphasized what the two religions had in common and often identified "paganism" as their common enemy. An address he delivered in Washington in 1950, for example, declared that Christians "share with Islam many of our prophets and much of our scripture; the Muslims revere Jesus as a prophet, and we hold Mohammed in very high respect." Eddy saw Christianity and Islam as potentially engaged in a "moral alliance" organized around what he asserted were the two faiths' joint devotion to "humility, charity, the brotherhood of mankind, and the family as the sacred unit of society."[43]

Thus, Eddy, while realistic in his understanding of the potential for jihad, was often romantic about Arabs and the Islamic faith.[44] In 1954, when Eddy published his account of the meeting between President Roosevelt and King Ibn Saud, he offered a personal postscript sketching a grand vision of "this moral alliance," in which "the guardian of the Holy Places of Islam," who was "the nearest thing we have to a successor to the Caliphs . . . cemented a friendship with the head of a great Western and Christian nation."[45]

Eddy was reluctant to find fault with any of the world's classic religions, including Judaism. He sometimes listed Judaism along with Christianity and Islam as Abrahamic siblings. He was on good terms with the leaders of the American Council for Judaism, an organization of anti-Zionist Jews. But in many contexts Eddy was religiously judgmental. At the end of his life he faulted in Christian terms the behavior in which he and other agents of the OSS and the CIA had engaged while serving the interests of the United States. These reflections of the mature Eddy are worth quoting here because they are among the most probing of the meditations left by any of the missionary children who served in any capacity in the US government.

"The OSS had no conscience," Eddy wrote amid a series of memoir fragments composed during the last year of his life. "It is still an open question whether an operator in OSS or in CIA can ever again become an honorable man." The Gestapo chiefs engaged in the same deceits and betrayals as the Americans, Eddy recalled, and some of the German officers were better family men than the Americans and British, who often took local concubines. OSS officers "used Communists, telling them that we would help them overthrow Franco, which we did not do," and falsely promised the "Moors"—as Eddy called the Moroccans—that the Americans would "work for the independence of Morocco from Spain." The Moors were desperately poor and would sell anything, even their sisters, Eddy mused, so the Americans exploited this vulnerability. Even if a fellow "might be a wife-beater or an opium-addict, it mattered not if he knew how to get around. It is permitted to walk with the devil until you have crossed the bridge." Eddy did not explain where the bridge was, but in these reflections, apparently drafted for an autobiographical book for which he had signed a contract in 1961, he was clearly pondering that question. "We deserve to go to hell when we die," he wrote.[46]

What most troubled the mature Eddy was his own relationship with a group of two hundred underground Communist guerillas who had escaped the Franco regime after the Civil War and were clandestine operators in Spanish Morocco, waiting their chance to renew the struggle against the Fascists. They readily assisted Eddy in sabotage and other intrigues. "To use Communist spies today would bring down on my head the John Birch Society and other Neo-fascists, but that did not worry me," he observed, because in 1942 "we were Brothers-In-Arms of Uncle Joe Stalin." In a six-page sketch entitled "Our Communist Allies," Eddy invented the pseudonym of "Carlos" for the leader of this group, with whom he dealt regularly in Tangier, and offered these rueful thoughts:

> What worries me most about Tangier is the sheer immorality of exploiting under false pretenses sincere patriots like those Spanish Republicans who served us in the OSS. We wanted to win the war; they wanted to win Spain, and we let them think we would help. When I dream of men like Carlos, I wake in a sweat. I try to alibi, to curse and swear saying, I know not this man of whom ye speak.

Seeing himself in the role of Peter denying Jesus (Eddy here invokes Mark 14:71—Peter "began to curse and to swear, saying, I know not this man of whom ye speak"—KJV), these lines of Eddy's are perhaps the most fiercely self-interrogatory he ever wrote. But would he do the same again, Eddy asks himself? He answers "Yes, in wartime, I would, but that melancholy conviction does not make it easier for me to live with myself."[47]

Had Eddy lived long enough to continue these autobiographical writings, might he have addressed what might be seen as another ethical conflict: his willingness after he left government service to maintain friendly relations with Grand Mufti Muhammad Amin al-Husseini, the Palestinian leader who had openly collaborated with the Nazis? To be sure, the Grand Mufti was the general secretary of the Arab League, therefore hard to ignore. But this ferociously anti-Jewish Arab actually argued that the United States had been on the wrong side in World War II, and should have joined the Germans in fighting against the Bolsheviks. If Eddy ever felt qualms about his occasional conversations with the Grand Mufti, there appears to be no record of it.[48]

Did Eddy ever feel moral qualms about anything he did for the oil industry, with its effectively Jim Crow labor practices, and for the Saudi regime with its notorious inequalities and cruelties? If he did, he kept them to himself. Eddy was a top adviser to ARAMCO during the escalating labor conflicts of the 1950s. Unlike that corporation's leadership, he was sometimes willing to say that the workers had some justification for their strikes and other agitation. But surely he was deeply implicated in the perpetuation of a labor regime that scholars now agree was not only racist, but required workers to live in dreadful circumstances. Eddy's own style was radically different from the Texas roughnecks who dominated the ARAMCO's fields in the 1950s, but his memoranda and correspondence say little about those aspects of the scene.[49] Eddy was forthright in castigating medieval theocracy and arbitrary use of power when he encountered them in Yemen in 1946, but, as Thomas W. Lippman observes, "Eddy's affection" for the Saudis "evidently led him to overlook" the "arbitrary justice and horrifying cruelty" that were almost as visible in Saudi Arabia as in Yemen.[50]

Eddy did characterize as naïve the belief of Ibn Saud and other Saudi leaders that modern technology could be brought into their country without cultural consequences, leading eventually to the education of women. He reported at least one conversation with the old king in which he tried to defend the education of women, but Eddy seems to have made his peace with the view that the path to modernity was a long one, at least in Saudi Arabia, which was, for all its faults, a stolid bulwark against the Zionism that Eddy so much abhorred. Practices to be condemned as cruel if found in Eddy's own culture were, if found among the Arabs, best left to local dynamics to be diminished over time. Eddy's almost total absence of recorded reflection about his years at ARAMCO, during which he regularly advised that company's leadership how to deal with the Saudi government, may also derive from promises he had made to the CIA. Eddy was good at keeping secrets. Moreover, it has long been the policy of the US government—during Eddy's life and since—to guarantee continued access to Saudi Arabian oil while keeping to a minimum any attention to human rights violations and to the slow pace of democratization. Eddy, while highly moralistic in many contexts, was surely a party to this understanding, which he only voiced on rare occasions.[51] He was remarkably quiet about how he reconciled this and other features of his post-government career with his personal belief system.

Eddy's uncritical attitude toward the Saudi regime and his embrace of an American political hegemony organized around the Dhahran military base reveal the extent to which his anti-imperialism was directed against the old European powers and against Israel. Eddy's feeling for the Arab peoples was deep, but so, too, was his embrace of American stewardship of the developing world. It would not do to equate Eddy's loyalty to the Saudis with Luce's loyalty to Chiang Kai-shek, but the two commitments do have something in common. Nor would it be fair to equate Eddy's vision of the world with Luce's "American century," but recalling the latter can remind us of the limits of Eddy's anti-imperialism. Eddy took a generous view of American power, and was slow to find fault with the Arabs, who welcomed it in the form of either military assistance or the development of the oil industry.

But Eddy had no cause to brood about one monumentally important, ethically freighted CIA venture in the Middle East, because in it he was not a player. This was the 1953 coup in Iran that ousted the nationalist leader Mohammed Mosaddeq and installed the pro-Western Shah who held power until the Islamicist revolution of 1979. Now seen by most scholars of the Cold War as the most problematic of the CIA's activities not only in the Middle East, but in the entire era, this coup was led by the Oyster Bay-reared aristocrat Kermit Roosevelt and assisted by Miles Copeland and other CIA operatives and government officials with no missionary connections. Among these was Eddy's old boss, Loy Henderson.

Hugh Wilford and other historians of the CIA and the State Department agree that the Mosaddeq coup marked a shift toward greater acceptance of the legacy of British and French imperialism in the Middle East. The gap noted by Kaplan between the missionary-influenced American Arabists and the empire-oriented British Arabists narrowed during the Eisenhower years, when Secretary of State John Foster Dulles and his brother, Allen Dulles, as director of the CIA, began to see nationalism more as a dangerous step toward Communism rather than a potential bulwark against it. A major theme of Wilford's *America's Great Game: The CIA's Secret Arabists and the Shaping of the Modern Middle East* is the decisive turn of the CIA toward shoring up conservative Arab regimes that were more or less clients of their imperial predecessors.

"The story of the CIA involvement in the Arab world during the early years of the Cold War," Wilford argues, was in large part an internal struggle "between two contradictory influences: the British imperial legacy and the American missionary tradition." The latter "more moralistic, idealistic impulse" eventually lost out to the more "pragmatic, realistic, even cynical" impulse that "came to dominate" after the 1953 coup in Iran. The Eisenhower administration "came down decisively on the side of the old imperial order," and the CIA—"ironically," in view of the earlier, Eddy-style anti-imperialism—"became the main instrument of the new antinationalist policy." Wilford notes that in 1958, when the United States sent troops to Lebanon, one of the few voices to oppose American military invention was "the old Arabist William Eddy," who wrote from Beirut to his contacts in Washington that "armed intervention" on the side of the local Christian militias "would be a disaster to American interests." Eddy "earlier had used his knowledge to prepare a World War II bridgehead for American forces to liberate North Africa," but in 1958, his advice rejected, he watched "aghast as US troops returned to the Arab world to defend the old imperial order." Prominent among the other voices speaking to the same effect was Eddy's cousin, Hoskins, by then also retired, who bluntly told the State Department that military action in Lebanon at that time would "align the U. S. with the colonial powers and against the Moslem majority," but his advice, too, was rejected.[52]

Harold B. Hoskins (1898–1982) had always been outspoken in the series of assignments he held in the State Department, the OSS, and as an army lieutenant colonel. He was on excellent personal terms with Undersecretary of State Sumner Wells and with President Roosevelt himself, who in 1942 appointed Hoskins as his representative in Palestine and later as the first American envoy to Saudi Arabia, preceding Eddy in that role. Hoskins was never zealous, but often represented the State Department in explaining to members of Congress why the government cared about Arab interests. Hoskins regarded the Middle Eastern region to be a single, strategically important entity, while other officers were inclined to focus on particular national regimes. Hoskins was more willing than most of the Arabists to welcome Jewish migration to Palestine so long as numbers could be limited and the integrity of the region as a Arab homeland be guaranteed.[53] Like Eddy, Hoskins maintained close connections with the missionary community of Lebanon and served until the end of his life as a trustee of the American University in Beirut.

A younger generation of missionary sons carried on the same tradition. Two of Eddy's nephews, Arthur Close (1925–2010) and Raymond Close

(1928–), were leading CIA officers in Syria and Saudi Arabia for several decades.[54] As with so many CIA officers, just what they did and did not do is not open to view. But long after his retirement in 1977, Raymond Close emerged as a vocal critic of American foreign policy, finding fault with President Bill Clinton's actions in Afghanistan and Sudan and later with President George W. Bush's policy in Iraq. In 1998, he wrote that the US government was relying too much on military means to defeat "terrorism," which, Close insisted, "can only be defeated by better ideas, by persuasion and, most importantly, by amelioration of the conditions that inspire it."[55]

Beirut-born missionary son Talcott Seelye (1922–2006) had a distinguished Foreign Service career that climaxed with ambassadorships in Tunisia and Syria. William Stoltzfus (1924–) was another prominent Beirut-reared Foreign Service officer of that generation who, after a variety of important postings, became ambassador to Kuwait. Stephen B. L. Penrose Jr. (1908–1990) stood between the two generations. He served in the OSS and later in the State Department, and after leaving government service became president of the American University in Beirut.

Stoltzfus and Seelye vigorously defended their work in the Foreign Service against charges that they were subject to a pro-Arab bias.[56] A big part of the job was to stay on good terms with Arab leaders, Stoltzfus observed, and "you don't stay in touch with them by rubbing their faces in your differences. You make clear what American policy is and then you show some personal sympathy for some of their points of view."[57] Seelye, who quit the government when he found the policies of President Ronald Reagan and Secretary of State Alexander Haig too extreme in their deference to the Israeli government's wishes, insisted that he and those with whom he worked did not think of themselves as anti-Israeli. They did believe that the United States "should not tilt so heavily toward Israel," and "of course, when you took that position, in the eyes of the Israeli lobby or those who were 100 percent pro-Israeli, it meant that you were anti-Israel," and thus "we got into trouble."[58]

The point is not that Eddy, Hoskins, and their fellow missionary sons got everything right— obviously, they did not—but that their anti-Zionism was part of a general view of the American role in the Middle East. These missionary sons were enduringly suspicious of the European imperial legacy, and eager to find varieties of Arab nationalism with which the United States could cooperate. Were some missionary-connected Americans enabled by their deeper engagement with Arabs to recognize American national interests less visible to others, perhaps on account of an ethnically-driven identification with Jews that created its own blinders? Whose understanding was the most capacious, and whose was less so? Were the missionary sons who served the US government inappropriately swayed by their own immersion in the Arab world? Were Zionists in possession of a wiser understanding of modern history than their critics? Surely, blind spots were widely distributed, even if not equally; I have indicated some of Eddy's. But he and John Badeau, as I have also observed, saw that the Muslim Brotherhood was a growing force in the Arab world when virtually no one outside the extended missionary community did.

That community was almost always on the losing side of the policy debates it most cared about. The King-Crane Commission's notion of an American-supervised Greater Syria, designed to thwart European imperialism and to facilitate Arab political development outside the framework of the Balfour Declaration, achieved instant oblivion. The efforts of Eddy's generation to protect Palestinians from the sovereign authority of a Jewish state failed spectacularly. The hopes of Seelye and his contemporaries that the United States would develop a more critical stance toward the decisions of the Israeli government were not fulfilled.

World War II did little to change the Middle Eastern issues that engaged missionary-connected Americans, but that war transformed issues in the Pacific. The Pacific issues were different from the start, moreover, because they were much less entangled with the interests of the European colonial powers. Neither China nor Japan had ever been a colony of a European state, or the domain of a United Nations mandate. In the Pacific, the Asia-centered cosmopolitanism of missionary-connected Americans faced challenges very different from those it confronted in the Middle East.

CHAPTER SIX

Who Is My Brother?

THE WHITE PERIL AND THE JAPANESE

THE WHITE PERIL *in the Far East*: the title is provocative. The book of 1905 was written by Sidney Gulick (1860–1945), a son and grandson of missionaries to Micronesia who himself had been a Congregationalist missionary to Japan for seventeen years and would later serve for eight more.[1] Gulick reversed the "Yellow Peril" of contemporary discourse, a term which originally referred to a threat to Western civilization ostensibly posed by all East Asian peoples but by 1905 was most often applied to the Japanese. The big problem in the Pacific, Gulick insisted, was not the yellows but the whites, not the Asians but the Westerners. European powers wanted to exercise too much control over Asia. Japan had absorbed so many good things from the West that it was a more natural ally of the United States than was Russia, Germany, or France. The racism of Europeans, and of too many Eurocentric Americans, stood in the way of greater acceptance of the Japanese as defenders of modern civilization.[2]

Missionary-connected Americans later became more critical of Japan, but even during World War II they were conspicuously antiracist in two contexts: the interrogation of Japanese prisoners of war, and the confining of Japanese Americans in camps as if they were enemies. This and the following chapter are about missionary-connected Americans in relation to Pacific issues. This first chapter takes the story through the war against Japan; the next chapter begins with the war years in China, when the conflict between the Nationalist government of Chiang Kai-shek and the Communist movement led by Mao Zedong vexed Americans and led to controversies during the McCarthy era. The division between the two chapters follows from the nature of the Pearl Harbor divide. Prior to American entry into the war, Pacific issues were generally confronted together: almost everything Americans said about China referred also to Japan, and vice versa. That changed on December 7, 1941. Japan was an enemy belligerent, and China a military ally. The two became sharply separate challenges.

Although this chapter begins with a series of events prior to Pearl Harbor, it is most concerned with two issues that arose in the setting of the war. How were Japanese prisoners of war to be treated? How were Japanese Americans to be treated? The missionary contingent was right in the middle of the processes by which each of these two questions were answered. In both cases, missionary-connected Americans acted in keeping with Gulick's suspicion of the power of white racism.

During the decades before Pearl Harbor, Gulick and like-minded Americans of missionary background advanced a number of initiatives in the private sphere. They were usually limited to nongovernment roles because the US government dealt with the independent states of Japan and China differently from the way it dealt with the heavily colonized Middle East. The government employed fewer missionary-connected individuals. In the nineteenth century, to be sure, the United States had occasionally appointed China-based missionaries to represent it in the Peking legation and in local consulates.[3] But by the start of the twentieth century the United States looked more to business than to missions as the foundation for its policy making. It assigned standard-issue diplomats to represent the United States in Asian capitals and port cities. Only during the missionary-friendly Wilson administration was there a former missionary in a senior position, even briefly. E.T. Williams (1854–1944) headed the State Department's Far Eastern Division from 1914 to 1918. The one unusual case does require brief attention here.

Williams had been a missionary in China for a decade when, in 1896, he began to serve as an interpreter in the American legation in the Chinese capital. He later became an officer of the Foreign Service stationed in China and was called to Washington in 1914. Once in his post in the State Department, he entered the Wilson administration's debate over Japan-friendly versus China-friendly policies. Commercial ties were greater with Japan, but the Japanese—as allies of the British in World War I—had seized German holdings along the China coast, especially at Shantung, and had imposed a regime no less exploitative than the Germans'. The new government of the Republic of China protested this, supported by many American missionaries, although never with the standing of the missionary lobby concerning the Middle East during the same era. Secretary of

State Robert Lansing favored letting Japan have a relatively free hand in China, in exchange for a promise that the Japanese government would send no more immigrants to the United States and would stop complaining about discriminatory treatment of Japanese Americans on the West Coast. Like most missionaries, Williams took the other side, but his chief argument was commercial rather than humanitarian; he insisted that China would eventually modernize and become a much greater market. Williams prevailed. Wilson maintained diplomatic pressure against the Japanese.[4]

Debates between "pro-Chinese" and "pro-Japanese" approaches continued to dominate Pacific-related discussions within the administrations of Harding, Coolidge, Hoover, and Roosevelt. But after Williams left Washington for Berkeley in 1918 to become a professor at the University of California, these policy debates were led by career diplomats.[5] The most important of these were Nelson T. Johnson and Stanley K. Hornbeck, both of whom were suspicious of missionaries as sentimentalists lacking in political savvy. The drift in Washington was more sharply pro-Chinese after 1931, when the Japanese invaded Manchuria, and all the more so after 1937, when Japan conquered most of coastal China.

Long before Japanese imperial expansion became the central issue in all discussions of the Pacific, Gulick and his associates were active in other causes. Of special concern in the 1910s and early 1920s was the controversy over immigration. Relatively few Anglo-Protestants opposed the enactments of 1917 and 1924 that drastically restricted immigration from Eastern and Southern Europe and eliminated it entirely from Asia. Representatives of immigrant-intensive districts of eastern cities led the congressional fight against immigration restriction. Outside of government, immigrant scholars like the great anthropologist Franz Boas were prominent. But the Anglo-Protestant voices raised in defense of continued immigration came largely out of the missionary community and the missionary-influenced Federal Council of Churches. In 1913, the council employed Gulick as its expert on Japan, and charged him with campaigning for the continuation of immigration from Asia and Europe.[6] Gulick spent a decade as a traveling lecturer, popular writer, and organizer of committees and forums on issues of immigration and anti-Asian prejudice. Historian Roger Daniels describes Gulick as "a mass movement all by himself."[7]

In basic outlook, Gulick was far from alone. Daniel J. Fleming and Robert Speer, whose leadership of the missionary project I noted in an earlier chapter, wrote extensively against the racism they found in the desire to exclude Asians. Both of these leading churchmen developed the idea that diversity, rather than homogeneity, was a healthy social ideal. Their assumption in the 1920s that Christianity, rightly understood, was a sufficiently commodious canopy for ethnoracial diversity distinguished them from the multiculturalist writers of the 1990s, but in their opposition to homogeneity-promoting assimilation they anticipated popular themes of seventy years later. Speer wrote his antiracist treatise of 1924, *Of One Blood*, while serving as president of the Federal Council of Churches.[8]

While Gulick and his associates in the Federal Council of Churches were losing in the immigration debates in Washington, Gulick was inspiring a group of missionary activists in California. Their chief vehicle, the Survey of Race Relations on the Pacific Coast, mixed Social Gospel reform with social science research. The group was organized by three former YMCA secretaries, each of whom had served for many years in Japan. Galen Fisher, George Gleason, and John Merle Davis persuaded the FCC and the Rockefeller Foundation to support a fact-finding inquiry into anti-Asian prejudice. The YMCA group understood this prejudice to be especially widespread on the West Coast, the location of the largest population of Asian immigrants. That prejudice not only fueled the movement to restrict immigration, but created legal limits on where ethnic Asians could reside and own property.[9] Although the Japanese were the most contested of the Asian groups of interest to the Survey, it also attended to other immigrant-ethnic populations, especially the Chinese, the Korean, and the Filipinos.

During the first half of the 1920s, Fisher, Gleason, and Davis—who, along with Gulick, were known in ecumenical Protestant circles as the "Japan gang"—organized and supervised the survey. The language facility of the former missionaries enabled them to enlist many immigrants and children of immigrants to assist in the project. They wrote hundreds of family histories and collected thousands of pages of data. Yet this formidable five-year project never resulted in the major publication that was anticipated. Robert Park, the University of Chicago sociologist who had been hired to head the survey, lost interest in it. He sat on it for years, and never produced the massive volume he had promised. Despite the merely ad hoc dissemination of the survey, however, the enterprise served to create a substantial community of scholars and reformers who were aware of the actual circumstances of Asian Americans.[10] Some were active years later in protesting the confinement of Japanese Americans.

While the survey left no lasting institutional legacy, "the Japan gang" in 1925 helped to create something that did: the Institute for Pacific

Relations (IPR). As an early NGO, this organization was the Pacific equivalent of the missionary-driven Near East Foundation, but with purposes more intellectual and policy-focused than philanthropic. IPR sponsored hundreds of books, published the journal *Pacific Affairs*, and organized countless conferences, workshops, and forums throughout the Pacific Rim. IPR emerged directly from the YMCA, which stationed officials in Hawaii, especially, but also throughout the Pacific, and was certain that Pacific affairs had a distinctive character and were being largely ignored by the governments, scholars, and business elites of the United States and Europe. YMCA leader John R. Mott used his unmatched convening power to call a series of meetings of YMCA officials. Gulick was included, but the driving force was Davis, who had grown up in Japan as a son of missionaries prior to his serving as a YMCA secretary there. Davis obtained funding from the Rockefeller Foundation and a diverse group of wealthy Protestants in New York.

The Rockefeller Foundation was ideally suited to finance IPR. It was under the influence of Raymond Fosdick, one of the period's most zealous Wilsonians and a close adviser to the Rockefeller family. He was the brother of Harry Emerson Fosdick, the most listened-to of ecumenical Protestant preachers of the interwar years and a leader of the modernist fight against fundamentalists. Raymond Fosdick was eager to advance the cause of international cooperation. He was first a trustee and after 1936 was president of the foundation. Although not himself a missionary, he was highly cognizant of the missionary project. His sister was a career missionary to China.

The YMCA group at the center of IPR had strongly anticolonial tendencies that were kept in check by IPR's business constituency, which encouraged the fact-seeking, expert-commissioning side of the Wilsonian heritage at the expense of the moralistic. Davis had hoped to mobilize IPR for a new campaign to reopen immigration from China and Japan after it had been cut off by Congress. The business group cautioned against a priority with so little hope of success. Yet the somewhat conflicting instincts of IPR's supporters did not prevent missionary cosmopolitans from dominating its administrative leadership. Davis recruited Edward C. Carter, another protégé of Mott's, who had been a YMCA secretary in India for fifteen years. Carter succeeded Davis as executive director of IPR in 1933 and remained in that position until 1946.[11]

Carter, recalled his co-worker William L. Holland, was "a rather old-fashioned Christian liberal" who always showed "a deep concern for the ordinary people" of China, Japan, and other nations of the Pacific.[12] Carter was accountable to Jerome Greene (1874–1959), a New York City lawyer who coordinated the YMCA group's relations with the business elite. Greene himself had grown up in Japan as the son of the Congregationalist missionary Daniel Crosby Greene. The elder Greene served in Japan for forty-four years and was a leader in the development of the liberal, service-oriented programs that gradually replaced conversion-centered agendas. Jerome Greene's brother, Roger Sherman Greene (1881–1947), long headed the Rockefeller Foundation's medical work in China and facilitated the YMCA group's connection to Jerome Greene and his circle in New York. Hence IPR was missionary-grounded not only in its origins and its staffing, but even in its commercial and philanthropic connections. IPR was a child of the missionary-engaged elite of ecumenical Protestantism, and a primary site for the elaboration of missionary cosmopolitanism. The missionary theorist and antiracist writer Daniel J. Fleming was an enthusiastic participant in IPR's founding and proclaimed its significance in *The Missionary Review of the World* as soon as IPR was established.[13]

IPR would not be so important had there been other institutions in the pre-World War II era providing opportunities to study the countries of the Pacific and to engage in policy debates about their relation to one another and to the United States. People with these interests were dismayed by the blatant Eurocentrism of the League of Nations and its affiliated bodies, and by the paucity of American university programs in Asian Studies of any kind. From its founding until the disruptions of World War II, IPR sponsored a succession of conferences in Kyoto, Shanghai, Banff, and other Pacific Rim locales, bringing together a diverse collection of journalists, scholars, and business leaders. Memoranda for these meetings were sometimes prepared by scholars of distinction. The British scholar R. H. Tawney's book of 1931, *Land and Labor in China*, was first drafted as a discussion paper for one of these meetings.[14] Beginning in 1940, IPR became, in the words of the most careful student of its history, "a think-tank for the allies."[15]

Well before that, IPR functioned as a relatively comfortable meeting ground for parties increasingly at odds with one another, especially the delegations from China and Japan. Although IPR was an American-centered organization, it established subsidiary councils of scholars and officials from Japan, China, Australia, and New Zealand, in addition to those from British and Dutch colonial outposts. One of these councils, made up of Japanese officials, remained associated with IPR even after Japan left the League of Nations in 1933. Many of the quarrels within IPR had to do with Japanese military actions, most of which are beyond the scope of my purposes here. In the absence of more extensive

American-Japanese diplomatic relations during the 1920s and 1930s, however, IPR was all the more important a scene for "private diplomacy," or "cultural diplomacy," as Pacific discourse has been described by historian Jon Thares Davidann.[16]

In addition to filling a diplomatic gap, IPR was a home for scholars and journalists who had few other places to go. IPR was long the chief institutional base for the distinguished China scholar, Owen Lattimore, who edited *Pacific Affairs* from 1934 to 1941.[17] The German refugee scholar, Karl Wittfogel, was an affiliate of IPR during the 1930s when working on his eventually famous book, *Oriental Despotism*.[18] IPR was a second professional residence for several young academics trying to get their campuses to build Asian-centered programs. These included John K. Fairbank at Harvard and Hugh Borton at Columbia. IPR Research Associates T. A. Bisson and E. H. Norman produced under IPR auspices some of the most ambitious writings on East Asia to appear in the United States in the World War II era. IPR commissioned Kenneth Landon's book on the Chinese population of Thailand, which was a foundation for Landon's later career in the OSS and the State Department.[19] Most of these individuals figure largely in later chapters of this book.

Lattimore, Wittfogel, Fairbank, Borton, Bisson, Norman, and Landon all understood that IPR's office in New York was where the action was in the 1930s and early 1940s. So did the period's Foreign Service officers, many of whom met informally at IPR with journalists and scholars, casually conversing about topics of mutual interest. During and immediately after the war, when John Service was told by his State Department superiors to hang out with journalists and to try to influence public opinion about China, he knew that IPR was the best place to go.[20]

IPR did not constitute itself as a lobby, but many IPR regulars, especially Bisson, were active in creating one in 1938. The awkwardly named American Committee for Non-Participation in Japanese Aggression soon became one of the most prominent organizations opposing the isolationist sentiments still widespread in American politics. The missionary community, with few exceptions, gravitated toward the idea that the United States needed to use its economic power to stop Japanese expansion.[21] A number of missionary cosmopolitans were annoyed at the white bias that condoned imperialism in Asia when practiced by Europeans but not by Japanese, but most were so outraged by Japanese aggression that they took the Chinese side of the conflict. Missionary lecturer Sherwood Eddy witnessed the Japanese invasion of Manchuria and the reports he wrote about it circulated widely among ecumenical Protestants. The full-scale invasion of China in 1937 intensified these anti-Japanese feelings, especially in the light of missionary reports of details of the Nanking Massacre.

The aims of the American Committee for Non-Participation in Japanese Aggression differed from those of other anti-isolationist organizations that flourished in the years running up to Pearl Harbor. For example, the largest of these initiatives—the Committee to Defend America by Aiding the Allies, led by William Alan White—took little interest in the Pacific. Many missionary-connected Americans supported that lobby, too, but what distinguished the American Committee for Non-Participation in Japanese Aggression was its focus on the vulnerability of China, rather than of Britain, and on Japanese conquests rather than German. The American Committee for Non-Participation in Japanese Aggression pressed for the embargo on oil and metal that the United States eventually put in place. By 1940, public opinion, thanks in part to the labors of the Non-Participation Committee, was more supportive of a stronger US stance toward Japan. This made it easier for President Roosevelt and Secretary of State Cordell Hull to take the diplomatic steps that virtually assured a Japanese attack.[22]

The Non-Participation Committee was often called "The Price Committee" because it was created by Harry B. Price and Frank W. Price, missionary sons from China who had served there as missionaries themselves. Harry B. Price was the committee's executive secretary. The brothers were not related to Ernest B. Price, who had served as a Foreign Service officer and later in the OSS, and is mentioned elsewhere in this book. Both Henry Luce and Pearl Buck, who disagreed about the Kuomintang, were affiliated with the committee right up until Pearl Harbor. [23] Its most energetic speaker was the former missionary doctor Walter Judd, whose success in the cause of China led to his election to the US Congress in 1942.[24] The committee did have nonmissionary affiliates, including writer Van Wyck Brooks, theologian Reinhold Niebuhr, and diplomat Henry L. Stimson, but the figures most associated with the committee were without exception missionary-connected: the Price Brothers, Judd, Buck, Luce, and Bisson, in addition to the organization's chief staff person, Geraldine Fitch, a longtime missionary in China. But none were more important than the committee's chair, the illustrious and well-connected Roger Sherman Greene.

The Price brothers sought Greene's services and were delighted to get them. Greene had resigned as head of the Rockefeller medical program in China and was available in New York. Greene and his brothers could count among their ancestors Roger Sherman, a signer of the Declaration of Independence. The Greene family was recognized as one of the most prominent of old New England families. Jerome Greene became the protégé of

Harvard President Charles W. Eliot during Eliot's final years in office, and was Eliot's choice over A. Lawrence Lowell to succeed Eliot as president in 1909.[25] Another brother, Evarts Boutell Greene, a historian at Columbia University specializing in early American history, was president of the American Historical Association.[26] All three missionary sons took active, lifelong interests in East Asian affairs. Roger was an intimate acquaintance of Stanley Hornbeck, the head of the State Department's Far Eastern Division, and enjoyed easy access to Secretary Hull. He was even able to meet occasionally with President Roosevelt, who wrote to him as "Dear Roger."

Roger Sherman Greene brought to his lobbying efforts a sense of entitlement that worked extremely well in some circumstances, but less so in others. He was forced out of his position as resident director of the Chinese Medical Board, and as head of the Peking Union Medical College, because he would not suffer the meddling of John D. Rockefeller III. The Rockefeller Foundation had assigned to the young heir a large measure of responsibility for overseeing its China operations. Greene knew China and the issues in medical education very well, and refused to defer to the wishes of the self-important young billionaire. A central issue was religion. The original Rockefeller vision for medical education in China included the inculcation of Christianity. Greene believed the time for that had long since passed. The college did not need a department of religion, and should stop linking medical education with Christianity. But to Greene's annoyance and disbelief, the young tycoon insisted on defying him, and demanded that the program's traditional affirmation of Protestant Christianity be renewed and perpetuated. The copious correspondence between Greene, Rockefeller, Fosdick, and Greene's brother Jerome shows Roger Sherman Greene to be more self-righteous than diplomatic.[27]

Diplomacy, ironically, was something Roger had practiced professionally. He had been a Foreign Service officer for a dozen years before entering the employ of the Rockefeller Foundation. He developed a reputation for telling his superiors exactly what he thought, whether or not they wanted to hear it. His egalitarian principles got in the way of his work in the Foreign Service. "He wanted to see an end to the privileges of the unequal treaties in China," historian Warren I Cohen explains, "and an end of discrimination against Chinese and Japanese in American immigration policy."[28] Greene accepted appointment with the Rockefellers in 1914 as a way out of this dilemma. His superiors in the Far Eastern division of the State Department, especially the old missionary E. T. Williams, whom Greene revered, regarded him as a fine officer and unsuccessfully pled with him to stay.

Even friends and family who usually agreed with Roger's principled stands found him austere and sometimes insensitive.[29] Once the United States was in the war, Greene's less frequent interactions with people in power had less historical significance. He was never happy with the Kuomintang, but was more suspicious of the Communists than were most of his friends in the missionary community. He was also in poor health, and died in 1947 at the age of 66. Cohen concludes that Greene was "the most important nongovernmental advocate of American intervention in the war in Asia."[30]

Pearl Harbor ended the committee's work, and it also changed almost everything concerning American relations to the peoples of the Pacific. Emblematic of the change was the fact that among the first wave of US Marines to hit the beach at Guadalcanal on August 8, 1942, was a man who had been a Congregationalist missionary to Japan for twenty-six years.

Sherwood F. Moran (1885–1983) had been home on furlough on December 7, 1941. Immediately, he went to US Marine headquarters in Washington.[31] Volunteering for service, he told the Marines there that his idiomatic Japanese was probably better than any other American's. The Marines sent him to the South Pacific, and put him in charge of interrogating POWs. He had radical ideas about how this task should be carried out: "By the expression on your face, the glance of your eye, the tone of your voice" you must "get him to know" that you really do regard all men as "brothers," he instructed other Marines. He proved to be so good at extracting intelligence from captured soldiers that he was told to write an instruction manual for others assigned to this job. The resulting document systematically rejected the beliefs of many Marines that Japanese prisoners should be shot, if not tortured. The American interviewer, Moran's manual advised, should speak to the Japanese prisoner "as a human being to a human being," treating him with respect.[32]

On Guadalcanal, Moran was by far the oldest man around. He was soon being called "Pappy" by the young men working under his supervision. Language fluency was what got Moran to the South Pacific, but what he did with his Japanese is what made history. Moran may have been, as his family liked to say of him, "probably the only Marine of his era who never took a drink, never smoked a cigarette, and never cursed."[33] He was much more than that. He was, among other things, a classic ecumenical Protestant missionary.

Educated at Oberlin College and at Union Theological Seminary, and inspired more by Jane Addams's social work than by any ideology of religious conversion, Moran was a devoted follower of the Student Volunteer Movement's greatest orator, Sherwood Eddy. Moran and Eddy were sometimes called "the two Sherwoods" because Moran served for a year as Eddy's personal secretary, traveling with him and absorbing his liberal views about the missionary project. Worldly enough to have become an accomplished tap dancer, and to have considered a career in vaudeville before a trusted female friend warned him against the unwholesome characters he would meet in the New York theater milieu, Moran was anything but retiring in his ways and was far from orthodox in his theology. Moran married his Oberlin sweetheart, Ursul, and settled down with her in Japan to raise a family and exemplify what the two understood to be a Christian life, and to help local Japanese in whatever way they could. Moran quickly took a serious interest in Buddhism and in Japanese art—on which he published several monographs late in life—and became an outspoken critic of the militarism of the Japanese ruling elite.

Moran's manual instructed the interrogators to speak to a Japanese prisoner not only as a brother, but almost as a seducer. In his very first paragraph Moran compared the "interviewer"—a label he preferred to "interrogator"—to a "lover." Each interviewer must develop his own skills, so that each "will gradually work out a technique of his own, his very own, just as a man does in making love to a woman! The comparison is not merely a flip *bon mot*; the interviewer should be a real wooer!"[34] Some Marines in their "hard-boiled" manner will "sneer that this is a sentimental attitude," Moran predicted, but he urged resolution and persistence in the face of such banal scorn. The central theme of "Suggestions for Japanese Interpreters Based on Work in the Field," as the manual was entitled, was the need to establish rapport with the prisoner. Moran insisted that "the Japanese soldier is a person to be pitied rather than hated," a man who has been misled, deceived, and manipulated by his government and his officers. Every prisoner actually had a story he wanted to tell, and the job of the interviewer was to create an atmosphere in which the prisoner would tell it. The interviewer should learn as much as he could about Japan and its history and culture. Those like himself who had lived in Japan had a great advantage, yes, but others should do all they could to inform themselves so as to do a better job.[35]

Of course one must never forget the goal of extracting intelligence. The interviewer must be "wise as serpents but harmless as doves," cautioned the old Congregationalist, casually quoting Matthew 10:16 without identifying the source. The ideal interviewer must have patience and tact, and he

should be a man of culture, insight, resourcefulness, and with real conversational ability. He must have "gags"; he must have a "line". He must be alive; he must be warm; he must be vivid. But above all he must have integrity, sympathy; yet he must be firm, wise. . . . He must have dignity and a proper sense of values, but withal friendly, open and frank.

In all this it was essential to be "absolutely sincere." The soldier will be able to tell if the interviewer is faking it; "he will know the difference." Facial expression and tone were crucial. After all, "'the men of the four seas are brothers,' to quote a Japanese (and Chinese) proverb."[36] Here, as so often in Moran's utterances, the Christian universalism of Oberlin and Union found its way into a comfortable synthesis with East Asian culture.

Moran's approach worked. His colleagues in First Marine Division intelligence soon realized that Moran was wise to design a strategy aimed at extracting small bits of information, rather than at the ticking time bombs that the average soldier is not likely to know about in the first place. Several months after his methods had proven effective, his superiors sent him back to Australia to write the manual and to train new recruits.[37] Among the new intelligence officers were several missionary sons, including Roger Hackett, later a historian at the University of Michigan but at that time a twenty-year-old who had known Moran in Japan. Hackett had no trouble understanding Moran's prescriptions and putting them into effect. In one case, Hackett later recalled, it was especially easy: a soldier flushed out of the jungle by his unit turned out to have been a classmate of Hackett's in the missionary high school his father ran in Japan.[38]

Hackett kept his own copy of another classified document written by Moran which is in some respects an even more striking indicator of Moran's ecumenical missionary perspective than his interrogation manual. "The Psychology of the Japanese" is a twenty-seven-page, single-spaced typescript Moran submitted to Marine intelligence on June 4, 1942, more than two months before the landing on Guadalcanal. The document was issued to all Marine intelligence personnel on September 6, 1943, as part of the training packet for newly arriving intelligence officers like Hackett. "The Psychology of the Japanese" combined respect for the particularities of Japanese culture with a fervent affirmation of the fraternity and solidarity of all humankind. Always direct, Moran went right to the point in his very first sentence, like Jefferson in the Declaration of Independence, whom he echoed: "All men, no matter of what race or nation, are in their fundamental nature and general characteristics, the same," and all men are thus "brothers."[39] Moran was at great pains to explain that liberalism had made substantial gains among the Japanese people. He expected the Japanese liberals would struggle after the war to regain control of their country from the militarists and imperialists who had led Japan into this disastrous war. Moran insisted that Americans must not fight them on racist grounds (i.e., because they are "Japs"); that would undercut the liberals. We must "attack Japan as hard as we can," even with devastation, but

If our only object is that expressed by a fellow officer of mine, "I don't know why I want to fight Japan except that I want to knock s—t out of the Japs," we can never hope to bring the liberals and other fair-minded people in Japan to see that we are, in the last analysis, fighting their fight, for a victory that will be for the good of Japan itself.[40]

Though the good Congregationalist could not bring himself to write out a four-letter word—even in a Marine setting where such speech was common—he delivered a political and cultural history of Japan since the Manchurian incursion of 1931, calculated to get the Marines to take a generous view of the average Japanese soldier. That soldier was the victim of a society that was simply "sick," but would eventually get well. What had happened since 1931, Moran explained, was an intensification of Japanese nationalism that had been layered over a range of more attractive traits. Yes, there were conventions about who should bow to whom, and when, and, yes, there was a tradition of emperor-worship that helped explain the soldier's reluctance to surrender, but Americans should not be misled by cultural peculiarities. Beneath the post-1931 imposition of militaristic nationalism there resided a wealth of human traits that Americans could well connect with after the war. The last thing Americans should do is to demonize the Japanese people and their soldiers.[41]

After the war Moran tried to live out his idealistic vision of Japanese-American relations. He and Ursul went back to Japan in 1948 to resume their missionary work. Eventually the Morans left Japan, and moved into a facility for retired Congregationalist and Methodist missionaries in California. Moran died there in 1983 at the age of ninety-eight.

But Moran's work was rediscovered during the Iraq War. Suddenly, in 2003, an independent group of Marines and Marine veterans made Moran's story public for the first time, posting his interrogation manual on the internet.[42] Critics of the regime of Dick Cheney and Donald Rumsfeld pointed to the insights Moran had developed sixty years before. The manual was the topic of a widely discussed 2005 article in *The Atlantic*. In the decade following, amid growing outrage at the barbarities of Abu Ghraib and Guantanamo, Moran's ideas were hailed in *Time* and a variety of books, articles, and blogs. Moran's manual was described by one prominent blogger as a "wrecking ball for torture's apologists."[43] Moran was a compelling witness, from the grave, against the American military's torture of its captives in Iraq.

The missionary foundation for Moran's work with POWs becomes all the more significant when we recognize two counterparts in the army and the navy who adopted virtually the same approach, and who were both mission-ary sons. The notorious service rivalries in the Pacific war prevented Moran from knowing about it, but Army Col. John Alfred Burden (1900–1999) and Navy Lt. Otis Carey (1921–2006) were operating on the basis of the same instincts. That the anti-torture policies and practices of all three services in the Pacific War were instituted by missionary-connected Americans has gone unnoticed until now. [44] A sign of just how thoroughly this episode had been forgotten by the 1980s is the fact that none of these three men is men-tioned in two books written in that decade by the leading students of the war in the Pacific: Akira Iriye's *Power and Culture: The Japanese-American War, 1941–1945* and John W. Dower's *War Without Mercy*.[45]

"Otis Cary's name," reports Ulrich Straus, "was the only one cited re-peatedly" many years after the war, when Japanese veterans "wrote up their wartime experience in prison camps." Cary, who was remembered with respect, even affection, "was determined," writes Straus, "to treat prisoners not as enemies but as human beings, individuals who deserved to have a bright future aiding in the reconstruction of a new, democratic Japan."[46] The son and grandson of Congregationalist missionaries, Cary, who always considered Japanese his native language, had come "home" in 1936 to attend Deerfield Academy and then Amherst College, as did so many missionary sons. He enlisted in 1942 and by early 1943 was the navy's primary officer for interrogation. He was stationed first in Hawaii and then in Alaska's Aleutian Islands, where he led in the interrogation of POWs captured in the fighting there. Cary was first hampered by the army, which was in control of the American operation in the Aleutians and wanted nothing to do with the navy's Japanese language specialists. Still, Cary managed to win acceptance when he had the astonishing luck of encountering, as his first POW, a soldier from his own hometown in Japan. Carey extracted information from this man that was deemed highly valuable by the top brass.[47]

But Cary did not operate on a large scale until later in the war, in the Marianas, especially on Saipan in the summer of 1944. It was there that Cary, confronted with a flood of captives, made such a lasting impression on the soldiers he interrogated. "Following lengthy discussions," notes Straus, many of the prisoners "eventually found persuasive Cary's argu-ment that [they] had given their all in the service of their country, had nothing to be ashamed of, and should look forward to contributing to the reconstruction of a post-war Japan."[48]

Cary's successes in the Aleutians and the Marianas would be better known if he had written about his exploits in English instead of only in

Japanese.[49] As translated by Straus, Cary explained that the soldiers "were used to being coerced and knew how to take evasive measures," but "if treated humanely, they lost the will to resist." While there were rumors about high pressure methods used on the POWs, Cary insisted that nothing of the sort happened on his watch. The unanimous postwar testimony of the POWs in his charge vindicates the claim.[50] Cary went back to Japan after the war and headed the American Studies program at Doshisha University, the close partner of his US alma mater, Amherst. Largely unknown in the United States, to which he returned ten years before his death in 2006, Cary was an important and widely celebrated figure in Japanese academia.

Cary apparently had no contact with his Army counterpart, John Alfred Burden, who was a medical doctor in Hawaii at the time of the Japanese attack on Pearl Harbor. Burden immediately enlisted in the army, ready to use the language skills he acquired as a Tokyo-born son and the grandson of Seventh-day Adventist missionaries. He was able to speak the Tokyo dialect more fluently than most of the Nisei with whom he worked in the South Pacific.

As a captain posted to Fiji in October 1942, Burden was frustrated that his superiors did not quickly send him into the combat zones where his language facility could be of immediate use. He finally persuaded them to send him to Guadalcanal in December, accompanied by two Japanese Americans who, Burden complained bitterly, had been stuck in a prejudice-filled atmosphere on Fiji driving trucks around the base. Burden went on to lead the first joint Caucasian-Nisei team of interrogators, eventually establishing an impressive record. Even Major Gen. Alexander Patch, the army commander in the Solomons who had first opposed relying on the ostensibly untrustworthy Nisei, was won over quickly. Later, Patch was proud, while fighting in Europe, to have under his command the all-Nisei 442nd Regimental Combat Team, which was the most decorated American unit in the war. The standard history of the Nisei linguists recognizes Burden's role in diminishing prejudice against the Japanese Americans and in facilitating their contributions to the war effort.[51]

Once on duty in the Solomon Islands, Burden found that his fellow soldiers were inclined to kill Japanese prisoners rather than treat them according to the Geneva Conventions and bring them in for interrogation. Burden ascribed part of the army's bad treatment of Japanese POWs to the legacy of the Marines who preceded the army on Guadalcanal.[52] Yet it was there that Moran had operated in a virtually identical fashion as a Marine, and had left more extensive records of his work. Burden's entire lack of connection with Moran is ironic in view of the fact that Burden had no idea of how the Marine interrogators actually did their work, and assumed merely on the basis of a stereotype that the Marines were not taking prisoners, but just killing any Japanese soldiers they captured.[53] Burden struggled to change the practices he encountered. Many officers had dehumanized the Japanese to the point of treating their physical remains as souvenirs for friends and families.[54]

In a brief autobiography written many years later, Burden recalled an army major asking him to provide "some Japanese skulls" so he could send them as gifts to his four daughters.[55] Burden's memoranda and oral presentations frequently condemned the mistreatment of prisoners. "Several times," he reported to his army superiors, "word was telephoned in from the front line that a prisoner had been taken, only to find after hours of waiting that the prisoner had 'died' en route to the rear." This attitude was not limited to the lieutenants and captains who made these decisions in the field. One regimental commander actually censured the field grade officers of one unit for bringing in prisoners at all, saying, "Don't bother to take prisoners; shoot the sons of bitches." In one memo of July 1943, Burden protested that the army's intelligence manuals gave exactly the wrong instructions for interrogation. Kindness, not violence and threats of violence, was needed. Japanese prisoners were trained to deal with violence and were able to face it with patriotic confidence and great stoicism. They were not prepared for a humane reception by their captors. Once the prisoner learns he is going to be treated well, he is often very eager to talk, Burden explained, offering examples from his own experience.[56]

Although Burden's arguments for the humane treatment of POWs were instrumental and strategic, they were also principled. The torturing and killing of Japanese POWs and the whole idea of "a war of extermination," he wrote, is "directly against American principles—the principles which we are fighting to uphold." Burden was a forceful presence, not afraid to criticize his superiors. Upon finding the field grade officers and enlisted men reluctant to take POWs, Burden ventured into the field himself at great risk, determined to monitor the situation. He won two Purple Hearts, the Bronze Star, the Silver Star, and the Legion of Merit badge. A blistering report on the army's failure to understand the value of the intelligence that could be gathered from POWs finally had an effect. A long memorandum of Burden's was circulated within the Fourth Army in November.[57] By that time Burden had been called back to Hawaii to train new groups of interrogators.[58]

Promoted to major and then to lieutenant colonel, Burden was sent from Hawaii to China in 1944 to serve under Lt. General Joseph Stillwell. There he was for a short time a member of the "Dixie Mission," visiting the Communist outpost in Yenan, where he met Mao Zedong and Zhou Enlai before being called back to Chungking to assist Stillwell in military planning.[59] Finally, Burden was stationed in occupied Japan, and left the army as a full colonel in 1946. He returned to Hawaii, where he resumed his medical practice and became a prominent civic leader in Maui. He moved to Tennessee shortly before his death at the age of ninety-eight.[60]

The job of interrogating Japanese military prisoners came suddenly to those who did it. The call to support Japanese Americans who were confined[61] during the same war came to Galen Fisher (1873–1955) in the context of two decades of antidiscrimination activities. The ex-missionary Fisher had been active in the Survey of Race Relations on the Pacific Coast. Fisher's experience with anti-Asian discrimination led him to anticipate what would happen if the United States found itself at war with Japan. He prepared for it.

In the summer of 1941, half a year before Pearl Harbor, Fisher launched his Committee for American Principles and Fair Play. By then he had settled in Berkeley and was serving as chair of the board of trustees of the Pacific School of Religion (PSR). A strongly liberal seminary serving mostly Congregationalists and Methodists, PSR was the closest West Coast equivalent of Union Theological Seminary in New York. Fisher was also a research associate in the Political Science Department at the University of California, Berkeley, and was a friend of David Barrows, a former president of the university who earlier had been a military officer and government official in the Philippines. Fisher and Barrows worked together to create a committee of influential citizens prepared to defend Californians of Japanese descent in the event of war with Japan. The committee was designed to influence policy and to counteract prejudicial attitudes toward Japanese Americans. When the time came to use it, the committee had its apparatus firmly in place.[62]

Once the US government announced the confinement policy, a handful of other groups without missionary influence opposed it. These included the American Civil Liberties Union, the Socialist Party, the Fellowship of Reconciliation, and the Society of Friends. They did so following their own well-defined centers of political and ethical gravity. So it was, too, with several other parties that later joined in the criticism of the government's practices, including a number of churches and the National Association of Colored People. From the beginning, George Schuyler was an outspoken

African American voice in *The Pittsburgh Courier*, the newspaper he led.[63] US Supreme Court Associate Justices Robert Jackson and Frank Murphy acted independently of a missionary matrix when they wrote eloquent dissents from the court's 1944 decision in *Korematsu v. United States* to uphold President Roosevelt's executive order. Jackson declared Mr. Korematsu the victim of "an attempt to make an otherwise innocent act a crime merely because this prisoner is the son of parents as to whom he had no choice, and belongs to a race from which there is no way to resign." Murphy insisted that "all residents of this nation are kin in some way by blood or culture to a foreign land," and every one should be protected from "the ugly abyss of racism."[64]

But Fisher was there first. And he "played the key role," concludes historian Robert Shaffer, in coordinating "religious, academic, and secular liberal opposition to evacuation policies."[65] Fisher wrote articles in national magazines condemning the racism of the confinement, mobilized others to lobby against confinement, and sought means of aiding the internees. The "uprooting" of Japanese Americans from their homes on the West Coast was "a testing by fire" of the devotion of white Americans "to the letter and spirit of the federal constitution," Fisher proclaimed in his first article on the matter, which appeared in the *Christian Century* in April 1942. For white Christians there was an additional challenge: do they or do they not believe that "Christian brotherhood transcends blood and skin color?"[66]

To staff the Fair Play Committee, Fisher turned to local missionary-connected individuals. For his executive director he chose Ruth Kingman, a daughter of Methodist missionaries to China. Kingman had missionary experience of her own in China during the 1920s, accompanying her husband, Harry Kingman, a YMCA secretary who had been born in China of missionary parents. "My parents were completely without race prejudice, and of course they influenced me," Harry later explained.[67] He was well known for having been a professional baseball player with the New York Yankees before signing up with the YMCA to return to the country of his birth. Harry Kingman, like his wife, was part of Fisher's operation, as was Frank Herron Smith, another former missionary living in Berkeley. After Pearl Harbor, Smith led the Commission on Aliens and Prisoners of War, an organization created to aid the Japanese Americans.[68]

Fisher and Barrows put together a list of distinguished figures, including Stanford University President Ray Lyman Wilbur, several corporation presidents, and Berkeley's two top administrators, Provost Monroe Deutsch and President Robert Gordon Sproul. Fisher and Barrows made a point of not including known pacifists in order to avoid the impression that the committee was insufficiently supportive of war, should it come.[69] When the war did come, the committee was in a position to navigate the political waters carefully; it stopped short of officially opposing any removal at all of Japanese Americans, and focused instead on ways in which the confinement might be limited in scope and duration, and on the conditions under which the people being confined might live. Were there no means by which a Japanese American could prove his or her loyalty? Were there to be no hearings, just wholesale rounding up of everyone of Japanese ancestry? Were there no evacuation processes short of sending these people to camps in the desert? Where did American citizenship come into play?

The committee lost the debates about these and other questions. But by raising them at all, Fisher's group won some friends within the government. A number of officials proved glad to have the committee as a modifying influence on public attitudes. Among these was U.S. Attorney General Francis Biddle, who had actually opposed the president's executive order authorizing the confinement, but was overruled. The committee managed to maintain working relationships with John J. McCloy of the War Department and Dillon Myer of the War Relocation Authority, the two officials most directly responsible for managing the camps.[70]

Fisher's committee produced and circulated memoranda and flyers designed to educate the public and to influence the opinions of well-placed elites. He and several co-workers testified before the Tolan Committee of the House of Representatives—chaired by Democrat John Tolan of Oakland— investigating "National Defense Migration," swelling the small ranks of witnesses who were willing to speak out critically.[71] Fisher himself traveled extensively, lecturing to community and church groups, and visiting more than half of the seventeen camps distributed from Idaho to Arkansas to California. Perhaps most importantly, Fisher published a series of sharply argued articles in *Christian Century* and *Far Eastern Survey*. While keeping his relations cordial with many government officials, Fisher never let up on the military and civilian leaders who persisted in racist characterizations of the Japanese. In the summer of 1943, Fisher denounced Gen. John L. De Witt for having told a committee of the House of Representatives that "a Jap's a Jap" and therefore citizenship papers had no meaning when dealing with persons of Japanese ancestry.[72]

Thanks in large part to six articles by Fisher himself and one by E. Stanley Jones, *Christian Century* was the largest national magazine consistently opposed to the confinement.[73] Indeed, during April 1942 alone—very early in the national conversation, when many antiracists remained unsure how to react—*Christian Century* published six items about it. In a bitter editorial of April 29, 1942, the editors declared that the United States was on the verge of treating its Japanese citizens the way the government of Germany was treating its Jewish citizens.[74] No other national periodical displayed remotely this level of engagement.

One strong criticism of the government's policy appeared in *Christianity & Crisis*, the "realist" magazine founded by Reinhold Niebuhr to counter the pacifist tendencies of *Christian Century*. Henry Smith Leiper, a former Congregationalist missionary to China and longtime executive of missionary organizations, was the author. Leiper compared President Roosevelt's policies to the Nuremberg Laws of the Third Reich. This stark provocation generated a ferocious set of letters disagreeing with Leiper. Niebuhr himself responded in defense of his friend, and characterized as "racist" the very idea that Japanese Americans were any less loyal than Americans of German ancestry. Yet the issue of internment was sufficiently contested in Niebuhr's adamantly antipacifist councils that *Christianity & Crisis* never mentioned it again.[75] That the only member of Niebuhr's close circle to explode so angrily against President Roosevelt's policy was a missionary is another index of the demography of the opposition. In the meantime, it was another prominent former missionary, Charles Iglehart, who wrote the *Nation*'s first attack on Roosevelt's order.[76]

While missionary-connected critics of the confinement were from the start highly visible in the national press, other scattered voices joined. By the end of 1943 the liberal Catholic magazine *Commonweal* and the smaller radical magazine *Common Ground* emerged as forthright opponents of the policy.[77] The only elected official of note credited with condemning the confinement at the time it was happening, Republican Governor Ralph Carr of Colorado, claimed that his defense of the men and women confined destroyed his political career. Yet Carr's actual record on the issue was mixed, and scholars have concluded that while Carr was correct about the political atmosphere in Colorado, he grossly exaggerated his record as a friend of the Japanese-Americans.[78] Few Americans of any affiliation outside of missionary circles opposed a policy that by the 1980s became so universally lamented that the US Congress then paid reparations to many of the families that had been confined, and those who did oppose the policy usually registered their opposition later than the missionary contingent.[79]

Missionary-connected Americans were strikingly overrepresented in supporting the people in the camps and helping them to find jobs and housing when they were released from captivity. Herbert Nicholson (1892–1983) quickly became one of the more ubiquitous of the allies of the Japanese Americans. He logged what he estimated at more than fifty thousand miles as he traveled from camp to camp delivering gifts from church groups, retrieving desired items left behind with the friends in the communities from which the Japanese Americans had been evacuated, and trying to facilitate their return to their homes. Nicholson had been a Quaker missionary to Japan for twenty-five years before 1940, when he took up residence in Pasadena. After the removal, he turned a local church with which he was affiliated into a warehouse to save and protect as many possessions of the Japanese Americans as he and his co-workers were able to salvage from the widespread looting that accompanied the evacuation. An exceptionally energetic organizer, Nicholson managed to get one hundred and fifty thousand letters sent to Assistant Secretary of War McCloy asking that the families of the Japanese American soldiers serving in uniform be released from the camps. After the war, Nicholson and his wife, Madeline, returned to Japan for another decade of service as missionaries.[80]

Nicholson worked out of Southern California, while other former missionaries and their allies ran a similar support operation out of Seattle. The Japanese Americans from the Seattle area were held for about six months in the nearby town of Puyallup before most of them were transferred to the Minidoka camp in the desert of southern Idaho. The US Army's public relations office gave the name "Camp Harmony" to the Western Washington Fair Grounds, a name that was widely used for the Puyallup facility even by those who objected to the entire confinement policy. The Seattle Council of Churches sent many volunteers to support the more than seven thousand Japanese Americans held there in structures designed for race horses and farm animals. The council employed a former Methodist missionary to Japan, Everett Thompson, to serve as the minister for the heavily Protestant population. Thompson and his wife, Zora, then moved to the Minidoka area to be near the Seattle Japanese Americans, and worked there for the remainder of the war. A handful of others from the Seattle support group did the same, including Margaret Peppers, who had been an Episcopalian missionary in the Philippines for more than a decade.[81]

The Japanese Americans at Minidoka and at many of the other camps "benefited from the experience of American missionaries who were forced to leave Japan or its occupied territories when the United States entered the war," writes Anne Michele Blankenship. In a detailed study of the Seattle support group, Blankenship found that the missionary-connected whites manifested what many of the Japanese Americans considered a "unique perspective on racial problems," markedly more generous than the more prejudiced outlook the Japanese Americans were accustomed to discerning in whites. The Seattle clergy and lay workers set up housekeeping in Twin Falls, the city closest to the Minidoka camp, and persuaded the military officials at the camp to allow frequent visits to their homes. Blankenship describes the atmosphere:

> The households [of the whites from Seattle] served as lodging houses, tea parlors and wedding chapels throughout the war. In a typical week, Minidoka's administrators issued shopping passes to three or four hundred incarcerees. . . . Military police or camp administrators drove Nikkei to town and picked them up at an appointed time, leaving them to conduct business without escorts. . . . Incarcerees shopping in town would frequently stop for a visit to talk about a particular problem or simply to enjoy the comfort of a normal home. . . . Youth groups of sixty or more descended on a pastor's house during outings. . . . [Incarcerees] got to leave camp, spend time in a real home, and receive special food and other treats.[82]

In this setting, one indefatigable minister's wife reported having entertained in her home an average of two hundred Japanese Americans per month throughout her years in Twin Falls. Her husband, Baptist minister Emery Andrews, performed the same errand-running tasks as Nicholson, working from Pasadena. Andrews, who had served as pastor of a Japanese American Baptist church in Seattle since 1929, drove back and forth to Seattle frequently. "Andrews determined that he traveled 151,413 miles, wrote 3,538 letters and attended 644 meetings during this time," Blankenship discovered in records Andrews had kept. Japanese Americans were overheard describing Andrew as "the ideal Christian missionary."[83]

Many West Coast whites did not want the Japanese Americans to return at all. Missionary son Van Harvey recalled how his Episcopalian family, then living in Merced, California, braved local opposition by welcoming into their home a Japanese family released from Manzanar.[84] Harry Kingman, who in 1945 was the West Coast regional head of the Fair Employment Practices Committee (FEPC), accompanied Harry Bridges to an important meeting of longshoremen. Bridges tried to persuade his members to welcome the returning Japanese American workers, thereby accepting the ruling of the FEPC that they do so. But the union members vehemently refused. When the otherwise popular Bridges defended

Japanese American laborers, he was actually booed by members of his own union.[85]

The War Relocation Authority (WRA) also worked extensively with professional anthropologists, many of whom they employed to assist in dealing with unrest among the prisoners. While generally opposed to racism, the anthropologists rarely criticized the racial basis of the confinement and often spoke of the episode as a helpful means by which the assimilation of the Japanese ethnic group into American society could be accelerated. Some even described the camps, as "model cities." They offered extensive praise to the WRA for providing a humane environment within the camps. Protest on the part of the incarcerated population was described as pathological. The most careful student of the role of anthropologists in the camps, Orin Starn, concludes that

> WRA anthropologists reformulated the classic Boasian axiom: instead of confronting power with truth, anthropology was to supply information to power. A fusion of administration and social science was the consequence. The people studied became objects of control and manipulation, and scientific methodology a means to the ends of government policy. The problem was not simply that anthropologists broke disciplinary taboos about mixing science and politics. In fact, WRA ethnographers were unequivocal in claiming neutrality and objectivity, as if their work had no political content.[86]

The missionary-saturated support groups also worked with WRA officials, to be sure, but in the frame of consistently articulated moral solidarity with the Japanese Americans and in the larger context of deep and well-articulated dissent from the confinement policy itself. The church workers sometimes refused to be housed in the Caucasian-only compounds where the government officials and the anthropologists lived. "We came to feel very uncomfortable living in separated and better conditions," recalled one Church of the Brethren teacher at Manzanar, who with her husband was eventually allowed to live in the barracks with the Japanese Americans.[87] The anthropologists "tended to represent internment as a process independent of federal control," Starn explains, taking place within a larger, longterm process of structural assimilation.[88]

One anthropologist who worked at Manzanar is something of a special case. Morris Opler ghost-wrote the legal briefs the Japanese American Citizens League submitted in the two important constitutional cases that addressed the confinement, *Korematsu* and *Hirabayashi*. He also vehemently disagreed, albeit privately, with the military leaders at the

Manzanar camp. Although Opler was an ally of the Japanese Americans, Starn observes that Opler "never published his oppositional views." For Starn, "Opler's silence exemplified the public role" that anthropologists accepted during the war, thus passively "validating" the whole confinement project despite "behind-the-scenes" opposition.[89]

In 1989, Elizabeth Colson, who had spent the war working the WRA at the Tule Lake Camp in Northern California, explained herself as follows: "I can only say that we regarded the internment as a gross violation of civil rights. But I thought then as I think now that witnesses were needed and that anthropologists had skills suited to that task."[90] If any professional anthropologist published a repudiation of the government's confinement policy while it was in effect, I have not found a record of it.

Distant from Fisher's California and from Moran's South Pacific, missionary-connected individuals in China were making history in very different ways. As diplomats and spies, they tried to make sense of the Chinese civil war and were then obliged to navigate American domestic politics. The following chapter explains how they came to be among the most famous of all the missionary-connected Americans, and how their own lives became the field in which much of modern America's political engagement with Asia's largest nation took place.

CHAPTER SEVEN

Telling the Truth about the Two Chinas

THE STORY of the "China Hands" is one of the great dramas of twentieth-century American political history. It unfolded in the context of wartime conflict between the Nationalist government of Chiang Kai-shek and the insurgency of the Communist Party led by Mao Zedong. Missionary-connected Americans were prominent players in this drama, which began when Pearl Harbor suddenly made China more important to the United States.

Chiang's government was then a military ally. The Foreign Service and the OSS maintained large contingents in China throughout the struggle against Japan, but their work was complicated by the reality of civil war. The Americans understood that both parties were maneuvering to defeat the other once the Japanese had been vanquished. The center of American operations was Chungking, the Nationalist capital after the Japanese had occupied coastal China. The Communists had their own capital in the northern city of Yenan. Chiang preferred that the Americans have nothing to do with Yenan, but the Americans saw the Communists as another military ally against the Japanese. Foreign Service officers who reported weaknesses of the Kuomintang and strengths of the Communists were later accused of undermining Chiang and facilitating the "loss" of China to Mao's forces in 1949. Four of these officers—two of whom were missionary sons—were dismissed in one of the McCarthy era's most notorious episodes. Eventually, the meaning of the affair came to be understood in terms expressed by J. Stapleton Roy, a missionary son too young to have participated in the events, but later an ambassador to the People's Republic of China. According to Roy, the purged China Hands

> saw clearly and accurately the corruption and decay in the Kuomintang government and military leadership. And they pulled no punches in reporting it even when this brought them into conflict with their superiors. They were right in doing so, because this was the factor more than any other that explained the inability of the Kuomintang government after World War II to use its superior man power and resources in the civil war against the communists.[1]

The two missionary sons central to this saga were John Paton Davies Jr. (1908–1999) and John S. Service (1909–1999). The other dismissed Foreign Service officers, O. Edmund Clubb and John Carter Vincent, are sometimes wrongly assumed to be missionary sons, too. While they were not, both were close enough to the missionary community to make this impression understandable. Clubb's daughter married a missionary son. Vincent toyed with the idea of becoming a Baptist missionary himself, before and even after he entered government service.

The careers of Davies and Service demand extended attention in any study of missionary-connected Americans. Their names are among the most recognizable of all the men and women who have ever served in the Foreign Service of the United States. Their two careers constitute another instance of the centrality of missions to the process by which Americans came to grips with modern Asia. Moreover, Davies and Service exemplify the greater sensitivity missionary cosmopolitans often showed to the promise of indigenous political movements not sponsored by the Western powers. This chapter also takes up the careers of other missionary-connected individuals who served the US government in relation to China, and explains how their fates were different from Davies's and Service's. How did the China Hands form their opinions, and how did the purge come to include Davies and Service and not others who shared their views of the Kuomintang?

Service was the first of the China Hands to be accused and the first to be dismissed. What happened to him affected what happened to Davies. I begin with Service.

In 1906, the YMCA sent Service's father to the interior city of Chengtu to open a Y station there. The town "was little different in appearance, amenities, and life style from a thousand years before," the son later recalled of the atmosphere of his childhood.[2] Service grew up in a religiously observant but theologically latitudinarian household of Northern Baptists.

"Both Mother and Father were religious liberals," Service observed; they believed that religion "was a matter of personal belief." No other missionary home in the Chinese interior of the 1920s was liberal enough to appreciate *Christian Century*, Service surmised in his unpublished autobiography. The coastal provinces were strongholds of the liberal missionaries, while the interior, even at Y stations, was more conservative. The *New Republic*, to which Service's proudly progressive mother was devoted, shaped his own "broader political horizons." All this made it easy for him, later on, to migrate into the secular modernity he encountered at Oberlin College, where, ironically, he was turned into an agnostic by the one course Oberlin required on religion. The assigned textbook was William James's *Varieties of Religious Experience*. It convinced him religion was not for him. Service was not sure what he wanted to do after college, but when he heard that his boyhood friend, Davies, had taken the Foreign Service exam and passed, Service decided to follow in his footsteps. He was sent to China in 1933 and quickly won the respect of colleagues for his skill with the Chinese language and his deep knowledge of Chinese society. In Shanghai in 1940, he distinguished himself by greatly increasing the number of Jewish refugees the local authorities were willing to accept.[3]

During the war, Service was posted to Chungking as political adviser to the American commander, Lt. General Joseph Stillwell.[4] Both Stillwell and Ambassador Clarence Gauss were frustrated by what they perceived as Chiang Kai-shek's unwillingness to commit his soldiers to greater engagement with the Japanese invaders. Chiang seemed to be saving his strength for an anticipated war against his Communist enemies. Stillwell and Gauss received credible reports that substantial quantities of the war material given to Chiang were being sold by warlords for profit to the Japanese, and that a disturbing number of Chiang's soldiers had deserted to join the Communists. Repeatedly, the Americans asked Washington if they could send a mission to Yenan, a step which Chiang vigorously opposed. Finally, in 1944, Washington approved.

Stillwell and Gauss had no doubt that Service was ideally suited to find out what was going on in the Communist capital. He had already been their liaison with Zhou Enlai and the other Communists who still maintained an office in Chungking. Indeed, Service got along with Zhou all too well from the point of view of Chiang, whose police kept a close watch on the Chungking Communists and their visitors. Accompanying Service on the "Dixie Mission," as the US station in Yenan was called because of the "rebel" character of the Communist camp, were more than a dozen US Army soldiers and several agents of the OSS.[5] The soldiers were under the command of Col. David Barrett, who had long been stationed in China and could speak Mandarin. Davies, who was then based in India as the State Department's head of operations throughout the China-Burma-India theater, had chosen OSS officers known to be independent of an existing OSS operation working out of Chungking that had been merged with the Kuomintang's secret police, led by the notorious Tai Li.[6] Davies and OSS Director William Donovan knew Tai Li's reputation for torture and double-dealing and preferred to have nothing to do with him.

Service went to Yenan at a point in his life when he was personally more invested in things Chinese than ever before. Two months before this trip, he began living with a prominent actress on the Chungking stage who had taken for herself the English name of Valentine. "I was in love with China and with the hopes and aspirations of my young intellectual friends," he told an interviewer while in his eighties. "It is not surprising perhaps that I made this more personal by falling in love with a Chinese woman." He wrote to his wife, Caroline, who was in the United States with the Services' two young children, and asked for a divorce. His friends in Chungking adjusted to Service's new living arrangements but warned him that "Val" was probably an agent of Tai Li's secret police or of the Communists. The FBI in later years promoted rumors that she was a Communist agent, but no evidence has ever emerged that she was. The affair soon ended, but when Service went to Yenan in 1944 he assumed his marriage was over and supposed that should the affair with Val cause the termination of his career in the Foreign Service, he would stay on in China as a journalist.[7]

From Yenan, Service's dispatches reported that the Communist capital could not be more different from Chungking. Service and other American diplomats in Chungking had long been troubled by what they perceived as Chiang's self-serving, corrupt associates and their cruel treatment of the populace and of military conscripts. But at Yenan, unity and shared sacrifice were everywhere, along with a hopeful, upbeat spirit. Service was impressed with the efficiency and cooperative practices of Mao's forces, and with the popular support those forces had won and retained in the surrounding region. Service was reminded of the student atmosphere of a religious college. During his several months in Yenan, Service collected evidence that the Communist forces were more numerous than suspected and controlled a much larger terrain than was realized. The Communists were eager to cooperate with the Americans in the war against the Japanese; Mao Zedong proved readily accessible and seemed to enjoy long talks about topics both light and weighty. He allowed unrestricted access to Japanese prisoners of war. Service reported with greater and greater confidence that the Communists would be useful military allies and that, simply by virtue of their demonstrated ability to garner and keep popular support, they were bound to be a much larger factor in China's future than American policy had taken into account. "Unless the Kuomintang goes as far as the Communists in political and economic reform," he warned, "the Communists will be the dominant force in China within a comparatively few years."[8]

As for Chiang, the generalissimo's "dealings with us have been an opportunistic combination of extravagant demands and unfulfilled promises, wheedling and bargaining, bluff and blackmail," Service reminded a sympathetic Stillwell, who was already fed up with the man he privately called "Peanut." It is a mistake, Service added, for the United States to continue "the hollow pretense that China is unified and that we can talk only to Chiang," because this conduct on the part of the United States "puts the trump card in Chiang's hands."[9] Service recommended that they provide direct and immediate military aid to Mao.

In fact, as recent scholarship has shown, Nationalist forces were somewhat more engaged against the Japanese than Service and the other Americans perceived at the time. Moreover, by asking the Chinese government to relinquish command of its own military, the Americans were asking more of Chiang than virtually any head of state could possibly agree to do.[10] But the Americans in Chungking were not wrong to suppose that greater cooperation with the Communists could be of real military value in the war against the Japanese, nor were these Americans mistaken in their perception that Chiang did not want Communist actions during the war to enable Mao to topple the Nationalists once the Japanese were defeated. The Americans were correct, also, to warn that the Kuomintang regime was slow to enact reforms that might increase the regime's popular support.

Service's awareness of the deeply nondemocratic character of Nationalist China undoubtedly made him see the Communists as moving in democratic directions, and has having a lot in common, spiritually, with Americans.[11] He also commented on the potential for ruthlessness he saw in Yenan. He recognized the Yenan Chinese as genuine Communists, unlike some in Washington who were calling the Yenan group "so-called" Communists.[12] Stanley Hornbeck and some others in the State Department found Service's perspective on the Communists to be naïve. But overall Service's dispatches played extremely well in Washington.[13] In the short run.

Gen. Patrick J. Hurley, whom Roosevelt liked personally and sent to troubleshoot the problematic relationship between Stillwell and Chiang, fell immediately into line with Service's basic outlook on the Communists. In a visit to Yenan in early November 1944, Hurley got along famously with Mao and enthusiastically accepted a detailed plan Mao presented for military cooperation with the Americans and the Nationalists. Hurley even endorsed Mao's proposal of a coalition government, in which the Communists would share power with the Nationalists. Hurley rewrote Mao's proposal to include lengthy quotations from the American Constitution and Lincoln's Gettysburg Address, presenting a united China as indeed democratic. Hurley made the Yenan Reds seem considerably more "American" than Service ever had or ever would.[14]

While Hurley was outdoing Service in his appreciation for the contributions the Communists were making to world democracy, Service himself was in Washington. Davies had sent him there in the hope that Service could generate a reconsideration of America's China policy. John Carter Vincent, who was Davies's and Service's State Department superior, encouraged Service to meet with journalists and politicians to share with them his understanding of what was happening in China. Service did exactly that, and in the meantime reconciled with his wife. Caroline gave birth to the Services' third child the following year, and the couple remained married until Caroline's death in 1997. Service's understanding of the situation in China did not change following the breakup with his Chinese mistress. He carried out his Washington rounds with the full support of his State Department superiors. Yet the reevaluation of the China policy that Vincent and Davies both desired did not take place. Many other things were moving rapidly in the late months of 1944.

Hurley did a total about-face when Chiang refused Mao's proposals and insisted on the Nationalist government's total control of any cooperation with the Communists. Having been effectively turned by the Kuomintang, Hurley refused from then on to go against Chiang, in whose hands he was suddenly willing to entrust China's democratic future. Roosevelt promoted Hurley from his personal representative to ambassador, replacing the frustrated and exhausted Gauss. Roosevelt also deferred to Chiang's demand that Stillwell be recalled. But even more indicative of the force fields in which Service was caught were two additional, portentous developments.[15]

For one, Roosevelt was well into the process of secretly writing off the military effort in China. He had decided to depend instead on an arrangement whereby the Soviet armies would assist the Allies in the Pacific, whose main assault on Japan would come from the islands rather than the mainland. Roosevelt in 1944 and early 1945 blithely allowed the somewhat chaotic diplomatic situation centered on Hurley to continue while privately looking beyond China for a military solution in the Pacific war, then expected to last well into 1946.[16] The second major development was equally secret, and in complete contradiction to the first. The newly arrived Gen. Albert Wedemeyer, Stillwell's successor, began to carry out on his own secret negotiations for American military aid to the Communists. Wedemeyer was impatient for the expected agreement between Mao and Chiang and acted on his own. His actions remained classified for many decades, and, under this convenient cover, he later undermined the China Hands when his testimony in their defense could have made a difference. Later, he gave aid and comfort to the John Birch Society. But in 1944 Wedemeyer's outlook was virtually identical to Service's. Indeed, he asked that Service be sent back to China, causing the State Department to drop its plans to send Service to Moscow to work with Harriman.[17]

Service's return to China in early 1945 coincided with yet more conflicting policy trajectories. While Hurley now forbade any cables to Washington that were in any way critical of the Kuomintang regime, Service in Yenan was engaged in the most intensive conversations yet with Mao, who was more eager than ever for an alliance with the United States. The Communist leader even wanted to fly to Washington to meet with Roosevelt, but neither he nor Service knew that a message Mao had sent through OSS channels asking for exactly this had been intercepted by Tai Li. The Kuomintang spymaster doctored the document, then showed it to Hurley as an example of how out of control the American conversations in Yenan had gotten.[18] Service's dispatches became more urgent and prescriptive: he recommended the "Tito option," the pluralistic approach to warfare against the Axis being implemented in Yugoslavia, where the Communist leader Josef Tito was a recognized ally in the struggle against the retreating *Wehrmacht*. Frankly advocating a "two Chinas" policy, Service insisted that if the United States supported Chiang's government "to the exclusion of the Communists, disunity will be stimulated and the consequences will be disastrous."[19]

Service managed to get this particular, very important cable approved by the other State Department officers in Chungking and by Hurley's own chief of staff, Gen. Mervin Gross. Service sought their protection because he knew he was going further than ever before. Upon receiving this cable in Washington, Acting Secretary of State Joseph Grew found it reasonable enough and sent it on to the president with a favorable cover note. Roosevelt, of course, unbeknownst to Service and Wedemeyer, was no longer paying attention. But Hurley, who happened to be visiting Washington, was most attentive, and exploded when Vincent showed him the dispatch. Hurley recognized Service's hand in it, and told Vincent that he would "get that son-of-a bitch if it is the last thing I do."[20]

Meanwhile, Tai Li again managed to penetrate the secrecy of the Americans. He found out that Wedemeyer and the OSS were pressing for more military cooperation with the Communists without informing Chiang. Wedemeyer was deeply embarrassed and lied to Chiang, claiming falsely that he knew no details. He fired Chief of Staff Gross, countermanded Dixie Commander Barrett's provisionally approved promotion to brigadier general, and began what turned out to be a drift toward his eventual public denial that he had ever viewed the Chinese Communists in the same terms that Service did. The apoplectic Hurley replaced the entire Foreign Service staff in Chungking with new officers, few of whom could speak or read Chinese. He demanded that Service be recalled, which he promptly was. When Service left Yenan on April 4, 1945, he had no idea why he was being recalled, that this would be his last visit there, or that it would be twenty-seven years before any diplomat of the United States would again have direct contact with the Chinese Communists.

Service was also unaware of what awaited him in Washington. At first it was pretty much as before. Vincent urged Service to make the rounds of journalists again, to explain what was happening in China. From the middle of April though early June, Service was an animated presence in Washington and New York, expanding the circle of communication he had developed the previous fall. He did not know that the FBI was following him in relation to a series of illegal raids agents had made at the *Amerasia* office adjacent to the Institute of Pacific Relations, where they found copies of hundreds of classified documents, including many written by Service himself.

The FBI knew on the basis of illegal wiretaps that *Amerasia* editor Phillip Jaffe was a regular source for Soviet agent Joseph Bernstein.[21] Service was one of a number of government employees who had frequented the IPR office, although Service had not met Jaffe until Jaffe sought him out in mid-April. But the FBI, following up on their discovery of the classified documents in the *Amerasia* office, listened illegally to Service's conversations with Jaffe. On June 6, the FBI arrested Service, Jaffe, and several other journalists and government employees. This was a press sensation, but federal prosecutors, finding that they had very little evidence of espionage, soon reduced the charges to the lightweight crime of stealing of government property. Many people, including most of the press, began to wonder if this might not be such a big deal, after all.[22]

The State Department knew that there was no case against Service. There was no evidence then, nor has any ever been discovered, that Service had any inkling of Jaffe's connection to Soviet intelligence. Davies, then posted in Moscow, sent a six-page personal letter to Raymond E. Ludden, his colleague in the Far Eastern Division, describing in detail how documents were classified, and explaining the standard procedures for sharing information with journalists. "What about all of the other officials in Washington and elsewhere who have done the same" as Service did, he asked? Davies also reminded Ludden of the poisoned atmosphere surrounding the Kuomintang and provided evidence of Hurley's animosity.[23]

A unanimous grand jury refused to indict Service. There was no proof that the relevant documents had reached the *Amerasia* office though his hands. Service was able to explain that he had classified many of the documents himself, and only for technical reasons. Nevertheless, during the month between his arrest and grand jury's vote, FBI Director J. Edgar Hoover leaked suspicious bits of information to right-wing journalists and spread the word that Service had been saved by higher-ups in Washington. Hurley announced his resignation as ambassador in a vitriolic press conference attacking career officers of the Foreign Service for sabotaging his efforts to bring political unity to China. Hurley then testified to the same effect before the Senate Foreign Relations Committee. The rebuttal testimonies of George Kennan and the new Secretary of State James Byrnes were highly effective in discrediting Hurley, but Hoover kept encouraging conservative congressmen to believe the worst about Service and those who stood by him.

In this context, the State Department was afraid to post Service anywhere in Asia, and sent him instead to New Zealand. But this was only the beginning. The State Department issued a White Paper designed to douse the political fires with facts about what had actually happened in China, but its chief effect was to create more headlines about the "loss" of China. Hurley blasted the White Paper as an "alibi for the pro-Communists in the State Department who have engineered the overthrow of our ally." Hurley and others demanded to know why the officials arrested in the *Amerasia* case of 1945 "were white-washed and released." Republican Congressman Walter Judd, about whom I have more to say below, read into the *Congressional Record* some of Service's 1944 dispatches containing negative comments about the Kuomintang, treating these comments as indisputable proof of the Foreign Service's treachery. Judd complained that Service had been promoted by the State Department even though his apparent crimes "were hushed up under circumstances never disclosed or explained." The FBI was hard at work. In 1949 alone the Bureau produced for various recipients seven investigative reports on Service.[24]

When Senator Joseph McCarthy delivered his epoch-defining speech in Wheeling, West Virginia, early in 1950, Service was his exhibit A of the "traitors" he alleged were in the State Department at that moment. "Please remember that name, ladies and gentlemen," McCarthy said of "this man Service."[25] Service testified compellingly before the Senate committee, led by Maryland Senator Millard E. Tydings, that was assigned to assess McCarthy's allegations. The Tydings committee resoundingly vindicated Service, and savaged McCarthy for "deliberate and willful falsehoods." But Tydings was unseated in the next election and, in the tense atmosphere of 1950, the Tydings inquiry served more to publicize the charges against Service than to discredit them.

Simultaneously with the Tydings Committee hearings, Service was called before the State Department's own Loyalty Security Board. This body's inquiries were very different from a grand jury. No legal charges were at issue, and no rules of evidence prevented a discussion of the by then widely leaked stories of Service's conversations with Jaffe. Davies testified in defense of Service, explaining the well-established practice of relying on some documents that were technically classified while briefing journalists "on background."[26] After four weeks of hearings, the board found no cause to question Service's loyalty. But irate Republican politicians and conservative journalists kept up a stream of accusations, leading the board to open the case again and receive yet more information from the FBI. The State Department's Loyalty Security Board again found in favor of Service. But that was not the end of it.

Because of the case's extraordinary importance, the Loyalty Review Board of the Civil Service Commission decided to hold its own hearing. Along the way, this body, having been repeatedly told that it was not vigorous enough in finding the security risks among government employees, asked that its charge be altered. Earlier, the board was tasked with determining if there were reasonable grounds for finding disloyalty. The new charge enabled it to find only that there was any reasonable doubt whatsoever about someone's loyalty.[27] The Civil Service Commission's Loyalty Review Board eventually ruled that there was "reasonable doubt" about Service's loyalty. Even so, Secretary of State Dean Acheson did not want to dismiss Service. He took the matter to Truman, who told him that Service simply had to go. Neither the president nor the secretary of state had read the actual reports of any of the proceedings. In late December 1951, Acheson dismissed Service.[28]

Six years later, the US Supreme Court invalidated Service's termination. The court found, in *Service v. Dulles*, that Acheson had violated the State Department's own regulations in deferring to the Civil Service Commission's Loyalty Review Board.[29] Now exonerated once and for all, he thought, Service returned to duty in the Foreign Service. But Dulles's State Department was unwilling to locate the experienced China Hand in any job more interesting than the consulate of Liverpool, England. Service soon resigned and moved to Berkeley, California, where he became a senior staff employee of the Center for Chinese Studies at the University of California campus from which both of his parents had graduated before going to China. Service became an antiwar activist during the Vietnam era.

During those years in Berkeley, Service, like the retired William Eddy in Beirut, brooded self-critically about what he had done. Had he "gone native," one interviewer asked him in 1977, and identified too strongly with the Communists that so impressed him in 1944? Service replied that he had "tried hard to avoid" this fate in Yenan, but it was a struggle. He and the others in the Dixie Mission did wait until they'd been on site awhile before drawing conclusions. But the atmosphere was simply amazing, and all the more so to those who knew China as well as he did. Yenan had a very strong impact, especially if one was coming from Chungking:

> The confidence that we ran into, the difference in the morale, esprit, this was something that hit us right away. The ways things got done. If you asked for things, yes, they said they'd do it, and it was done, promptly, in fact, efficiently. In Chungking nothing was efficient. Nothing seemed to work and everything took a long time.

Service told his interviewer that his old friend C. Martin Wilbur, whom he had known growing up in the missionary community of China and who was also an Oberlin graduate, warned him even in 1945 that he was becoming too much of an advocate for the Communist side in the Chinese internal conflict. Wilbur, who became a prominent professor of Chinese history at Columbia University, always remained less critical of the Kuomintang than Service, and more skeptical of the Communists. But Wilbur defended Service's integrity and remained his devoted friend throughout the lifetimes of the two missionary sons. Wilbur had identified "a real danger," Service acknowledged in the interview of 1977.[30]

Two decades later, Service admitted to his biographer that, as a diplomat, he had shown "too much zeal" and overreacted when his proposals were rejected by his government. "I had become very much involved" with China, and this feeling "probably compromised my impartiality."[31] Service saw in the Communists of Yenan something he liked, and of which he had seen absolutely nothing in the company of the Kuomintang: the feeling of a missionary community. "The Communists," he wrote in his memoir, were also "missionaries" of a kind, "and had no doubts that their mission would succeed."[32] Service often compared his own labors in the Foreign Service to his father's work in the mission field, just as Eddy described his own career as an extension of his family's. Service carried this even to the point of reflecting on neglected family responsibilities: I am a bit like "my father," he mused in the 1977 interview, "devoting himself to the interests of the YMCA and to China over the interests of the family, his staying out in China when he really should have come home on home leave."[33]

In none of these pensive reflections did Service imply that his critics had been justified in faulting him as they did. But he admitted that he and his colleagues missed the fact that the Communists were playing a game rather like Chiang's:

> We took too much at face value some of the things the Communists were saying. I think we didn't realize that they were stalling and playing for time, in much the same way the Kuomintang was. It just happened that they strengthened themselves by expanding and taking more territory when they could. They weren't really fighting as wholehearted a war against the Japanese perhaps as we thought.[34]

Service lived until the age of ninety but, like Eddy, died before he finished his memoirs. Davies, however, managed to complete his own memoirs, *China Hand*, covering his life through the year 1950. This book was not published until 2012, thirteen years after Davies's death at the age of ninety-one. It is one of the most firmly written and carefully detailed of any of the memoirs written by missionary children in any walk of adult life. Davies admits to some of the same blind spots mentioned by Service. Davies, too, allowed that in 1944 and 1945 he had "underestimated the commitment of the Chinese Communist ruling party . . . to ideology and the dexterity with which Mao and company manipulated it." In keeping with that error, Davies had probably exaggerated the potential of an alliance with the Communists. Had the United States responded to Mao's overtures and signaled that he had friends outside China other than the Soviets, things might have been different, but might not.[35]

Davies's perspective on the missionary project itself was less generous than Service's, and considerably more skeptical than Eddy's. Christian missions "did much to shatter a civilization that had endured for millennia," he observed at the end of his 1972 book about American-Chinese relations. Davies acknowledged that some good came from some things missionaries did, but overall he felt the missionary project was a failure. "The western businessmen, missionaries, and educators" had failed in their efforts to "modernize and Christianize" China, just as the Japanese had failed to conquer it militarily. So, too, had the American government failed in trying to "democratize and unify" China, as had the "Soviet rulers who tried to insinuate control over it failed."[36] I am not aware that Davies ever had any contact with John Hersey, but Davies ended up with a resigned and rueful perspective similar to Hersey's as expressed in *The Call*.

Davies's career-defining frustration with the imperative to view China in patronizing and pro-Kuomintang terms began at the same place as Service's. Davies was born a year earlier in the same Chengtu missionary compound, the son of Baptist missionaries more conservative and evangelically inclined than Service's parents. But Davies became a religious skeptic early on, enduring the ritual of baptism as an adolescent to please his parents but soon enamored of the *American Mercury* and its notoriously anti-religious editor H. L. Mencken. College experiences at the University of Wisconsin, where he was inspired by the ethically intense liberal educator Alexander Meiklejohn, and later at Columbia, moved him further into a confident secularism.

Reflecting years later on the various strands in his education, Davies connected his father's Protestant witness with secular lines of Epictetus to which Meiklekjohn introduced him. The old Baptist missionary John Paton Davies, Sr. admitted in a letter to his post-Protestant son in Madison that he, the career evangelist, might have been wrong about just what God was asking of him, but he declared to the youth that "I must obey the light I have, and not only walk in this way but also try to induce others to do the same." Meanwhile, Epictetus invoked for the younger Davies an ancient hero who refused to be silent even when his emperor was obliged to slay him for speaking prohibited lines that the hero took to be true. "You will do your part, and I will mine," the hero says to the sovereign. "It is yours to kill and mine to die intrepid; yours to banish, mine to depart untroubled." How could such a solitary witness do any good? Epictetus explains that it was the same good that purple does to a garment: "to be beautiful in itself, and to give examples of beauty to others."[37] Characteristically, Davies found the moral intensity of the Protestant missionary tradition of greater value when linked in this way to the moral intensity of pagans.

As a junior officer in the Foreign Service, Davies quickly developed a reputation for telling emperors—his superiors in the US government— exactly what he thought, whether they wanted to hear it or not. Nobody appreciated this quality more than Gen. Stillwell, to whose staff he was sent early in 1942 as a political adviser, but plenty of Davies's auditors, including Chiang Kai-shek and Patrick Hurley, were displeased by this in- dependence. Davies was called to assist Stilwell just when the general took command of the China-Burma-India theater. By then Davies had experi- enced nearly a decade of postings in Kunming, Beijing, and other Chinese cities, as well as time on the State Department staff in Washington. In his new post, Davies travelled extensively through the CBI region, getting to know Stillwell in Chungking while dealing also with political and military figures in India and Burma, including B. R. Ambedkar, Mohandas Gandhi, and Louis Mountbatten. Davies became an early advocate of contact with the Communists, and a forthright analyst of Kuomintang administration and governance. In a long dispatch of June 1943, more than a year before he was able to send his friend Service to Yenan, Davies wrote that the Communists were winning more and more of the country to their side while Chiang Kai-shek remained "a political hostage to the corrupt system which he manipulates." Not since 1938, he complained, had any American official or military representative visited the Communist- controlled re- gions of China.[38]

Once the Dixie Mission was in place, Davies visited it twice in the fall of 1944 and had confirmed for himself the dynamism and eagerness to cooperate with the United States that Service had reported. Davies's own dispatches predicted that civil war would follow the expulsion of the Japanese, and that the Kuomintang could not win without "foreign inter- vention on a scale equal to the Japanese invasion of China." Davies thought his superiors appallingly naïve about how much American aid it would take to keep Chiang in power. "The Communists are in China to stay," he said bluntly. "China's destiny is not Chiang's, but theirs." Yet as a practical matter the United States "should not now abandon Chiang Kai-shek," he added, because keeping Chiang in the war against the Japanese served American interests. This was a temporary expedient. "We must not indef- initely underwrite a politically bankrupt regime."[39]

Davies also found Washington slow to appreciate how different American interests were from those of the British. Davies had extensive ex- perience dealing with Mountbatten and other British leaders. Davies's tren- chant critique of imperialism takes his story importantly beyond Service's and fits a pattern of anticolonialism found in many other missionary sons,

Missionary son Henry Luce (1898–1967), shown here with his second wife, ambassador Claire Booth Luce, was the most successful magazine publisher in American history. His essay of 1941, "The American Century," asked that the United States become a "Good Samaritan" to the world. Photo by George Karger/The LIFE Picture Collection/Getty Images.

Missionary daughter Pearl Buck (1892–1973) allegedly did more to affect Western ideas about China than anyone since Marco Polo. Her *The Good Earth* enabled American readers to appreciate the basic human qualities of Chinese people. She is shown here receiving the Nobel Prize for Literature from the king of Sweden in 1938. Courtesy of the Pearl Buck Foundation.

Pictured here as a war correspondent, John Hersey (1914–1993) was born to missionary parents in China and became a prolific writer. He was best known for *Hiroshima*, his extraordinary account of how people on the ground experienced the atomic bomb. Courtesy of Associated Press.

Margaret (1903–1993) and Kenneth (1903–1993) Landon were missionaries in
Thailand before becoming influential figures in the United States during
the 1940s. Kenneth served the government during World War II as an
expert on Southeast Asia, while Margaret wrote *Anna and the King of
Siam*, the bestseller which became the basis for *The King and I*.
Courtesy of Wheaton College Archives and Special Collections.

Often called "the American Lawrence of Arabia," Col. William Eddy (1896–1962) served as translator for both President Franklin D. Roosevelt and King Ibn Saud of Saudi Arabia at their meeting of 1945. Born in Lebanon to missionary parents, Eddy was one of the most valuable agents of the Office of Strategic Services. Courtesy of National Archives and Records Administration.

Shown here in his official portrait as president of the City College of New York, Buell G. Gallagher (1904–1978) distinguished himself as a writer and activist who opposed racist practices and institutions throughout the United States. Although never a missionary, his major book, *Color and Conscience*, was a distillation of what he had learned from missionaries. Courtesy of the City College of New York.

Robert Goheen (1919–2008) was born to missionary parents in India, where he later served as the US ambassador. Goheen was a distinguished classical scholar before becoming president of Princeton University, the role in which he is pictured here. Courtesy Princeton University.

Former missionary Ruth Harris (1920–2013) inspired many young white people to devote their energies to the civil rights Movement. Beginning in 1955, she led a series of interracial church youth conferences. Courtesy of Pat Patterson.

One of the legendary "China Hands" wrongly blamed for the defeat of Chiang Kai-shek, missionary son John Paton Davies Jr., is shown here in Yenan in 1944 in the company of Zhou Enlai, Mao Zedong, and other Communist leaders. Courtesy of Tiki Davies.

Another of the State Department officers purged
during the McCarthy era, John S. Service,
missionary son, had the pleasure in 1972
of renewing his acquaintance with Zhou
Enlai, with whom he is shown here.
Courtesy of the Service family.

Rosamond Frame (1917–1960) was
a resourceful agent of the Office
of Strategic Services, known for
her ability to converse in nine
Mandarin dialects. She directed
an extensive network of anti-
Japanese activists while reporting
to the OSS on the activities of
Chiang Kai-shek's inner circle.
Courtesy of Pierre de Saint Phalle.

W. Norman Brown (1892–1975) was
the prototypical academic "empire
builder." A missionary son from
India, Brown began as a Sanskrit
specialist but gradually expanded
his interests to the entirety of
South Asian history and culture.
Courtesy of the University
of Pennsylvania.

Shown here with Chinese Nationalist President Sun Yat-sen, Sherwood Eddy (1871–1963) was an indefatigable organizer and lecturer for the YMCA. Under the leadership of Eddy and John R. Mott, the YMCA downplayed doctrinal and liturgical differences between denominations. Courtesy of Duke University Libraries.

Lt. Col. Sherwood Moran (1885–1983), shown here with his back to the camera while interrogating a Japanese POW on Guadalcanal, spent twenty-six years as a missionary in Japan before volunteering his services to the US Marine Corps. Moran had great success in extracting information from POWs, whom he insisted should be treated as "brothers." Courtesy of Oberlin College Library, Special Collections.

Margaret Flory (1914–2009) held the official title "missionary at large" in the Presbyterian Church. Although she served abroad (in Japan) only briefly, she was a central figure in missionary support organizations and in promoting the civil rights movement. Courtesy of Yale Divinity Library, Special Collections.

This is the Office of Strategic Services identity card of Duncan Lee (1913–1988), a missionary son from China. Although he became a conservative business executive following the war, it was revealed after his death that in 1943 he had provided Soviet intelligence with classified information from the OSS office in Washington. Courtesy of John Lee.

Shown here teaching a class at Harvard University, Edwin O. Reischauer (1910–1990) was the most influential of the many missionary children and former missionaries who developed the study of Asia in American universities after World War II. In the 1960s he served as ambassador to Japan, the country of his birth. Courtesy of Harvard University Archives.

Historian and diplomat E. H. Norman (1909–1957) was born in Japan to Canadian missionaries. He falsely assured his government that he had never been a member of the Communist Party. He took his own life while serving as ambassador to Egypt when he learned that the truth about his past was about to be discovered. Courtesy of University of British Columbia Special Collections.

Top left: Here shown with Bayard Rustin, with whom he was a co-founder of the Congress of Racial Equality, missionary son George Houser (1916–2015) was an antiracist activist in many settings. In 1947, he and Rustin led the first "freedom ride," in which an interracial group rode busses in two Jim Crow states. Courtesy Congress of Racial Equality.

Top right: Harry Kingman (1892–1982), shown here on a baseball card, quit the New York Yankees to go to China as a YMCA leader. He had been born there as a son of missionaries, and is the only major league baseball player to this day to have been born in China.

Bottom left: As editor of the chief periodical of the Protestant missionary community in China, *The Chinese Recorder*, Frank Rawlinson (1871–1937) stirred up controversy by voicing liberal ideas. He was experiencing profound doubts about the missionary enterprise when he was killed by a bomb during the Japanese invasion. Courtesy of Yale University Divinity School.

Bottom right: Harvard philosopher William Ernest Hocking (1873–1966) was the chief author of *Re-Thinking Missions*, a church-commissioned report recommending that the primary activity of missionaries should become social service instead of preaching. Courtesy of Shady Hill School.

Japan-born missionary son Edmund D. Soper (1876–1961) emerged in the 1940s as a premier theorist of missions and a forceful critic of racism. His *Philosophy of the Christian World Mission* recast the missionary project in terms of greater respect for indigenous peoples. His *Racism: A World Issue* connected racism in the United States to white supremacy throughout the globe. Courtesy of Ohio Wesleyan University Historical Collection.

Shown here speaking to the Chinese Communist encampment at Yenan in 1937, T. A. Bisson (1900–1979) was one of his era's leading East Asian experts. Although never a Communist, this former missionary teacher's associations with Communists sidelined his career during the McCarthy era. Courtesy of University of Maine Archives.

In his book of 1955, *Encounter with Revolution*, Richard Shaull (1919–2002) declared on the basis of his experience as a missionary in Latin America that Christianity required political action to help the oppressed populations of the world. He was later recognized as a prophet of "Liberation Theology." Courtesy of Princeton Theological Seminary.

China-born missionary daughter Molly Yard (1912–2005), shown here in conversation with fellow activists, devoted herself to pro-labor and antiracist causes before becoming president of the National Organization of Women in 1987. Courtesy of the Pittsburgh Post-Gazette.

Dressed here in the Indian manner he often preferred, E. Stanley Jones (1884–1973) argued that all cultures should be encouraged to develop their own versions of the Christian faith. He was the world's most famous missionary after the celebrated Alsatian surgeon, Albert Schweitzer. Courtesy of Asbury Theological Seminary.

A classic example of the missionary transition from conversion to service activities, Frank Laubach (1884–1970) left the mission field in the Philippines to become his generation's leading promoter of literacy. He is credited with helping several million people to read. Courtesy of Historical Images.

Grace Hutchins (1885–1969) was a missionary teacher in China before becoming a writer for the Communist Party of the United States. She focused on the injustices suffered by women and by African Americans. Courtesy of University of Oregon Special Collections.

Republican Congressman Walter Judd (1898–1994) was largely responsible for ending the "white only" proviso that had long prevented Asian immigrants from becoming naturalized US citizens. Before his election to Congress, Judd was a missionary physician in China. Courtesy of Hoover Institution Archives.

including William Eddy, and, as taken up in the next chapter, Kenneth Landon of the State Department's Southeast Asian desk. "The resurrection of British Empire in Asia may be said to lie outside the scope of our mission," Davies wrote. The Americans should be wary of the "subjugation, exploitation, privilege, and force" entailed by imperial rule, and should expect that colonized peoples will look "to any nation or group of nations" that will assist them in changing their condition for the better.[40]

Davies's tense relationship with British commander Mountbatten concerning issues of empire added to the pressure in Washington to have Davies recalled. Chiang and Hurley very much wanted this. Shortly after these same parties had succeeded in getting Stillwell recalled, they succeeded with Davies. Hurley accused the departing Davies to his face of being a Communist. He vowed, in the presence of Wedemeyer, to get Davies fired from the Foreign Service.[41] In January 1945 Davies was transferred to the US embassy in Moscow to work with Ambassador Harriman.

Davies's closest co-worker in Moscow was George Kennan, with whose classic "cold war" analysis of the Soviet Union as an expansionist power Davies agreed. Kennan would later defend Davies in the face of loyalty inquiries. By then Davies and Kennan were both back in Washington, working on the State Department's Policy Planning Staff. All along, Davies's dispatches and memoranda had stressed the importance of preventing China from becoming a Soviet satellite. Rather than acquiescing in the flourishing of China under Soviet influence through the ideology of Communism, as Davies was later accused of doing, Davies had looked for ways the United States could have its own relationship with what would surely become a Communist China.[42]

But Davies, while in no way connected with the *Amerasia* imbroglio, was caught up in the political dynamics of the era, and underwent eight security investigations between 1948 and 1953. None were as sensational as Service's, and all resulted in findings in Davies's favor, much to the consternation of his enemies. Along the way, O. Edmund Clubb was forced to accept early retirement in 1952, and in 1953 John Carter Vincent was dismissed for disloyalty, chiefly on the grounds that "throughout the period when it was the declared and established policy of the Government of the United States to support Chiang Kai-shek's Government," Vincent had instead offered "studied praise of Chinese Communists and equally studied criticism of the Chiang Kai-shek Government."[43]

The investigations of Davies were kept going by advice he had given to the CIA in 1949. Asked if he thought some of the folks he knew might be enlisted to find out what was happening in the councils of the new regime in China, Davies obliged by listing people whom he thought had good contacts in those circles. He named journalists Edgar Snow and Agnes Smedley, and Harvard historian John K. Fairbank. But one of the CIA officers later leaked news of this advice to Senator McCarran and others, who claimed it was evidence that Davies had tried to bring Communist sympathizers into the government of the United States.[44] The State Department's Loyalty Security Board held more hearings, and finally in 1954 the decision was against him. He was offered a chance to resign, but instead he insisted on a meeting with Dulles himself. The secretary of state dismissed him to his face.[45]

"If I were ever in deep trouble," the radio and TV newsman Eric Sevareid told his national radio audience after Davies's dismissal was announced that "the man I would want to be with" was John Paton Davies Jr. Sevareid met Davies during the war. The two had parachuted into a Burmese jungle when the plane carrying them and several others crashed. In the character-revealing ordeal that followed, Davies showed the qualities that led Sevareid to say that of all the men he had ever known, Davies was "more the whole man" than any other, the one most complete "in modesty and thoughtfulness, in resourcefulness and steady strength of character."[46]

Such testimonials were not enough to live on, especially with a growing family. Davies returned to Peru and began a new career as a furniture maker. He and his wife and seven children later moved back to Washington and then to Spain, and finally back to the United States, where Davies lived in North Carolina until his death in 1999. During these decades he wrote *Dragon by the Tail*, his history of Chinese-American relations from 1931 to 1945, and worked on his memoirs, *China Hand*. His security clearance was restored in 1969 and he experienced the same vindication in the early 1970s as his fellow victims.

What happened to Davies is cast into bold relief by an incident involving Dulles shortly before Dulles dismissed Davies. Dulles was at a diplomatic meeting in Geneva where he encountered another American missionary son. Chester Ronning (1894–1984) was born in China to American Lutheran missionaries. But shortly after his mother died in 1907, Ronning's grieving father accepted a pastorate on the Alberta prairie and took up Canadian citizenship for himself and all seven of his children. Son Chester was a full-fledged Canadian when he began his diplomatic career, taking his Chinese language skills and deep engagement with China into the Canadian rather than the American Foreign Service. In Geneva in 1954, Ronning, as a representative of Canada, happened to be walking a few steps behind Dulles when the two encountered the Chinese representative Zhou Enlai, who put out his hand. Dulles refused to shake it. But Ronning hastily took Zhou's hand and shook it firmly, in a gesture Zhou never forgot. Ronning watched in dismay as Davies and others he knew in the United States were being victimized while he, even as an avowed leftist who had run for office in Alberta as a socialist, was enjoying a successful career as a Canadian diplomat.[47]

Many of the US China Hands managed to escape the purges. How so?

Robert W. Barnett (1912–1997) who, like Service, was the son of a YMCA leader in China, narrowly escaped likely dismissal after Senators McCarran and McCarthy discovered that he had been active in the Institute of Pacific Relations and was thick with the whole cast of characters then thought to be subversive. Barnett's opinions were essentially those of his old friend Service, but during the crucial late years of the war Barnett had been attached to the pro-Chiang Gen. Claire Chennault in Chungking. Barnett had far fewer occasions to be on record the way Service had, but after the war he spent several years in Washington as the State Department's officer for economic affairs in China. McCarthy, in a speech on the Senate floor in 1951, named Barnett as a Communist. Barnett survived five hours of grilling by the McCarran Committee, which he later compared to living a scene from Dostoevsky. His superiors took the heat off him by transferring him to a division of the State Department dealing with the economic affairs of Europe, and then posting him to France and Luxembourg.[48]

Barnett's friend and fellow missionary son William Lockwood (1906–1978) also narrowly escaped. He had served briefly in the OSS before being transferred to the Foreign Service. McCarthy and McCarran discovered that Lockwood had been active in the Institute for Pacific Relations, and indeed had coedited *Amerasia* with Jaffe. But Lockwood was lucky enough to get a job offer from Princeton University, to which he decamped. Lockwood later expressed gratitude to Princeton for having supported him at a time when the absence of such support from a major academic employer might have been fatal to his career.[49]

William Gleysteen (1926–2002) was another Foreign Service officer with views highly critical of Chiang Kai-shek. He was born in China to Presbyterian missionary parents and interned by the Japanese during much of the war. While never close to being purged, he was long under suspicion. When posted to the Nationalists' post-revolutionary capital of Taipei, Gleysteen was transferred from political to consular duties because of his view of Chiang's government. His brother, Culver, also posted to

Taipei, was pointedly asked by his superiors if he was "a Red."[50] William Glysteen survived and had a distinguished career as ambassador to Korea and Indonesia. Arthur Hummell Jr. (1920–2001), a future ambassador to the People's Republic of China, was yet another missionary son who served in the Foreign Service. He said he escaped the McCarthyites because he was "too small a fish." But he was surely helped by the fact that, upon escaping from a Japanese POW camp in 1944, the guerilla army he happened to fall in with was loyal to the Kuomintang instead of the Communists. It could easily have gone the other way.[51] Missionary son Armistead Lee (1916–1998), a brother of the Duncan Lee discussed later in this chapter, was slated for a posting in Chungking in 1948, but the American ambassador to New Zealand was determined to keep Lee in Auckland. So, Lee missed "being blamed for the loss of China."[52]

Edward E. Rice and Everett F. Drumright were not missionary-connected, but their destiny illustrates the contingencies of the McCarthy era as it applied to all China Hands. Rice had the good fortune of postings that put him beyond the cross hairs of the China Lobby's artillery. Stationed in Chungking along with Service in 1944, Rice asked to go on the Dixie Mission. But Ambassador Gauss insisted on keeping Rice around to monitor the Kuomintang. "So that's what I did," he later recalled, "and that's how, solely by being lucky, I survived the purge."[53] Drumright was, like Rice, kept in Kuomintang territory during the war. Some of his reports on the state of Chiang's military were as uncomplimentary as those posted by his colleagues, but Drumright was not always critical of Chiang and this seems to have been the basis for his survival.[54]

John Leighton Stuart (1876–1962) was a somewhat special case. As the US ambassador to Nationalist China starting in 1946, Stuart was obliged to deal with Chiang Kai-shek constantly. Stuart endlessly nagged his fellow Christian Chiang for democratic reforms of the same sort advocated by the younger China Hands, but Stuart was more patient. "Stuart treated Chiang like a promising but wayward student," write two historians who have studied Stuart's dispatches with great care; he spoke with Gen. George Marshall as if Marshall was Chiang's "exasperated parent."[55] Although Stuart often advocated cooperation with the Communists, his formulations remained sufficiently general to enable the Kuomintang to put up with his talk of Chinese unity under the noble principles of Sun Yat-sen, whom Stuart had known well during Stuart's long tenure as the president of Yenching University. "Even as Ambassador," observes a historian sympathetic to him, "Stuart saw himself in a continuing missionary role, dreaming of a peaceful, united, progressive China, helped by the

United States."[56] Stuart finally gave up on the Kuomintang's ability to lead China and asked Washington for permission to meet directly with Mao and Zhou. But Truman, even after his electoral victory in 1948, was unwilling to allow such high-level official contact with the Communists. By the time Stuart was recalled in 1949, he had begun to sound more like his younger colleagues, but he attracted few complaints from the China Lobby. He had stayed the course with Chiang long enough to escape censure.[57]

Beyond the Foreign Service, a number of missionary-connected China Hands made their marks in the OSS and later in the CIA. Prominent among these was Rosamond Frame (1917–1960). Born and raised in China as the daughter of missionary educators, Frame was held in awe by her co-workers for her fluency in nine Mandarin dialects. Her mother was the Congregationalist Alice Browne Frame, long-time dean of Yenching Women's College.[58] The elder Frame was known for her refusal to leave China at the time of the Japanese invasion. The widowed Alice Browne Frame managed for four years to avoid capture and internment by the Japanese, then returned to the United States in 1941 to become president of Mt. Holyoke College but died of cancer before her inauguration. Daughter Rosamond became one of Gen. Donovan's most trusted operatives in Chunking and Kunming, supervising networks of Chinese who engaged in sabotage behind Japanese lines and who disseminated false and morale-undermining news reports among the occupying Japanese troops. From endless rounds of social events, Frame gleaned helpful information from dance partners who were in Chiang Kai-shek's diverse and factionalized governing elite. By switching dialects within a conversation, she was able to tell whether someone was likely to be truthful about exactly where they had been born and raised. This enabled the OSS to better assess the trustworthiness of Chiang's personnel. During a posting in New Delhi, Frame and another female agent infiltrated Chiang Kai-shek's embassy there and found the secret sharing of information with Japanese intelligence that the OSS had correctly suspected of Chiang's double-dealing staff. For this caper, Chiang's secret police classified Frame as "dangerous" and injured Frame's co-worker when they tried to run her over with an automobile.[59]

Frame's colleagues in the OSS described her as an "enigma." Working in an atmosphere where the gender ratio was twenty-to-one male to female, Frame was said to have broken countless GI hearts. Anthropologist Gregory Bateson, who was serving the British government in India during the war, described Frame as a "practiced tease." Yet there is no evidence that she was ever part of "operation mattress," the sexual seduction of enemy agents.[60] Eventually Frame married fellow OSS officer Thibaut de Saint Phalle, an American of French aristocratic ancestry. She met de Saint Phalle through her OSS co-worker Julia Child, destined through her cookbooks and television career to become the most famous of the OSS women. De Saint Phalle's socially conscious mother referred to Frame condescendingly as a "missionary's daughter from China" and pled with her, to no avail, to pull out of the marriage. Frame had three children with de Saint Phalle, and died of cancer in 1960 at the age of forty-three without ever having written anything about her experiences in China and India.[61]

Burma-born missionary son Ernest B. Price (1890–1973) was another figure of consequence in the China-focused wing of the OSS. He had served as a Foreign Service officer in the 1920s before going into business in China and was then recruited to the OSS in 1942. Price was briefly head of Donovan's Far Eastern Division but quarreled with Donovan over the extent to which the OSS should work in tandem with the Kuomintang's own intelligence operations. Price was obliged to resign when he insisted that OSS independence from Chiang was a serious diplomatic and military mistake.[62] Much more reliable, from Donovan's point of view, but of lower rank, was Henry Lacy. A fourth-generation Methodist missionary, Lacy proved to be an indefatigable and diligent organizer of anti-Japanese networks. He "not only set up a print shop in the basement of a convent near Canton," notes the officer to whom he reported, "but caused such havoc in Japanese thought-control circles that they organized special teams to track down the bashful little missionary and wipe out his subversive press."[63] Missionary son Charles Steele served in the OSS throughout the war. He was stationed in Yenan for many months, reporting on the latest diplomatic requests of the Communists there, but left little trace beyond being remembered as one of the OSS's heaviest drinkers. Another missionary son, Oliver Caldwell, was, according to one of his co-workers, the missionary "who most readily assumed the cloak and dagger."[64] Caldwell later wrote a sensational autobiography about his OSS work in China, which historians have dismissed for its exaggerations and self-aggrandizing postures.[65] Charles Fahs, scion of an old missionary family, spent the war in the OSS's Washington office and became head of its Far Eastern Division, where he worked closely with Kenneth Landon, a former missionary extensively discussed in the next chapter.[66]

There was one real Soviet agent within the company of these OSS officers. Duncan Lee (1913–1988), like his brother Armisted, was born in China to Episcopalian missionary parents. During the war he served as an assistant to Gen. William Donovan at the Washington headquarters

of the OSS, and made several trips to China on Donovan's orders. Lee
spied for Soviet intelligence for about a year, then in 1944 stopped doing
so and upon leaving the government had a long career as a conservative
lawyer. He vigorously denied the espionage charges leveled against him
shortly after the war. Lee was fingered by Elizabeth Bentley, the notorious
"Red Queen" witness before the House Un-American Activities Committee. Only in 1995, seven years after Lee's death, did the government release
the Venona transcripts which proved that Bentley, so often unreliable, had
been correct about Lee. Had the FBI been willing to use the still-secret
evidence against him when he swore to his innocence before the House
Un-American Activities Committee, Lee would likely have been convicted
of espionage or perjury. His journey to spying began in the hothouse political atmosphere of Oxford in the late 1930s, when, as a Rhodes Scholar,
he became infatuated with the Bolshevik project. Lee's biographer, Mark
A. Bradley, convincingly treats Lee's brief enthusiasm for Communism as
a case of the transferal of missionary idealism from his Episcopalian upbringing in China.[67] Given the enthusiasm of that historical moment, perhaps it is surprising that there were not more. But Duncan Lee is the only
missionary-connected officer of the OSS, CIA, or Foreign Service known
to have violated the trust of the US government.

At the opposite political extreme was John Birch (1918–1945), whose
name today is better known than any other of the OSS agents operating
in China. What makes him famous is the organization named after him
thirteen years after his death, the John Birch Society. Birch was born in
India to Presbyterian missionary parents and had gone to China as a missionary himself shortly before the outbreak of the war. He was an army
captain serving in the OSS when he was murdered by Communist guerillas in the weeks immediately following the war's end in 1945. His own
politics were sufficiently far to the right to make him an appropriate hero
for opponents of American membership in the United Nations and critics
of the Supreme Court leadership of Earl Warren. As a student at Mercer
University before the war, Birch asked that several of his professors be dis-
ciplined because of their liberal theological views. Birch's death was generally understood by his OSS contemporaries, and later by historians, to be
the result of his own incautious, impetuous actions.[68] Had Birch survived
and returned to the United States to become politically active, he might
well have been a striking and important exception to the liberal pattern of
missionary-connected careers of his generation. But Birch's chief historical
significance is as a political instrument designed and wielded by people
with few missionary connections.[69]

Birch became a great hero of the "China Lobby," a highly organized political pressure group the character of which invites clarification here because of its vilification of the China Hands and the popular misconception that its base of support was heavily missionary.[70] Devoted to the interests of Chiang Kai-shek, the China Lobby was dominated by secular anti-communists motivated more by political economy than religion. The wealthy Jewish textile importer Alfred Kohlberg was its chief funder, along with the Soong family of Chiang's wife and in-laws, and its leading spokesperson Republican Senator William F. Knowland of California. A number of evangelical missionaries supported the China Lobby, as well as a number of churchgoers on the ecumenical side of the great Protestant divide. Many of the latter had been pleased by the widely publicized return of four hundred missionaries to China after the war in 1946, which made their expulsion a few years later all the more dramatic an event.[71] But on the ecumenical side, the missionary contingent was conspicuous by their reserve.[72]

The missionaries from ecumenical denominations who returned to the United States after the revolution were not of one mind about the outcome of the Chinese civil war, but many of them told their fellow churchmen and churchwomen that the new regime might well prove to be better for the Chinese people than the Nationalist government had been.[73] It was partly in response to such testimony that the National Council of Churches was the first major American organization to publically advocate "normalization" of relations with the People's Republic, in 1958, a decade and a half before Nixon took that step. But well before 1958, prominent ecumenical voices, such as the ex-missionary president of Princeton Theological Seminary, spoke in favor of it. As a result, Mackey brought upon himself bitter attacks from evangelicals.[74] The chasm between the ecumenical and the evangelical Protestants widened in the course of the 1950s debates about American policy toward China.

Three highly distinctive individuals are largely responsible for the popular and mistaken impression that the China Lobby was to a significant degree an extension of the Protestant missionary project. Henry Luce's unswerving devotion to the Kuomintang is discussed in chapter 2. Yale historian David Nelson Rowe, a missionary son, attacked his fellow academics recklessly. He told a subcommittee of the US Senate that Owen Lattimore was "an agent of Stalinism."[75] The third was Congregationalist ex-missionary Walter Judd, one of John Service's most zealous pursuers and one of Chiang Kai-shek's most consistent supporters in the US Congress. Judd was a singular figure, whose combination of antiracism and pro-Kuomintang sentiments invite attention here. If there was a "China Hand" in the House of Representatives, it was Judd.

In 1942, after an early career as a medical missionary to China, and after great success as a speaker for the Committee for Non-Participation in Japanese Aggression during the years immediately preceding Pearl Harbor, Judd was elected to the House in a Minnesota district.[76] He proved to be a narrowly focused legislator, indefatigable in his insistence on the strategic importance of Asia. He was a leading advocate of the legislation of 1943 that eased restrictions on immigration from China. During his twenty years in the House, he made few alliances, even with other Republicans. One factor in his relative isolation was his racial egalitarianism. Judd was a strong advocate of statehood for Hawaii and attacked those who doubted that so heavily Asian a population could be trusted. But Judd flourished mostly as an anti-Communist orator in public spaces beyond Congress. He was best known to the public for his performance as the keynote speaker at the 1960 Republican National Convention that nominated Richard Nixon for president.

Judd was celebrated during his lifetime for what is by far his most important achievement: his successful campaign to eliminate the barrier to naturalized citizenship for non-white immigrants. The "Judd Bill" bobbed around in Congress until its substance was finally incorporated into the McCarren-Walter Act of 1952. This act is most mentioned for retaining the racist quotas on immigration in place since the Johnson-Reed Act of 1924. But thanks to Judd, this new law also erased the "whites only" limitation on naturalization dating back to 1790. This barrier had been eliminated for Mexican immigrants by the treaty that ended the Mexican War and for African immigrants by congressional enactment after the Civil War, but it was still in effect for Asia. This change in American immigration law was not a priority of other leaders in the China Lobby.

Was there a "lost chance" in China? Had the advice offered by Davies and Service been taken, would the course of history have been different? If the US government had been willing to risk cooperation with the Chinese Communists at the conclusion of the war against Japan, or at least immediately after the revolution of 1949, might the regime of Mao been less repressive because less isolated? Might the Great Famine or the Cultural Revolution or both have been avoided, or at least been somewhat less destructive? Might the international politics of the Cold War have been different? Perhaps the American relation to anticolonial and postcolonial movements of Asia might have been less driven by a preoccupation with the spread of Soviet power?

Such counterfactual questions have no clear answers. Historians now do not doubt that Mao's policies killed millions of his own people, but these scholars are not agreed on what, if anything, the United States might have done to prevent this.[77] Nor do scholars agree that the loss of the China Hands to the government was decisive in leading the United States into Vietnam. The US government did have others in the early 1960s with the relevant experience.[78] But the idea remains appealing that the United States had an opportunity to use its tremendous power in the late 1940s and early 1950s differently, less tied to the interests of the Kuomintang and of the indigenous clients of the retreating European empires.[79] It is far from clear that had the ideas of the China Hands been adopted, the direction of history would have been different. But it will not do to suppose that this bit of history, any more than any other, had to happen exactly as it did.

The careers of Davies, Service, and others in the missionary contingent were primary sites in which the US government engaged the two Chinas. Although each of the individuals discussed in this chapter did exercise some agency, they were more often on the receiving end of power. The significance of the China Hands is as much in what was done to them— and what their fate revealed—as in what they achieved. A pair of ex-missionaries from Thailand had a very different experience. Between the two of them, this couple shaped America's diplomatic and cultural relationship with Thailand. The next chapter is about Kenneth and Margaret Landon.

CHAPTER EIGHT

Creating America's Thailand in Diplomacy and Fiction

COL. WILLIAM DONOVAN, not yet a general and not yet known as "Wild Bill," was desperate in the summer of 1941 to find someone who knew something about Thailand. President Franklin Roosevelt was worried about the Japanese armies crossing Thailand from recently occupied Indochina to make war against the British in Burma. If the United States ended up at war with the Japanese, what were the American forces to make of the situation in Southeast Asia? Donovan, as leader of an "information coordination" project that soon became the Office of Strategic Services, finally came up with a former missionary to Thailand who was teaching at a small college in Indiana. Donovan called Kenneth Landon (1903–1993) and urged him to come to Washington immediately. As soon as he arrived, Landon asked his initial host, President Roosevelt's son, James, to show him what was already in the government's intelligence files concerning Thailand. The young Roosevelt drove Landon to army intelligence head-quarters, where he was handed a slim folder. It contained, Landon later recalled, "four articles written by me."[1]

Many years would elapse before anyone else in the US government knew as much about Thailand as Landon. Upon visiting the Library of Congress, Landon found "most of the Thai language publications lying in heaps on the floor, unprocessed because they had no one to read and classify them."[2] Landon was quickly in place as the US government's top expert not only for Thailand, but for most of Southeast Asia, including Indochina.

Working from posts in the Office for the Coordination of Information, the Office of Strategic Services, the Board of Economic Warfare, and the

State Department, Landon was central to Washington's diplomatic, military, and intelligence operations concerning Southeast Asia throughout the war and its aftermath. Landon was the single person most responsible for the postwar alliance between the United States and Thailand that diplomatic historians have long called "a special relationship."[3] He extracted from President Roosevelt a written expression of FDR's wish that the French not be allowed to return to Indochina after the war. Landon was the author of the document of earliest date in the Pentagon Papers, a dispatch of early 1946 informing President Truman of his conversation with Ho Chi Minh, in which Ho proposed that the United States administer for Vietnam a path to independence modeled on its handling of its own colonial possession, the Philippines.[4] Landon later moved from the State Department to the National Security Council, where he served under Presidents Eisenhower, Kennedy, and Johnson, and finally to American University, where he taught international politics and Southeast Asian Studies until his retirement in 1974, building upon the pioneering works of scholarship he had written before and during his period of government service.

But that is only part of the Landon story. Landon's wife, Margaret Landon (1903–1993), created an enduring popular image of Thailand. In 1944 she wrote *Anna and the King of Siam*, the historically inspired, fictional account of mid-nineteenth-century Siam that led to the Rex Harrison and Irene Dunne film of 1946. Margaret's book was eventually the basis for three other Hollywood films and one of Rogers and Hammerstein's most successful Broadway musicals, *The King and I*. The 1956 film version of that musical, starring Yul Brynner as the king of Siam and Deborah Kerr as the British governess who wins his respect, remains one of the most iconic and highly romanticized images of East-West cultural interaction in American popular culture. Yet another production of *The King and I* opened in New York in the fall of 2015.

Today the Landons are largely unknown. As the writer who inspired *The King and I*, Margaret is the more widely recognized of the two. Even so, most people who have encountered the flamboyant Siamese monarch and the elegant English lady on stage or screen have no idea that their story was written by a missionary woman whose husband was the US government's chief authority on Thailand. The literature on the history of American foreign relations analyzes Kenneth's own exploits episodically, but rarely mentions his connection to the woman behind *The King and I*. The few accounts we have of either of the two Landons are scattered in disparate literatures and almost never address the compatibility of the wife's fiction with the husband's diplomacy. A rare exception is literary scholar Susan Morgan, who, as an afterthought to a book on the life of the real Anna (the woman on whose 1860s experience Margaret's volume was based), comments: "Together, this husband and wife controlled or significantly directed American attitudes toward Thailand for several decades."[5] Other accounts may mention their missionary background in passing, but none analyze in detail the missionary matrix for either of their careers.

I begin with the Landons' missionary experience and the circumstances under which the couple put missionary work behind them and settled in a small midwestern college town. After Donovan's call, the two lives played out in a sequence of sometimes interlocking events on national and global stages. The two intertwined lives are all the more remarkable given that both Landons went to resolutely fundamentalist Wheaton College. How did this pair become so anomalous: Wheaton graduates making a stir in domains largely inhabited by graduates of Princeton, Yale, Oberlin, and Swarthmore? How did Margaret as a writer and Kenneth as a diplomat and scholar help to articulate visions of America's role in the world largely consistent with that of their ecumenically-originating contemporaries? Just how did the Landons get from a Presbyterian mission in Thailand to the very center of the process by which the United States defined its relation to Asia?

The Landons went by default to Siam, as Thailand was known until 1938. They wanted to become missionaries in the Middle East. This preference followed from scholarly interests Kenneth had developed while a student at Princeton Theological Seminary, where he specialized in Semitic philology and Hebrew literature. The Presbyterian missionary board to which he and his then-new wife Margaret applied had no openings in the Middle East. So, in 1927, the Landons agreed to fill an opening in a country about which they knew nothing. They threw themselves with great energy into the standard project of converting the local population to Christianity. The Landons were fast learners and were soon highly visible figures in the long-standing Presbyterian missionary community. But there were tensions.

Kenneth was exceptionally good at languages and quickly upstaged the older missionaries with his ability to preach in Thai and in several Chinese dialects. He made a number of converts among the Chinese, who proved more receptive than the Thais to a new religion. Margaret, in keeping with the norm for missionary wives, ran a school while raising her own three children. But Margaret came across to the other missionaries as willful and pushy. She and Kenneth were both strong personalities and felt confined by a missionary community that seemed to them complacent and resistant to innovation. Kenneth was a devoted evangelist, especially in his earliest years in the field, but his interests broadened when he came to realize that he was living in a complex social order and a natural setting with many remarkable features. He became curious about the entirety of Thailand's culture and geography. Although stationed in the Trang region, in the far southern part of the country, Landon spent much of his time traveling throughout Thailand, photographing and collecting Thai artifacts and texts of every description.[6]

The Landons were involved in a series of fractious disputes within the missionary community. They developed especially hostile relations with the Eakin family—members of which had been leaders of the mission since the 1880s—and the McFarland family, which had served the mission since 1908.[7] Kenneth enjoyed the role of rebel in this context. He later recounted with pride how he publicly accused his fellow missionaries of being poor speakers, even when speaking English, and of being more interested in living a comfortable life than in attending to the needs of the indigenous population. Margaret loved to write, but on her own terms. Other missionaries reacted coolly to her newsletter-like writings designed to energize and better inform the missionary endeavor in Thailand. The Landons favored the granting of more authority in mission affairs to indigenous Christians. "They can't be our children forever," Kenneth declared as part of his witness on behalf of the increased autonomy of which he was certain the Thais and the Chinese were capable.[8]

Policy disagreements of this order were not the chief problem, which was personal. The Landons' contemporary letters and later reflections leave no doubt that their fights with other missionaries turned on the refusal of the confident young couple to fall in line with existing practices and hierarchies. Margaret was outraged when the missionary leadership diminished her authority and placed a teacher in her school she did not want. She had a bitter relationship with another missionary woman who appears to be the model for an unpleasant character in her novel of 1949, *Never Dies the Dream*.[9] That book, which did not achieve the popularity of *Anna and the King of Siam*, tells a story of petty jealousies and intrigues among missionaries in Siam. That she wrote it a dozen years after leaving the mission, and well after experiencing the satisfactions of literary fame, shows how deeply the imbroglios of the Presbyterian mission affected her.

It was in part to escape these increasingly antagonistic relationships that the Landons left the mission field. They physically departed Thailand in the summer of 1937 to spend a year on furlough in the United States, but they extended their leave another year, and then another. In 1940 they formally resigned. Their twenty-one-page letter to the Presbyterian Missionary Board was a relentless attack on the leadership of the Presbyterian mission in Thailand, alleging partisanship, secrecy, authoritarianism, and insufficient commitment to the missionary project itself. They declared that the member of the Eakin family then in charge was "totally unfit" to lead the mission: "We left the mission in 1937 with our health seriously impaired, profoundly convinced that we had been discourteously treated." In Margaret's case, "a nervous breakdown had occurred" as a result of being treated unjustly and antagonistically.[10] The petulance of this document is uncharacteristic of Kenneth and at variance with his other writings during the same period. While jointly signed, the missive was clearly an expression of Margaret's feelings. Both Landons were undoubtedly fed up with the people they had been obliged to deal with in the Thai mission, but the couple had other reasons, too, for deciding to make their lives within the United States.

Kenneth wanted to pursue an academic career. He spent his 1937-38 furlough year as a graduate student at the University of Chicago, picking up studies he had begun several years earlier on a previous furlough. This time he threw himself into the study of philosophy, and completed his qualifying examinations and his dissertation in that single year. In the commodious atmosphere university president Robert Hutchins had created at Chicago, even a detailed study of Siam's recent political history could count as a dissertation in philosophy. Kenneth's contemporary private writings and his later recollections show that he enjoyed the intellectual atmosphere of academia. By the fall of 1939 he was an assistant professor of philosophy at the respected Quaker institution Earlham College. The Landons were also motivated by concerns about the traumas of missionary children. They knew of specific disturbing cases and speculated that their children might be better off growing up in the United States.[11]

Kenneth's declining commitment to Christianity was also an important, but strictly private, basis for the decision. While he continued to formally profess the faith, and to attend church, Kenneth's year of philosophical study at the University of Chicago under the supervision of Albert Eustace Haydon was a turning point for him. "The year with Haydon," he remarked to Margaret in a pensive letter of 1942, "gave me two very consistent alternatives." One was "what I had had." This was the Calvinism he had defended in animated debates with the freethinking Haydon, who was a signer of *The Humanist Manifesto* of 1933, and a well-known ally of John Dewey, Max Otto, Roy Wood Sellars, and other leading secular philosophers of the generation.[12] Kenneth loved to tell the story of his classroom debates with Haydon, entertaining a gallery of other students. The second alternative was the "more humanistic position" toward which Haydon pointed. "I chose the latter because it answered to my great need," Kenneth reminded his more conventionally God-talking wife. "Your universe is different from mine because it is absolute," wrote Kenneth, accepting a declaration Margaret had made to him about their increasingly apparent spiritual differences. Kenneth explained that, for him, the universe was a mystery and the only Gods he had were "truth" and "Margaret."[13]

Kenneth had not become an open agnostic. But by the summer of 1938 he was well launched on a path of passive participation in churchly activities while doubting their substantive foundation. He seems not to have fully shared with Margaret the measure of his distance from the old faith until the long letter of 1942, unusual for having been handwritten. It is the most intense of all the letters Kenneth wrote while in Washington. The Landons attended Quaker Meeting during their years at Earlham, and Kenneth did the same in Washington when there without Margaret in 1941 and 1942. Eventually, the couple attended Presbyterian services in Washington but were not, their son later recalled, formally affiliated. They went to church "because it had meaning for Mother," Kenneth Landon Jr., recalls of his 1950s childhood. "It no longer held any meaning for Dad."[14]

Kenneth acknowledged, at least privately, the discomfort he came to feel with Wheaton's religious tradition. In his early years as a missionary, he wrote to Margaret in 1942, "I would have felt that my religion was going fast if I compromised anything." But he changed his mind, and gradually adopted an outlook similar to that of his ecumenical Protestant and post-Protestant contemporaries. "Strong fundamentalist religion so often is merciless," with its advocates "harsh" to themselves and to "those about them," he reflected; too often "my religious convictions made me quite implacable and hard on so many things." In the same letter he admitted that he began to make this turn even during their years as missionaries. It was probably a mistake to go back to the mission after their first furlough in 1932-33, he allowed, given the fact that Margaret had "hated Siam" and that he himself had been so confused religiously. They went back to Siam because Kenneth had not yet been willing to face up to his own religious doubts. Once home on furlough for the second time, he realized what a mistake it had been, and that his wife, while not subject to his own religious transformation, was so unhappy in Siam that a permanent return to the United States was imperative if their marriage was to survive.[15]

Once he determined to make it as an academic, Kenneth proved no less enterprising in career planning than he was fast in learning languages and in mastering philosophical texts. He solicited the help of Mortimer Graves, the executive secretary of the American Council of Learned Societies (ACLS), who was known for his active promoting of the study of Asia. Graves asked deans and librarians at one major university after another if they could possibly find a place for this brilliant young man who had privately collected what Graves thought to be the largest library of Thai materials anywhere in the English-speaking world. Landon obtained interviews at several of these campuses. Years later, Landon claimed that Harvard's head librarian for Asia, Keys Metcalfe, told him bluntly that Harvard was interested in China and Japan but not Southeast Asia and probably never would be.[16] Finally, in 1939, Kenneth, who had hoped for an appointment at a major university, was glad for the job at Earlham.

Landon loved his new life, even in the relative backwater of Richmond, Indiana. From the start, he was highly productive as a scholar and teacher. He published *Siam in Transition: A Brief Survey of Cultural Trends in the Five Years Since the Revolution of 1932*, a detailed, 328-page account of the political, economic, ethnic, and religious history of Siam during its epic transition to what was soon called Thailand. A central theme in the book was the relative success of the revolution's leader, Pridi Panomyong, in modernizing the old country, imposing limits on what had been the absolute monarchy of the Chakri dynasty that had ruled Siam for many centuries. Pridi was a French-educated social democrat, often wrongly accused of being a Communist. Landon later described Pridi as "the hero" of *Siam in Transition*.[17] This deeply informed volume of 1939 made Landon the leading American authority on contemporary Thailand. Unbeknownst to him, it was similarly regarded in Japan. Landon later learned that his book had been immediately translated into Japanese and was an important source of information for Japanese intelligence during Japan's occupation of Thailand. During his first year at Earlham he attended the annual meeting of the Eastern Division of the American Philosophical Association and made satisfying contacts with philosophers at Columbia University and elsewhere.[18]

Landon kept writing. In the summer of 1940, only a year following publication of his first book and after completing his first year of teaching at Earlham, Landon sent the manuscript of another substantial book off to Oxford University Press. *The Chinese in Thailand* was commissioned by the Institute of Pacific Relations, then at the point of its greatest standing as an arena for the discussion of Pacific affairs. Landon was not the first to notice that the Chinese were "the shopkeepers and tradespeople of

Thailand," the "Jews of the Orient," but he did more than anyone else to explain just how the Chinese constituted "the middle class of the nation."[19]

While writing and publishing at this remarkable pace, the young professor was also introducing at Earlham what he believed to be the nation's first undergraduate course in Chinese philosophy.[20] The next year, 1940–41, this missionary cosmopolitan taught a course in Indian philosophy. By then his written Chinese was good enough that he translated some of the Chinese philosophy texts into English. He also dabbled in Sanskrit. Landon was in a philosophy department, but his essential goal was to teach and write what was yet to be called more broadly Asian Studies, and he set about this with his characteristic resolve. During the same years, Margaret began working on her book about Anna Leonowens, the exotic woman whose memoirs about life in the Siamese court of the 1860s Margaret had come across while in Thailand. By chance, Kenneth met a distant relative of Leonowens, who in turn arranged a meeting between Margaret and Leonowens's elderly granddaughter, then a resident of Canada.[21] Margaret was delighted to be writing a book of her own. Both Landons, free to write as they wished and having escaped at last from the scrutiny and backbiting of the Presbyterian missionaries, were pleased in the summer of 1941 with their new lifestyle. Neither expected the phone call from Washington that changed their lives.

Kenneth liked to tell the story of being out on a lake in a rowboat, fishing, when Margaret shouted to him from the shore about a long-distance call from Washington.[22] Donovan had asked the Ivy League universities of the east to provide him with an expert on Thailand. The academics, recalling the recent lobbying of the ACLS's Graves on behalf of Landon, referred Donovan to the philosopher at Earlham. So it was that Landon drove his car to Washington and discovered that army intelligence had collected nothing more about Thailand than a smattering of his own published work.

In that first encounter with army intelligence, Landon learned something that defined much of his subsequent work in Washington. When the US government wanted to know something about Southeast Asia, a senior officer explained to the newcomer, the practice was to "ask our allies, the British, the French, or the Dutch."[23] From the outset, Landon was skeptical about the assumption that American interests in Southeast Asia were at one with the interests of the European colonial powers. This skepticism came into important diplomatic play in discussions of the one issue that most immediately concerned Roosevelt: could significant resistance to the Japanese be expected, and should Thailand be classified as an occupied country, rather than as a collaborationist power, as the British insisted? The Thai government had been cooperating with the Japanese, and been rewarded with a chunk of Indochina. What to make of this?

Landon insisted that the Thai government's working relationship with the Japanese invaders was not the whole story. There was potential for resistance to the Japanese, but it could not be expected from the Thai government itself. Moreover, the British had self-serving designs on Thailand. They were eager to treat Thailand as an enemy belligerent because it would give them a freer hand. Landon explained that Thailand was an independent dynastic power, precariously positioned between the Japanese on one side and the British on the other. From a governance point of view, Thailand was more like China and Japan than like India or Indochina. His massive collection of photographs taken of Japanese businesses in Thailand enhanced his credibility. Many people in Thailand and in Washington wrongly surmised that he had been a US spy all long, under the cover of his missionary activities.

Kenneth's letters to Margaret during the fall of 1941 include a fair amount of bragging about the influence he was having with people whose names she would recognize from the newspapers, had he been free to identify them. Yet had he been just trying to impress his wife, he would not have been invited repeatedly to consult with military and diplomatic officials, and of higher and higher rank. In the first major meeting of the research group with Donovan and James Roosevelt, a week after the group was assembled in August, Kenneth reported that John K. Fairbank "and a couple of others on China and Japan" were visibly anxious because Landon was "the only one who knew his stuff and they were out on a limb." It was a bit "embarrassing," because Kenneth was ready "to write up a finished report" while the others needed to do much more research.[24]

After two months Landon found himself at a roundtable meeting with twenty of "the key men" from "the State Dept., Army, Navy, Air Force, Foreign Affairs, etc. . . . the biggest collection of big names I ever sat with." He told the group that the Thais understood something very few others did: that "Britain was done for as the prime power in the Far East unless we won her battles for her." This assertion "brought down the house on me and we had glory halleluia for another hour with things centering on me." It was like teaching a philosophy seminar, except everyone was "bright" and "kept treading on my heels."[25] A week later he met with a similar group from all over Washington's military and diplomatic map. He was dismayed at "how belligerent some of them were." They were saying the thing to do about the Japanese was "to wipe the bloody bastards off the face of the earth, they aren't human, etc." In this open meeting the former missionary objected to these officials' crude and brutal understandings of the peoples of the Pacific. "How foreign . . . to my way of thinking," Kenneth remarked to Margaret. Several of the officials in the room spoke to him appreciatively afterwards. "In my quiet way I get in my opinions."[26]

Throughout these months of 1941, Kenneth worked closely with others Donovan had recruited. Landon befriended Fairbank and his wife, Wilma, whom Kenneth described as "our kind of people." The Fairbanks tactfully refused to drink as heavily as was the Washington norm, a trait that won Kenneth's respect. W. Norman Brown, Edwin Reischauer, Arthur Hummel, Gordon T. Bowles, and Charles Fahs—all missionary-related and all mentioned elsewhere in this book—were present at many of Landon's meetings, and intermittently occupied adjoining offices or desks. Landon appreciated Bowles, who had grown up in Japan as the son of Quaker missionaries, and Hummel, who had been a missionary in China. Pleased as Kenneth was to be in the company of other scholars, missionary-related and otherwise, he told Margaret that he did not think most of them knew their own terrains as intimately as he knew his. After all, Landon had already published two substantial books on his assigned turf. Landon rose quickly through the chain of consultancies. His report on the Burmese people and the war "made a hit" and was "being printed by the thousand and distributed throughout every government agency."[27] He discovered that he was being paid a higher salary than the other scholar-consultants. This meant a lot to him and to Margaret, both of whom were always conscious of money and status.[28] At the end of 1941 he was offered an annual salary of $4,600 for the remainder of the war.[29] For a college professor of that time, this was a lot of money.

Pearl Harbor made Landon look even better as a result of a remarkable diplomatic event. When the Thai government officially declared war on the United States, in keeping with that government's working relationship with the Japanese marching through their country, the Thai ambassador to the United States refused to present the war declaration to American officials. Rather, Ambassador Seni Pramot walked into the office of Undersecretary of State Adolph Berle, repudiated the declaration, and proclaimed solidarity with the Allies. Landon had been correct: there was genuine opposition to the Japanese among the Thais, even at the ambassadorial level. Back in Bangkok, Landon's favorite Thai leader, Pridi, opposed the war declaration and as a result was forced to accept a lesser role in the government. Landon was able to explain the intricacies of Thai politics to his superiors in Washington, who continued to act as if Seni Pramot represented Thailand.[30] A few days later Kenneth reported to Margaret that his own connection with Seni Pramot led to his being "brought into close touch with the higher ups again."[31]

By early 1942 there was no longer any doubt that the United States "officially considered" Thailand "an occupied nation rather than a willful collaborator," as R. Harris Smith notes in his classic account of this episode.[32] When Donovan became an army general and transformed the administratively marginal Office for the Coordination of Information into the full-fledged OSS, his protégé Landon was all the more empowered. Landon helped organize clandestine Thai resistance, relying on former missionaries to help recruit Thai students from various universities in Britain and the United States. Landon identified a coastal cave where guerilla fighters and supplies could be landed by the OSS without detection. The Free Thai Movement first worked through Chungking and the Kuomintang's spymaster Tai Li, but, as I explained in the previous chapter's discussion of the intrigues involving the China Hands, Donovan and most American officials did not trust Tai Li. After "Tai Li had a couple of Thai killed and also interfered in other ways," Landon recalled, Landon and his OSS colleagues "changed to Ceylon as a way station en route to Bangkok," preferring to cooperate with even the British imperial officials rather than the yet more treacherous operatives of Chiang Kai-shek.[33]

When Landon moved from the OSS to the Board of Economic Warfare and then to the State Department, he was in an even stronger position to ensure that Washington's perspective on Thailand differed from what the British or the Chinese Nationalist allies were advising. He remained informally very much part of Donovan's operation, and moved comfortably back and forth between the Board of Economic Warfare, the State Department's Asian section, and the OSS. He mediated disputes within the Free Thai forces and placated Seni Pramot, reconciling him with feuding adversaries when the movement almost fell apart in 1943.[34] The Free Thai networks that Landon helped create and maintain proved to be of lasting diplomatic significance. It was partly through these networks that the United States was able to maintain its close connection with Thailand during the succession of governments that nation later experienced.

Landon cut a distinctive figure in Washington during those early war years. His own droll account of a session with the Joint Chiefs of Staff provides a glimpse of Landon's flair as a raconteur. The Joint Chiefs asked how much they could rely on elephants instead of tractors for logistics in the jungles of the China-Burma-India theater. Forty years later, Landon recalled the meeting as follows:

> They wanted to know how many miles an elephant could go in a day. Well, that was easy. I said 16 miles. They were dumbfounded to think that I knew that, and so I explained that after a elephant has gone 16 miles he won't go any farther because he's got to eat. . . . Then they wanted to know how many hours an elephant would work if he was pulling things and I said about 4 hours. He had to eat 20 hours a day to keep his belly full of leaves and bark, which he dragged down out of trees, and even then if he was required to do heavy work he required a bucket of rough rice. . . . They asked how steep a hill an elephant could go up. I said that if need be he could go up on his knees, if the load was not too heavy. And how steep a hill could an elephant go down? And I said they were just like boys when it came to going down. If the hill is very steep they would sit down, put their trunk up in front and tail up behind, and slide on their bottoms, trumpeting all the way.[35]

Amid the Washington whirl in February 1942, Landon found himself at a dinner with a number of high-profile individuals, including Pearl Buck and her husband, Richard Walsh, who ran the John Day publishing house. Landon told Walsh that his wife, Margaret, still in Indiana with their children, was having trouble finding a publisher for a book she was writing about mid-nineteenth-century Siam. This conversation proved to be a crucial intervention. A month later the John Day house told Kenneth that Margaret's book was going to be "great."[36] *Anna and the King of Siam* appeared in 1944 and immediately became a commercial success. The book sold nearly eight hundred thousand copies.

Anna and the King of Siam told the story of a British-born widow employed at the Thai court as a governess for the king's children. Anna was a forceful but tactful woman who gradually won the king's confidence and became his trusted consultant on a wide range of concerns. Margaret had based the story on Anna Leonowens's two books from the 1870s, *The English Governess at the Siamese Court* and *Siamese Harem Life*.[37] But the tale was much more Margaret's invention than she acknowledged. Margaret described her book misleadingly as about three-quarters "fact" and about one-quarter "fiction based on fact."[38] Her extensive use of the original Anna's writings lent verisimilitude to *Anna and the King of Siam*. But Margaret ascribed to Anna countless reflections that are not to be found in the real Anna's two books, and of dubious relation to those that are. Landon also made Anna thoroughly American. Reviewers in

England had no trouble recognizing Anna as an American counterfeit of a well-born Englishwoman.

Margaret's Anna displayed enthusiasms that broad-minded American readers of the 1940s recognized as their own: personal autonomy, fair-mindedness, democratic institutions, the progress of science and technology, and a belief in expanded opportunities for women. Landon's Anna urged the Siamese royalty to read Harriet Beecher Stowe's *Uncle Tom's Cabin*, and to adopt the liberal and reformist views Stowe advanced in that novel of the 1850s. Medieval ideas, whether found in the West or the East, were to be overcome by the civilizing forces of the modern West. American readers warmed to Anna in her capacity as the willing ally of progressive King Mongkut, who wanted to protect his country by equipping it with the tools of modernity being developed in the West. The king was a decent, intelligent, but headstrong man who served to remind American readers that the Siamese were capable of responding positively to what Americans had to offer. Anna was a great Westernizer who gradually convinced the king that many aspects of the West he had not understood were even sounder than he had suspected. King Mongkut was an ideal American client.

Landon's themes were fully consistent with the classical missionary project's ideal of the tutelage of the East by the West, but in this story Christianity is not the defining element of what is being taught. Landon never leaves any doubt that Anna is a Christian, and that she sees herself as an instrument of God, but Anna's cultural agenda is not to convert the Buddhists and Hindus she encounters in Bangkok. Hence, as a text of the 1940s, *Anna and the King of Siam* fit smoothly into the secularization of the missionary project. The West's gifts to the East were less explicitly religious. In Landon's version there remains a strong patronizing element. She often presents the Siamese as essentially childlike in relation to the wiser and experienced West. A central passage from *Anna and the King of Siam* expresses cogently the self-conception that Landon gave to Anna. At this point in the narrative, Anna is worried that the king will not support her as he had led her to believe, and she fears she will be obliged to abandon the life in Siam that she has just begun.

> She had imagined herself helping an enlightened monarch found a model school that would set the pattern of education for a country just emerging from medievalism. She had looked forward eagerly to influencing a nation through its royal family. She believed so passionately in human freedom, in human dignity, in the inviolability of the human

spirit, that she had thought when the chance came to penetrate the harem, the very heart of the Siamese system of feudalism and slavery, that God had meant her for a liberator.[39]

Slavery was a fact of life in Siam in the 1860s. Landon made it a major context for Anna's actions. Landon's Siam becomes a kind of retrospective America of the Civil War era. Anna's greatest triumph is the decision of King Mongkut's son, when he ascends the throne, to do away with slavery in Siam. The American voice speaking through the ersatz Englishwoman is that of triumphant emancipators. Landon did not remind her readers in 1944 that the United States was, or ever had been, anything other than an exemplar of the modern, progressive values reflected in emancipation.

Landon's King Mongkut is a man of real character. Landon invites readers to appreciate him because of his amenability to Anna's arguments in favor of Western ways, but Landon's king has his own center of gravity. He presides over a country with a highly organized, extensively articulated cultural and political system of its own. Siam maintained its independence century after century while all the Asian societies around it were successfully colonized by Europeans. Landon offers her readers an Asian people that can do quite a lot on its own, and is capable of producing a leader with the strength of King Mongkut. Hence *Anna and the King of Siam* partakes of standard Orientalism by depicting Asian peoples as decidedly lacking in the qualities that make Westerners proud of themselves, but the king's admirable traits and the sheer fact of Siamese independence complicate the picture. Anna does not propose that Siam be added to the British Empire; rather, she helps the king maintain his dynasty's traditional control.

Anna and the King of Siam's simultaneous rejection of British imperialism and acceptance of the idea of Western tutelage of an Asian population fit wonderfully with a popular American geopolitical mood in 1944. The postcolonial world awaited the generous and sensible help of the United States. Luce's *Time* invited readers of *Anna and the King of Siam* to see contemporary parallels. *Time*'s reviewer even described as "gestapo" the henchmen of the Siamese king to whose nefarious activities the courageous Anna puts an end. Literary scholar Alfred Habegger exaggerates in describing Landon's book as "at bottom" an argument "for an American crusade to bring freedom and democracy to the corrupt and authoritarian East," but there is something to his point.[40]

Landon does not endorse Luce's vision of an "American century," but readers caught up in that vision would find little in Landon's book to give them pause. It was easy for Landon's wartime and early postwar readers to view the globe as saddled with twisted political regimes that American power could make straight. Landon's book appeared at the same historical moment as John Hersey's *A Bell for Adano*, which helped accustom Americans to a stewardship role for foreign peoples while announcing informal rules for just how Americans should perform this service.

This stewardship could be all the easier to perform if the foreign populations were understood as fully human. Landon's Siamese characters are like Hersey's Japanese and Pearl Buck's Chinese in one important respect: they have distinctive personalities. For example, the king's chief wife, Lady Thing, with whom Anna develops a close relationship, is very much an individual. For American attitudes toward Asian peoples in the 1940s, this depiction of Asians as individualized human personalities was significant in itself. Yet Margaret's Siamese are more stereotyped than Buck's Chinese and Hersey's Japanese. Moreover, unlike so many other missionary-connected Americans of her generation, Landon stops short of suggesting that Americans have anything to learn from a foreign people. Upon leaving Siam, Margaret's Anna remarks that "the capacity of the Siamese race for improvement in any direction" is well demonstrated, but she does not add that she takes back to England a deeper sense of life's dimensions.[41] Anna's own ideas are rarely challenged by her experience in Siam. The great popularity of the book and its later film and stage spin-offs may indeed follow from the absence in the novel of a more direct challenge to American self-conceptions. "Americans," as Susan Morgan puts it, "could not get enough of this version of themselves" and its apparent welcome by peoples abroad.[42]

The film and stage versions of Landon's story reproduced her basic images of Anna and of Anna's guiding values, as well as her representation of the king and of nineteenth-century Siam. Although Landon signed away all rights and did not have a direct hand in any of the later renditions of her story, she was justified in feeling that the moguls and writers of Hollywood and Broadway were amplifying something that was truly hers. The most important innovation was made by Rogers and Hammerstein through *The King and I*'s most popular song, the climactic "Shall We Dance."[43] The Broadway musical presented the relationship between the king and Anna as "a heterosexual romance of unconsummated trans-racial love," as Christina Klein rightly describes it.[44] This dynamic was not part of Landon's bestselling book or even of the 1946 Harrison-Dunne movie. But the innovation was consistent with Landon's antiracist tendencies and contributed greatly to the enduring appeal of *The King and I*'s version of her tale.

What the real Anna was like is marginal to my concerns, but several facts about her enable us to understand Landon's *Anna and the King of Siam* as even more distinctly a product of her own time and place than we might otherwise suspect. The Anna Leonowens who wrote the books that inspired Landon had never been to England, was never married to a British military officer, and was never even a governess. She was born in about 1831, in India, as Ann Edwards. Her maternal grandmother was probably Indian, not British. Anna's father was a sergeant, not a colonel. Her husband was not the "Major Thomas Leonowens" of her autobiography, moreover, but a man named Tom Leon Owens. The husband died while working as a hotel manager, not killed by a tiger, as she claimed.[45]

Ann Edwards reinvented herself upon arriving in Singapore in the late 1850s. She worked there as a teacher, and cultivated friendships with local Americans less likely than the Singapore British to discern that she was passing as a native of Wales and the daughter and widow of British military officers. Habegger, the most thorough student of the life of the original Anna, concludes that she was "mendacious to the bone." In Bangkok she was not a governess, but a schoolmistress, and the books she wrote about her experience in the Siamese court are rife with fabrications that Landon accepted uncritically. Yet the original Anna was a formidable woman, highly intelligent and enterprising. Upon leaving Siam she lived in New York, where she was supported by wealthy Quakers who were charmed by her amazing stories. She then moved to Canada and managed a serious career as a reformer and writer. She died in Halifax in 1914 at the age of eighty-three.[46]

Landon's straightforward, chaste, white, British-born widow of a British officer embodied an idealized version of American womanhood. It played well. But this conventionally attractive figure was socially very distant from the tough lower-class woman of racially mixed ancestry who, through ingenious self-fashioning, made a better life for herself and her children. When skeptics warned Landon as early as 1950 that she had taken Anna Loenowens's autobiographical writings too seriously, she was displeased and preferred to ignore the distraction.[47]

Margaret reveled in the success of her book and its spin-offs, and enjoyed the resulting money. Kenneth, too, was thrilled on her behalf, even as he continued his government work during the pivotal years of the war's end and the onset of anticolonial struggles. At the same time Margaret's book appeared and the first of the films it inspired was released, Kenneth, as the State Department's desk officer for Southeast Asia, became increasing entangled in deep disputes over American policy in Indochina as well as Thailand.

Kenneth wrote memoranda directed to Roosevelt himself. This intensified the tension between Landon and the European desk officers, who, as managers of American relations with the British, French, and Dutch, had always been in charge of Southeast Asia. "I think I must have re-written" those Indochina memos "30 times," Landon recalled, "before I could get the language well enough" for the European desk officers to approve before the documents could be sent to the president. FDR was skeptical about the French before hearing from Landon, but Landon remembered "the thrill I got" when one of these memoranda "drifted down the line back to me and in the margin, in fine, clear handwriting" the president had written "I want no French returned to Indochina."[48]

But the French did return. Truman mandated "a definite shift in American policy," as historian Bradley F. Smith describes the situation in the wake of Roosevelt's death; "Truman had decided to let the Anglo-American military assist the French in recovering their position in the colony."[49] Driven largely by the concern of Truman's Washington advisers about the weakness of France and the other European allies after the war, this shift was also influenced by the growing uncertainties about future relations with the Soviet Union. American officials were sympathetic with the struggles of the British in Asia, but, thanks partly to Landon's influence, they were willing to help the Thais resist a series of demands made upon them by the British. The State Department sent Landon to Bangkok in October 1945, and with instructions to go on to Saigon and Hanoi to take soundings on the situation in Indochina.

In Thailand, Landon and others from the American embassy proudly stood down the British, who continued to insist that Thailand had collaborated with the Japanese and should therefore be subject to allied disposition in the postwar era. The British were determined to "bleed Siam," Kenneth wrote to Margaret.[50] Landon personally went head-to-head with his British counterpart, Hugh Bird, contesting on the basis of his own knowledge the British claim that there had been no significant opposition to the Japanese.[51] By December the British had abandoned most of their demands. The way was clear for the United States to develop the strong alliance with Thailand that was a highly unusual feature of the Cold War in Asia.[52]

It was during his visit to Indochina in early 1946 that Landon posted the legendary dispatch that was destined to open the Pentagon Papers. Landon first flew to Saigon and spent two weeks there. He was impressed with the Vietnamese, and formed increasingly negative impressions of the French. He complained to Margaret about their cruelty, noting that politically suspect Vietnamese were being routinely tortured. Kenneth's non-French sources made it clear to him that the Vietnamese "were well armed and busy training troops" and "intended to fight the French to the last man." Already they were matching the French for cruelty, "snatching Frenchmen off the streets in sudden raids" and depositing "their muti-lated bodies" a few days later.[53] Landon recorded a visit to the consul gen-eral of the Chinese Nationalist government who claimed that the French had committed more than two thousand documented atrocities against ethnically Chinese individuals in Vietnam. Reports of French violence against suspected indigenous enemies were confirmed by a highly credi-ble Australian journalist who told Landon he had personally witnessed the torturing of Vietnamese prisoners in a Saigon prison. Landon persuaded a French general to let him ride in one of the regular planes from Saigon to Hanoi, but was dismayed to find that this sympathetic Frenchman was operating a brothel in Hanoi for his own profit.[54]

Once in Hanoi, Landon walked up to the front door of Ho Chi Minh's residence and knocked. Remarkably, he was ushered in to see the revo-lutionary leader without being asked for any documentation.[55] Ho was eager to reestablish and strengthen the ties he had lost with the United States when the OSS withdrew at war's end, having ruffled the feathers of America's ally Chiang Kai-shek by cooperating with the Vietnamese Communists. After the Japanese defeat, the joint allied command had assigned responsibility to Chiang's Nationalist troops for receiving the surrender of Japanese soldiers in the northern parts of Indochina. By early 1946 the Kuomintang army was close to armed conflict with Ho's Vietnamese troops. The only Americans left in Hanoi after the exit of the OSS were military personnel charged only with finding the bodies of American fliers downed during combat missions. Before the OSS departed Hanoi, its officers had informed Washington of Ho's hope that the United States would make Indochina an American protectorate.[56]

This was exactly the idea that Ho wanted Landon to convey to the new president of the United States. Having lost his OSS link to America and now facing both the hostile Kuomintang and the recolonizing French, Ho promptly provided Landon with excellent living quarters and a car and a driver, and insisted that he join him at dinner, which Landon did several times during his ten days in Hanoi.[57] Landon found Ho to be a formidable intellect with vast knowledge of world history and impeccable English. Landon had taught a course in political philosophy at Earlham, but Ho knew the classics of the field much better than he did. Landon was not modest about his own abilities and learning, but he admitted being outclassed by Ho, whom he described as a "genius."[58] Ho knew about Roosevelt's negative view of the French, and in conversations with Landon emphasized democratic rather than Communist elements in the movement he led against the French colonizers. Landon was able to brag that he, Landon, had actually drafted FDR's Indochina policy.[59] No wonder the two got along so well.

Landon also met twice in Hanoi with Bao Dai, the deposed emperor who had cooperated with both the French and the Japanese. Landon regularly saw the local representatives of Chiang's government, which at that time had about fifty thousand troops in the vicinity. In addition, Landon debriefed local French officials, the handful of American military personnel stationed there, and several journalists who hopped in and out of Hanoi. Landon learned that the French were offering Ho what they called "independence" as part of a "French commonwealth," with an ample supply of French "advisers." While the French expressed hope that the deal for limited autonomy might work, Landon learned how adamantly all of the Vietnamese were united in their "opposition to the French." Ho gave Landon "a beautiful tortoiseshell vanity case" for Margaret and a letter to Truman suggesting that the United States accept the responsibility for supervising the transition to Vietnamese independence on the model of the then-unfolding independence of the American colony in the Philippines.[60] Landon did not himself pronounce on the wisdom or viability of this proposal, but dutifully reported it to Washington as a live piece of diplomacy. Neither Truman nor the State Department ever replied to Ho's overture.

As early as 1947, Landon grudgingly accepted the Cold War framework for American diplomacy in Southeast Asia. He wrote memoranda endorsing an expansion of American political and military influence, even in opposition to indigenous Communist movements, in the interests of establishing the stability he concluded was necessary for the eventual triumph of democracy.[61] During these postwar years he interacted regularly with the Siamese royal family— descendants of King Mongkut and of the Chakri dynasty that had ruled Siam for centuries—and entertained them at his Washington home.[62] Landon proved willing to work with the dictatorial regime that in November 1947 pushed aside Pridi and the democratic reformers Landon had long defended. Historian Daniel Fineman notes that Landon "took a pragmatic approach to Thai politics and US foreign policy," while the US ambassador to Thailand Edwin Stanton "viewed matters with a moralistic bent." Stanton, a career diplomat, operated with "a strong sense of right and wrong," while Landon, "the former missionary," was "quick to recognize the limits of American influence and based his decisions on hard political realities."[63] Yet Landon did not cut off contact with the groups and individuals who were out of power after 1947. In his periodic visits to Bangkok in the late 1940s and early 1950s, he met openly with James Thompson, a former OSS officer for whom he had great respect, and who continued to side with Pridi's group in Thailand and with Ho's forces across the border in Indochina. Thompson is now remembered as a reminder of a road not taken in American policy in Vietnam.[64]

Landon was never happy with the French reoccupation of Indochina. In several visits in the early and mid-1950s, he was again impressed with the discipline and determination of the Vietnamese. After driving past the old Hanoi home of Ho Chi Minh in 1950, Kenneth wrote Margaret that he "felt a little sad at all that has happened since" his visit to Ho four years before.[65] Kenneth came to know Vietnamese president Ngo Dinh Diem during a visit to Saigon in 1960, by which time Landon had moved from the State Department to the White House office of the National Security Council. Landon was appalled at the administration of John F. Kennedy for having Diem assassinated in 1963. Diem, Landon was certain, was as good as the United States could possibly expect from anti-Communist leaders in Vietnam and it was foolish of Kennedy and his advisers to suppose otherwise. Landon had contempt for Kennedy; he "couldn't take his mind off the girls." Landon, a member of the White House staff, knew long before the general public that Kennedy brought women in and out of the White House with some frequency. Landon thought Kennedy's approach to foreign policy was almost criminally casual and that Kennedy's personal grasp of Southeast Asian politics and society was abysmal.[66]

Yet Landon did not use what influence he had in the Kennedy and Johnson administrations to actively oppose the escalation of the war in Vietnam at a time when he might have made a difference. He was right there as a senior staffer for the National Security Council until 1963, when he moved back to the State Department to lead the Foreign Policy Institute's transformation in the direction of more comprehensive Area Studies on the model then being developed on university campuses. Two years later he left the State Department to become a professor at American University. Even there, no longer an employee of the government, Landon was sufficiently quiet about his misgivings that student demonstrators took him to be more in favor of American military action in Vietnam than against it. In private letters to his son, Landon was more critical of the war. In later years he excoriated both diplomatic and military leaders for having so badly bungled an anti-Communist cause that he believed might have had some chance of succeeding if handled differently. By the 1980s, he was telling his son that the war in Vietnam "was a historic mistake," not "worth the life of a single American boy."[67] Just as Landon had long suppressed his religious doubts (and finally admitted to himself that he had no faith in God), he long suppressed his doubts about American policy in Vietnam. He could have acted sooner on his sense of what was right. But he did not.

Landon's caution probably had something to do with his survival as a government employee into the 1960s. He might have been purged well before the Vietnam War had the McCarthy era's investigators known what he had said about Ho Chi Minh in his diary in 1946, as noted above, and in some of his private letters. In 1947 he told Margaret that "the French [didn't] have a chance" to defeat Ho Chi Minh's Vietnamese revolutionary armies because of "the psychological solidarity" of the Vietnamese nation.[68] Such defeatism about the "right side" and respect for the "wrong side" was the classic recipe for trouble in China. Landon survived, but just barely.[69] Government gumshoes ransacked his office. FBI agents repeatedly grilled him. They were chiefly interested in a brief passage about Ho Chi Minh in his 1949 book, *Southeast Asia: Crossroad of Religion*, about which more below. Landon had indeed offered a favorable view of Ho. Here is Landon's account, offered more than thirty years later, of how his conversations with the FBI proceeded:

> "[FBI:] 'Did you know Owen Lattimore? . . .' [K:] 'Sure I knew Owen Lattimore, why?' [FBI:] 'Well, he said something about you, why would he like you?' [K:] 'Well, everyone liked me, I said, what's new about that?' [FBI:] 'Well he said something very favorable about you? Did you agree with Owen Lattimore?' [K:] 'Well, I certainly agreed that I was a nice fellow, if that's what he said. . . . [FBI:] 'Well, why did you write this paragraph very favorable to Ho Chi Minh?' [K:] 'What makes it favorable, I said? [FBI:] 'Well you said he's a very able man.' [K:] 'Well he is, I said. Don't you think it's a good idea to know your enemy and not underestimate him?' "[70]

Landon's wit no doubt helped him avoid being purged, but what really mattered was that his most generous accounts of the Communists and his most skeptical comments about the anti-Communist French were not on the public record. It also helped that the French regime did not fall until 1954—late in the McCarthy era—and that the resulting Communist sovereignty was then limited to the northern half of Vietnam. Moreover, Landon's scholarly publications, of which the 1949 book was another distinguished example, were not focused on the conflicts between the Communists and their rivals.

The 1949 volume was based on Landon's Haskell Lectures at the University of Chicago in 1947. The honor of giving the Haskell Lectures, a prestigious forum for religious studies, meant so much to him that he wrote frequently to Margaret about their preparation and delivery. Landon had maintained a connection to academia despite his demanding schedule as a federal official. He had also done the Taft Lectures on Chinese Philosophy at the University of Cincinnati in 1943, and was a regular reviewer of books on Asian thought for *The Journal of Philosophy*. In 1947 he considered leaving Washington to return to academia, and was moved personally when his old professor Albert Eustace Haydon, who had just retired, told him that he could easily have Haydon's chair at Chicago if he wanted it. But by then Landon was earning more than double what Chicago was paying even for senior professors, so he quickly dismissed the idea, even while producing, in the book based on the Haskell Lectures, a distinctive piece of scholarship.[71]

Landon opened *Southeast Asia: Crossroad of Religion* by explaining the difficulty of the very concept of Southeast Asia, given the great variety of political traditions, languages, religions, and social structures found in the part of the world that included Thailand, Burma, Cambodia, Vietnam, Malaya, and the varieties of peoples once subject to Dutch colonial rule and recently joined together in the newly independent Indonesia. Landon wrote shortly before the concept of "modernization" came into vogue among American scholars, but his account of what he called "Westernization" displays a vision of the gradual transformation of the cultures of Southeast Asia by the economic, political, and culture forces of the North Atlantic West. What most distinguished this volume was Landon's learned discussion of religion, and the detail with which he analyzed the practices of the Buddhists, Muslims, Hindus, Christians, and other faith communities. This book reads today as a deeply historical as well as anthropological work, tracing the multi-century processes by which the various major religions had come to the various cultures of Southeast Asia and merged with local religious practices to produce syncretistic faiths that preserved old spiritual practices within new rituals and symbols.[72]

Although massively sympathetic with nationalist efforts to create what a later generation of writers would call a "postcolonial" world, Landon took a relatively generous view of Western colonialism as a means through which indigenous elites learned science and technology, and began to appreciate the dignity of each individual rather than "the authority of the village or clan."[73] Landon was decidedly on the side of modernity, and for all of his frequently expressed sympathy for what he referred to as the "pains" of growth, held to an essentially progressive vision of history as it was unfolding in Southeast Asia. His choice of language reveals his paternalism; at one point he even compares the experience of the Southeast Asian peoples to that of children experiencing the traumas of adolescence.[74] Still, the "genius of the peoples of Southeast Asia" had produced wonders like Angor Wat, and in the future they could do great things again, in interaction with the West.[75] He believed missionaries were part of the process, but ultimately less on account of any Christian message than because of their instrumentality in the cause of what he called "westernization." Nowhere in this book of 1949, or elsewhere in his writings from the late 1930s on, does Landon identify conversion to Christianity as a worthy contemporary objective. He thought of missionary work, and colonization, as particular historical episodes, charitably understood as stages in a progressive narrative of enlightenment and democracy. With his characteristic cogency, he summed up his perspective on missionaries:

> They went to save souls and stayed to open dispensaries, to build modern hospitals, to erect modern leper homes, to urge prison reform, to advise on the proper treatment of the insane, to initiate education for females, to lecture on modern science and physics, to invent alphabets for people who had none, to introduce printing, to invent typewriters, to compile dictionaries, to produce in many cases the first written or printed literature, to advise women on new methods of obstetrical treatment, to indoctrinate the public on proper methods of public health such as how to behave during a cholera epidemic, to introduce physical education, and indeed to lend a new vocabulary to the languages of Southeast Asia.[76]

It was the total impact of the West on local elites through missions, commerce, and colonization that Landon had in mind when calling attention to the promise of men like Ho Chi Minh. The passage that aroused the suspicion of the FBI was one in which Landon cited Ho as a prime example of the influence of the West on indigenous peoples. He accurately quoted Ho's respect for the "immortal" words of the American Declaration of Independence and Ho's pledge to ensure a future for Vietnam based on the political values classically associated with the United States.[77]

Southeast Asia: Crossroad of Religion, along with Landon's two earlier books on Thailand, formed the foundation for his brief academic career at American University, beginning in 1965, when, at the age of sixty-two, he left the government's employ. By then he was a respected senior figure in the emerging project of Area Studies for Southeast Asia.[78] Before leaving the State Department, Landon worked to persuade his colleagues, in keeping with his book of 1949, that religion mattered to the formation of foreign policy.

Landon's perspective on religion had become largely pragmatic and detached long before he wrote *Southeast Asia: Crossroad of Religion*. But Margaret remained much closer to the faith the couple had both encountered in their youth and especially at Wheaton. Just when Kenneth published his geopolitically sophisticated book on Southeast Asian religion, Margaret published her resoundingly faith-affirming novel of missionary life, *Never Dies the Dream*.

This novel has little in common with *Anna and the King of Siam* other than a Siamese setting and a strong female protagonist. Margaret's new book is entirely about missionaries to Siam in the 1920s and 1930s and their interaction with the indigenous population. Many of the characters and events are inspired by her own experiences in the mission field as recorded in her contemporary letters and her later recollections. The protagonist, India Severn, is the leader of a missionary school who, though single, is clearly modelled on Landon's own experience as a missionary wife.

Yet the bitterest squabble in *Never Dies the Dream* diametrically reverses the roles that Landon and her archenemy actually played in 1930s Siam. In real life, it was Margaret who wanted to dismiss a Siamese teacher known for her notorious sex life. The busybody whom Landon hated is the person who defended the unsavory influence at the school.[79] By contrast, in the novel, it is the virtuous India Severn who defends the errant young woman while Severn's priggish and biased enemy, Grace Rutherford, successfully mobilizes the missionary leadership to get rid of the ethnically Siamese sinner and drives the heroine, India Severn, into private meditation on the goodness of God.[80] Had Margaret changed her mind since her missionary days, and felt more comfortable tolerating and trying to help an indigenous woman who had strayed, instead of casting her out?

Be that as it may, India Severn clearly resembles Margaret's Anna as a force for Western wisdom in Southeast Asia. Yet Landon's new heroine has extremely limited ambitions and achievements. Anna got rid of slavery and convinced an ancient dynasty to change a multitude of its ways of doing things, while India Severn's greatest triumph is the rescue of a young American woman who had foolishly married an unfaithful and unprincipled Siamese prince. The few scholarly discussants of *Never Dies the Dream* focus on Landon's ungenerous construction of some of her Siamese characters, and note her implication that mixed-race individuals are less likely than full-blood Caucasians to become honest and effective citizens and co-workers.[81] But Landon's most unforgivingly negative constructions are, in fact, of other white Americans, including boorish businessmen and, above all, self-serving missionaries. In this respect, Landon's *Never Dies the Dream* contributes to the genre introduced by Hersey's *A Bell for Adano*, making distinctions about how Americans should behave in the developing world. The book lacks the authorial control of *Anna and the King of Siam*, and leaves the impression that Landon is not altogether sure what she wants to say. The *New York Times* reviewer lamented that *Never Dies the Dream* was "a testament of faith, rather than a human drama played at the level of human nature."[82]

Margaret's novel of 1949 and Kenneth's scholarly treatise of the same year are reminders of how the two parties to this intimate and enduring marriage differed religiously. Margaret was more interested than Kenneth in the Wheaton tradition, but both attended college reunions and agreed to deposit their papers in the Wheaton archives. The ninety-five hours of oral history the pair recorded together, moderated by their Wheaton-graduate son, show them in their eighties as genuine partners, even while Kenneth's wit and sardonic detachment remove him from Margaret's earnest insistence on being right about every detail of their recollections.

Kenneth did not directly challenge Margaret's religious sensibilities, nor did he pretend to share them. When he was sixty, he wrote to his son acknowledging that while culturally he felt deeply Protestant and Presbyterian, he had no belief in God. The son later summarized what he took to be the father's core spiritual orientation:

> He never pointedly rejected Christianity, but neither would he have fitted within any segment of the Christian world. And he sometimes expressed a distaste for every segment of the Christian world. Still, he might say a formulaic Christian blessing at meals, though only on special occasions like birthdays. If Mother wanted to go to church, he would go with her. But when she no longer felt up to going, he wouldn't go on his own. Couldn't be bothered.[83]

Kenneth retained a conventionally Protestant social imagination even as he proudly walked Washington's corridors of power and appreciated the cosmopolitan world through which he travelled decade after decade. This old-fashioned side of Kenneth's personality is apparent in his letters, and is vividly revealed in an entry he made in his diary on the evening of his arrival in Saigon early in 1946. On the plane from Bangkok, he was captivated by a French woman of about thirty who would be "ideal as a character in a boudoir scene if I should ever describe one." This inspires a moralistic tale that he imagines himself writing, complete with Presbyterian-style redemption: "I have been thinking for a possible story of a girl who might be used in her sex life to portray the fall into evil at adolescence of so many people and her achievements of a normal good life," he began. The girl has a wholesome boyfriend.

> She finds him dull and in her senior high school year gets in with a college frat crowd on the occasion of a house party is given the works by all the boys. She is hysterical and goes home for help and sympathy but her mother flies into a rage and throws her out for the rest of the night. This hardens her spirit and she goes wild bad and leads others into it. She gets worse into various eccentricities of evil and is forever bumping into the hero who has gone to Princeton Theo Seminary and then becomes a minister . . .[84]

Indeed, the old boyfriend, now a clergyman, comes to the rescue.

> The minister not only redeems the girl but makes her a very success-ful pastor's wife with a happy normal home and children. As chapter headings I might use phrases from the story of the woman taken in adultery and also some out of the Proverbs and Song of Solomon to give significance and direction to the story. A scene along the way she might have a Lesbian phase, a sex showoff phase, periods of remorse and self hatred to condemnation of all men—with a final phase when things begin to come into focus and she realizes how distorted life has been for her. Normal life and right perspective come by and of the hero when she marries.

Yet Kenneth was more worldly than most of the men of his genera-tion who might be capable of this particular fantasy. Amid his sentimental attachment to the culture of his upbringing, he used as an emblem for provincial ignorance "a bunch of Presbyterian preachers and their wives" gathered for church functions.[85] He could speak this way to his more conventional wife with the confidence that Margaret was sophisticated enough to understand, which she certainly was.

Throughout his career as a government official and scholar he was a post-Protestant. Kenneth devoted his critical powers to the sympathetic understanding of indigenous peoples, including their religious beliefs and practices. He struggled against contemporaries who were slower than he to repudiate traditional imperialism. His embrace of the globe's diversity was more capacious than Margaret's, but the cosmopolitanism he es-poused remained Americo-centric until his disillusion with the Vietnam

War. For his entire career in government service, Landon assumed that the best interests of the indigenous peoples of Asia lay within a geopolitical hegemony of the United States, even in cooperation, sometimes, with authoritarian regimes like that of Thailand from 1947 onward.

Kenneth performed many important actions as a government official and scholar over the course of several decades, while Margaret made her mark with one dramatic public act, the publication of *Anna and the King of Siam*. What Margaret did can be more quickly described, on account of its singularity, but Kenneth's place in the history of his times was more substantial than one would infer from the fact that in 2016 there was a *Wikipedia* article for Margaret, but not for him.

When Kenneth Landon decided after the war to stay in Washington, and not to return to academia, he made the opposite choice from most of the scholars he had come to know in the OSS and the State Department. Three of Landon's wartime colleagues in Washington—W. Norman Brown, Edwin Reischauer, and John K. Fairbank—became leading empire-builders in the expanding academic space of Area Studies. To their careers, and of the many missionary-connected scholars with whom they worked, I devote the next chapter.

CHAPTER NINE

Against Orientalism

UNIVERSITIES AND MODERN ASIA

THE MAN WHO came to be called the "viceroy" of South Asian Studies had a high position in government during World War II and used it to promote the academic study of India. Missionary son W. Norman Brown (1892–1975) got to know Kenneth Landon in the Washington headquarters of the Office of Strategic Services. But unlike Landon, who had heavy policy responsibilities, Brown was in the research division, where he headed the South Asian section. In 1943, Brown convened a "private IPR roundtable" at Princeton to talk about India. The main item on the agenda was Brown's memorandum, "Suggested Program to Promote the Study of India in the United States." The memorandum called for the creation of institutes, teaching programs, and public lectures designed to advance knowledge of India.[1]

That an officer of the OSS could run a private event under the auspices of the Institute of Pacific Relations highlights the easy back-and-forth between IPR and government officialdom. The roundtable also shows how an OSS officer could promote an academic cause not immediately related to the war effort. The roundtable is revealing, further, for the individuals who participated in it. Brown knew how to light a fire under people located in potentially relevant networks. The recently elected congressman Walter Judd was there. So was the prominent Asian affairs writer T. A. Bisson, who was then serving on the wartime Board of Economic Welfare. Present, too, was Harry B. Price, the lobbyist who had been Executive Director of the "Price Committee"—the American Committee for Non-Participation in Japanese Aggression—and who by 1943 was coordinating the Lend-Lease program for China. Brown made sure that the Rockefeller Foundation sent representatives. The group also included journalist Varian Fry, already a legend in Washington circles because of his death-defying work for the Emergency Rescue Committee in Vichy France, smuggling more than two thousand anti-Nazi refugees out of Marseille. The presence of Judd, Bisson, and Price, all of whom were former missionaries to China, shows how Brown mobilized the missionary network for his own purposes, and how that network easily bridged different mission fields.

After the war the enterprising Brown established himself as one of the most successful empire builders in an academic generation legendary for its empire building. Whenever there was a committee related to his interests, Brown ended up chairing it. Whenever there was a center or an institute to be established, Brown was invited to serve as its director. Whenever there was an academic position to be filled, Brown's advice was taken into account. Whenever there were funds to be distributed, Brown was part of the decision process. Whenever there was a major event concerning India, Brown's views about it were quoted. Focused, efficient, and determined, Brown was the prototype of the academic operator.

Brown's counterpart in postwar Japanese Studies was another missionary son, Edwin Reischauer. The Chinese Studies equivalent was John K. Fairbank, who was neither a missionary son nor a former missionary but whose formation as a scholar was heavily influenced by the missionary contingent. This chapter is devoted to the careers of these three men and the attendant growth of what came to be called Foreign Area Studies.

By 1967, missionary son and Japan scholar John W. Hall was justified in claiming that the success of Area Studies in the previous twenty years had rendered obsolete the old charge that American academia was parochial. The universities of no other nation had achieved as wide a global range as those of the United States.[2] This could happen as rapidly as it did because so many missionary-connected individuals were ready to make it work. In no other institutional setting was missionary cosmopolitanism more visible than in academia, and nowhere was its Asian center of gravity more consequential.

Some participants in this transformation had begun academic careers before the war, and were in a position to take the lead when postwar opportunities arose. Others came along later, when they recognized that their language facility and foreign experience were vital assets in this suddenly booming professional domain. Missionary-connected Americans were scattered in many regional fields, but the most numerous and influential in the study of China, India, and Japan. These were the three largest mission fields, producing a greater supply of potential scholars. But additional conditions help to explain this concentration.

There were few American missionaries in Russia and Eastern Europe. Programs for that part of the world developed without significant missionary background. This was also true for programs focused on Western Europe and its sub-regions. Latin American Studies had no special need for missionary-connected individuals because Latin America was the subject of extensive academic study before the war and its major language—Spanish—was widely spoken in the United States.[3] There were plenty of missionaries in sub-Saharan Africa, but the Foreign Service and the OSS did little recruiting there because that region was not a major theater in World War II, and its strategic significance in the Cold War was not recognized until much later.[4]

No matter what the specific region, Area Studies in its broadest sense embraces all types of scholarly study of a given region, without methodological, chronological, or ideological particularity. It is in this broad sense that I use the term. Yet Area Studies also has a more narrow meaning. Area Studies first referred to the ways in which academic agendas of the postwar world differed from "Oriental Studies," the earlier, heavily classical and humanistic tradition of scholarship. Area Studies included social science and presented itself as a resource for understanding the contemporary world. This narrower understanding of Area Studies was assumed when it came under attack during the Vietnam era for allegedly compromising scholarly integrity by working too closely with the US government. Some Area Studies scholars, indeed, had done counterinsurgency work for the Central Intelligence Agency, assisting the US government in defeating Communist movements in several postcolonial locales. Critics calling for a more genuinely independent study of Southeast Asia or the Middle East or Latin America began to refer to "Area Studies" as a largely social scientific enterprise closely associated with American imperialism. Area Studies in this sense was something for progressive scholars to renounce.[5]

I use the more inclusive sense of the term because much of the scholarship produced about China, India, and Japan since World War II does not fit the narrower definition. In the most comprehensive and judicious review of Area Studies scholarship, David Szanton argues that when the whole body of Area Studies scholarship is assessed, the connection between it and the priorities of the US government is episodic—genuine in some cases but not in others.[6] This is the case even for social scientists, but all the more so for the historians, literary scholars, and students of the arts who also flourished in what were called Area Studies programs.[7]

I turn first to Brown's leadership of South Asian Studies, then to Reischauer's and Fairbank's leadership of Japanese and Chinese Studies.

Brown was not a reflective man. He left few traces of his feelings about himself or about how his background affected his work as a scholar. His personality was antithetical to that of the demonstrative and loquacious Kenneth Landon. What Brown left was a record of concerted action.[8]

It all began with the study of Sanskrit, to which Brown's scholarly father introduced him as a child. Brown was born in the United States in 1892 while his parents were home on furlough, but grew up in India, immersed in things South Asian. So close was the intellectual relationship between father and son that the two enrolled together at Johns Hopkins University in 1908, the elder Brown to study the Upanishads as a doctoral student, the younger to major in Greek as an undergraduate. The younger Brown quickly followed his BA with a Hopkins doctorate in Indology, beginning a lifelong engagement with Vedic Studies. The pivotal step in Brown's career was his appointment in 1926 to the University of Pennsylvania's chair of Sanskrit. In that year he reorganized the American Oriental Society's Indic and Iranian Committee, which was soon absorbed by the American Council of Learned Societies (ACLS).

It was natural for the ACLS to look to a Sankritist to head the committee. India had a classical past with its own language, one of the most complex and inspiring in the world. American scholars had less incentive to study the modern period because it was so well covered by British scholars in relation to the British Empire's long tenure in South Asia. American interest in the modern period increased only during the 1920s and 1930s as greater appreciation for Gandhi grew along with mounting suspicion of British authority. Brown was in the middle of this transition. By the mid-1920s he was a regular contributor to *The Nation*. Brown was among the many missionary-connected voices that condemned the British propagandist Katherine Mayo's 1927 best-seller *Mother India* for its scornful dismissal of the habits, customs, and religion of the peoples of South Asia.[9]

Gen. Donovan had no trouble identifying Brown as the OSS chief for India, but paid relatively little attention to him thereafter. The British presence in India meant that the OSS was less engaged there than in Europe, the Middle East, and East Asia. Brown could get away with treating his government job as an instrument for advancing South Asian Studies. The 1943 IPR workshop exemplified this practice, but the following year Brown did something else that promoted his own agenda even more boldly.

Brown sent Robert I. Crane (1920–1997) to India on an unabashedly academic mission. Crane, also a missionary son from India, had finished college at Duke University just before the war. In 1944 he was serving the State Department as a junior officer of the Division of Cultural Relations.

Brown brought him into the OSS and, in cooperation with the Library of Congress, concocted the idea of authorizing Crane to travel anywhere in India he wished, to purchase as many ancient and modern books, magazines, and manuscripts he could find. All these materials would then enrich the South Asia collection of the Library of Congress. Working under the cover of an agency called the Interdepartmental Committee for the Purchase of Foreign Publications but bankrolled by the OSS, Crane had virtually unlimited funds at his disposal. He spent many months buying everything in sight that his India-sensitive eyes found of interest.[10]

This assignment would surely not have been given to Crane had Brown or Donovan known that Crane was the source of a politically embarrassing leak of a top-secret document to newspaper columnist Drew Pearson earlier that year. At issue was a report written for President Roosevelt by the veteran diplomat William Phillips, whom Roosevelt had sent to India to assess the war effort there and to advise him on how the United States should handle its delicate relationship with the British imperial authorities. The Phillips report castigated the British as obstacles to victory over Japan and argued that the war would go much better if the British granted independence to India. Crane, an ardent supporter of the Congress Party, shared the document with Indian friends in Washington who knew exactly what to do with it. The Pearson column created a diplomatic firestorm. No one seems to have suspected Crane, who admitted decades later that he had leaked the report.[11]

Crane's conduct was consistent with the most politically engaged of the American missionaries in India during the late 1930s and the war years. Several missionaries were forced out because they refused to keep quiet about their belief that Britain should give India its independence in return for the support many Indians were giving to the war effort against the Japanese.[12] OSS relations with the British in India were always tense. "British rule in India is fascism, there is no dodging that," one OSS office wrote to his wife.[13] Official documents were usually softer than this in tone, but nonmissionary as well as missionary-connected OSS personnel were generally appalled at the British attitudes toward the indigenous populations.

After the war Brown lectured frequently at the Naval War College and spoke in other government forums. He was elected president of the American Association for Asian Studies and of the American Oriental Society. He led the ACLS South Asia Committee that became a joint committee with the Social Science Research Council, and the chief source of individual research grants in the field. Brown's career as a promoter of South Asian Studies reached its climax with the establishing in 1961 of the American Institute of Indian Studies, an international research center with sites in India as well as in the United States. Brown had been the key agent in this enterprise, leading the campaigns for public and private funding and working out details with officials and scholars within India. Under the aegis of this institute, heavily supported by the Ford Foundation, scholars from the United States and throughout the world were more easily able to work in India. Brown served as director of this institute for a full decade after its founding, relinquishing the controls only in his seventy-ninth year, 1971, four years before his death. His tenure as viceroy of South Asian Studies was long.

For all his entrepreneurship on behalf of South Asian Studies, Brown was not a leading trainer of doctoral students. John K. Fairbank and Edwin Reischauer exercised much of their influence through their large networks of students, but Brown did not.[14] Nearly all of the leading South Asian scholars in the generations following Brown's earned their degrees elsewhere, and almost always in discipline-defined departments of anthropology, political science, or history. This pattern formed in part because of Brown's reputation as a controlling personality.[15]

Brown's leadership was more decisive institutionally than intellectually. But he did write *The United States and India and Pakistan*, first published in 1953 and revised in several later editions.[16] Reischauer and Fairbank published books of the same genre and for the same series in 1946 and 1948, respectively, on modern Japan and modern China. Brown's work, like theirs, was the standard popular book on its topic for a generation and more. Although Brown covered an impressive expanse of political and social ground, he emphasized the role of religion and of the classical literary heritage in making India what it was.[17]

Brown's celebration of India's ancient contributions to world civilization downplayed the dynamic creativity of South Asian peoples in more recent times. While his counterparts in the study of China, Japan, and other regions fought against what a later generation of scholars called "essentialist" and "Orientalist" understandings of Asian societies, Brown continued to speak in the older idiom that emphasized the civilizational difference between East and West. Moreover, for all his support for Indian independence, Brown described the British imperial era generously, as "preparation" for "modernization."[18] He had little to say about how the British Empire had restricted the terms on which the peoples of South Asia experienced the modern industrialized world.

Brown's critics were impatient with his relative tolerance for colonialism and his unwavering emphasis on the importance of religion. "While

Brown's intentions were framed within his own larger goals to increase understanding and exchange between India (and Pakistan) and the United States," observes Nicholas B. Dirks, "it seems obvious now that his sense of modern Indian history was profoundly shaped by his disciplinary concern with issues of religion and classical Sanskritic (and in his terms 'Hindu') civilization."[19] Politically, all the missionary sons in South Asian Studies were on the left except for Brown. He was understood to be a Republican, but this did not put him importantly at odds with his colleagues. Brown was quick to defend Owen Lattimore in 1950 when Lattimore was accused of being a Communist, and carried on a cordial correspondence with him for some years afterward.[20]

Ironically, the most intellectually creative of the missionary-connected scholars in South Asian Studies had no contact with Brown, and did not occupy academic posts. Presbyterian missionaries Charlotte Viall Wiser (1892–1981) and William H. Wiser (1890–1961) produced in 1930 the first detailed ethnographic study of an Indian village. *Behind Mud Walls* was like no other book on India. It described the daily lives of all castes residing in the North Indian village of Karimpur, based on the Wisers' observation over the course of five years of increasingly extensive friendships.[21]

Driven from start to finish by the social gospel version of the missionary project, the Wisers believed in providing agricultural assistance as a form of Christian service. The pair met as students at the University of Chicago's School of Social Services, where they were inspired by a lecture by Samuel Higginbotham, the missionary reformer discussed in chapter 3. They arrived in 1916 and lived there until their deaths, William in 1961 and Charlotte in 1981. The Wisers followed Higginbotham's example and developed their own local program of agricultural education and development. Along the way they kept detailed records of their experience. *Behind Mud Walls* would surely have achieved its standing as an ethnographic classic more quickly had the Wisers come to the United States and pursued academic careers. But the couple, even while they continued to publish scholarly studies of contemporary India, remained in India as missionaries, where they served as advisers for a variety of development projects.[22]

The Wisers did little to promote themselves as anthropologists, and only gradually did their work receive professional recognition. On their periodic visits to the United States they concentrated on building support for their own social service program, the India Village Service. Eventually the Wisers did win a large and appreciative following among scholars. In 1963, the Berkeley anthropologist David Mandelbaum edited a new edition of *Behind Mud Walls*, incorporating Charlotte Wiser's later ethnographic study of changes experienced by villagers of Karimpur. Anthropologist Susan S. Wadley edited other editions in 1989 and 2000. By the early twenty-first century the book had sold more than fifty thousand copies, a very high number for a study of its kind.[23]

The Wisers spoke to local Indians in their own languages, but the role of language marked a striking difference between South Asian Studies and Japanese Studies, to which I now turn. Some South Asian specialists, especially the historians, mastered Hindi, Urdu, or others of the dozens of widely spoken languages in the Asian subcontinent, but the prominence of English in India made foreign language fluency less essential than it was in Japanese Studies.[24] So taken for granted was fluency in Japanese that meetings of the joint American Council of Learned Societies-Social Science Research Council Committee on Japanese Studies were often conducted in Japanese.[25]

The high language threshold made missionary-connected individuals all the more in demand. An inquiry of the mid-1930s by a leading scholar from Japan illustrates this. The Institute of Pacific Relations commissioned Yasaki Takagi, who taught American Constitutional Law at the Imperial University of Tokyo, to survey the resources for Japanese Studies in the United States. Takagi found a handful of language-and-literature specialists, including several distinguished Japanese scholars who had immigrated before the US Congress curtailed migration from Asia in 1917. The most eminent was Ryūsaku Tsunoda of Columbia University. Takagi could find only one chair of Japanese Studies in the entire country, at Stanford University, and it was held by a professor who did not speak or read Japanese. There was also a small but sophisticated body of scholarship created outside universities, largely by missionaries, including J. C. Hepburn's romanization of the Japanese language.[26] In 1934, Harvard University recruited from France the highly accomplished Serge Elisseeff, who was skilled in both Chinese and Japanese Studies. But Takagi discovered something else, apparently not noticed by others: a handful of "young scholars who were born in Japan and who sp[oke] excellent Japanese" and should be encouraged to use their language skills, and might well develop "future centers of Japanese studies in various American universities." Takagi named five such individuals: Hugh Borton, Gordon Bowles, Burton Fahs, Edwin Reischauer, and Robert Reischauer.[27]

All five came from missionary families. Takagi did not mention this fact, nor did Marius Jansen in 1988, when he called attention to Takagi's prophetic analysis. It was prophetic because, to one degree or another, the five did exactly what Takagi hoped. Hugh Borton, who had missionary experience himself with the American Friends Service in Japan, became a historian and was for many years the leader of Japanese Studies at Columbia University before accepting the presidency of Haverford College in 1957. Gordon Bowles, also a Quaker, was born in Japan to missionary parents. Bowles taught anthropology for most of his career at Syracuse University. Edwin Reischauer and his older brother, Robert, were both born in Japan to a Presbyterian missionary couple and spent most of their childhood there. Robert had just begun his career as a historian when he was killed in Shanghai in 1937 during a Japanese bombing attack. Edwin, also a historian, became the most recognized Japan specialist of his generation in any discipline. Burton Fahs's missionary connection was more attenuated: he was the son of Sophia Lyon Fahs, a daughter of Presbyterian missionaries to China who herself built a distinguished career as a Unitarian leader and as one of the first female professors at Union Theological Seminary. The younger Fahs did not pursue Japanese Studies, but became an Asian specialist for the Rockefeller Foundation, which was credited with gaining Rockefeller support for Area Studies in many regions. Fahs, Bowles, and Reischauer were among the individuals Kenneth Landon met in Washington during the war.

All five of the young men identified by Takagi got some measure of support from Elisseeff, an anti-Bolshevik refugee who had been educated in Japan and had no missionary connections of his own. Harvard recruited Elisseeff to head the Harvard-Yenching Institute, which, while heavily focused on China, also supported the study of Japan. Elisseeff enlisted what few intelligent Japanese speakers he could find within his reach, and showered them with attention and resources.[28] Wherever they went, they were rare for their fluency.

Reischauer (1910–1990) served in the 1960s as the US ambassador to Japan, of which more below, but he was less important in diplomacy than in the development of Japanese Studies. As ambassador, he carried out the instructions of his government, but in academia he made a real difference. For several decades Reischauer and his Chinese Studies counterpart Fairbank co-taught a course at Harvard on East Asian history that enrolled several hundred students every year and inspired many imitations on other campuses. The two co-wrote textbooks that were assigned virtually wherever East Asian history was taught.[29] As a teacher of graduate students, Reischauer, again working closely with Fairbank, trained the young men and women who then took up the new Japan-defined jobs that opened up in other universities, including in departments of history and political science as well as in expanding language and literature departments.[30]

Reischauer was acutely conscious of his missionary heritage and its relationship to his career. Reflective and expressive, Reischauer referred to himself as a missionary of sorts, committed to a mission of educating Americans about East Asia in general and Japan in particular. "Without doubt, I drew many of my ideals as well as personal traits from my missionary background," he proclaimed in his autobiography. Resolutely proud of his parents and of "their achievements as missionaries," he allowed modestly that their contributions to the development of a modern educational system in Japan were "much more tangible and lasting than anything" he himself ever did, as a scholar or an ambassador.[31]

The Presbyterian missionary leader A. K. Reischauer was an adamant proponent of the shift from preaching to social service, especially the providing of better schools. His wife, Helen Oldfather Reischauer, who had grown up in Persia as the daughter of a prominent missionary family there, was also active in establishing schools in Japan.[32] The elder Reischauer was one of the most scholarly of the American missionaries to Japan, and one of those most determined to understand Japanese culture from the inside. He published learned studies of Buddhism as early as 1917, and, upon finding it impossible to return to Japan after being caught in the United States on furlough at the time of Pearl Harbor, finished his career as a professor of Comparative Religious Studies at Union Theological Seminary in New York.

A. K. Reischauer's reputation as an extreme liberal was based not only on his strongly expressed empathic identification with Buddhists, but even more on his sharply formulated attacks on imperialism and racism. His *The Task in Japan: A Study in Modern Missionary Imperatives* was, like the works of Daniel Johnson Fleming and E. Stanley Jones, among the forerunners of *The Layman's Report* of 1932.[33] When conservative Presbyterians protested that book, as explained in chapter 3, they singled out Reischauer along with Pearl Buck as heretics. The younger Reischauer never wavered in his respect for his missionary parents. When a group of Japanese Christians brought out a volume of appreciations for A. K. Reischauer in 1961, the son wrote an affectionate account of the personal integrity, exemplary parenting skills, and sound values of both of his parents. The elder Reischauers were, the son insisted, "two sane, balanced, mature people."[34]

It was indeed the antiracism and anti-imperialism of his missionary upbringing that the younger Reischauer most emphasized when trying to explain the relevance of that upbringing to his own career. "The fundamental attitude that I encountered in my own home," he recalled in the 1980s, "was one of deep respect for the Japanese." It was of "immense value to me in my career" to grow up "free from racial prejudice," with "a strong dislike for Western imperialism," and with "a corresponding enthusiasm for Asian nationalism." At age of thirteen he was already prepared to be "indignant" over the decision of the US Congress in 1924 to exclude Asians from immigration. Later in life, when his first wife died at age forty-five, "it seemed completely natural to me to marry a Japanese woman," he observed.[35] Although Reischauer attributed some of this racial egalitarianism to simply having been born and raised in Japan, rather than to the specifically missionary milieu, he persistently defended the missionaries he had known against the charge of "cultural imperialism." Racist and imperialist outlooks could be found among the missionaries, he granted, but on the whole the missionaries he knew were "usually motivated by the noble desire to share with others what they value most."[36]

Reischauer, like his classmate John S. Service, abandoned religion while at Oberlin. As a college student too, Reischauer decided he wanted to share the Asia he valued with those in the West who knew nothing about it. At first, his idea was to concentrate on ancient rather than modern history. From the time he left Oberlin in 1931 to study at Harvard until his older brother, Robert, was killed in 1937, Edwin Reischauer left the modern period to Robert, in an informal division of family labor. Instead, Edwin began as a classicist of sorts, pursuing a dissertation under Elisseeff's direction on the life and work of a ninth-century Japanese Buddhist monk, Ennin (also known as Jikaku Daishi).[37] But with Robert's death, Edwin took up his brother's engagements, too, and gradually broadened his interests as the likelihood of an American-Japanese war increased. "If Bob had been alive, he would have been the obvious person for the State Department to task to join it in 1941," Edwin wrote many years later to a former student and friend. [38] Finding himself as the only Reischauer son, his sense of his mission in life was to embrace what had been his brother's presumed destiny as well as his own.

Long before Reischauer began in earnest his academic empire-building at Harvard in 1947, he displayed in the context of the war a set of dispositions about Japan that he continued to voice in his later career. Reischauer's war-related utterances resisted the demonization of the Japanese people and looked to a postwar future in which Japan's least militaristic and imperialist proclivities could flourish. He insisted that, for all its authoritarianism, Japanese culture had a democratic potential. Most strikingly for the times, he equated the Japanese empire with the European empires to the defense of which the United States was then massively committed.[39]

This last point was at the heart of the disagreements Reischauer had with nearly all of the State Department's Far Eastern Division during the summer of 1941. The United States was in the process of deciding to embargo oil shipments to Japan unless it agreed to withdraw from its conquests in China. In the then-secret, eighteen-page memorandum "The Adoption of Positive and Comprehensive Peace Aims for the Pacific Area," the youngest and newest of the State Department's Far Eastern hands opposed the embargo on the grounds it would certainly lead to a Japanese attack on the United States for which the United States was not prepared. Reischauer also referred to some Japanese imperial interests as "legitimate," treating Japanese control over some of the Pacific region as no different from the British, Dutch, and French empires. Forcefully rejecting the racist assumption that Japanese imperialism differed substantially from the colonialism of the white empires, Reischauer asked his superiors if the United States was "prepared to oppose and even to fight Twentieth Century imperialism while tolerating and actually maintaining the injustices of Nineteenth Century imperialism?"[40]

Reischauer went on, in this memorandum of 1941, to demand that the United States publically proclaim a vision for peace in the Pacific that would be based on the principle that "all the peoples and nations of the Pacific Area are by nature equal as nations, peoples, and individuals." Every nation was to "enjoy complete sovereignty and Territorial Integrity" and to have access to the products of the region, subject only to any restrictions imposed by the indigenous peoples themselves. Moreover, the Pacific region should be administered "in the interests of the permanent inhabitants of these territories and . . . directed toward preparing their inhabitants for self-government and independence." While Reischauer made no mention of the Philippines and admitted in memoirs that "a lingering Japanese bias" had probably led him to omit Korea and Taiwan from the areas to be liberated from colonial rule, his memorandum was, in the words of his biographer, "an amazing departure from the conventional wisdom of the day." Reischauer recalled that his memorandum was treated "with condescension" by those with whom he discussed it.[41] But on the specific issue of the embargo, the American ambassador Joseph Grew did entertain the idea of secret negotiations with Japanese moderates believed to be close to the emperor. The initiative was scotched by the State Department's Far Eastern chief, Stanley K. Hornbeck, who was said by Grew's principal aide to have accused Grew of being "more Japanese than the Japanese."[42] Secretary of State Cordell Hull did impose the embargo, and the Japanese did attack just as Reischauer, and a few others, had predicted.

The young Rieschauer's departures from standard thinking about the Pacific were manifest from the beginning of his government service. He had less of a monopoly on things Japanese than Kenneth Landon had on things Thai, but there was enough of a parallel to keep Reischauer in loops from which he would have been excluded had there been someone else to call on. The discussions in which Reischauer participated were of less strategic importance than the ones in which Landon was involved, and those in which the China Hands participated. The diplomatic issues concerning an enemy belligerent were less numerous and complex. Hence there is no chapter in this book on "the Japan Hands." Reischauer's work for the State Department was less consequential than his career as an academic, but Reischauer himself was hooked on his government role as soon as he got a taste of it. His "first experience with the State Department" that summer of 1941 transformed him, his biographer correctly observes, "from a quiet scholar" into "an active, impassioned policy advocate."[43] Reischauer was quick to accept a commission in the army as an intelligence officer.

Reischauer served in uniform from the summer of 1942 until the end of the war, first as a major and then as a lieutenant colonel. It was upon his arrival in Washington that he found the first unit he headed to be made up exclusively of men with missionary experience in Japan. Reischauer spent most of the war with a handful of other Japanese speakers, deciphering Japanese cables and helping the American military understand the movements and plans of enemy forces. It was in this capacity as a senior intelligence officer that he was among the first to learn of the atomic bomb dropped on Hiroshima. At the time, Reischauer thought the use of the atomic bomb was "a terrible mistake." He and others in his office, having read the latest secret communications within the Japanese leadership, "knew how near to defeat Japan already was and how eager some elements in the government were to bring an end to the fighting." Reischauer changed his mind in later years, informed by the additional information about the Japanese military discovered by later researchers. Without Hiroshima, he conceded, the Japanese military might not, after all, have allowed "the civilian government to surrender." He remained adamant throughout his life that the second, Nagasaki bomb was without justification.[44]

Although Reischauer did not participate in any of the discussions about whether to drop the bomb, or how many to drop, he was at least a minor player in another policy issue: what to do with the emperor once the Japanese had been defeated. His advice was to leave the emperor alone, rather than treat him as a war criminal. This course was eventually followed, but during most of the war it was by no means assured. "From early 1942 on," his biographer notes, "Reischauer worked tirelessly to educate American policymakers about the nature of the emperor system in Japan." He was joined in this endeavor by his friend Borton, who was also working in the State Department from 1942 to 1948. That an observant Quaker could be the State Department's chief Japanese specialist during the Pacific War is another indicator of how dependent the government was on missionary-connected Americans for Japanese expertise. It is also a reminder that the wartime State Department did not have much to do concerning Japan. Borton and Reischauer apparently persuaded the State Department to oppose the army and navy leaders who wanted Emperor Hirohito tried as a war criminal. But Gen. Douglas McArthur ended up with the power to make the decision. He broke a Washington deadlock, and decided to keep the emperor in place as a foundation for a postwar Japanese political order. Reischauer had little authority, but he had played a role in the debates, "and he loved it," notes George Packard.[45]

Reischauer marked his transition from government service back to academia by writing what turned out to be his most widely appreciated book. *Japan: Past and Present* pulled together into a cogent artifact the perspective that had informed its author's policy advice and that he would soon develop further as a teacher and scholar. The militarism of the recently defeated regime, Reischauer argued, was an aberration in the context of Japanese history as a whole. This became his central interpretive idea in all that he wrote from then on. Japan, contrary to what was widely assumed, had so extensively participated in the industrialization process that it was no exception to the pattern of development in the North Atlantic West. Reischauer identified strongly with the Japanese liberals of the 1920s, and, when his first wife died, married the daughter of one of the leading figures in the liberal bloc. Reischauer downplayed the fascistic elements of Japanese politics and society of the 1920s. Against those who saw Japan as vividly in contrast with the West, in the thrall of an essential Japanese national character at odds with the democratic United States and Western Europe, Reischauer insisted—even in 1946 and in later, revised editions of this book—that Japan was very much a "modern" nation. That Japan differed from other East Asian norms, and was more like Germany,

France, Britain, and the United States, became, Andrew Barshay has observed, "the argument for which he became widely known."[46]

While Reischauer continued to develop his ideas about Japanese history, he made a more decisive impact institutionally. In 1952 he succeeded Elisseeff as director of the Harvard-Yenching Institute, by then a very rich operation that placed in Reischauer's hands resources that were the envy of all the generation's academic empire builders. He and Fairbank together recruited the finest of the country's graduate students in modern East Asian history. Among their students and admirers was James C. Thomson Jr., a missionary son who described the contrasting temperaments of the pair in this way: "Fairbank confronted the tragedy and irony of the human condition, especially in the 20th century, and was deeply pessimistic about the future," while Reischauer "was more of a Manchester liberal of the 19th century variety, always upbeat about the future."[47]

Reischauer's generous view of Japanese history, focusing more on its harmonies than its contradictions, did not persuade everyone. As research in the field expanded and deepened through the 1950s, Reischauer's conception began to seem superficial. Throughout the 1960s and 1970s, Reischauer's ideas were debated, sometimes contentiously. Reischauer downplayed internal conflicts between defenders of a "feudal" past and the largely unsuccessful reformers and revolutionaries who tried to establish a more egalitarian society. Reischauer presented the Tokagawa period (1603–1868) as an incipiently democratic episode, in which significant degrees of urbanization, increases in literacy, and mercantile and technological development set the stage for the more aggressive modernization of the Meiji era (1868–1912).

Modernization, indeed, was at issue, as Japan became one of the principal cases for debating the value of "modernization theory" as then favored by social scientists and also by some historians. These scholars argued that industrialization, urbanization, and scientific-technological advances were part of an integrated process driving societies in the same basic direction. Although Reischauer later insisted that he did not regard modernization theory as a weapon in the Cold War, it was so regarded by many discussants at the time. And with good reason: Reischauer, as ambassador from 1961 to 1966, upheld the Japanese case of modernization-from-the-top as a model for other nations in East Asia. Arguments over the Japanese case were sharpened at a 1960 conference at Hakone, Japan, organized by two of Reischauer's students, John W. Hall and Donald Shively, both missionary sons.

At this conference, government officials, as well as scholars from Japan and the United States, quarreled over the extent to which Tokagawa and

Meiji Japan had paved the way for democracy or made democracy harder to achieve than it would have been had workers been able to achieve greater power. Hall, who was just then publishing his most important book, *Government and Local Power in Japan, 500 to 1700*, pressed the "modernization" framework. Many of the Japanese participants, however, Marxist and liberal, believed that a more complete democracy might have prevented the militarists from taking control of Japan and plunging them into a disastrous war. These scholars were impatient with the modernization framework which seemed to downplay the power that the militarists achieved and deployed with such devastating consequences.[48] Some of Reischauer's critics at Hakone invoked the early 1940s scholarship of E. H. Norman, a Canadian and another missionary son.

Norman was not present at the Hakone conference—he had died three years before—but the critique of the modernization-centered narrative of Japanese history voiced there was very much in line with Norman's Marxist-oriented works of the early 1940s. Norman stressed the limitations of democratization throughout the Tokagawa and Meiji eras, and called attention to the power by which traditional elites kept peasants and workers subservient. These wartime works published by the Institute of Pacific Relations—especially *Japan's Emergence as a Modern State* and *Soldier and Peasant in Japan*—became in the 1970s the basis for the claim that Norman had created a great alternative to Reischauer's way at of looking at Japanese history.[49] In a field-transforming critique of Reischauer published in 1975, historian John W. Dower resuscitated Norman's ideas as the antithesis of what Dower saw as the American empire-friendly modernization thesis. Reischauer was deeply wounded by the attack. He downplayed his own genuine resistance of Marxist ideas, and reminded colleagues in print that his own *Japan: Past and Present* had drawn upon Norman's work. He explained that as the years went by he had become less and less convinced that Norman's reading of Japanese history was correct.[50]

These scholarly discourses about the Reischauer-Norman interpretive divide were complicated politically and personally by the circumstances of Norman's suicide in Cairo in 1957, while he was serving as the Canadian ambassador to Egypt. Long affiliated with left-wing politics and, indeed, according to his most reliable biographer, Roger W. Bowen, a member of the Communist Party for at least a few years in the late 1930s, Norman was repeatedly accused of disloyalty. No evidence has ever come to light that Norman committed any acts of espionage or that he was anything other than faithful to his calling as a representative of Canada, the government of which cleared him in investigations of 1950 and 1952. But in those inquiries, Norman had lied by declaring that he had never been an actual member of the Communist Party. He might have gotten away with this deceit, but a committee of the US Congress continued to pursue the matter, claiming that US security interests were being compromised by Norman's high position within an ally's diplomatic corps, and the FBI continued to search for evidence that could nail Norman as a dangerous "red." Early in 1957, word reached Norman as these agitations intensified in Washington, causing him increasing distress. Bowen argues convincingly that Norman believed it likely that his deceit was about to be discovered, which would lead not only to his own disgrace, but to the discrediting of his close associates. Norman jumped to his death from the rooftop of the Swedish embassy in Cairo.[51]

Reischauer later joined in the condemnation of Norman's persecutors, but Reischauer, while remaining in direct contact with other members of Norman's family, had not seen Norman himself since a brief meeting in Japan in 1948.[52] The paths of the two missionary sons had diverged, although there is no reason to conclude that they became personally hostile to one another. It is not clear that Reischauer knew that Norman had been a member of the Communist Party, had deceived his government about it, and felt so defenseless in the time leading up to his death.

What most matters to *Protestants Abroad* about the Reischauer-Norman interpretive divide over the dynamics of Japanese history is not so much its rights and wrongs, about which much has been written by and for specialists in Japanese Studies.[53] Of significance here is the remarkable fact that the divisions within the field did not proceed along the lines of who had a missionary background and who did not.[54] Disagreements over modernization theory and Marxism did not have their origin in the missionary/non missionary distinction.

Missionary experience is not of a single piece, as I observe often in these pages. Differences between the immediate social environments of these two scholars may help explain their contrasting views of Japanese history. Although Reischauer and Norman were together for several years as boys, most of Norman's upbringing was in a countryside mission far from the more urban, educated population of Japanese to which Reischauer was almost exclusively exposed. Norman's father was a devoted preacher who, even after forty years in Japan, never learned to read and write the Japanese language, which he used only orally, for his sermons and other evangelistic labors. Norman's preoccupation with "the struggle of ordinary people," observed Cyril Powles, and his skepticism about the ability of elites to accomplish much good, followed in large part from the aspects of Japanese society he knew growing up. Powles, also a Canadian missionary son, remembered how easily Norman made the transition from religion to Marxism, and cited letters in which the mature, long-since secular Norman wrote that "Jesus certainly taught Communism." Reischauer himself offered a similar suggestion about Norman's rural upbringing. "Herb's father" had done "direct evangelistic work in rural mountainous" regions, making his son Norman more "aware of the poverty and problems of rural Japan" than Reischauer himself, the son of the scholar and educator A. K. Reischauer. Norman's peasant-intensive background "may have had a profound influence" on the kind of history he wrote, Reischauer speculated; Norman was driven by "deep concern and sympathy for the peasantry and moulding his views of the modernization process in Japan."[55] Norman also rejected the missionary heritage more decisively than Reischauer; the two were both secular but Norman did not retain the warm feelings about the Protestant missionary project that Reischauer continued to voice until the end of his life.

Yet the contrasting interpretations of Japanese history offered by the two most prominent missionary sons in that field were developed within a common frame of anti-exceptionalism that the missionary-saturated generation put firmly in place. Norman's use of Marxist theory was even more vigorously opposed to exoticism than Reischauer's use of modernization theory. To be sure, one did not have to have a missionary background of any sort to embrace anti-exceptionalist understandings of Japan, but it was in fact scholars of just this background who most energetically and effectively advanced such understandings in the 1940s and 1950s. By contrast, Ruth Benedict's popular 1946 book *The Chrysanthemum and the Sword*—even while it advanced a substantial measure of sympathy for the recently hated Japanese people—reinforced the cultural exceptionalist perspective.[56] Reischauer and Norman, in their contrasting ways, diminished even further than Benedict the potential gap between the kinds of humanity found in Japan and the kinds of humanity found in the North Atlantic West.[57]

Close identification with the Japanese people was also a theme of Reischauer's service as ambassador, which invites attention here as an extension of his academic career.

The prominent professor's appointment was something of a surprise to observers of American Asian policy, since Reischauer openly favored the diplomatic recognition of the People's Republic of China. It was no secret that Reischauer had contempt for Secretary of State Dean Rusk, who professed to know a great deal about East Asia but did not. Rusk could not read either Chinese or Japanese. Reischauer loved being the American representative to Japan, but at that historical moment the job of representing the administrations of Presidents Kennedy and Johnson obliged him to defend a Vietnam policy to which he was privately opposed. That he should have resigned and publically repudiated the Vietnam War is a major conclusion of his sympathetic biographer, George Packard, who had been Reischauer's aide at the time and himself had left the Foreign Service in 1965 because of Vietnam. Reischauer "enjoyed the power and importance of his position too much" to walk away from it, Packard concludes ruefully.[58]

Reischauer's willingness to defend the American war in Vietnam was all the more troubling to people who had followed his leadership in the past. This behavior seemed out of keeping with the policy positions Reischauer had taken throughout his career. His *Wanted: An Asian Policy*, especially, argues for a sympathetic engagement with anticolonial, nationalist movements. That book of 1955, while classically "Cold War" in its acceptance of a Communism-vs-democracy frame for world affairs, continued to voice the perspective Reischauer had displayed during World War II and in his postwar writings. This book resolutely defended the "neutralism" of nationalist movements as appropriate expressions of independence, and took issue with the American commentators who insisted that the new nationalists had to join in the anti-Soviet alliances of the Western powers. Written against the policies then being put in place by the Republican Secretary of State John Foster Dulles, Reischauer lamented the inability of the United States to capitalize on what he insisted was the common commitment to anti-imperialist, democratic governance. In a lengthy disquisition on the situation in French Indochina, Reischauer assailed as foolish and dangerous the continued defense of a colonial regime against Communist insurgents. The United States was "absurdly wrong," he declared in the midst of his analysis of American support of the French policy in Indochina, "to battle Asian nationalism instead of aiding it," and the mistake might eventually, he warned, have great cost in money and American lives.[59]

Reischauer was prone in later years to quote his book of 1955 by way of reassuring his critics that he saw through the mistake of the Vietnam War all along. He had gone along with it, he said in his autobiography, because once "we had become so deeply enmeshed" he was "ready to accept the administration's argument that the quickest and easiest way to end the war was to force North Vietnam by military might to desist from trying to conquer the South."[60] Reischauer's biographer insists that Reischauer was never actually consulted about the Vietnam policy developed by his enemy, Rusk, even though he was willing to defend it in public.[61]

Reischauer's slowness to repudiate American policy in Vietnam greatly damaged his relationships with his academic colleagues in the United States, threatened many of his personal friendships, and caused conflicts with his adamantly antiwar children. Reischauer returned to Harvard in 1967 carrying very different baggage from what he had taken with him when he left Cambridge for Tokyo. As a major figure in national politics, Reischauer was surrounded for many years to come with contentions deriving from the Vietnam War. Even as he resumed his academic role and was widely appreciated for his extremely successful leadership in advancing the cause of Japanese Studies, his Washington connections continued to define him. He eventually admitted that he had been wrong in 1967 to write the book *Beyond Vietnam: The United States and Asia*, which continued to defend the pro-war view that he "changed completely not long afterward."[62]

The dependence of Japanese Studies on missionary-connected scholars like Reischauer gradually changed. The war brought Japanese language training to a number of people with no missionary connections at all, who then joined the academy and had distinguished careers.[63] But as late as the mid-1960s, the missionary footprint was substantial. Missionary son Donald Shively taught at Stanford, Harvard, and Berkeley, and was a highly successful fund-raiser for Japanese Studies wherever he worked, especially at Harvard, where he picked up Reischauer's responsibilities when Reischauer became ambassador to Japan. Missionary sons John W. Hall and Roger Hackett made the University of Michigan a leading center for Japanese history, as did Hall at Yale when he moved there. At Princeton, political scientist William Lockwood, also a missionary son, worked in Japanese as well as Chinese Studies and was also a president of the Association for Asian Studies. Historian Delmer Brown had taught Japanese history at Berkeley since 1946. Brown was not a missionary child, but had married a missionary daughter and was quick to express his closeness to the missionary community that had sustained him when studying in Japan in the 1930s. The former missionary Hugh Borton taught at Columbia since 1937, was interrupted by his wartime service in the State Department, and left Columbia in 1957 to become president of Haverford College.[64] And Reischauer himself was by no means finished as a leader of Japanese Studies. He remained in place at Harvard until his retirement in 1981. And there he continued his productive collaboration with Fairbank.

John King Fairbank (1907–1991) was probably the most successful mentor of doctoral students in American academic history. He supervised one hundred PhD dissertations. He developed Harvard University's "China shop" alongside Reischauer's "Japan shop," as the two took shrewd advantage of the institutional opportunities afforded by their university and by the monies available during the era following World War II. Fairbank was neither a missionary nor a son of missionaries, but he was surrounded by missionary-connected friends, allies, students, and informants. His autobiography of 1982, *Chinabound: A Fifty-Year Memoir*, details his indebtedness to them. He casually attributed to himself, and to Reischauer, a certain "missionary impulse" in preaching the importance of East Asia to any and all who would listen.[65] The story of how missionary-connected individuals participated in the development of Chinese Studies revolves around Fairbank. The relevant people included his predecessor as the China team's captain, the one-time China missionary Kenneth Scott Latourette (1884–1968).

Fairbank acknowledged the debt Chinese Studies owed to this professor at the Yale Divinity School. But Fairbank said his only religion was Harvard, while Latourette viewed all history as a Christian cosmic drama for which China and the United States were sites. Latourette began as a student of Chinese history in the round, but gradually narrowed his interests to the history of Christian missions. Fairbank shared with Latourette a belief that missions were important, but Fairbank studied missionaries as actors in secular time.[66] The differences between these two great figures in the study of Chinese history were neatly encapsulated in their two presidential addresses to the American Historical Association. Fairbank's address of 1968 identified "the missionary in foreign parts" as "the invisible man in American history." Latourette's address of two decades earlier said that God was missing.[67] The dynamics of the transition in the leadership of Chinese Studies from Yale to Harvard is partly a story of Latourette's narrowness and of Fairbank's more capacious vision.

The place to begin the story of Chinese Studies is a 1928 decision of the American Council of Learned Societies (ACLS) to establish a Committee on Far Eastern Studies. Nearly all of the scholars qualified to serve turned out to be former missionaries or the children of missionaries. The obvious leader of the new committee was Latourette, who, while a missionary in China, served briefly as a traveling secretary for the Student Volunteer Movement before taking up a professorship at Yale. Latourette wrote the state of the art articles on Chinese Studies for several decades.[68] Only one

of the seven members of the ACLS committee lacked missionary experience. Berthold Laufer, a German-trained art critic and museum curator,
was neither a former missionary nor a child of missionaries. Latourette's
other colleagues were three former missionaries—Arthur Hummel,
Lucius Porter, and Lewis Hodus—and two missionary sons, L. Carrington
Goodrich and Carl Bishop.[69]

Mortimer Graves, the Permanent Secretary of the ACLS, appointed
this committee at the encouragement of the ACLS's oldest specialized
constituent society, the American Oriental Society.[70] This organization,
which dated from 1842, had long sought to deal with the entire expanse
from Morocco to Japan. Graves wanted to get beyond the ornamental
scholarship and connoisseurship the American Oriental Society had
indulged, even while it sponsored some scholarship of enduring value.
The idea of a more uniformly *wissenschaftliche* approach, and one not
confined to antiquity, was enthusiastically endorsed at an organizational
meeting of some forty scholars, including virtually all of the Asian specialists of professional standing in any discipline then resident in the
United States.[71]

Latourette had been abroad for less than two years, returning to the
United States in poor health in 1912, but worked stateside in missionary
support organizations and soon became a prolific author of books about
China. Starting at Yale in 1921, Latourette for nearly three decades was
the D. Willis James Professor of Missions and World History.[72] His early
writings indicated a strong commitment to Chinese history as a whole.
In 1934 he published an important two-volume work, *The Chinese: Their
History and Culture*.[73] Yet for all its range of coverage, this contribution
was recognized as lacking in analytic depth. Even Latourette's most
distinguished doctoral student, M. Searle Bates—mentioned in chapter
4 for his role in promoting Human Rights—was disappointed in it. Bates
complained in the *American Historical Review* that Latourette merely
summarized existing studies, used documents only in English translations,
and "[did] not claim familiarity" with the actual sources needed for anything beyond amateur scholarship.[74] Moreover, shortly after publishing
this work, Latourette's interests then took a turn that made Chinese Studies at Yale wholly different from Harvard, where Serge Elisseeff was just
then advancing the secular-oriented study of both China and Japan.

Latourette decided to focus on the history of the missionary project
itself, where his weak fluency in Chinese was less of a barrier. Between
1937 and 1945 he produced the seven-volume *History of the Expansion of
Christianity* that remains an indispensable source of detailed information

for the history of missions.[75] In chapter 3 I quoted from this work's conclusion as an example of the triumphalist view of the missionary project characteristic of many ecumenical leaders during the mid-1940s. Latourette became a highly visible and esteemed leader of ecumenical Protestantism, appearing regularly at conferences and symposia on the state and future of Protestantism and its place in the nation and the world.[76]

Latourette thus shifted inward, to a more Protestant-intensive engagement with China exactly at a time when other China scholars, including most of those who shared Latourette's missionary background, were doing the opposite.[77] That a professorship of missions in a divinity school was a major foundation for the early development of Chinese Studies is a reminder of how poorly that field was represented in mainstream academia during the 1920s and 1930s.[78] But this fact can be a reminder, too, that Latourette's career was a bridge from an earlier tradition of missionary sinology that included contributions of some consequence, especially at Yale. Latourette's immediate predecessor, Harlan Page Beach, was a representative of that tradition. So, too, was the earlier case of Samuel Wells Williams, who came to New Haven as a professor of missions in 1877 after forty-three years in China and Japan. Williams translated many books of the bible into both Chinese and Japanese. His greatest achievement was a two-volume work, *The Middle Kingdom*, which remained a standard reference work in Chinese history for more than half a century.[79]

The same combination of diplomacy, scholarship, and missions defined the career of the Berkeley sinologist mentioned in chapter 7, Edward Thomas Williams, who was not related to Samuel Wells Williams. E. T. Williams's 613-page survey *China Yesterday and Today* appeared in 1923 and was widely circulated as one of the few authoritative books available on the subject. One of its most conspicuous features was its resolutely sympathetic outlook on Buddhism, Confucianism, and Taoism. In a characteristic utterance, Williams concluded his chapter on Buddhism with the injunction to American Christians to remember that "no matter what our faith, we should love truth above all things and be willing to acknowledge it wherever it may be found."[80]

Edward Thomas Williams was not a scholar of Samuel Wells Williams's distinction, but his career is of special interest because he left such a detailed record of his own transformation from an ethnocentric, conversion-engaged missionary to someone who regularly made the kinds of statements just quoted. He became what his biographer more than thirty years ago called "a multicultural man," directing his energies against anti-Chinese prejudice and Protestant parochialism. Williams's life was indeed an early example of the pattern that most defines *Protestants Abroad*. Williams went to China in 1887 but soon "experienced a profound transformation" in his views of religion, China, and himself, writes Dimitri D. Lazo. Williams left the mission after nine years, resigned his ministry, soon "abandoned conventional Christianity," and came to invoke "the moral pronouncements of Confucius as often as the teachings of Jesus." Williams retired in 1927, but remained an active advocate of Chinese Studies until his death in 1944 at the age of ninety.[81]

Latourette inherited this tradition of sinology and was essentially charged by the ACLS with modernizing it. But until Fairbank took over, the China field did not have what would later be understood as professional leadership. In the early 1980s, Fairbank recalled visiting Yale in the 1930s and meeting "Dr. Latourette," who had "moved into the China vacuum" and who wrote

> standard volumes of dispassionate knowledge, compiled by a fair-minded and indefatigable seeker after the facts. Ken Latourette was a benign bachelor, helpful to all who came to know him. He covered mountains of sources and produced manuscript, I believe, every morning except Sundays. His presidential address to the American Historical Association was on the Christian interpretation of history.[82]

Even after Latourette completed in 1945 the seven-volume study of mission history for which he is most remembered, he continued to produce at a prodigious rate. He wrote, among other books, the five-volume study *Christianity in a Revolutionary Age: A History of Christianity in the 19th and 20th Centuries*.[83] His *Festschrift* of 1962 was entirely devoted to the history and contemporary state of the Protestant missionary project and, although of genuine importance in the context of that period's debates within ecumenical Protestantism about missions, was virtually irrelevant to the Chinese Studies of that era.[84]

Fairbank was more intellectually capacious than Latourette, and more savvy professionally. When Fairbank began teaching in the History Department at Harvard in 1937 he quickly engaged potential colleagues and allies throughout the campus, especially his Japanese history counterpart, Reischauer. The two began to teach together. Just as Reischauer had placed Japanese history on the Harvard map before heading off to Washington, Fairbank did the same for Chinese history before he left for OSS service in China and in Washington, where he, too, made the acquaintance of Kenneth Landon.

In these early efforts at Harvard, Fairbank was greatly helped by the existence of the Harvard-Yenching Institute, which dramatically distinguished Harvard's China engagement from Yale's. When a wealthy donor left eight million dollars to Harvard "to promote Christian higher education in China," Harvard's leaders in 1928 cleverly entered a partnership with the leading missionary-operated college in China.[85] The bequest was thus, in a fashion, directed to Christian education, but also to scholarship on things Asian as understood by Harvard. It was to staff the Harvard-Yenching Institute's Cambridge installation that Elisseeff was recruited from Paris. Fairbank thus had a highly promising institutional setting to which he could return after the war.

Once Fairbank started rolling, especially from the very early 1950s, when large amounts of money from the federal government and the big foundations came within his reach, he proved his mettle as doctoral mentor. The one hundred students who completed their Harvard doctorates under Fairbank's supervision included many from outside the history department. They worked in the disciplines of political science, sociology, and East Asian languages and literature, and gravitated to Fairbank.[86] Fairbank's doctoral alumni who became visible China scholars in American universities and around the world in several disciplines included Paul Cohen, Albert Feuerwerker, Merle Goldman, Charles Hayford, Aikira Iriye, John Israel, Philip A. Kuhn, Joseph R. Levenson, Marion J. Levy, Lilian Li, K. C. Liu, Rhoads Murphey, Andrew Nathan, John L. Rawlinson, David Roy, John Schrecker, Benjamin I. Schwartz, James C. Thomson Jr., Philip West, Mary C. Wright, Ernest P. Young, and Marilyn B. Young.[87]

In addition to his specialized scholarship, Fairbank's textbooks and conference volumes—often produced in collaboration with others—made him all the more central to his field. His popular book, *The United States and China*, first published in 1948, went through four editions. There was no more important Area Studies scholar in any of the geographic regions than Fairbank, who, two years after his death in 1991, was still called "Father of the Field" in the dedication of a volume of essays on *American Studies of Contemporary China*.[88] Fairbank liked to compare his own labors to those of the missionaries; when he began teaching at Harvard, he later recalled, he was "already embarked on that missionary-in-reverse role of the area specialist, telling our fellow citizens about foreign parts."[89]

The numerous missionaries and missionary children who populated Fairbank's path were highly important to him intellectually and professionally. This was true in both of his long residencies in China, first in the mid-1930s as a dissertation student from Oxford, and second during

World War II as a roving intelligence officer. Those two highly formative episodes in Fairbank's life invite attention here because they show how ubiquitous the missionaries were in the American relation to China as late as the 1930s and 1940s, and how missionaries could affect someone with no personal connection to missions and even no commitment to Christianity.

Fairbank first went to China in 1932 after having been talked into studying Chinese diplomatic and economic history by Charles Webster, who had been Fairbank's British mentor while Fairbank was a Rhodes Scholar at Oxford. Fairbank grew up in a reasonably prosperous South Dakota family with a long line of Congregationalist ministers in its ancestry, including some missionaries. But his own upbringing had been "irreligious," as he explained in his autobiography, adding that his own religion had come to be "Harvard and what it stands for in the secular world." Once in China, however, Fairbank resourcefully sought out and profited from any support he could get, and very often those helping him find his way were missionaries.

Upon his arrival in Beijing he immersed himself in the society of the local missionary colleges. He relied on the experience and expertise of their faculties and administrators, including Roger Sherman Greene, the missionary child from Japan then serving as the dean of the Peking Medical College who later chaired the American Committee for Non-Participation in Japanese Aggression. Greene gave "moral support when I needed it," Fairbank recalled. There in Beijing, Fairbank first met John H. M. Lindbeck, then in his late teens, who would later lead the Ford Foundation's support of Chinese Studies and would serve in senior staff positions at Harvard and Columbia. "Nearly all the missionaries offered more than the evangelical message that had preoccupied earlier generations," Fairbank noted, although he was quick to register the vast theological differences between the old-fashioned, conservative missionaries of the China Inland Mission and the more liberal ones he met in Beijing and Shanghai. Typical of his new friends was a missionary clergyman who married Fairbank and his bride, Wilma, when she arrived in China not long after he did.[90]

The young dissertation student and his wife met a remarkable cast of characters during their two years in China, including many Westerners who were not connected with missions. These included the radical writer Agnes Smedley, the journalist Harold Isaacs (who became Fairbank's lifelong friend), the great sinologist Owen Lattimore, and the writer Edgar Snow, whose 1937 book, *Red Star Over China*, was the first and for long the most authoritative account of the Communist guerillas led by Mao

Zedong.[91] Fairbank also met Ida Pruitt, a daughter of missionaries who had rejected the old faith and was then making her way as a social worker and journalistic commentator on Chinese life.[92]

But it was the missionaries themselves, with their long-standing base in local communities, to whom Fairbank turned again and again in his travels. "We were impressed with the hospitality and hostelry function of the missionaries," he recalled in 1982 on behalf of himself and Wilma.

> There they were in each town, ready without notice to take us in at any hour, provide local news, guides, and connections, and accept only our nominal contributions of cash for expenses incurred. Even in the 1930s, past their heyday, they functioned in almost as many places as the China Travel Service of today and would tell you at least as much about local conditions.

Such recollections prompted Fairbank to ponder a question he pushed as a mature scholar but remained unsure of the answer: "How to evaluate the contribution of Christian missions to China is a real poser," perhaps a question that "cannot be answered in any conclusive way."[93]

Fairbank's engagement with this question was all the deeper as a result of the missionary element in his later residencies in China, in 1942-43 and again in 1945-46, both in official capacities. He was first working for the OSS, and later for the Office of War Information and then for the Department of State. While so doing he met up occasionally with missionary sons John Paton Davies and John S. Service, and with others dealt with in this book's treatment of the Foreign Service, the OSS, and the CIA. But a major theme of his autobiographical account of these years, as with that of his earlier time in China, is the help he got from missionaries. Many were new acquaintances, and others he had come to know during his previous time in that country. Again and again the missionaries filled him in on what was happening, enabling him to write credible reports to his OSS superiors in Washington. Fairbank found missionary leaders Frank W. Price, Daniel Dye, and Andrew Roy to be particularly convincing analysts of the scene. Andrew Roy's son, Stapleton Roy, would eventually become an American ambassador to the People's Republic of China, and his other son, David Roy, would become one of Fairbank's doctoral students. The missionaries reinforced Fairbank's growing skepticism about the government of Chiang Kai-shek.[94] The missionaries warned him repeatedly of the failings of the Kuomintang to supply basic government services and to hold the loyalties of the local populations. Fairbank got the same message from the many left-wing American intellectuals he got to know better in his 1940s residencies in China. He was willing to describe the Kuomintang as an essentially fascist operation.

Fairbank's dispatches from China during and immediately after the war would have gotten him into the same trouble that destroyed the Foreign Service careers of his friends if only he had been more prominent. But there were bigger fish to fry. Fairbank's experiences in the McCarthy era were relatively mild, although he was several times accused of being a conduit for the Communist line, most painfully by China specialist George Taylor of the University of Washington, whom he had known in China and who had been his initial boss in the OSS. Fairbank had, after all, been an affiliate of the Institute of Pacific Relations, written disparagingly about the Kuomintang, and reported regularly to Alger Hiss when Hiss was in the State Department. Fairbank had been friendly with Owen Lattimore, O. Edmund Clubb, John Service, John Paton Davies, Agnes Smedley, Edgar Snow, Ida Pruitt, and others whose names peppered the hearings of the early 1950s. Fairbank had recommended the Canadian leftist E. H. Norman for an appointment at Harvard.[95] But by the time Fairbank became a minor player in the dramas of the McCarthy era, he was protected by Harvard and well launched into his career of building Chinese Area Studies, and also of contributing to the public discussion of Chinese affairs and American policy toward China.

As soon as he got back from China, Fairbank published an article in *The Atlantic* arguing against interventions to save the Kuomintang, declaring further that it was a mistake to see the Chinese Communists as mere puppets of the Soviet Union.[96] The article was soon followed, in 1948, by the book *The United States and China*. In these actions Fairbank followed an identical course with Reischauer, and one very close to that of W. Norman Brown. Reischauer's *Japan: Past and Present* and Brown's *India and Pakistan* were both part of the same series. All three books illustrate how closely the postwar development of Area Studies proceeded in step with the project of educating politicians and the general public about Asia. All were identical in genre, written and published within a few years of one another, and went through many editions. *The United States and China* was widely regarded as the finest and most influential of all of Fairbank's books.[97]

Chinese Studies, even more than Japanese Studies, was closely entangled with American politics from that immediate postwar period down through the Vietnam era and following. Paul Evans found that, of Fairbank's fifty correspondents between 1946 and 1950, no fewer than thirty-five were officials of the State Department.[98] As late as the early

1970s, China scholars more often worked with the Central Intelligence Agency than did scholars in the other regional fields. Chalmers Johnson, a leader of Berkeley's Center for Chinese Studies in the 1960s and early 1970s, was open about his use of the center in his work for the CIA, only later excoriating what he came to regard as American imperialism. At some scholarly meetings, nametags included the affiliation "CIA," which meant that the bearers were analysts based in Washington, not agents in the field. Prominent among these CIA analysts was missionary son John Seabury Thomson, brother of James C. Thomson Jr., who left the government when he found he could not support the Vietnam War.[99] It was not unusual for Chinese Studies scholars to serve on the National Security Council. Fairbank's East Asian Studies Center welcomed CIA analysts for year-long study. As late as 1993 a volume assessing the state of Chinese Studies included a chapter on "Government China Specialists: Scholar Officials and Official Scholars."[100]

The career of Fairbank's contemporary T. A. Bisson (1900–1979), who began his Chinese engagements as a missionary teacher in the 1920s, further illuminates this intimacy of academic Chinese Studies with the politics of American foreign policy. What happened to Bisson also illustrates the great difference could be made during the McCarthy era by institutional support of the kind Fairbank enjoyed at Harvard. While Fairbank in the late 1940s and early 1950s was comfortably going back and forth between his academic program-building and his exchanges with government officials, Bisson was becoming more and more marginal. Bisson's case also illuminates the transition between the IPR era, when the line between scholarship and journalism was blurred, and the later, academic era, when that line became much sharper.[101] Before attending further to Fairbank and other sinologists, I will take a brief detour through the career of this extremely talented but ill-fated former missionary.

The story began in China, where four years of missionary experience in Anhuei and Beijing convinced the young Congregationalist Bisson that he wanted to pursue an academic career. He left missions in 1928 and enrolled at Columbia University. He stopped short of the completion of his doctorate when he was enticed away by a substantial salary offer from the Foreign Policy Association. This well-funded private organization had been founded in 1918 by staunch Wilsonians eager to instruct and influence American public opinion and officialdom about world affairs. By the time FPA beckoned, Bisson was married—to a daughter of China missionaries—and the father of two children. "I went into politics to make a living," he later explained.[102] Bisson had the experience and expertise the

FPA wanted. During the 1930s he used this position to establish himself as one of the most respected American commenters on East Asian affairs. He published more than one hundred articles. "Bisson's scholarship of the 1930s was of the highest standard," notes the most careful student of his career, "and usually won him praise from scholars and statesmen alike."[103]

Bisson's book of 1938, *Japan in China*, provided a detailed account of the recent Japanese occupation based on his own extensive travels, which were financed by the FPA and the Rockefeller Foundation. It was the standard work of the period, relied upon by popular writers like John Gunther as well as government officials and academics.[104] His journeys included an automobile trip of 1937 he and several friends, including Owen Lattimore and Philip Jaffe, made from Beijing to Yenan to interview Mao Zedong and other Communist Party leaders. Although *Japan in China* drew on that trip, Bisson did not publish his detailed account of the Yenan visit until 1973, immediately after the United States recognized the People's Republic of China. *Yenan in June 1937: Talks with the Communist Leaders* is a compelling journal of a harrowing journey, complete with photographs of the Communist leaders and of the travelers' canvas-topped touring car being towed out of mud by oxen and by local Chinese peasants. The journal's sympathetic perspective on Mao Zedong, Zhou Enlai, and the other Yenan Communists may have led Bisson to put it aside during the 1950s, when such close contact with the Chinese Communists was more damaging than helpful to one's reputation.[105]

Bisson was recruited into government service within a few weeks of Pearl Harbor. His assignment was the Economic Warfare Board, charged with advising the government on ways in which the mobilization and redirecting of economic resources could affect the war effort throughout the globe. The board was chaired by Vice President Henry Wallace and was reputed to be a shelter for left-wingers. In April 1943, Bisson was one of several called to testify before Martin Dies's subversive-chasing congressional committee. Bisson's positive assessments of the Chinese Communists were indeed at issue. He defended himself vigorously, but that same month escaped the volatile atmosphere in Washington to accept an appointment as a research associate of IPR in New York, to which he had strong ties for many previous years.

During the next two years at IPR, Bisson produced a large body of articles and books arguing for the self-determination of Asian peoples, whose legitimate claims on their own destiny had been thwarted by indigenous militarist and Western imperialists. Shortly after he got to IPR he published the article in *Far Eastern Survey* for which he became the most famous, an attack on the Kuomintang even more severe than the one Pearl Buck had just published in *Life*.[106] In a sentence that would later haunt him, Bisson wrote that the Chinese Communists were practicing "bourgeois democracy" in an agrarian setting, and "by no stretch of the imagination" could be regarded as genuine Communists.[107] Bisson brought out a new, revised version of *American's Far Eastern Policy*, a detailed historical and contemporary study that he earlier published at IPR in 1940.[108] He moved from a focus on China to a deeper engagement with Japan. Drawing on the work of his long-time IPR co-worker E. H. Norman, Bisson projected a future for Japan that would involve fundamental political and economic restructuring.

It was as a Japanese expert that Bisson moved back into government service in October 1945 and served as an economic analyst in the occupation of Japan, resulting in another volume published by IPR, *Prospects for Democracy in Japan*.[109] After more than two years in Japan, Bisson was ready to join the suddenly expanding academic domain for East Asian experts. His friends back at IPR successfully promoted him for an appointment in political science at the University of California at Berkeley, where he began teaching in 1948. But Bisson, having been enticed away from graduate studies to take the job at the FPA, had not completed his doctorate. His faculty appointment at Berkeley was temporary, subject to periodic review.

The appointment was soon under severe attack from Republican Party politicians within and beyond California well aware of his proclaimed sympathy for the Chinese Communists. Bisson was called to testify in 1952 before the same senatorial committee of Senator McCarran that gave such a hard time to the Foreign Service officers. Bisson was confronted repeatedly with the ostensibly bad company he had kept, including Lattimore and another of his co-travelers to Yenan, the writer and editor Philip J. Jaffe, whose Communist sympathies were not disguised. Bisson's interrogators would have been even more belligerent, and his career yet more decisively damaged, had they known what was then a well-kept secret: that between 1934 and 1937, Bisson, under the pseudonym of Frederick Spencer, wrote dozens of articles supporting the Communist cause in China in *China Today*, a magazine edited by Jaffe.[110]

Bisson managed to stay on at Berkeley through 1953–54. But there were no more renewals. At that time campus officials had their hands full defending tenured faculty from political purges, and it seems that Bisson was too marginal to be worth a fight. Without the tenured job for which the doctorate had become almost always a necessity, Bisson was vulnerable. "At age fifty-two," Howard B. Schonberger observes, "Bisson found himself without a job and unable to get one," despite a continuing publication record of some distinction. Bisson finally found employment at a tiny religious college for women in Ohio, and "never again," in Schonberger's words, "had the time or the facilities for further major research."[111] Bisson did speak up politically from time to time, and was an adamant opponent of the Vietnam War.[112] Bisson eventually moved to Canada, and died there in 1979.

Were it not for his political difficulties, Bisson might have survived as adjunct or lecturer in the academic world of the 1950s and 1960s, but the transformation of academia made universities less hospitable to scholars like Bisson who lacked doctorates. Moreover, Bisson's major work of his Berkeley years, *Zaibatsu Dissolution in Japan*, cited no Japanese language sources.[113] This book offered a view of Japanese economic and political history similar, again, to that of Norman, but Norman's work had a deep research base in Japanese documents while Bisson relied on what could be learned from reading English. By the 1950s, academia had vastly expanded the opportunities for people of Bisson's interests and expertise, but the linguistic standards for scholarship had become much higher. When Bisson moved his primary focus from China to Japan, he diminished his academic credibility.

Bisson's political difficulties persisted beyond his death in an episode that demands clarification here. As explained in an earlier chapter, when the Venona transcripts were released in 1995, it was established that Duncan Lee had participated in espionage while in the OSS. At that time, too, it was widely noted that Bisson was mentioned by name and given the code name "Arthur" for the purposes of Soviet intelligence. Some scholars have since classified Bisson as a spy.[114] But I find it unlikely that Bisson consciously participated in espionage. The Venona transcripts do record that Joseph Bernstein, who was indeed passing information to Soviet military intelligence, had befriended Bisson at the New York offices of IPR shortly after Bisson arrived there from Washington in the spring of 1943.[115] It is clear from the transcripts that Bisson did share with the group of Asia specialists at IPR, including Bernstein, documents from his recent experience at the Board of Economic Warfare. Yet there is nothing in the record to indicate that Bisson understood Bernstein to be passing information on to the Soviets. The atmosphere in the offices of IPR and the closely associated magazine of FPA, *Amerasia*, edited by Bisson's friend Jaffe, was very casual. Foreign Service officer John S. Service, as discussed in chapter 7, showed classified documents to the circle of scholars and journalists gathered in those offices during the war. Bisson was surrounded at IPR by old friends with whom he shared a positive view of the Chinese Communists, and, while it is conceivable that he was aware that he was being used as a source for Soviet intelligence, I have seen no evidence that he was. It seems more likely that Bisson was given a code name in his capacity as a source for Bernstein, not as a co-conspirator.

Bisson's virtual disappearance in the early 1950s has made it too easy to forget what a prominent figure he had been in learned as well as popular discussions of contemporary East Asia during the 1930s and 1940s. During the years that Bisson was being pushed out of scholarship, a number of other missionary-connected individuals managed to make their marks in Chinese Studies. None of them had been as publicly identified with the Chinese Communists as Bisson had. The missionary contingent was especially strong at Columbia University. Missionary sons L. Carrington Goodrich (1894–1986) and C. Martin Wilbur (1907–1997) together led the Chinese history program there for four decades. Former missionary M. Searle Bates (1897–1978), also a historian, worked across the street at Union Theological Seminary, and was closely connected with Columbia.[116] This group was eventually joined by two other China-born missionary sons. Career administrator John H. M. Lindbeck (1915–1970) served as director of Columbia's East Asian Institute, for many years chaired the Chinese Studies Joint Committee of the American Council of Learned Societies and the Social Science Research Council, and led the Ford Foundation's inquiry into the resources available for Chinese Studies in the United States, *Understanding China*.[117] A. Doak Barnett (1921–1999), a leading political scientist, had been an official of the Ford Foundation before moving to Columbia.[118]

Missionary sons and daughters were scattered elsewhere. Political scientist Lucian Pye (1921–2008) spent most of his career at the Massachusetts Institute of Technology and was known as a persistent defender of modernization theory.[119] Literary scholar Harriet C. Mills (1920–2016), a missionary daughter famous for surviving a long imprisonment and traumatic interrogation at the hands of Communists after the revolution of 1949, was a noted professor at the University of Michigan.[120] Richard Mather taught history at the University of Minnesota. David M. Rowe, the anomalously right-wing member of his cohort, taught at Yale University, along with George Kennedy, who worked primarily on antiquity in the older, philologically-centered tradition of sinological scholarship.[121] Historian James C. Thomson Jr. joined Fairbank at Harvard, having left the US government's employ in 1966 in protest against the Vietnam War.

The Chinese Studies "establishment," as critics called the Fairbank-centered enterprise by the end of the 1960s, was accused of promoting perspectives on China that were too oriented to the political interests of the American government and insufficiently driven by a vision of what was best for the Chinese people. These disputes ran parallel to those in Japanese Studies, and often focused on the concept of "modernization." Had the leading China scholars—despite their troubles in the McCarthy era, their long advocacy of the normalization of relations with the People's Republic of China, and their opposition to the Vietnam War—been too inclined to promote a liberal rather than Marxist perspective on modern Chinese history? And had some of these government-connected academics been in effect "bought" by the powers in Washington? Fairbank, Lindbeck, and Barnett were accused by name of betraying academic ideals.[122] Fairbank's own place in these debates was long defined by his slowness in joining the bulk of East Asian academics in clearly and unambiguously opposing the Vietnam War. His biographer provides a detailed account of the Vietnam debates and Fairbank's role in them, concluding that "there was no single moment" when Fairbank "turned from being a reluctant supporter to a hesitant, then impassioned, opponent of the war."[123]

The rights and wrongs of these debates, like those in Japanese Studies, are beyond the scope of this book. But the question arises: were missionary-connected scholars more likely than others to come down on one side or another of these disputes, and did these scholars have any more distinctive a view of Chinese history than the missionary-connected specialists in Japan or India?

The missionary/nonmissionary distinction provides very little purchase on the charges and counter-charges of the late Vietnam era. Political scientist Robert Scalapino of Berkeley, primarily a Japanologist but also active in Chinese Studies, long defended the Johnson administration's policy in Vietnam. His political science contemporary Alan Whiting, a China specialist, was so dismayed by that policy that he severed his connection with the State Department. Neither of these strongly disagreeing scholars had any missionary connection. David Rowe of Yale vigorously supported the war, while another missionary son, A. Doak Barnett, continued for several years to be reserved about it, like Fairbank, even when Barnett's own siblings were adamantly opposed to it.[124] Most of the missionary-connected scholars active in Asian Studies during the Vietnam years were lined up with the majority of nonmissionary colleagues in basic support of Fairbank, who did believe that the Communist path toward an industrialized, public-serving society was less defensible than the path taken by the capitalist democracies. Fairbank's more zealously antiwar critics included some younger China specialists like Jim Peck and Marilyn Young, who were graduate students at the time, but many of the most adamant and professionally established of these critics were not Asian specialists.[125]

One of the most active players in the Vietnam era disputes of Chinese Studies was Fairbank's student and colleague Thomson. This missionary son served in the State Department and in the White House in several capacities between 1961 and 1966, all the while "trying," as George Packard summarizes Thomson's brief government career, "to change China policy from within." It was Thomson, more than any other voice close to John F. Kennedy, who was responsible for the appointment of Reischauer as ambassador to Japan. Thomson was a skilled political operator, working closely with Chester Bowles, McGeorge Bundy, and other major foreign policy figures of the historical moment.[126] But he lost the argument in Washington. And finally, in 1966, as noted above, Thomson resigned from the government in opposition to the Johnson administration's Vietnam policy. He went back to Harvard, produced a respected monograph on Chinese history, and began a long tenure as head of the Nieman Fellowship program for visiting journalists. In a 1968 article in *The Atlantic*, Thomson fumed at the inability of the Kennedy and Johnson administrations to overcome the legacy of the Dulles years:

> In 1961, the U. S. Government's East Asia establishment was undoubtedly the most rigid and doctrinaire of Washington's regional divisions in foreign affairs. This was especially true at the Department of State, where the incoming administration found the Bureau of Far Eastern Affairs . . . purged of its best China expertise and . . . committed to one policy line: the close containment and isolation of mainland China, the harassment of 'neutralist nations' . . . and the maintenance of a network of alliances with anti-Communist states on China's periphery.[127]

While Thomson was writing things of this sort, his older brother, John, continued the work in Washington as a CIA analyst that he had begun in 1957. Did the two brothers ever speak? Yes, and cordially, according to family members. John Seabury Thomson is remembered by his son as having been totally supportive of the youth's decision to become a conscientious objector in 1968. Christopher Thomson was a student at Swarthmore College when his father—himself a Swarthmore alumnus—visited the campus and dealt calmly with the son's antiwar contemporaries. The son declares that at the time and for many years after, he and other members of the family were never sure exactly what John Seabury Thomson thought about the Vietnam War. But shortly before his death in 1998 the former CIA man said to the son: "You know Christopher you were right about Vietnam." The son's account of the political and personal relationships with his father and his uncle is worth quoting here as a window on how at least one missionary family dealt with the issues of that era.

> Freshman year at Swarthmore. . . . I turned in my draft card in protest of the Vietnam War. I sent Dad a copy of my letter to my draft board. He replied "that is a position I can support." A few months later he sent me a copy of Uncle Jimmy's Atlantic Monthly article. I believed at the time and still believe he was proud of his younger brother. Dad hired a good lawyer for me and also took me to speak with pro and anti-war experts. I never felt he was trying to talk me out of my position. . . . I eventually decided I could be of more service doing alternative service as a conscientious objector than trying to argue my position in court. When it was time for my draft board hearing Dad invited Jimmy to come down from Harvard, stay at our house, and speak in support of me. They both spoke eloquently. I sensed no tension between them at the hearing or during the day and a half before. . . . Both men had a deep sense of duty and morality that manifested itself differently.[128]

"Uncle Jimmy," collaborating with colleagues Peter W. Stanley and John Curtis Perry, went on to write in 1980 what remains after several decades one of the finest popular books ever written about the relations of the United States to the peoples and governments of East Asia, *Sentimental Imperialists: The American Experience in East Asia*.

Beyond disagreements over Vietnam, did the missionary/-nonmissionary divide mark differences in interpretation? Was there a "missionary school" of Chinese Studies? No, there was not, any more than for Japanese studies. There, the big divide was between two missionary sons, Reischauer and Norman. In the case of China, missionary son Pye was adamant: throughout the entire period postwar era "there was no suspicion or counter-suspicion among scholars of China that being a child of missionaries created a bias."[129] The same is true of South Asian studies. The cases of Brown and the Wisers illustrate the great range of topical interests and methodological approaches of the missionary-connected scholars in South Asian Studies.[130] In all three Area Studies specialties—India, Japan, and China—missionary cosmopolitanism was expressed across rather than within the lines of interpretations over which scholars argued.

A handful of missionary-connected individuals worked in the Area Studies programs for three other Asian regions: Southeast Asia, Korea, and the Middle East. Kenneth Landon, discussed in the previous chapter, was by far the most important example in Southeast Asian Studies. But not until the Vietnam era did Southeast Asian studies become a major player in American academia.[131] Korea was long seen as too small and too marginal to inspire ambitious Area Studies programs. In what little work there was in mainstream academia on modern Korean Studies, however, a conspicuous leader was missionary son George M. McCune.[132] An entirely different set of circumstances explains the relative lack of missionary involvement in Middle Eastern Studies.[133]

What had long been called the "Near East" was the scene of many of the oldest and most robust of American missionary endeavors, but one overwhelming reality made this mission field unique: this part of the world was the original home of Christianity and Judaism, and was "the cradle of civilization," including ancient Babylon and Egypt. Missionaries participated in the study of the ancient Near East from the start, but there was no special need for them. The leading American practitioner of Near Eastern Studies, James Henry Breasted of the University of Chicago, was trained in Berlin, had no personal connection to missions, and focused on ancient history.[134] Antiquity in this part of the world was so rich and appealing that it overshadowed the study of the modern period more fully than in any of the other regions for which Area Studies were later developed.

Moreover, when scholarly engagement with the Middle East's modern period finally flowered, there was available a supply of qualified Arab, Persian, and Turkish scholars. The most important of these was Philip Hitti, whom Princeton brought from his native Lebanon in 1927 to lead the nation's first program in Arabic and Islamic Studies.[135] American universities could also draw upon the scholars trained in the French and British universities, which had developed programs connected to colonial empires. Eventually, the field attracted Jewish scholars with a special interest in Palestine and the new state of Israel. These included political scientist Leonard Binder, who had fought as an Israeli soldier in 1948–49 and became one of the leading modern Middle East scholars in the United States.[136]

Historian Albert H. Lybyer was one of few missionary-connected Near Eastern specialists who got beyond antiquity and who found a place at an American research university. Earlier in this book, I discussed his role in the King-Crane Commission of 1919. An Ottoman specialist, Lybyer left Istanbul's Robert College in 1913 and was teaching at the University of Illinois when, in 1917, he offered his services to the Woodrow Wilson administration as an expert on contemporary Near Eastern affairs. After the war, Lybyer returned to Illinois and taught there until 1944. Within the relatively small world of Ottoman Studies, Lybyer was known for "the Lybyer thesis," explaining Ottoman success through the administrative practices developed with the greatest efficiency by Suleiman the Magnificent in the sixteenth century. But Lybyer did not read Ottoman Turkish, and depended on sources in European languages and on translations from Ottoman sources. His reputation did not survive into the postwar era, when Middle Eastern Studies was developed more extensively.[137]

Missionary cosmopolitanism massively increased the sheer magnitude of East Asia and South Asia in American higher education's representation of the world. Although first concentrated in a few Ivy League universities, this expanded and deeply respectful attention to China, India, and Japan was soon common to all research universities and gradually affected curriculum at colleges throughout the United States. Missionary cosmopolitanism also directed the study of Asian societies away from the older, "Orientalist" preoccupations and toward modern history and contemporary methods in the social sciences and humanities. The disagreements between Reischauer and Norman took place within the decidedly post-Orientalist framing of academic Asian Studies after World War II.

Beyond academia, other missionary-connected Americans engaged the regions of the globe in secular service projects that functioned, in many respects, as successor-projects to missions. They were the model for the Peace Corps established by the US government in the early 1960s. To these endeavors in post-missionary service the next chapter is devoted.

CHAPTER TEN

Toward the Peace Corps

POST-MISSIONARY SERVICE ABROAD

"WHAT CANNOT BE overemphasized," writes a close student of the origins of the Peace Corps, "is how closely the Peace Corps actually copied IVS."[1] The "IVS" to which Paul Rodell refers is International Voluntary Services, a secular NGO founded in 1953 by churches eager to expand missionary-style service projects abroad without entangling them in the ideological and institutional framework of missions. IVS is one of several missionary-inspired foreign-aid programs designed to serve the needs of populations in what came to be called "the underdeveloped world." This chapter is about three such programs. One is IVS. A second is the battery of development projects created and led by the missionary-educated and supported organizational genius C. Y. James Yen. The third is the literacy-advancing campaign of former missionary Frank Laubach.

Post-missionary service operations were usually community-centered, featuring face-to-face contact and focusing on education, literacy, agriculture, and public health. Individuals and groups who had performed service through missions became extensively involved in the technical aid programs of NGOs and of the US government that proliferated and expanded after World War II. The character of post-missionary service projects was well captured in 1956 by a foreign aid officer of the State Department who admired them. "The missionaries," reflected Arthur Raper, have shown Americans how they could "be of help in India, or China, or the Sudan, or some other part of the world generally identified by Americans as underdeveloped." Raper wrote in the middle of a distinguished career as a government supervisor of development projects throughout Asia, Africa, and the Middle East. In his meditations on

foreign aid efforts, Raper returned repeatedly to the ways in which public and private agencies were carrying on the service role pioneered by
Protestant missionaries. Indeed, even in the setting of the Cold War, he
singled out the missionary project, with italics of his own, as an important
cultural foundation for foreign aid: a major reason we are providing all
this technical aid to developing countries was to "provide the American
people an opportunity to *elongate and broaden the Foreign Missionary
effort* of the Western churches."[2] Raper was struck by how different the
missionary style—of close-to-the-ground attention to local conditions—
was from many of the aid projects he had witnessed. He found value in
the large-scale development projects that sought to modernize underdeveloped countries through the building of dams, electrical systems, and
other macro systems.[3] But the missionaries were different. They lived in
closer proximity to the local people, Raper explained, "without the benefit of clubs or other escapes from the rigors of local life" favored by other
Westerners. "Most basic of all," he continued, "the missionary effort assume[d] the individual worth of the native," promoting an element of
"equal footing" that was essential to any successful "community development endeavor." What the missionaries most have to teach secular development workers was the inspiration for doing things on one's own: "In
summary, what the missionary has done *for* the people is limited; what
he has done *with* them is greater; but greatest of all is what he has helped
them to do *among themselves*."[4]

   Laubach's project was the most famous of the three cases I discuss
here, and the one most closely connected with the missionary experience; I begin there. Then I will turn to Yen, who was, from the American
Protestant perspective, the "complete convert": he had a life and career
exactly in the mold prescribed by the missionary project to create for the
world. I will then take up IVS and its connection to the Peace Corps, and—
equally revealing—its traumatic experience in the Vietnam era.

   Laubach (1884–1970) had spent fifteen frustrating years as a
Congregationalist missionary in the Philippines, making very few converts, when, in 1930, he went to a mountaintop near his village on
Mindanao to pray and meditate. There, God spoke to him, and bluntly.
Laubach later reported that he felt God was chastising him for secretly
negative feelings about the Moros, the people among whom he lived. "You
have failed because you do not really love" the people you are trying to
serve, God scolded him. "You feel superior to them because you are white."
God told Laubach that "if you can forget" your American whiteness and
think only of love for the Moros, "they will respond."[5]

The troubled missionary decided that loving the Moros meant stopping all proselytizing. God wanted him to study the Quran, to engage in sympathetic dialogue with the predominately Muslim local inhabitants, and to find ways to actually help them live better lives. Soon, Laubach hit on the idea of teaching the Moros how to read. This was a practical tool, useful without reference to any religion. The inspiration was mystical—Laubach wrote as if he were Saul being struck down on the road to Damascus—but the outcome was decidedly down-to-earth. Laubach went on to become the twentieth century's most illustrious promoter of literacy, rivaled only by the much younger Brazilian educational reformer Paulo Freire, who surfaced shortly before Laubach died.[6] Starting with the rendering of the Moro tongue into Roman characters and establishing many schools designed to teach people to read in it, Laubach and the organizations he created eventually produced language primers in 312 languages. By the time he died in 1970 he was popularly credited with enabling several million people to read in more than one hundred countries, and had been awarded honorary degrees by Columbia, Princeton, and other universities. He wrote forty-three books. At the centennial of his birth in 1984, the US Postal Service issued a stamp in his honor.[7]

Laubach was absorbed into the missionary endeavor at the time of its highest confidence. Like so many in his cohort, he was well educated and committed to the social gospel. When Laubach went to the Philippines in 1915, he had recently earned a PhD in sociology from Columbia. His dissertation, a study of the social and economic causes of the large population of homeless men seen on the streets of New York, was written in the classic social gospel mode of the period.[8] Earlier, he had been an undergraduate at Princeton and a ministerial student at Union Theological Seminary. There is no doubt that his experience in the field had a deep effect on him, but he illustrates well the ways in which dispositions brought to the missionary experience could render individuals responsive to the redeeming qualities in foreign cultures. He was prepared to see in Filipinos and Muslims human qualities that some others were slower to celebrate.

Laubach liked to say that "God killed my racial prejudice" at that mountaintop moment of great spiritual intensity.[9] But long before his epiphany of 1930 he had been soberly reflective about the challenges of the missionary enterprise. Within a few years of his arrival he was well on his way toward a principled antiracism. In the 1920s, Laubach wrote several popular books about the Filipino people and about the wrong-headed character of traditional missionary activities directed toward them. He introduced his five-hundred-page volume of 1925, *The People of the Philippines: Their Religious Progress and Preparation for Spiritual Leadership in the Far East*, with confidence that the Filipinos were capable of sharing global leadership with other peoples. Laubach looked to them and other Asian peoples to take over Christianity.

In his extravagant idealism, Laubach essentialized his subjects and ascribed to them as a group the traits he most admired: "the Filipinos" were not at all like what Americans supposed, but instead "meek, quiet, gentle, kindly, hospitable," and in every respect what a human being should be. He castigated the many American businessmen who mistreated Filipinos, and reported that the Protestant missionaries would "overwhelmingly" support independence "as soon as the Philippines can be guaranteed security from international complications."[10] In a book of 1929, Laubauch denounced the zoo-like presentation of Filipinos at the St. Louis World's Fair of 1904, which, he correctly saw, had reinforced the prejudicial notion that all Filipinos wore g-strings and carried spears.[11] Laubach criticized American imperial authorities; he wrote in missionary publications of the predatory nature of American corporations who were gaining control over arable land that Laubach believed should be reserved for Filipino farmers and their families.[12]

It was in the context of these concerns that Laubach in 1936 wrote a celebratory biography of Jose Rizal, the great hero of Philippine nationalism. A writer and physician who had converted to Protestantism, Rizal was executed in 1896 by Spanish colonial authorities angered by his reformist, nationalist writings. Laubach declared that Rizal "means to the Filipinos" what Lincoln means to America, Bolivar to South America, and Gandhi to India. Witnesses said Rizal died quoting Jesus on the cross ("it is finished"), and forgiving his executioners in the spirit of Jesus's "forgive them, Lord, they know not what they do."[13] No doubt Rizal's Protestant faith enabled Laubach to treat him worshipfully. Laubach's *Rizal: Man and Martyr* retains the notion of Filipino meekness that permeated his earlier books, but here Laubach insists that meekness not be confused with any lack of courage. His portrayal of the Filipino reformer was designed to make Rizal as attractive as possible to Laubach's American, churchgoing readers:

> His consuming life purpose was the secret of his moral courage. Physical courage, it is true, was one of his inherited traits. But that high courage to die loving his murderers, which he at last achieved— *that* cannot be inherited. It must be forged out in the fires of suffering and temptation. As we read through his life, we can see how the moral

sinew and fiber grew year by year as he faced new perils and was forced to make fearful decisions. . . . When the sentence of death and the fateful morning of his execution brought the final test, 30 Dec 1896, he walked with perfect calm to the firing line as though by his own choice, the only heroic figure in that sordid scene.[14]

Laubach remained based in the Philippines until the Japanese occupation early in World War II prevented his return from a furlough in the United States. By that time he and his co-workers had managed to spread a phonetic-centered, highly individualized method of literacy instruction throughout many regions of the islands. This "each one teach one" method was more labor-intensive than the traditional classroom approach, but Laubach was able to inspire hundreds and eventually thousands to devote themselves to do it voluntarily even while engaged in other vocations. By then, Laubach had also joined a number of ecumenical Protestant leaders in various antiwar protests and efforts to expand the size and visibility of the pacifist contingent then demanding peaceful solutions to international conflict. He was prominent among American advocates of the independence of India from the British Empire.[15]

Laubach always regarded the advancement of literacy as the doing of Christ's work, and thus a direct extension of his missionary calling, even if literacy itself was without particularistic religious meaning. His work was appreciated beyond the Protestant company he kept. His 1938 book, *Toward a Literate World*, was published with an enthusiastic foreword by Edward L. Thorndike—John Dewey's successor as the leading educational theorist in the United States— of Columbia Teacher's College.[16] Many of Laubach's books described and celebrated his literacy programs, but a number of others were spiritual meditations that, while Christianity-inspired, emphasized the common ground of all religions.[17]

Laubach contrasted Christianity to Communism, but differed from many of his religion-invoking contemporaries in identifying poverty and injustice as the chief causes of Communism's appeal. He held the privileged white peoples of the West responsible for the inequities that rendered Communism one of the few options available to the world's poor. In a book of 1951 entitled *Wake Up or Blow Up: America, Lift the World or Lose It!*, Laubach warned his own tribe that their failures to help their fellow human beings was the root cause of the world's problems. Always the preacher, Laubach let his constituency have it frontally: "So let it hurt! Your pain is part of the birth pangs of a new world."[18]

Historian Matthew Hedstrom is correct to identify Laubach as "a dramatic instance of mysticism facilitating spiritual cosmopolitanism."

Laubach's multiple volumes of mystical meditations blurred distinctions between Christianity and other faiths, yet promoted a generalized spirituality in the tradition of William James's *Varieties of Religious Experience*. Laubach's devotional writings played extremely well with an ecumenical Protestant public of the midcentury decades that also appreciated the biblically-inspired fiction of Lloyd C. Douglass and Thomas B. Costain. That Laubach lived a life of Christian service, as his readers understood his literacy campaign, made his meditations all the more acceptable to a readership that was dubious about doctrinal distinctions. "Laubach's mystical cosmopolitanism reached beyond devotional life and became, more expansively, the basis," notes Hedstrom, "for a global ethics of peace and justice for the poor."[19]

Laubach criticized Jim Crow racism in America and apartheid in South Africa, but his political utterances were usually as abstract as his literacy campaign was concrete. His devotional writings performed the important function of making American Protestants more comfortable with other faiths without having to engage any of their diverse particulars. Laubach made as smoothly as anyone the emotional transition from religious evangelism to secular service. His god-talk diminished the appeal of his writings to persons outside the Protestant community of faith, but within that large community Laubach was one of the most deeply admired individuals of his generation. For several decades he was a sought-after church speaker for Sunday nights, holding aloft in his hands a globe on which he had indicated by brightly colored markers exactly where could be found the greatest concentrations of illiterate persons in need of his program.[20]

Expanding literacy was also a major goal of Y. C. James Yen (1890–1990). This world-traveling Chinese Christian was a remarkably complete fulfillment of the missionary project's ideal of indigenization: here was a man born and raised in China who converted to Christianity and then showed impressive initiative in building organizations of his own that served local populations and thereby fulfilled the service goals of the missionary project. Although Yen began as a YMCA employee and always described himself as a "follower of Christ," his organizations in China, the Philippines, and elsewhere were independent and secular. He offered Americans attractive means of helping the peoples of East Asia, unencumbered by any missionary apparatus or theology, yet fully consistent with the service-orientation of the ecumenical missionaries. He was, in a fashion, a Chinese Laubach.

Yen was first known for Mass Education Movements, a literacy-focused, vocationally oriented program he organized in China in 1923. The operation later moved to the countryside and merged into the Rural

Reconstruction Movement, focused increasingly on agriculture. By 1930, Yen operated 423 schools in regions throughout China, serving more than ten thousand students. In one of these schools, Mao Zedong first learned how to be a community organizer. Mao went his own way, however, and his Communist Revolution eventually shut down Yen's enterprise because Yen had cooperated closely with the Kuomintang regime. Upon finding he was no longer welcome in China after 1949, Yen operated in India and Brazil and, especially, in the Philippines, where he eventually became almost as important a figure as he had been in China.[21] "Jimmy Yen," as he was often called, was the obvious model for "Johnny Wu," the influential community development leader who is a character in John Hersey's The Call.

In the 1940s and early 1950s, Yen's name seemed to pop up everywhere in internationalist circles within the United States. He was profiled in the Reader's Digest more often than any other individual at any time in the magazine's entire history. In 1943 he was one of ten "Copernican figures" honored by the Carnegie Corporation on the occasion of the four hundredth anniversary of the birth of the great astronomer. Albert Einstein, John Dewey, Walt Disney, Orville Wright, and Henry Ford were also honored.[22]

How did Yen get into this company? He was a charismatic, canny, and optimistic man with a knack for organizing programs that changed the lives of hundreds of thousands of people. It would not do to underestimate his talents and agency. But his fame, and his ability to command resources for his empire of service activities, depended heavily on missionaries. Yen got his start in missionary schools in China and was quickly absorbed into the YMCA network there. Sherwood Eddy and John R. Mott were impressed with his intelligence and energy and provided him with connections. Yen studied at Yale and Princeton, and served with the YMCA in France during World War I before returning to China. He invented a thousand-character primer used by more than twenty million Chinese. The leadership of the Institute for Pacific Relations was devoted to Yen, and made sure he met the right people. In a visit to the United States in 1928, Yen paid a call on President Calvin Coolidge, and, at the personal invitation of John D. Rockefeller Jr., spent a week at the Rockefeller family compound on Maine's Mt. Desert Island. That visit of Yen's enabled him to finance his transition from literacy to a more comprehensive program of community development.

In China, one missionary connection after another advanced Yen's reputation. Edward Hume and John Leighton Stuart, key leaders of Chinese missionary-related institutions, were among Yen's promoters. In 1932, the

Layman's Inquiry— the nine-month investigation I discuss at length in chapter 3—commissioned one of the United States' most respected agricultural reformers, Kenyon L. Butterfield, to assess Yen's operation.[23] Butterfield could not say enough good things about Yen. The missionaries who accompanied Butterworth were more taken with Yen than ever; one of them proclaimed in *The Chinese Recorder*—the missionary periodical edited by Frank Rawlinson—that "if Jesus Christ were to return to earth today," he would likely be found working with Yen in the villages of rural China.[24] Yen gradually pulled away from the missionary project itself, and presented activities like his own as successors to missions in service to the Chinese people. But Yen continued to appear in missionary circles, where he was always welcome.[25]

Yen's star in the American political and cultural firmament was unrivaled by anyone from China other than the Chiangs. Shortly after Yen received his "Copernican Citation" in 1943, Pearl Buck published a volume of interviews with him.[26] Her husband, the publisher Richard Walsh, put together the American-Chinese Committee of the Mass Education Movement, filled with corporate giants in addition to First Lady Eleanor Roosevelt and the philosopher William Ernest Hocking. Supreme Court Associate Justice William O. Douglas was also a member of the committee. Douglas compared Yen to both Jesus of Nazareth and the Apostle Paul.[27] Even Henry Luce signed up with Walsh's organization, an indication of Yen's ability to win support across the political spectrum and across the lines of personal rivalries.

Enthusiasm for Yen peaked at the same historical moment that Gandhi was most revered, Margaret Landon presented a Siamese king as an ideal American client, and John Hersey depicted war-devastated Italians as eager for the good deeds of an American military officer. Yen was a sophisticated, adroit figure emerging from what would soon be called "the Third World," who did exactly what progressive Americans most wanted their foreign friends to do. He gratefully accepted American aid and used it to do things that virtually everyone could agree was productive. Unlike Chiang Kai-shek, Yen did not bear the burden of political and military responsibility.

American ecumenical Protestants much preferred Yen's operation to another widely publicized development project that competed with Yen for support. The Chinese Industrial Cooperatives (Indusco) was led by Rewi Alley, a New Zealand expatriate social activist.[28] Alley established a network of vocational training schools and small-scale village factories that made wartime materiel. Alley stayed in China after the revolution of

1949 and served its government as an official "Friend of China" until his death in 1987.[29] Indusco's most devoted supporter in the United States was the writer Ida Pruitt, a missionary daughter who moved to the United States in 1939 after spending most of the first fifty years of her life in China. But Pruitt was deeply alienated from the missionary project. While never a member of the Communist Party, she was not troubled by Alley's close connections with the Chinese Communists.[30]

For a brief time, the Institute for Pacific Relations took an interest in Alley and Yen, as did Harry W. Price. But Alley had no religious connections and was not Chinese, so he carried less symbolic capital than Yen. Moreover, there were negative rumors about the private life of the unmarried Alley, who adopted many young Chinese boys.[31] Yen and his wife lived like ideal American Protestants. "The family eschewed cards, social gambling, alcohol, and tobacco," notes Yen's biographer, Charles Hayford, and in the Yen home "novels were thought frivolous." Yen was so uncomfortable with divorce that on at least one occasion he cut off his friendship with a man who divorced his wife.[32]

While Alley's Indusco was folding at the end of the 1940s, Yen was achieving his greatest triumph. When the US Congress enacted the China Aid Act in 1948, the "Jimmy Yen provision" mandated that ten percent of the 275 million dollars go directly to Yen's programs. The provision was piloted through Congress by the conservative Republican congressman Walter Judd. While Congress was deliberating, Secretary of State George Marshall arranged for Yen to visit President Truman, who told Yen that his own preference would have been to allocate one hundred percent of the Chinese aid package to Yen.[33] Truman and Marshall knew that Yen had nothing to do with the Communists but was also independent from, and privately critical of, the Kuomintang. The Reader's Digest Association gave Yen a gift of $600,000. Yen's other bankrollers included Nelson Rockefeller, Henry Ford, J. P. Morgan, Philip Morris, General Electric, and the Carnegie Corporation.

Yen continued to garner strong corporate support after he moved his chief base of operations to the Philippines in 1952. There, his "rural reconstruction" services worked closely with the anti-insurgency programs of the anti-Communist government of Ramon Magsaysay. "Although the nature of Yen's ties to the CIA is unclear," observes Daniel Immerwahr, "his work fell obviously in line with the CIA's mission."[34] In the 1960s and 1970s, Yen pushed well beyond the Philippines. He established projects in India, Ghana, South Korea, and Thailand. He also used what had become his primary institutional tool, the International Institute of Rural

Reconstruction, to train government officials from more than a dozen other countries in Africa and Latin America as well as Asia. In Vietnam, he helped train counterinsurgency workers connected with the American military. Yen himself kept a low profile during the Vietnam years, but his International Institute of Rural Reconstruction was very much part of the action.

Yen is also significant as an example of an Asian voice promoted by missionary-connected Americans in an environment in which nonwhite voices were regularly ignored.[35] It might be an exaggeration to describe Yen as the missionary community's gift to American public life, but not by much. If William Eddy seemed, to King Ibn Saud, too good an American to be true, Jimmy Yen seemed to American ecumenical Protestants too good a Chinese to be true.

While Yen's development projects operated in tandem with the US government during the Cold War and Vietnam eras, International Voluntary Services experienced a much more difficult relationship with American authorities. IVS's story leads not only to the Peace Corps, but to the Vietnam debacle's consequences for post-missionary service projects abroad.

IVS emerged from a confluence of church and government engagements with the decolonizing world. Shortly after President-elect Dwight Eisenhower announced late in 1952 that John Foster Dulles would be his secretary of state, Dulles declared in a radio address that US foreign aid programs needed to be supplemented by organizations of volunteers who would go abroad to help the peoples of the non-Western world to develop the resources of their own countries. This idea appealed to Harold Row, the director of the Church of the Brethren's social service agency, the Brethren Service Commission. Row approached his counterparts on the Mennonite Central Committee and the Friends Service Committee, the social service agencies of the other "historic peace churches" which, like the Brethren, had been eager to find foreign postings for the "alternative service" that conscientious objectors performed under the terms of the Selective Service Act of 1940. The Brethren, Mennonites, and Quakers all maintained missionary programs, but it had not been possible to assign conscientious objectors to missions because of the latter's official involvement in religious proselytizing. Hence, most of the conscientious objectors served their two years of alternative service stateside in a variety of medical, construction, and agricultural endeavors. Row rounded up his Mennonite and Quaker friends and they went to Washington together and started to knock on the doors of officialdom.[36]

While the churchmen were making their rounds, a middle-ranking officer of the State Department's Point IV Program—President Truman's foreign aid project—returned from a posting in Iran and voiced to colleagues his wish that churches or some other private party would send volunteers abroad to do vocational training and other work to enable the Iranians to modernize themselves. Dale D. Clark knew nothing of Dulles's speech, but had come up with this idea while contemplating the needs of people in Tehran. Clark had been a Mormon missionary in Europe for two years as a youth, an experience that may have influenced this episode, although he did not say so. Clark was delighted when his aides excitedly told him that there were church officials in town at that moment trying to get someone to listen to exactly such a plan of their own. Row and his friends had found an official who was ready to work with them. In February 1953, the Brethren, Mennonites, and Quakers established a new NGO, International Voluntary Services (IVS), a name suggested by Row as a variation on his own denomination's Brethren Volunteer Service.[37]

IVS came into being at a time when ecumenical Protestants were divided about the viability of their missionary programs but more committed than ever to the service ideal. IVS was a means for expanding service projects without having to deal with the uncertainties of missionary purpose and ideology. IVS's director for its first eight years was John S. Noffsinger, a Brethren minister who in his youth had been a teacher in the Philippines, then spent most of his career in the United States working for vocational training organizations, including the Federal Board of Vocational Education. Once in place, Noffsinger quickly dispatched young men and women abroad. They almost always operated "missionary style," interacting directly with local populations in villages and learning to speak the indigenous languages.[38]

IVS was a secular organization that welcomed volunteers with no religious affiliation, but throughout its history—including the volatile Vietnam years which I discuss below—its volunteers were overwhelmingly ecumenical Protestants. Noffsinger himself seems not to have pushed the analogy to missions, but some of his staff did. "You are still missionaries," one staffer told a group of volunteers, "for like Christ you are working to improve peoples' lives. Your job is to bring your great American know-how to Asia."[39] One volunteer from the mid-1950s recalled that the Foreign Service officers in Laos, where he was serving his alternative service, referred with some derision to his IVS group as "the missionaries."[40]

By the late 1950s, IVS had "won a reputation," historian David Ekbladh explains, "as an exemplar of community development with its programs in

Africa and Asia."[41] In 1961, immediately after President John F. Kennedy announced that Sargent Shriver would head such an agency, Noffsinger wrote to Shriver offering assistance. Members of Shriver's newly appointed staff began attending IVS staff meetings to get a sense of the operation. IVS was not only the ideological model for Shriver's agency, but the practical one as well. Historian Daniel Immerwahr notes that IVS staffers "showed Shriver's team how to set up payrolls for international work [and] screen recruits."[42]

IVS's role as a model for the Peace Corps is in itself a significant example of the missionary legacy in secular development projects. But the Vietnam episode in IVS's history further clarifies the character and boundaries of post-missionary development work.

In 1958, IVS became affiliated with the United States Agency for International Development (USAID), a portentous change which enabled government officials to push IVS programs in directions of the government's own choosing. This did not become a problem until government officials wanted IVS to send more volunteers to Vietnam. In 1961 there were only twenty IVS volunteers in Vietnam, but by 1967 there were a hundred and twenty.[43] Unlike most IVS operations, which depended heavily on private funding, IVS work in Vietnam was financed entirely by the US government.[44]

IVS personnel were increasingly skeptical of the American government's role in Vietnam, especially after the assassination of President Diem in 1963. Grumbling that the US government's anti-Communist priority was getting in the way of local humanitarian work intensified in 1965 when the United States sent ground troops to Vietnam. USAID placed IVS projects in areas relevant to military strategies. This was trouble enough for the humanitarian self-conception of the volunteers; then volunteers began to be killed. The high representation of conscientious objectors among them contributed to the tension, but objections to American policy in Vietnam were shared by most of the volunteers in Southeast Asia. In 1967 the top IVS leadership in Vietnam resigned and sent to President Johnson a letter signed by forty-nine of their volunteers, condemning American policy in Vietnam. IVS also released the letter to the *New York Times*.[45]

The IVS leadership's protest against the Vietnam War played into the escalating national debate. Dozens of Senators and Congressmen sought out the renegade leaders for consultations. IVS continued, under new leadership, to operate in Vietnam under increasingly dangerous circumstances. Volunteers were killed more often, and by 1972 eleven had died and several others had been imprisoned by Communists. Still others were under fire, and had to be evacuated by the US military from combat zones. As happened to so many Americans engaging the world in the context of the missionary project, Vietnam was a turning point. Many who had been able to make their peace with the global hegemony of the United States, and who believed the interests of indigenous peoples to be consistent with American goals, were struck hard by Vietnam. By 1975 all IVS personnel had left Vietnam and IVS itself was reconstituted on a more international basis, no longer primarily consisting of American volunteers. By the time IVS closed operations in 2002, it had little resemblance to the organization set up by missionary-connected Americans fifty years earlier.

The cases of Laubach, Yen, and IVS indicate how direct the transition from missions to secular development projects could be. I have cited major institutional cases, but the same transition was made by many individuals. An example is the well-traveled Harry B. Price, the missionary son and former missionary whom I mentioned above and in earlier chapters for his having led the American Committee for Non-Participation in Japanese Aggression and for having served in the OSS. After the war, Price worked in Washington, supervising aid to China through the Economic Cooperation Administration and the Mutual Security Agency. He then went abroad again, and for most of the 1950s was economic adviser to the government of Nepal, where he helped to design that nation's first Five-Year Plan. Later, he immersed himself in several development projects in the Philippines. Missionary Dwight Edwards spent forty-three years in China, alternating between church and secular sponsors for the sequence of technical aid projects he led.[46] Edwards returned to the United States in 1949, when there were no more development projects in post-revolutionary China that he as an American was allowed to lead.

Edwards's case is a reminder that the transition from missions to secular development had already been enacted on a smaller scale well before the war, including by Laubach and Yen. The Institute for Pacific Relations and the Near East Foundation, both of which were organized and led by missionary-connected men and women, were conspicuous examples. Both organizations made distinctive marks in their educational, agricultural, and other aid activities during the 1920s and 1930s. The Rockefeller Foundation, too, funded programs heavily influenced by missionaries and often staffed by them. The agricultural improvement enterprises of Sam Higginbotham in India and Lossing Buck in China were taken up by secular agencies. But the Peace Corps is the largest institutional legacy of post-missionary service projects.

A few missionary-connected Americans defended and designed initiatives of this macro-level variety. Political scientist Lucian Pye, a missionary son, was one. But the missionary legacy for development abroad was found largely in more modest, locally-centered programs of the sort celebrated in Burdick and Lederer's *The Ugly American*. The hero of that book was an engineer working for a government agency, not a missionary, but Hugh Atkins displayed exactly the traits Raper ascribed to missionaries. Burdick and Lederer consolidated the favorable image of the technical aid worker who was close to the people while the diplomats and the dam-builders were said to be arrogant and persistently oblivious to local needs.[47] This novel deeply affected President Kennedy, who looked for means of acting on its insights and found them in the IVS-influenced Peace Corps.

Some missionary-connected Americans discovered ways to be of missionary-like service abroad. Others looked inward, to American society, and committed their energies to the support of the African American civil rights movement. The next chapter is about them.

CHAPTER ELEVEN

Of One Blood

JOINING THE CIVIL RIGHTS STRUGGLE AT HOME

AS LONG AS we "refuse to hold all races equal" in our own country, how can we offer moral instruction to "China, Japan, and India?" Edmund Davidson Soper, dean of the Duke University Divinity School, asked this of his fellow Methodists at a national convention in 1926.[1] This concern was often voiced in the quarter-century that followed, and intensified in the mid-1950s. The murder of Emmett Till in Mississippi and the school integration crisis in Little Rock, Arkansas, made Jim Crow's relation to the missionary project harder to evade. Nationalist and Communist groups publicized these events throughout Africa and Asia.[2] Doing something about American racism was all the more strategic an imperative early in the next decade. The world could see news clips of violence perpetrated against peaceful demonstrators. Two hundred Southern Presbyterian missionaries petitioned their denominational assembly to renounce segregated churches and a segregated society in the interests of saving the missionary project from ignominy. The denominational authorities rejected the petition.[3]

While these strategic considerations brought many churchmen and churchwomen to ally themselves with the civil rights movement, that movement also attracted missionary-connected individuals who had lost interest in the missionary project. Institutionalized anti-black racism was not the only aspect of American life at odds with the notion of human "brotherhood." But it was the most visible. This chapter is about the efforts of missionary-connected Americans to fight Jim Crow and the larger edifice of racial prejudice. These efforts emerged from a single matrix: the ideology of Christian universalism expressed in the lyrics of a missionary hymn that we can suppose was heard and sung many times by every man and woman discussed in *Protestants Abroad*:

In Christ there is no East or West,
In Him no South or North;
But one great fellowship of love,
Throughout the whole wide earth.

Join hands, then, members of the faith,
Whatever your race may be!
Who serves my Father as His child
Is surely kin to me.[4]

Some acted on this idealistic vision by publishing critical attacks on racism. Others organized demonstrations, boycotts, workshops, and educational programs. Some worked through churches or transdenominational institutions. Others pursued the cause within secular organizations ranging from the Fellowship of Reconciliation to the Communist Party. Although both men and women were active in the cause, women were more prominent here than in any of the other domains where the missionary contingent made a historical mark. Moreover, many of these women were involved in secret or semisecret intimate relationships with other women. Hence the story of missionary cosmopolitanism with regard to race is also a story of gender, and of sexual orientation.

Soper's experience is a good place to start. He gradually moved from narrowly focusing on Jim Crow as a strategic problem for missions to a more comprehensive analysis of racism as a deeply offensive and widespread evil in itself, to be combatted at every level within the church, the nation, and the globe. Soper's case is all the more important because he was a major a figure in the Protestant International, and the author of his generation's most respected treatise on missions, *Philosophy of the Christian World Mission*.[5]

In the same year he published that book—1943—Soper was commissioned by the executive secretary of the Methodist Board of Missions to lead a year-long seminar in Chicago on "world racism."[6] Soper invited a number of black and white religious and political leaders from the greater Chicago area to meet in ten monthly seminars, culminating in a five-day national conference on "Racism and World Order," also sponsored by the Methodist Missions Board. The conference featured presentations by specialists on the status of nonwhite peoples in the United States as well as in countries throughout the world where missionaries had been active.[7]

Soper's labors in leading these seminars and the conference led to his book of 1947, *Racism: A World Issue*, which stands today as one of the most sweeping antiracist books written by any white American prior to the 1960s. He produced it at the age of seventy-one, at the height of his influence.

Soper wrote in a confident tone, displaying the proprietary feeling toward the entire human species characteristic of ecumenical Protestant leaders of the era. No problem was going to get fixed unless Christians got together and did something about it. Racism was just such a problem, and it had been unconscionably ignored for too long by people in power. Governments needed Christian guidance. *Racism: A World Issue* ended with the vision from Revelation, where there appears "a great multitude . . . out of every nation, and of all tribes and peoples and tongues, standing before the throne and the Lamb," praising God.[8]

Soper's argument was warranted with factual information and social analysis as well as scripture. He offered a region-by-region survey of the power of racism and of the forces being mobilized against it, treating the United States as a distinctive site of dynamics found on every continent. He identified white supremacy as the most common and most dangerous form of racism, but called attention also to racist attitudes and practices among Arabs, Jews, and the nonwhite populations of India and East Asia. He took a generous view of the Soviet Union, whose declarations of racial equality he accepted at face value, and of Brazil, which he contrasted to the more deeply anti-black regime of United States. Soper's pages are studded with citations to social science classics of the period, including the works of Ashley Montague, Franz Boas, Ruth Benedict, Gene Weltfish, and Clyde Kluckhohn.

Thus grounded in the latest anthropological critiques of the very concept of race, Soper went after multiple instances of injustice that had long been, and continued to be, justified by racist ideas. Repeatedly, he reminded his readers of the world-historical stakes, as in this prophetic passage near the end of the book:

> Should we of the West, the white man in Europe and America, persist in our attitude of superiority toward the people of color and treat them with disdain, as inferiors, we can only expect in due time to reap the whirlwind of retaliation and vengeance. . . . No power in the world can prevent the colored races, the peoples of Asia and Africa, from uniting because of common grievances against centuries of domination by the white man and ending this domination by the use of means we have taught them so well to use.

This violent end of colonialism and imperialism need not be so dreadful, Soper insisted, if only the whites of the North Atlantic West would start treating other people with "justice and respect." The United States "took the right step in giving independence" to the Philippines, he said, in a typical linking of the local with the global, "but it still has a long way to go in giving justice to the Negroes within its own borders."[9]

In addressing the American scene, Soper attacked racially restrictive real estate covenants, discriminatory labor practices, and the denial of voting rights to black citizens. He praised Gunnar Myrdal's *American Dilemma*, published three years earlier. He called special attention to Myrdal's emphasis on legal rights. Going well beyond the traditional talk of building "better race relations," Soper declared unequivocally that "Negroes" deserved the same basic political and economic rights white citizens enjoyed. He offered his own paraphrase of a famous quotation from Lincoln: "Our nation cannot continue to exist part oppressed and part free, a part of the people living under the stigma of perpetual inferiority and another part considering themselves inherently superior, part grinding under the yoke of arbitrary discrimination and part enjoying the full fruitage of unlimited opportunity and privilege." He mocked the practice by which "the slightest presence of Negro blood consigns the possessor and his family" to a host of disabilities and deprivations, and praised Brazil for openly accepting race mixing. He called attention to the sexual exploitation of slave women.[10]

In his frustration at how white people were ignoring "the ideals of brotherhood" at home and abroad, Soper allowed that "no single group in modern times" had exemplified those ideals "more than Christian missionaries." He lamented the racism that persisted among some missionaries, but by and large it was the missionaries who, Soper insisted, enabled white people to recognize its evil. The full debt of this book to the missionary matrix, however, is most apparent in Soper's acknowledgments and in his account of the wartime seminars he ran under the sponsorship of the Methodist Missionary Board. Soper thanked eight individuals for having read his entire manuscript, seven of whom had been missionaries themselves or executives of missionary organizations. Soper was so much a creature of the missionary project that shortly after publishing this book he retired from his seminary post and returned to Japan to work for several additional years as a missionary teacher.[11]

While Soper was taking on the world, his earlier concern about the relation of Jim Crow to the missionary project continued to engage many churchmen and churchwomen. The dramatic case of Harris Mobley (1930–2010) illustrates this, and also reveals the challenges faced within

Southern Baptist circles by the missionary lobbyists for civil rights. Mobley served for six years as a missionary in Ghana. He became uncomfortable with how his fellow missionaries distanced themselves from the indigenous population, and came to see this behavior as a reflection of the Jim Crow system at home. When he returned to his native Georgia on furlough in 1963, he soon discovered that his criticism of racism in both domains was unwelcome. In an address on the campus of his alma mater, Mercer University, Mobley linked the segregationist practices of the local community to the continued tendency of missionaries in Africa to segregate themselves from the indigenous, black population.

"Let the missionary have his houseful of servants," Mobley chided the white Baptists serving in the mission field in Ghana; "let him mimic the colonial past," driving "his big American car, horn blowing, dust flying, Africans running off the road." We Baptists were "distorting the Christian Gospel" in our refusal to integrate ourselves more fully into the lives of Africans, he declared. "Neither the NAACP nor the Kennedy administration" was responsible for our problems in the American South, said Mobley, challenging the locally preferred assignments of blame; rather, "we" were the ones responsible for these problems. The speech was too extreme even for the Missionary Board. Mobley's remarks were "sophomoric," complained Board chair H. C. Goerner. The address caused an uproar among the Baptists, and was reported even in the national press.[12]

Mobley's angry denunciation of local customs and values was all the more troubling because at the time he delivered his speech, he was engaged in another institutionally radical move. Mobley had befriended a young Ghanaian convert, Sam Jerri Oni, who wanted to enroll at Mercer but, as a black person, was ineligible. The admissions office admitted that Oni was highly qualified, and "were it not for his color" would have been accepted "without question." The university's president favored Oni's admission, and, thereby, the school's integration, but the board of trustees balked. A controversy developed over whether or not Oni could be admitted as a foreign student without creating a precedent for American blacks. The distinction was in use elsewhere, including in at least one other Southern Baptist college, but supporters of Oni and Mobley attacked that subterfuge as an immoral evasion of responsibility. The link between the missionary enterprise abroad and the race question at home was a constant theme in the debate. "We either admit him or we should have the courage to call home all of our missionaries and go out of the business," asserted the editor of the official magazine of the Southern Baptists of Georgia.[13]

Eventually, the trustees gave in. Mobley and Oni integrated Mercer University. Perhaps eager to get him out of the local picture, the denomination's missionary board urged Mobley to go back to Ghana, to continue his service there as a missionary. But even in the wake of his victory at Mercer, he was fed up. Mobley decided to leave the ministry to become an academic and an entrepreneur. After taking a doctorate in anthropology at the University of North Carolina, Mobley taught at Georgia Southern University for many years, and ran a chain of restaurants.[14]

Within the Southern Baptists and many other denominations, the women's missionary boards were the most consistent antiracist forces.[15] These boards originated in the late nineteenth century when male leaders had encouraged women to focus on missions. This gendering of missionary support had unexpected consequences. Churchwomen were more aware than churchmen of the strategic considerations Soper flagged in 1926. In addition, the liberalizing consequences of the foreign missionary project were funneled through these women's missionary boards, whose protests against lynching were also controversial for the churches.

The Women's Missionary Union of the Southern Baptist Convention provided the most reliable support for what historian Alan Scot Willis describes as T. B. Matson's "fight against Biblical racism." Starting in the mid-1940s, seminary professor Matson published under the auspices of the Women's Missionary Union a series of books and pamphlets invoking what he called "Christian principles" against the discriminatory and segregationist practices of his fellow Baptists. Most biblical scholars had long since rejected the connection between black people and the "curse of Ham"—according to which the descendants of one of Noah's sons were to be "servants of servants"— but Genesis 9:20-27 continued to be cited by countless Southern Baptists as a justification for segregation.[16]

The Methodists had more antiracist activists than the Southern Baptists, and women were in the lead.[17] One supremely important issue was the segregated governance structure put in place at the time of the merger of the Southern and Northern Methodists in 1939, as described in chapter 4. This was the price the white southerners demanded for agreeing to the merger with the descendants of the Yankees of old. Women led the fight against "the Central Jurisdiction," as the black defined administrative unit was called, until it was finally eliminated in 1968.[18] A further indication of the importance of the Methodist Woman's Division is President Harry Truman's appointment of its chair, Dorothy Tilly, to the President's Committee on Civil Rights, the fifteen-member body that two years later produced the landmark document *To Secure These Rights*.[19]

Another Methodist woman, Ruth Harris (1920–2013), became an exceptionally important antiracist organizer. She served as a missionary teacher in China before joining the staff of the Women's Missionary Board, and was employed by several cross-denominational youth organizations. In 1955, while serving as the Field Program Secretary for the Student Volunteer Movement (SVM), Harris was the intellectual leader of an SVM conference that brought 3,500 students from more than eighty countries to Athens, Ohio. This six-day, racially integrated conference addressed the decidedly non-Cold War theme "Revolution and Reconciliation." The conference's major affirmation, wrote the *New York Times*, was that a "primary task of the church in the modern world is to smash the barriers of racial segregation and prejudice everywhere." In the 1950s it was far from common for white American college students to meet black students even from the historically black colleges of the United States, to say nothing of those from Africa, and students of different ethnoracial groups from Asia and Latin America.

Harris never doubted the connection between racism in the United States and racism in the larger world. Harris organized the 1955 event in cooperation with the Presbyterian official Margaret Flory, whose leadership of the Frontier Interns in Mission project of the 1960s and 1970s I discussed in chapter 3. Flory came up with the original design for the SVM conference and invited the radical theologian and ex-missionary Richard Shaull to address it. But the more personally intense and charismatic Harris was remembered by participants as the dynamic center of the event.[20]

Harris and Flory worked together again four years later at the next SVM Quadrennial Conference, held again on the campus of Ohio University and just as large as the earlier gathering. This time Martin Luther King Jr. was among the speakers. A number of the 1959 conferees participated in the sit-in movements that began the following year in North Carolina. This conference was even more international than the earlier one, and included 109 students from Africa. Shaull spoke again and his book *Encounter with Revolution* was assigned reading.[21]

Harris was the chief organizer of a third SVM Quadrennial Conference at Athens, Ohio, in 1963, again with more than 3,500 participants. At this event she introduced another cohort of white American Protestant youth to a wider demographic and cultural world. Among those Harris inspired was Charlotte Bunch, later an editor of the Methodist youth magazine *motive*, and still later a prominent feminist writer and Rutgers University professor. Bunch reports that it was at this meeting that she "discovered the world."

Speakers from South Africa challenged us about Christian responsibility to confront apartheid, a Czechoslovakian theologian talked about Christian-Marxist dialogue while the right wing was outside protesting the presence of a communist on the program, and Latin Americans spoke of the CIA and the U.S. intervention in their region. . . . Theologically the conference was also a mind-opener, with Catholic, Protestant, and Orthodox liturgies and inquiries interspersed throughout. The vision of a politically engaged, interracial, ecumenical Christian community electrified participants.[22]

By the time of that third SVM conference Harris had moved her primary affiliation back to the Women's Division of the Methodist church. She organized groups traveling to Washington, DC, for Martin Luther King Jr's march there in 1963, and then in 1965 to King's demonstrations in Selma, Alabama. Harris later explained that the Selma demonstrations were the most exciting moments in her life as a Christian activist. Harris and her co-worker Peggy Billings—also a former missionary, to Korea—transported civil rights activists on the same highway where Viola Liuzzo, the white Unitarian activist from Michigan, was shot and killed while performing the same service shortly thereafter.[23] As Harris moved from one Methodist staff position to another throughout the 1960s and 1970s, she continued to inspire cathected admiration wherever she went. One example is Rebecca Owen, a student from Randolph-Macon Women's College, who met Harris at the 1959 SVM meeting and was later arrested in sit-ins against segregated public accommodations in Virginia. Owens recalls Harris's impact on her:

> Ruth Harris was utterly astonishing. Heretofore, what men were doing in the church and the world had been much more interesting to me than women's doings. . . . [but here was] a *woman* whose life I could wish to emulate. In Ruth I saw a tall, intelligent woman, also beautiful . . . it had long been part of my consciousness that only unattractive women found a place in church work. I had learned further that women in full-time Christian work must give up everything interesting, sexy, exciting, and embrace a pale, emaciated (or obese), asexual, diminutive, constricted role. This image . . . Ruth definitively shattered. . . . Ruth's Christian faith was, in retrospect, more liberating for me than her person. For her, "acting up" for Christ and thereby being thrown into the world as a full human being was an integral part of faith.[24]

The accounts of Owen and other Protestant women civil rights and feminist activists from the mid-1950s well into the 1970s leave no doubt that Harris's charisma, resilience, and organizational savvy had a lasting impact on their political as well as their spiritual lives. Harris "mentored generations of students," summarizes Sara M. Evans, "exposing them to international perspectives, liberation theology, and struggles for justice both at home and around the world."[25]

The careers of Harris and Flory are examples of how missionary cosmopolitans sometimes made a difference in relatively confined settings, overlooked in national discourses and largely invisible to historians. Harris remained a relatively low-level staff employee, without the standing in the Methodist church that Flory achieved with the Presbyterians. Harris did not even publish essays in denominational or transdenominational media. She became a significant antiracist activist by using her positions as a bureaucrat.

Harris's career illustrates how the missionary experience could crystalize preexisting egalitarian dispositions and channel them into a life of political engagement. "My life's real commitment to justice" began in China, Harris wrote several decades after she returned to the United States in 1951 in the wake of the Communist Revolution. While mobilizing Methodist youth brigades to support Martin Luther King Jr. in Montgomery and Selma in 1965, Harris reflected on her experiences as a missionary; her deep immersion in the struggle of black Americans for civil rights in Alabama enabled her to achieve "closure," she said, on a calling shaped in China.[26]

An intense but unfocused desire to perform Christian service is what sent Harris to China in the first place. Having grown up in a small Nebraska town, educated primarily to become a music teacher, Harris in her early twenties was searching for a way to be of greater service. In 1945, she signed up to become a missionary teacher in China. But even as she underwent pre-missionary training at a Methodist facility in Nashville, Tennessee, Harris began feeling that reducing inequality was part of her calling to Christian service. In that southern city, deeply affected by witnessing the Jim Crow system in operation and drawn by her musical interests to the Fisk Jubilee Singers, Harris was all the more receptive to the aggressively ecumenical and politically progressive messages that were central to the Methodist missionary ideology she encountered during her training. Hearing the missionaries talk about the diversity of the world at large drew Harris farther and farther away from sectarian understandings of her faith and toward what she later described as "a profound commitment to the ecumenical movement." In this context she found it "jarring," while sailing to Shanghai, to find some of the China-bound conservative missionaries "staying up all night praying for the souls" of liberal missionaries like her.[27]

But the inequalities of Tennessee did not prepare Harris for the shock of "human suffering and degradation" she encountered in Shanghai when she arrived in 1947. She was quickly overwhelmed by the abject poverty, the appalling cruelty of the labor system, and "the bundles neatly wrapped in straw mats" along the streets—"dead babies, placed there by their families to be taken away." Harris soon adopted the view that China "had to have a revolution." The Chinese Christian young people she met at YMCA-YWCA conclaves instructed her about "the fascist tendencies of the Chiang Kai-shek regime," and made her "ashamed" of Western imperialism. Her college education had been "almost totally" confined to music, and left her "completely unprepared" for China, even as she learned the Chinese language. Determined to educate herself "in the realities of those suffering oppression," Harris's missionary service as a teacher at a girl's school was increasingly driven by a radical egalitarianism. She left China in 1951 because by then—especially in the context of the Korean War—it was clear that as an American she was a liability to her Chinese friends; they were placed at risk merely by being seen with her in public.[28]

Upon her return to the United States, Harris was absorbed into the domestic Methodist missionary apparatus, working at first in the New York office of the Women's Division's highly activist Department of Christian Social Relations. In 1954, she became the Field Program Secretary for the Student Volunteer Movement for Christian Missions (SVM), where she exercised her most consequential leadership. The transdenominational SVM was no longer the huge operation it had been from the 1890s through the 1920s, when it was one of the nation's largest campus-related organizations and recruited to the mission field many of the men and women whose names appear in *Protestants Abroad*. But the organization's decline makes all the more striking what Harris, as a full embodiment of the service-centered, politically engaged, anti-imperialist ecumenical missionary, managed to do with it.

Harris's career illustrates how women who remained unmarried were often able, within the society and culture of the churches, to exercise more leadership than married women. "An unmarried professional woman definitely had more freedom and status than a married woman," notes Pat Patterson, who was a missionary to Japan and then served on the staff of the Methodist Church in the United States.[29] Quite a few of these women maintained households with other women in the tradition of what was once called "a Boston marriage"—the socially accepted two-woman household. This domestic arrangement did not in itself necessarily imply anything about sexual orientation.[30] But Harris and Patterson were lovers for forty-two years, a relationship known only to a few close friends. Not until 2013, after Harris's death at the age of ninety-two, did Patterson openly discuss their intimate relationship and agree to celebrate it at a special ceremony held in a liberal church near the Claremont, California, retirement community where the couple had lived.[31] "Ruth herself was never out," explains Patterson, whose poem about her deceased fellow missionary and long-term lover has sufficient emotional intensity and biographical specificity to warrant quotation here in full:

> In a certain sense
> It was enough
> That we had a circle
> Of knowing loving friends
> A kind of inner harbor
> Apart from the storming surf
> Of suspicious attack
> And restrictions
> Of the establishment
> It was enough
> And yet rights fighters
> Such as we
> Knew it might not be enough
> When brothers and sisters
> Suffered and died
> At the hands of bigots
> And people were excluded
> Because of those they loved
> We gave support in petitions
> Donations and prayers
> But we were silent ones
> Following the struggle from afar
> We did not have to deny
> Who we were
> We just did not
> Have to say outright
> The whole truth about our identity
> And sometimes we talked
> About what we should do
> Not fully agreeing
> For we had other causes to fight

But finally one of us died
How then could truth be denied
The wider world must know
We truly belonged to each other [32]

How important is sexual orientation to understanding the public lives of unmarried women who distinguished themselves in the civil rights movement? The answer is unclear. Similarly unclear is the relevance of men's sexual orientation. No doubt there were some gay men who held leadership positions, but there is almost no discussion of male church-men's sexual orientation. Activist Bayard Rustin was widely known to be gay, and, as a result, was subject to extensive discrimination, but he was not a figure within the Protestant religious establishment.[33] Within churches, the presence of an unmarried female employee did not always give rise to speculation about sexual orientation. For example, Thelma Stevens— who fits this model of independent, high-achieving single women—was a major figure in the United Methodist Church for many years. But even after her death, discussions of her life do not refer to her romantic involvement with anyone, male or female.[34]

Is some analysis of the sexual orientation of these unmarried women and its possible connection to their political activities warranted? Were at least some of these women expressing a passionate commitment to com-batting racism that in a later era could have been more openly and directly expressed through intimate sexual relationships with other women? Did their sense of themselves as belonging to an oppressed minority, in ef-fect, spill over to foster their sense of empathic identification with other oppressed minorities? Patterson's "Inner Harbor" implies an answer to these questions, in alluding to the limits the closet placed on public advo-cacy of sexual liberation: "We were silent ones" even while the two "rights fighters" were able to work for "other causes."

Several other cases render highly plausible this link between closeted sexual orientation and civil rights activism. Peggy Billings, the former mis-sionary to Korea who, together with Harris, drove demonstrators to and from Selma in 1965, was forced out of her job as a senior staff employee of the United Methodist Church in 1992 when conservative Methodists raised questions about her sexual orientation.[35] Jeanne Audrey Powers, an ordained minister who participated in Harris's conferences in the 1950s, withdrew from her likely election as a bishop in 1976 out of fear that her candidacy would provoke scrutiny of her private life. She then waited nearly twenty years, until her retirement from the active pastorate, to become, as she described herself, "the most prominent woman in the United Methodist Church to come out as a lesbian."[36] Margaret Flory's situation in the Presbyterian Church may or may not have been different. For more than thirty years she made her home with Margaret Shannon, but she says nothing about Shannon in her otherwise highly personal autobiography.[37]

The writer Lillian Smith (1897–1966) was not a church employee, but I mention her here because she is yet another former missionary active in antiracist causes who lived a closeted life. Her three years as a teacher at a missionary school in China were "the most intense and profound" for her personal development, according to her biographer. Smith's time there, writes Anne C. Loveland, "enabled her to see in bold relief the system of white supremacy she had more or less taken for granted in the South."[38] Smith was one of a handful of southern whites Martin Luther King Jr. invoked in his "Letter from the Birmingham Jail" in 1963. When she died in 1966, Smith's letters confirmed that for two decades she had lived in a closeted intimate relationship with Paula Snelling, a teacher she met after returning from abroad.[39]

In Harris's case, we do have a record of reflection on these personal issues and their relation to political activism. In her seventies, Harris pondered her own lack of interest in men, which started at an early age. She also mused about her struggle, during her thirties, to achieve what her psychoanalytically-trained psychiatrist told her would be a "more mature" intimacy with a male partner. Harris's formative social environment was overwhelmingly female. When she was nine her father ran off with another woman, leaving her mother with five children to raise. Life came to be defined by strong women, especially her mother, who "supported five children on a monthly salary of $125" as a census bureau employee in their small Nebraska community. The boys Harris met in school were only interested in sports and sex, she recalled—"just wanting to go as far as they could." Not until she was in China did she meet a man for whom she felt real attraction. Still, things did not feel right, so Harris broke off the engagement with her fellow missionary and, upon moving to New York, began seven years of psychoanalytic therapy while having several love affairs with women. By the 1960s, her exclusive attraction to women was clear to her and known to a handful of her friends, although she did not begin a sustained relationship until the early 1970s, when she met Patterson.[40]

Georgia Harkness (1891–1974) was not missionary-connected, but her case may be pertinent because of her exceptional standing among excumenical Protestants as by far the most accomplished female theologian of her generation. Another high-achieving, high-status single woman working in a churchly setting, Harkness was a professor for many years at Garrett Theological Seminary and later at the Pacific School of Religion. In middle age she began living with a Methodist co-worker, Verna Miller, who performed household and social duties like a spouse for thirty years until Harkness' death.[41] In the 1960s, Harkness and Miller were not allowed to cohabit in a church-sponsored retirement home.[42]

Negative views, common even in liberal churches, of same-sex relationships may mean that lesbians and gay men faced even more difficulties in church-supervised jobs than in other employments. Some women attracted to other women stayed within churches and tried to remain under the homophobic radar. Others, like Charlotte Bunch, one of the young women inspired by Harris's civil rights activism, proclaimed their sexual orientation and left churches behind.[43]

Another lesbian who departed the churches was Grace Hutchins (1885–1969), who, with her partner Anna Rochester, found a home in the Communist Party. Hutchins is relevant here for several reasons. As a young woman, she was a missionary teacher in China; anti-black racism later became one of her top concerns; and she is another instance of an unmarried woman in a largely hidden same-sex relationship who achieved leadership in one institution or another.[44]

No other missionary-connected individual attained remotely Hutchins's level of leadership in the American Communist Party.[45] She was the party's candidate for lieutenant governor of New York in 1938, and eventually became the chief owner of the party's newspaper, *The Worker*. Hutchins's path to radicalism began at Bryn Mawr College, where she encountered a robust chapter of the Student Volunteer Movement. Inspiring speakers visited the campus. The students often engaged in intense discussions of what they, as good Christian daughters of privilege, could do to help the world. Her own sense of what it would mean to be a missionary teacher at a girl's school in China was conventionally religious, but once she was in the field the social service aspects of the missionary project outpaced the theological and she returned home deeply committed to progressive social action.

Hutchins began attending the meetings of an organization of Episcopalian women that was originally a prayer group, but by Hutchins's time had become a vibrant outlet for women inspired by the Social Gospel. At the 1920 retreat of the Society of the Companions of the Holy Cross, Hutchins held forth on the Christian imperative to sacrifice one's wealth and privilege in the interests of humankind. The Apostle Paul had "sacrificed many of the privileges of his citizenship, his conservativism, his wealth," she reminded the group; Episcopalian women must be similarly "moved by the Spirit" to "act" in the world. "Some people fear a great bloody revolution," she added, but "the revolution" many good Christians wanted was already at hand. It meant that Episcopalian women needed to speak out loudly, and "to drop our so-called noble reserve."[46]

It was in this organization that Hutchins met Anna Rochester. The pair's first joint publication was *Jesus Christ and the World Today*, which argued in classical Christian Socialist fashion that Jesus's teachings, rightly understood, required the creation of a community of equals. Affirming that "Jesus Christ is the hope of the world," Hutchins and Rochester thanked the social gospel theologian Walter Rauschenbusch for pointing them in an egalitarian direction. Studded with scripture, *Jesus Christ and the World Today* is one of the best written ecumenical Protestant treatises of its time.[47] Both women were active in the pacifist organization The Fellowship of Reconciliation, and were editors of the internationalist and social gospel magazine *World Tomorrow*. Hutchins and Rochester were deeply moved by the injustices suffered by working class Americans and read earnestly in Marx and Lenin. Amid uncertainties about where to position themselves politically, the pair embarked on a world tour in 1926–27 that turned them firmly and permanently toward Communism. Their travels included the Soviet Union, where they happily accepted the Soviet regime's official self-representations.

Upon their return to the United States in 1927, Hutchins and Rochester joined the Communist Party, which would be their social center for the rest of their lives. Hutchins first attained wide notice with her book of 1929, *Labor and Silk*, a technically detailed analysis of the silk industry and its corporate ownership, and a carefully documented account of working conditions. The book made a morally intense but information-crammed case for unionization of the industry. It was illustrated by Esther Shemitz, a close friend who later married Whittaker Chambers.[48]

Hutchins and Rochester realized that the Communist Party disapproved of their relationship, which they had not concealed. Abruptly, in 1932, they stopped acknowledging it. Never again did they speak openly about their love for one another. Party spokespersons sometimes tried to discredit Nazism and McCarthyism by accusing their followers of homosexuality. Hutchins herself was a strict enough party-liner to go along with this practice— for example, telling attorneys for Alger Hiss in 1948 that Hiss's accuser, ex-Communist Chambers, had always been known within the Communist movement as a "homosexual pervert."[49]

Hutchins frequently wrote about labor issues in party publications, including the *New Masses* and the *Daily Worker*. Her book of 1934, *Women Who Work*, emphasized the crushing effect of the class structure on women.[50] Hutchins also wrote about world affairs. Her pamphlet of 1935, *Japan's Drive for Conquest*, praised Japanese workers who were struggling against fascism within their own country, and ridiculed the Japanese government's call for an alliance of the world's nonwhites. "Negroes in the United States and in other countries [we]re hearing demagogic appeals from Japan for a movement of all the dark peoples of the world against white imperialism," but this, declared Hutchins, was "but a smoke screen to cover Japan's own imperialist program for the exploitation of China, Manchuria, Mongolia and other areas in the Far East."[51]

Old friends on the Protestant left became increasingly impatient with Hutchins and Rochester in the late 1930s and 1940s, when Stalin's regime was harder to defend. The pair nonetheless clung all the more intensely to their community of party comrades, especially women, including Ella Reeves Bloor, the party's illustrious, militant organizer, whose maternal persona earned her the name "Mother Bloor."[52] The party's affairs from the late 1940s onward were dominated by government investigations and legal indictments; Hutchins's past as an open member was no secret. She invoked the Fifth Amendment's self-incrimination clause in 1951 when the House Un-American Activities Committee asked her if she was, or ever had been, a Communist. The following year, Chambers, in his bestselling autobiography, *Witness*, charged that Hutchins had been, like himself, part of the Soviet underground.[53] Chambers claimed that the party wanted him killed after he left the underground in 1938 and went into hiding, and that Hutchins had participated in the plot to get him.

How likely is it that Hutchins was a member of the Soviet underground? In 1938, Hutchins did visit the law office of Ruben Shemitz, the brother of her old friend Esther Shemitz, at whose marriage to Chambers in 1931 she had been a witness. Ruben Shemitz reported to the FBI the day after Hutchins visited him that she had told him the safety of his sister and her children would be guaranteed if Chambers himself could be produced. When the FBI then went to Hutchins, she denied the implied threat to Chambers, and claimed that she had only been trying to retrieve fifty dollars she had once loaned him to pay a dental bill. Not until the early 1960s did Hutchins admit that this highly implausible tale was false, and that she had indeed been on assignment from the party to find Chambers.[54] If Hutchins was unaware of at least some of Chambers's espionage work, it strains credulity to suppose that the party would have authorized her to try to locate him, whether or not she conveyed a threat to his life.

Whatever the truth about the extent of Hutchins's underground role, Chambers's widely circulated account exacerbated the isolation that she and Rochester experienced for the rest of their lives. Even if tempted to leave the party in 1956, when they were in their seventies with failing health, they would have found it hard to find another community. As its financial and political fortunes dwindled, Hutchins and Rochester became all the more central to the party's operation. It was their money, repeatedly, that provided bail for indicted comrades and kept the party's presses operating.[55] Hutchins and Rochester were supported by this dwindling community until their deaths in the 1960s—Rochester in 1966, after several years of partial dementia, and Hutchins three years later.

Hutchins's relationship to the Communist Party was different from Harris's relationship to the Methodist church. Hutchins had little impact on the party's direction, but accepted it as a force for equality and then supported it on its own terms, even as those terms changed with the political events of the times. She was a loyal soldier. Harris, by contrast, inspired many Methodists to do things that most Methodists did not do. But in the Methodist church Harris was dealing with an institution that allowed her far more autonomy than the Communist Party allowed Hutchins. At least if she kept quiet about who she loved.

George Houser (1916–2015) was never a Communist, but he, like Hutchins, moved from religious to secular settings for his political activities. His primary vehicles were the Fellowship of Reconciliation, the Congress of Racial Equality, and the American Committee on Africa. A white man who began life as the son of Methodist missionaries in the Philippines, Houser was unusual in the ease with which he worked across color lines within the civil rights movement. In 1942, Houser joined African American activists James Farmer and Bayard Rustin to found the Congress of Racial Equality (CORE), whose first executive director he became.[56] Five years later, Houser helped organize and then participated in the first "freedom ride" designed to desegregate buses in the Jim Crow South. In the early 1950s, he was one of the most outspoken white Americans who demanded an end to colonialism in Africa and promoted national independence for its peoples. Houser, Farmer, and Rustin were all admirers of Gandhi and active leaders of the Fellowship of Reconciliation (FOR), a pacifist organization made up chiefly of left-oriented Protestants and post-Protestants, and unusual for its interracial character.[57]

Houser insisted that the religiously-grounded egalitarianism he imbibed as a missionary child in the Philippines propelled his life as an antiracist and a pacifist.[58] He recalled that his childhood amid Filipinos was "an environment where racism was not a fact of life." Houser's missionary values were reinforced by a circle of radical Methodist youth he met as a high school student in Berkeley, California, then by a year living in China with a Chinese roommate, and, finally, by his time as a seminary student at Union Theological Seminary in New York in the late 1930s. Houser married a missionary daughter who had spent the first eighteen years of her life in China. Along with Rustin, Houser was among the adamantly antiwar FOR affiliates who refused to register for the draft when the federal government instituted the Selective Service Program in 1940. As a result, Houser, displaying the commitment that defined his later activism, served a year in prison.

Houser's actions were more than unusual among left-liberal white men of his generation. Houser was in the vanguard of activism within the African American company he kept. After his release from Danbury Federal Penitentiary Houser and his CORE colleagues "sat in" and managed to integrate several Chicago-area restaurants that refused to serve to black customers. Historian Thomas J. Sugrue notes that Houser and his CORE associates "formed interracial households" and actually "lived" an interracialism sharply at odds not only with Southern ways of life but "with white Northern customs" of those around them in New York and Chicago.[59] His most distinctive enterprise was the interracial bus ride that became the model for the famous and effective freedom rides of the early 1960s.

In 1947 CORE and FOR jointly sponsored a group of eight black and eight white men—including Houser and Rustin—to ride Greyhound and Trailways buses in Virginia and North Carolina. Although the US Supreme Court had ruled a year earlier in *Irene Morgan v. Virginia* that segregation in interstate travel was unconstitutional, the ruling was not being enforced south of the District of Columbia. In what turned out to be a rehearsal for the extensive freedom ride training sessions of the 1960s, participants practiced nonviolence when trainers pretended to intimidate and abuse them. "The Journey of Reconciliation" bore a title that reflected its pacifist matrix but obscured the radical nature of the project's defiance of Jim Crow laws. In fact, Walter White and Thurgood Marshall of the National Association for the Advancement of Colored People opposed the project. The riders got as far as Chapel Hill, North Carolina, without incident. But there, a local white man assaulted one of the white travelers, and four of the others, including Rustin, were arrested for violating the state law recently struck down by the Supreme Court but still treated as the law in North Carolina. Warned that severe violence awaited the group if it went on to the next stop, Houser and Rustin suspended the "Journey." But Houser and the other leaders felt the point had been well made. Houser and Rustin's pamphlet *We Challenged Jim Crow!* told the story of their journey and attracted some press attention.[60]

Houser continued his partnership with Rustin during the late 1940s and 1950s, leading under CORE's auspices the Interracial Workshop Program that brought together activists to consider such questions as how to integrate municipal swimming pools. But Houser, as historian Joseph Kip Kosek notes, always saw "support of African independence" and "justice for African Americans" as part of "the same struggle."[61] Even as the domestic civil rights movement downplayed global perspectives in response to right-wing accusations that it was part of an international Communist movement,[62] Houser not only kept his eye on Africa, but made it a priority. In 1953, he founded the American Committee on Africa and then served as its executive director. This committee, which Penny M. Von Eschen describes as "the major American political group concerned with Africa," kept its distance from Communist-connected groups but maintained a staunchly anti-imperialist perspective on Africa throughout the remainder of the 1950s and the 1960s.[63] When, in 1989, an elderly Houser wrote a book about ACOA's doings, *No One Can Stop the Rain: Glimpses of Africa's Liberation Struggle*, the Tanzanian leader Julius Nyerere contributed a foreword.[64]

When Houser died in 2016 at the age of ninety-nine, he was honored as a hero of the struggle for black liberation at home and abroad. The destiny of Houser's white contemporary Buell G. Gallagher (1904–1978) was quite different. Virtually unknown today, Gallagher was the author of one of the most penetrating critiques of racism written in the 1940s. *Color and Conscience*, the book of 1946 from which I have taken the notion of the "boomerang," was a twin in many respects to Soper's *Racism: A World Problem*. But Gallagher was also an on-the-ground participant in the civil rights movement at several points in his career.

Unlike Houser, Soper, and the other individuals discussed in this chapter, Gallagher had no personal experience in the mission field. Gallagher was socially formed, instead, by his experience as the president of the historically black Talladega College in Alabama. Yet in searching for the meaning of his years at Talladega, Gallagher turned to the missionary project. He described "the whole" of *Color and Conscience* as "nothing more than an elaboration" on ideas set forth at a series of missionary-dominated ecumenical conferences, including the great 1938 meeting of the International Missionary Council at Madras. The only friend to read his manuscript before publication was a former missionary to Japan, Galen Fisher, whose leadership of the movement to support Japanese Americans during World War II I discussed in chapter 6. And it was through the testimonies and treatises of missionaries that Gallagher came up with the idea of a boomerang, whereby the "cultural imperialism" of the West was smacked in the face by messages the missionaries brought back from ostensibly heathen peoples.[65]

Gallagher's critique was more sharply worded than Soper's. A generation younger, Gallagher had absorbed more secular discussions. He wrote in a more anxious spirit, less certain that Christians would eventually get their act together. Soper had gone well beyond the highly individualistic "we must change our hearts" approach to segregation and discussed other forms of discrimination that evangelicals and moderate ecumenists continued to favor. But Gallagher was more adamant, arguing that insistence on structural changes was the only meaningful sign of a sound heart and an active conscience. Getting to know other townspeople across the color line might be all well and good, but what really mattered were legal protections for fair employment, voting rights, unrestricted housing, effective and integrated schools, equal access to public accommodations, and even freedom to marry someone of a different race.[66]

Gallagher's complaints were not limited to the Jim Crow system in the South. He, like Soper, denounced real estate covenants, racist labor practices, miscegenation laws, and other abuses of black and similarly stigmatized people throughout the country. Soper was embarrassed that the Communists seemed to be doing more than the Christians to battle racism, but Gallagher was more blunt: the "Christian Church," he fumed, had "not produced an ethical attack on color caste which approache[d] the vigor and virility of the attack launched by the American Communists."[67]

Gallagher's defense of black-white marriage was bolder than Soper's, and his account of the history of race-mixing and of the "one-drop rule" even more searching. "Some defenders of white supremacy will accuse the integrationist of 'advocating miscegenation,'" Gallagher observed. But the charge "is not true." What is true is this: the integrationist holds "that individuals should be free to choose their life partners without arbitrary interference by the State or by their neighbors."[68] Gallagher's position was radical for 1946, more than twenty years prior to the ruling of the US Supreme Court in *Loving v. Virginia* that laws prohibiting interracial marriage are unconstitutional. Unlike Gallagher, most civil rights advocates during the 1940s and 1950s avoided the issue.

Gallagher was an uncompromising universalist, applying no less to the United States than to the entire world his understanding of human brotherhood. "There is enough dynamite in the Malvern declaration," he said of an ecumenical conference of 1941 in Malvern, England, "to blow the whole world of the white man's imperialism with its racial inequities off the face of the earth." The problem, Gallagher said, was that the empowered classes were too slow to act on the aspirations of the ecumenical Protestant leaders. European whites were as reluctant to part with their colonial empires as American whites were to abandon Jim Crow and the softer versions of racism found outside the South. He hailed the wartime study conferences of the Federal Council of Churches as efforts to bring the spirit of Malvern to America, and spoke with special enthusiasm about the FCC's advocacy of a "human rights" commission for the new United Nations.[69]

Gallagher acknowledged his indebtedness to the black intellectuals with whom he became familiar while at Talladega. In *Color and Conscience*, Gallagher thanked the black philosopher Alain Locke for advice, and repeatedly cited the works of W.E.B. Du Bois. At a time when the bulk of even scholarly opinion still held to the neo-Confederate idea that Reconstruction was an orgy of corruption by unqualified and dishonest black politicians, Gallagher referred readers to Du Bois's defense of the Reconstruction governments in the book of 1935, *Black Reconstruction*. On race in relation to contemporary world affairs, Gallagher praised Du Bois's recently published *Color and Democracy: Colonies and Peace* as an "amazingly detailed and courageous analysis."[70]

While he was writing *Color and Conscience*, Gallagher moved to California to become a professor of Christian ethics at the Pacific School of Religion. Immediately, he became active in local antiracist activities.[71] He helped organize the interracial South Berkeley Community Church, and, as an ordained Congregationalist minister, served for several years as its co-pastor. He joined the leadership of the local chapter of the National Association for the Advancement of Colored People and served on its national board. In 1948 he sought the Democratic Party's nomination for Congress and lost the primary election by only one percent of the vote. Observers were quite certain that Gallagher lost the election because he shared a platform at one campaign rally with Henry Wallace, the Progressive Party candidate for president.[72]

The perception that he was too uncritical of Communism remained a problem for Gallagher in later years, too. In 1961 he was named the first chancellor of the new California State College system, but resigned after only eight months amid a relentless series of red-baiting charges hurled by

Republican politicians and reported widely in the press. Gallagher served as president of the City College of New York (CCNY) during the remainder of the 1960s, but was forced out in 1969 at the time of CCNY's crisis over "open admission." The trustees thought he was too sympathetic to the black and Puerto Rican demonstrators, whom he was reluctant to have arrested, while the demonstrators regarded him as too closely linked with the established order they believed racist.[73]

This CCNY crisis destroyed Gallagher. Partisans on both sides of this bitter dispute seemed to agree that there was nothing good to be said about him. He lived in relative obscurity for another decade. He continued to write, but what he wrote found few admirers. His book of 1974 about American universities, *Campus in Crisis*, was largely ignored and, when it was noticed at all, was understood to be out of touch with the current scene.[74] When he died in 1978, there was no obituary in the *New York Times*, despite the paper's earlier reporting of his 1929 appointment as president of Talladega College and its extensive coverage of the 1969 crisis of his City College presidency. No library has ever collected his papers beyond the official presidential documents kept by Taladega College and by the City University of New York.[75]

Many Anglo-Protestants who participated in the civil rights movement had no missionary connections. A famous example is the Unitarian minister James Reeb, murdered in 1965 in Selma, Alabama, while taking part in the demonstrations led by Martin Luther King Jr.[76] But, prior to the mid-1960s, the missionary contingent was overrepresented among the Anglo-Protestants who worked in public against anti-black racism. The relevant activities of the YMCA and of the Federal and National Council of Churches, discussed in chapter 4, were prompted in part by the same missionary background that helps explain the cases I have taken up in this chapter. With some exaggeration, Gallagher wrote in 1946 that Christianity "from the seventh century until very recent times" had been "identified with the aspirations of white men in every quarter of the globe," but Christians were finally repudiating the racialization of their faith, thanks to "the modern missionary movement."[77]

CHAPTER TWELVE

Conclusion

CAIN'S ANSWER

WHEN SPOKESMEN for President Franklin Roosevelt and Prime Minister Winston Churchill explained that the Atlantic Charter's call for the self-determination of all peoples did not apply in any immediate way to the colonized peoples of the European empires, Buell G. Gallagher accused the great leaders of giving "Cain's answer" to the question of whether humans had an obligation to look out for one another. "Whitehall and the White House," Gallagher complained in 1946, had taken steps "to emasculate the Charter . . . making clear that it was not to apply to India, Africa, the Island Indies, or Puerto Rico."[1]

Missionary cosmopolitanism lost its most important battle: the struggle to gain acceptance for the idea that the interests of the United States were tied to the self-declared interests of decolonizing peoples. Missionary-connected individuals and groups changed the United States by putting more energy behind this idea than it otherwise would have had. But it was not enough to carry the day. They quarreled with some government policies and supported others, pushed here and pulled there. They did not always agree among themselves on particular cases. That they lost as often as they did no doubt reflects their lack of unity and the limits of their political skill. But their crushing defeats in Palestine, Vietnam, China, and elsewhere followed also from the strength of opposing forces. The record of their strivings in the domain of empire may be instructive for anyone who imagines that the United States can ever be an instrument serving anything other than itself.

Missionary-connected officials and lobbyists were often willing to take chances with regimes run by indigenous and decolonized peoples. Sidney

Gulick early in the twentieth century and Edwin Reischauer during World War II were annoyed at the willingness of their contemporaries to condemn Japanese imperialism while having little or no objection to European imperialism. The King-Crane Commission wanted the United States to supervise the development of Arab regimes independent of the European powers. Most of the China Hands were willing to keep the American client Chiang Kai-shek at bay in order to see if the United States could get along with Chinese Communists. Kenneth Landon did not think it a mistake for the United States to cooperate with Ho Chi Minh to develop an independent Vietnam. Landon and John Paton Davies Jr. repeatedly warned their superiors in Washington against aligning US policy with British and French interests. Robert Crane risked criminal prosecution in wartime to advance the cause of Indian independence from Great Britain, the United States' military ally.

Later on, missionary-connected Americans in government service, academia, and lobbying organizations were, with some exceptions, more tolerant of the anti-American postures of postcolonial regimes than were the administrations of Truman, Eisenhower, Kennedy, and Johnson. The main characters in *Protestants Abroad* promoted visions of American national interest independent of the Europeans and potentially sympathetic with the political movements of Asian peoples. It did not require a missionary background to have such ideas, but those with it were heavily represented among the men and women who voiced this outlook within and beyond the corridors of power. When the CIA overthrew Mossadegh in Iran in 1953, it marked a transition within the US government from an era of missionary-influenced operations in the Middle East to a policy more clearly allied with the old colonial powers. Foreign Area Studies programs were designed in part to help the United States manage its relations with decolonizing peoples. Activist George Houser convinced African nationalist leaders that he was truly on their side. Theologian Richard Shaull sided with revolutionaries throughout the "third world," especially Latin America. Church executive John Coventry Smith tired of preaching the same old sermon about the importance of greater solidarity with indigenous peoples around the world.

But until the Vietnam War, even outspoken opponents of colonialism were, by degrees, comfortable with American global hegemony.[2] It was a missionary son, after all, who coined the phrase "The American Century." Henry Luce was not the first to suppose that the American nation was an instrument to serve all of humanity, but many who were appalled at Luce's sweeping and chauvinistic formulations nevertheless agreed that their country was more a means than an end, and accepted his invoking of the Good Samaritan as the right model for Americans. Luce's critics knew, too, that he was correct that no American generation before theirs was powerful enough to make it incumbent to act with the entire species in mind. John Hersey sharply criticized the behavior of Americans abroad, establishing a genre later brought to full flower by Burdick and Lederer's *The Ugly American*. But Hersey encouraged readers to view the globe as an expanse in which Americans were uniquely positioned to help others find their way. Kenneth Landon was willing, in the end, to play along with a military government in Thailand that was pro-American. William A. Eddy understood that the air base he negotiated in Saudi Arabia served American as well as Saudi interests.

Vietnam deeply challenged the relatively uncritical assumptions about American global hegemony that had been the norm throughout the 1940s, 1950s, and early 1960s. The US government's prosecution of this war shattered the treasured belief that American leadership could be sharply distinguished from the colonialism of the old European powers. Americans of all political persuasions, except the extreme left, did not want to recognize how much the French regime depended on the United States. Even Ho Chi Minh did not want to believe it.[3] If the Communist Ho had a hard time giving up this vision of American power, it is no wonder that American liberals like Kenneth Landon and Edwin Reischauer were so reluctant to let go of it.

The Vietnam War was a curse for Reischauer, who, like Landon, was slow to realize how the policies of his own government went against what he most valued in himself. The missionary contingent faced up to the truth at different times and with different measures of conviction. James C. Thompson Jr. resigned from the government in protest of the war, while his CIA analyst brother sent mixed signals and finally admitted that his brother and his own antiwar son had been right all along. Vietnam destroyed the generous view of American power the International Voluntary Services and the Frontier in Mission Interns carried with them wherever they went. Missionary-influenced church groups were among the Vietnam War's most adamant critics, as were post-Protestants like John Hersey and John S. Service. The majority of missionary-connected scholars in every geographic specialty of Area Studies were either antiwar from the start, or became so well before the war was over.

Along the way, however, the missionary contingent was a significant force in the development of the human rights movement. During the interwar years this group often espoused what historian Andrew Preston calls "the imperialism of human rights."[4] The Wilsonian dream of a world order based on American notions of liberal democracy survived in the missionary-saturated progressive flank of ecumenical Protestantism long after it was discredited elsewhere. The Protestant International grew out of this tradition, opposing colonial empires, vigorously supporting world government, and enthusiastically embracing human rights. Missionary cosmopolitanism helped shape the formal commitments of the United Nations and the Universal Declaration of Human Rights. The human rights movement that accelerated rapidly in the 1970s had many sources, but it owed much to these Protestant-intensive events of the 1940s.

Eventually, the human rights movement became entangled in theoretical issues that missionary-connected Americans of the midcentury era had not found so urgent. Just what rights are "human"? Can interventions to defend human rights escape the hierarchies in indigenous societies? When does the humanitarianism predicated on differences in power become the egalitarianism that demands equal rights? Can the universalism of the human rights movement avoid functioning in countless local contexts as another version of Western superiority? This sharpening of issues in the relationship of human rights to empire came late in the day. Human rights appealed to the missionary contingent in the context of its commitment to "the brotherhood of man." The human rights movement was a potentially powerful tool against racism, nationalism, and imperialism, and as a formula for a world community informed by Christianity but not limited by it.

While missionary cosmopolitanism was often frustrated in the domain of empire, it got more traction elsewhere. It transformed the missionary project itself. Given the magnitude of this project and its place in American culture in the early twentieth century, this achievement was far from trivial. Missionary cosmopolitanism also drove the ecumenical movement within the churches to its farthest reaches, and was central to the expansion of academic research and teaching about the world beyond the North Atlantic West. In the Institute of Pacific Relations and the Near East Foundation, the missionary contingent established two NGOs exceptional for their attention to East Asia and West Asia. Missionary service practices inspired the Peace Corps. Missionary-connected Americans added visible strength to the civil rights movement when few other white Protestants did, and they made a distinctive egalitarian mark in supporting Japanese Americans during World War II. Henry Luce and Walter Judd broke from their Republican Party associates in opposing white racism at several crucial times. Without Judd, it is far from clear that Congress in 1952 would have ended the ban on naturalization for Asian immigrants that had been in effect since 1790.

When Marines protested the torturing of POWs in Iraq in 2003, it was a missionary's witness against such crimes that the Marines could invoke as a proper American ideal.

Missionary cosmopolitans also reduced the scope and intensity of "Orientalism." Edward Said and his followers gave that name to invidious images of the East as exotic, enigmatic, static, irrational, and often effeminate that were widespread in the arts and in academic and popular writings from the eighteenth through the twentieth centuries. Orientalist perspectives flattered the West and treated the East as potentially dangerous and as a domain properly subject to Western control.[5] Although many of Said's assertions about just where Orientalism existed and what caused it have not been sustained by later scholarship, his formulation continues to serve as a helpful caution in reading Western sources about the Middle East, and to a lesser extent about East Asia and South Asia.[6]

The missionary contingent's rejection of Orientalism was a matter of degree. Pearl Buck's revision of American conceptions of China was a signal expression of missionary cosmopolitanism, but later generations were sensitive to Buck's perpetuation of some old stereotypes. E. Stanley Jones depicted Gandhi as exotic and perhaps feminized, but he presented the Indian leader as the modern equivalent of the Christian West's greatest hero, Jesus of Nazareth. Kathryn Mayo's *Mother India* was the locus classicus of Orientalism for India, and the missionaries vehemently rejected it. Margaret Landon's *Anna and the King of Siam* and the many films and stage productions it inspired all reinforced Orientalist conventions, but it also called attention to the strength of character of the Siamese king and the resolute independence of Siam from European colonialism. Frank Laubach represented the Filipino peoples in Orientalist terms, but he looked to Filipinos and other Asians to take over the leading of Christianity, an archetypically non-Orientalist role. Searchers for Orientalism can find it in the work of the older leaders of the academic study of the East, but Area Studies as developed by the generation of Edwin Reischauer was heavily directed against Orientalist images of foreign peoples. The missionary-influenced scholars and teachers of the post–World War II era long preceded Said and his followers in combatting negative and patronizing images of Asian peoples.

If there were a standard for an authentic, noninvidious egalitarianism, according to which every people and every culture might receive the respect it deserves, the moral deficiencies of many missionary cosmopolitans of the midcentury decades would be easy to discern. Yet if we recognize historical figures as actors in generationally specific force fields, propelled in more than one direction, we can assess their place in history without expecting them to live up to whatever may be our own opinion about how people should behave.

Moreover, and perhaps of greater interest, there are some settings in which missionary-connected Americans made very little difference, even when they had the opportunity to do so.

Why did missionary-connected individuals and groups contribute so little to the cause of gender equality? When I began this book I expected the rights of women would be a priority for my cast of characters. I expected this on account of Pearl Buck's forthright feminism, the mission field's opening of opportunities for women, and the extensive missionary-connected participation in the civil rights movement.[7] I was wrong.

Missionary-connected advocacy of women's rights was modest. It expressed itself mostly in relation to governance issues within the churches and within transdenominational bodies like the Federal, National, and World Councils of Churches. Even there, the movement was limited in scope and in results. Dana L. Robert concludes that once women ceased to control the separate women's missionary boards, they struggled to maintain even the measure of authority they had exercised before World War II.[8]

Beyond the churches and transdenominational Protestant organizations, missionary-connected pressure for gender equality amounted to even less. Second-wave feminism as developed in the 1960s and early 1970s was overwhelmingly led by secular Jewish women.[9] It is one of the major triumphs of Jewish cosmopolitanism. Protestants and post-Protestants were sometimes involved, but with little indebtedness to missions. Ruth Harris puzzled in her later years why she, having been so active in the civil rights movement, had not attended to women's rights.[10]

A major exception is Molly Yard (1912–2005), a missionary daughter from China who became president of the National Organization of Women. Yet it was not until 1987, late in the feminist movement, and in Yard's own seventy-fifth year, that she achieved that office. Yard liked to say that she was "born a feminist" due to the radically left outlook of her missionary parents, but she devoted most of her energies to labor and race. What really mattered about being born into a missionary family, she declared, was that she felt "no racial prejudice whatever."[11] In 1933, Yard led a student protest against Swarthmore fraternities and sororities that discriminated against Jews.[12] Upon finishing college she worked in the American Student Union (ASU), of which she became co-chair. In his classic study of 1930s campus radicalism, Robert Cohen observes that within the ASU leadership, Yard was unusual in the intensity of her opposition to anti-black racism. Cohen also recounts the battles that Yard, as a democratic socialist, and her co-chair Joseph Lash fought against the substantial communist faction with the ASU, an organization with more than twenty thousand members.[13] In keeping with this left-but-not-communist outlook, Yard went on to be one of the founders of the Americans for Democratic Action and a campaign organizer for one prominent liberal democrat after another.[14]

Why did missionary cosmopolitanism have so little to say about women? Why were ecumenical Protestant women in general so marginal to the movement for gender equality? Perhaps exposure to the yet sharper gender hierarchies in China, India, and elsewhere led missionaries to be more forgiving of the patriarchy found in their own society? Perhaps, too, the sizable minority of missionary-connected women who were involved in same-sex relationships prompted circumspection: would agitation for women's rights invite unwelcome scrutiny of their own private lives in communities in thrall to popular readings of the New Testament?

Perhaps the Christian scriptures were themselves a problem: the New Testament contains few items that could inspire gender equality. Galatians 3:28 ("In Christ there is no male or female"; KJV) was quoted so often by gender egalitarians because it is so rare a passage in the New Testament. One dramatic example of its use, and of how easily this passage was neutralized by patriarchal males, was played out at the opening session of the World Council of Churches in Amsterdam in 1948. The Methodist theologian Georgia Harkness spoke of the need to place women in leadership positions and offered Galatians 3:28 as textual warrant. Karl Barth, then the world's most respected Protestant intellectual, rose to reject her claim. He cited Ephesians 5:24 to the effect that man was head of the family just as Jesus was head of the church.[15]

In fact, Ephesians 5:24 is but one of many verses in the New Testament that stipulate the subordination of women to men.[16] Other kinds of egalitarianism can claim a theological foundation in sayings attributed to Jesus of Nazareth and Paul the Apostle, but the biblical tradition that helped to shape the sensibility of Protestant and post-Protestant women offers little warrant for the equality of the sexes. Feminism has always been a heavily secular enterprise. Indeed, the most outspokenly feminist of all the missionary daughters, Buck and Yard, were living well beyond the churches by the time they surfaced as advocates of women's rights.

To be sure, the ecumenical denominations liberalized by the missionary experience were much quicker than their evangelical and Catholic contemporaries to welcome birth control and to encourage women to make lives for themselves beyond homemaking and motherhood. In so doing, the mainstream Protestants were in step with other well-educated Americans. Educated secular women gave birth to even fewer children than their ecumenical contemporaries. One does not need to invoke the missionary experience to explain this phenomenon.

Still, it is important to recognize that missionary cosmopolitanism advanced the larger process of religious liberalization and the attendant growth of post-Protestant secularism. The liberalized religious culture that proved conducive to the expansion of women's lives owed much to the missionary project. Experience in missions quietly and relentlessly reduced the relative size of Christianity and threatened its claim to a special place in the cosmos. "Secularization" has become a highly contested concept, especially when applied to religions other than Christianity. But the concept still has purchase in the historically Christian North Atlantic West when understood to refer to a decline of dependence upon supernatural authority and the institutions ostensibly authorized by that authority. Chief among the conditions enabling this decline are the movement of populations from the rural countryside to diverse urban environments, the advancement of science and literacy, the diminution of physical insecurity, and the strengthening of democratic political institutions that facilitated the social empowerment of larger populations.[17] All of these long- recognized secularizing conditions were present in the United States, and spurred liberalized versions of Protestantism and a drift to post-Protestantism. But the missionary project added something specific and powerful: it forced a gradual and deepening recognition of the historically particular status of Christianity.

The Higher Criticism had already established that the bible was the product of real people living in real time, but the more knowledge the missionaries accumulated about the world, the clearer became Christianity's embeddedness in Mediterranean antiquity and European culture. Sorting out the relationship of Christ to culture turned out to be no easy task. Was there, really, a Christianity that was not "cultural"? The essence of Christianity could be scaled back so it could be made to fit with a great range of cultures, but what then was it? And if it was not scaled down, was it not simply an expression of the accumulated reflections of the North Atlantic West?

The faithful devised a number of strategies for accommodating the world's cultural diversity. Versions of Christianity understood as orthodox could be replaced with liberalized versions that claimed to distinguish the essentials of the gospel from the time-and-place constructions that conservatives mistook for its core. The finest features of the West could be distinguished from the worst, and then interpreted as theologically viable instruments in the world's redemption. The historicity of Christianity could be reconciled with the redeeming features of other religions by interpreting them as steps in spiritual growth, leading eventually to a universal Christianity. Or, one could eschew this worldly progressivism and accept sectarian commitment to this or that particular version of the faith as a way of making sense of a hopelessly diverse, complex, enigmatic, and fallen world, while retaining at some level an apocalyptic vision of the Judeo-Christian deity eventually rescuing an elect. Alternately, one could downplay the transcendent claims of the community of faith and embrace it for its social value. The invention, elaboration, deployment, and critical revision of these devices have constituted a major part of the history of Protestant thought in modern times. The intensity of the missionary encounter with alterity accelerated and deepened this self-interrogation by Protestant thinkers.

The liberalization of Protestantism enabled many men and women reared in the faith to stay with it. This book is filled with the careers of those who flourished largely within churchly domains. Others had careers almost entirely in secular contexts, but remained committed to various churches. This book is also filled with post-Protestants: people who were importantly shaped by Protestantism but ceased to espouse it. Post-Protestants and religious liberals are not inhabitants of two spiritual camps, but distributed along a spectrum. A single set of circumstances can push individuals in the same basic direction, even if they end up at more than one place. Conditions that led some people to be more comfortable outside the churches led others to try to reshape their own religious communities or to find comfortable enclaves within them.[18]

By the 1970s most of what missionary cosmopolitanism did to Christianity had been done. This was also the case for what missionary cosmopolitanism did to understandings of Asian and other foreign peoples, to the prospects for a more culturally diverse and ethnoracially equal America, and to ideas about the place of the United States in the world. Although the missionary project's impact preceded the midcentury decades, and continued after them, the main action occurred between 1920 and 1970, and especially in the 1940s and 1950s.

During that era, the missionary contingent changed American public life in much the same manner as the immigrant contingent: by putting established Anglo-Protestants into sustained contact with people who were different from themselves. No one doubts that the massive immigration from Eastern and Southern Europe between the early 1880s and the mid-1920s gradually transformed the country, especially through the lives of the children and grandchildren of immigrants. The heavily Catholic and Jewish migration challenged Anglo-Protestant cultural hegemony so obviously that Congress in 1924 cut off its source by drastically reducing immigration from the nations that were producing so many Catholic and Jewish migrants. Immigration affected American public life out in the open, and in the face of outspoken resistance. Foreign missions influenced American public life almost by stealth. I do not mean that anyone tried to conceal the process; only that it took place by long distance and through the mediation of missionaries. At the time it was happening it went largely unnoticed.

To recognize a similarity in these two episodes in demographic diversification is not to imply that the two were of equal magnitude. Yet we can better grasp the missionary project's impact if we compare it with the more familiar story of immigration and assimilation. Both episodes of demographic diversification—immigrant and missionary-mediated—confirm the basic insight of "contact theory," according to which social interaction can change important aspects of culture, including inherited prejudices. Contact with Jews, and later with Catholics, as the latter gained stronger class position, gradually weakened Anglo-Protestant prejudice toward each group.[19] Similarly, contact with foreign peoples through missions gradually made the peoples of Asia, especially, more complete members of an expanding human community.

The notion that social contact can change attitudes may seem a truism. "Unless we make ourselves hermits," the philosopher Charles Peirce observed casually, "we shall necessarily influence each other's opinions." Social contact enables us to "see that men in other countries" hold "very different doctrines," perhaps just as sound as those we "have been brought up to believe."[20] But this insight, to which Peirce alluded in 1877, did not achieve currency as a formal theory in social science until 1954, when Gordon W. Allport developed it in his book *The Nature of Prejudice*.

It is not clear how Allport's own brief missionary experience affected him. As a young Methodist, Allport met Muslims while spending a year as a teacher at Robert College in Istanbul. Later in life he was an active Episcopalian and a regular speaker at religious events on his Harvard University campus.[21] In his influential study of prejudice, Allport argued that an empowered group's prejudice toward a stigmatized group could be reduced by close contact, provided both groups were proximate in social standing.[22]

The missionary case qualifies Allport's proviso. Missionaries, driven by a radically egalitarian ideology, engaged sympathetically with a range of low-status peoples abroad and championed their interests in international politics. At home, missionary-connected individuals and groups were conspicuous among privileged Anglo-Protestants in defending confined Japanese Americans, campaigning against Jim Crow, bringing African Americans into the YMCA, welcoming African American clergymen into the leadership of the Federal Council of Churches, and challenging the racist dispositions of American soldiers and sailors in the Pacific War.

Immigrants and missionary-connected Americans diversified the United States from nearly opposite starting points. Yet the Europe-centered cosmopolitanism of the Jewish intellectuals and the Asia-centered cosmopolitanism of the missionary contingent were rarely in conflict. Zionism was an exception. Although Jews were divided about this movement, the presence of Jews in the United States greatly increased sympathy for Zionism and, after 1948, for the state of Israel. Zionism had low credibility with missionary-connected individuals and groups, who associated Zionism with the advancement of European interests in Arab lands. For the most part, however, missionary cosmopolitanism and Jewish cosmopolitanism acted harmoniously and simultaneously. Together, they, along with World War II, did much to give the midcentury decades a distinctive character. Those decades were anomalous in the history of the United States for the absence of large-scale immigration from any quarter. In the context of this great immigration interregnum, the Jewish cosmopolitanism that was a legacy of an earlier period of immigration and the missionary cosmopolitanism produced by the Protestant foreign missionary project were all the more distinctive forces in American public life.

One benefit of looking at American history through the lens of contact theory is that it can help transfer the focus of analytic attention from a) the morally structural question of just how racist, sexist, imperialist, xenophobic, or otherwise deficient a given cohort was, to b) the morally developmental question of just what conditions have promoted and enabled the diminution of those evils. Too often, our preoccupation with the first, rather easily answered question gets in the way of our pursuit of the second, more challenging one.

Is it possible to exaggerate the role of missionary-connected Americans in making the United States what it had become by the 1970s? Of course. I have tried not to do that. But calling attention to any influence that has gone largely unrecognized always entails the risk of appearing to exaggerate it. Causal direction is not easy to measure, even in the dialectical process that produced missionary cosmopolitanism itself. I have tried to show how dispositions brought to the missionary experience affected understandings of that experience, generating in some individuals a more critical assessment of the home culture than in others. There is no need to put a fine point on the relative muscle exercised by experience in the field and by prior dispositions. The missionary project provided ample grist for liberal mills already in operation, but those mills would not have produced the Asian-centered cosmopolitanism of mid-twentieth-century America were it not for foreign missions.

Beyond the many specific arenas in which we can see missionary-connected Americans as historical actors, it is appropriate to remember them as explorers of the capacious and blurry world of Edward Haskell's prophecy, when the circumstances of modern history throw diverse peoples into each other's closer and closer company. In that world, where traditional boundaries are challenged, new affiliations rival inherited associations, and old authorities become discredited, how do you achieve solidarity?[23] How do you manage the tension between inclusion and identity, between an impulse to bring everyone together and a need to define a community in some specific set of terms? With just whom should one try to form a community, and for what purposes? When you refer to "we," who are you talking about? And just where, in all that, is the United States and the resources at its command?

Missionary-connected Americans offered only partial and often conflicting answers to these questions. They tried harder than did most of their contemporaries to take larger segments of humankind into account, intellectually, morally, and politically. They aspired to a world-wide human community that proved elusive. In their finest moments they grasped the profundity of the problem of solidarity. At least they knew that Cain's answer was not theirs.

Chapter One: Introduction

1. Buell G. Gallagher, *Color and Conscience: The Irrepressible Conflict* (New York, 1946), 56–57.

2. "Blowback" is a term the political scientist Chalmers Johnson has popularized to refer to the retaliation against the United States of a number of populations aggrieved by American actions abroad. Johnson developed this analysis first in *Blowback: The Costs and Consequences of American Empire* (New York, 2000), and followed up with several other books in the wake of the 9/11 attacks on the World Trade Center and the Pentagon.

3. Walter Russell Mead, *Special Providence: American Foreign Policy and How It Changed the World* (New York, 2002), 141.

4. In the still tiny literature on the domestic impact of missions, the following works have made the most notable contributions: John K. Fairbank, ed., *The Missionary Enterprise in China and America* (Cambridge MA, 1974); Sarah R. Mason, "Missionary Conscience and the Comprehension of Imperialism: A Study of the Children of American Missionaries to China, 1900–1949," PhD dissertation, Northern Illinois University, 1978; William R. Hutchison, *Errand to the World: American Protestant Thought and Foreign Missions* (Chicago, 1987); Lian Xi, *The Conversion of the Missionaries: Liberalism in American Protestant Missions in China, 1907–1932* (State College PA, 1997); Dana Robert, "The First Globalization: The Internationalization of the Protestant Missionary Movement between the World Wars," *Bulletin of Missionary Research* 26 (2002), 50–66; Daniel H. Bays and Grant Wacker, eds., *The Foreign Missionary Enterprise at Home* (Tuscaloosa, 2003); "Special Issue on Missionaries, Multiculturalism, and Mainline Protestantism," *Journal of Presbyterian History* 81 (Summer 2003); and Susan Haskell Khan, "The India Mission Field and American History, 1919–1947," PhD dissertation, University of California, Berkeley, 2006.

5. Dwayne George Ramsey, "College Evangelists and Foreign Missions: The Student Volunteer Movement, 1886–1920," PhD dissertation, University of California, Davis, 1988, 1. The Student Volunteer Movement has attracted little scholarly attention. Measured by its relative size and the public notice it achieved, it was the most important campus-centered organization in American history prior to the Students for a Democratic Society in the 1960s. The most authoritative study in print is Terrill L. Lautz, "The SVM and Transformation of the Protestant Mission to China," in Daniel H. Bays and Ellen Widmer, eds., *China's Christian Colleges: Cross-Cultural Connections, 1900–1950* (Stanford, 2009), 3–25. The most thorough examination of the topic remains an unpublished dissertation completed on the eve of World War II: William McKinley Beahm, "Factors in the Development of the Student Volunteer Movement for Foreign Missions," PhD dissertation, University of Chicago, 1941.

6. Harlan P. Beach and Charles H. Fahs, eds., *World Missionary Atlas* (New York, 1915), 82–86. The most substantial of the mission fields in 1925 other than China, India, and Japan were located in the Belgian Congo, Brazil, Egypt, Korea, Lebanon, Mexico, Persia, the Philippines, and Turkey. More than forty denominational and transdenominational societies sponsored the missionaries.

7. The lyrics for "Am I a Soldier of the Cross?" were written by the Anglican divine Isaac Watts in 1722 and put to music forty years later by Thomas A. Arne.

8. Joseph Esherick, *The Origins of the Boxer Uprising* (Berkeley CA, 1988).

9. Robert Priest, "Missionary Positions: Christian, Modernist, Postmodernist," *Cultural Anthropology* 42 (2001), 29–46. References to "the missionary position," often with an apparent wink at the reader, continue to be published without reference to Priest's discovery. See, e.g., Albert H. Tricomi, *Missionary Positions: Evangelicalism and Empire in American Fiction* (Gainesville FL, 2010).

10. *Cultural Anthropology* 42 (2001), esp. 48, 50, 53. The anthropologists in this symposium appear to be unaware that many voices within the missionary project advanced an empathic identification with foreign cultures no less sweeping than that advanced in the classic works of the Boasian anthropologists, including Ruth Benedict and Margaret Mead. For widely cited works within the often grumpy literature devoted to the relationship of anthropologists to missionaries, see Claude E. Stipe, "Anthropologists versus Missionaries: The Influence of Presuppositions," *Current Anthropology* 21 (1980), 165–179; Sjaak Van Der Geest, "Anthropologists and Missionaries: Brothers under the Skin," *Man* (N. S.) 25 (1990), 588–601; and "Anthropologists and Missionaries," Special Issue of *Missiology* 24 (April 1996).

11. Barbara Kingsolver, *The Poisonwood Bible* (New York, 1998). In an irony missed by most of Kingsolver's readers, as well as by the author herself, a chapter of *The Poisonwood Bible* entitled "the anti-missionary" gives eloquent voice to a noninvidious, service-centered, indigenous-appreciating outlook on Africa that for many years was expressed by ecumenical Protestant missionaries themselves. This outlook was not so much anti-missionary as revised-missionary. James A. Michener was less hostile to missionaries in his bestselling epic of four decades earlier, but his *Hawaii* (New York, 1959) also emphasized the ethnocentrism of missionaries. Mischa Berlinski's *Fieldwork* (New York, 2007) develops a more ethnographically accurate picture of evangelical missionaries in Thailand even as Berlinski emphasizes the limitations of their capacity to appreciate the culture of the indigenous peoples they try to convert. In earlier years, the most frequently mentioned representation of missionaries in popular culture was "Rain," a story by W. Somerset Maugham about a married, stereotypically repressed South Seas missionary who converts a prostitute but then commits adultery with her, and, overcome with guilt, kills himself while the woman, struck with the missionary's hypocrisy, renounces her new faith and returns to her trade: *Rain and Other Stories* (New York, 1921). The story was the basis for several films, including a 1932 Hollywood movie of the same title which featured Joan Crawford as the prostitute, in one of her most celebrated roles.

12. Nadine Gordimer, "Commentary," *Times Literary Supplement* (September 23, 2003), 14. The tradition of writing about African-based missionaries in the fashion that annoyed Gordimer remains alive, and is well exemplified by Larry Grubbs, *Secular Missionaries: Americans and African Development in the 1960s* (Amherst MA, 2010). For a well-argued demonstration of the role of Protestant missionaries in the critique

of racism and of the apartheid system in South Africa, see Richard Elphick, *The Equality of Believers: Protestant Missionaries and the Racial Politics of South Africa* (Charlottesville VA, 2012).

13. This has been acknowledged even by anthropologists Jean Comaroff and John Comaroff, whose *Of Revelation and Revolution: Christianity, Colonialism, and Consciousness in South Africa*, 2 volumes, 1991 and 1994, is most frequently cited for its emphasis on how the consciousness of the Tswana peoples of Africa was subtly but pervasively altered not only by formal discourse, but by the artifacts of quotidian life under colonized conditions. In their second volume, the Comaroffs confront more directly than they did in the first the range of uses to which indigenous populations were able to put the inventory of Christianity. Among the many critical discussions of the Comaroffs, the most trenchant is Elizabeth Elbourne, "Word Made Flesh: Christianity, Modernity, and Cultural Colonialism in the Work of Jean and John Cameroff," *American Historical Review* 108 (2003), 435–459.

14. For a qualified defense of the missionary project's legacy for Christianity in Africa by a leading apologist for missions, see Lamin Sanneth, *Translating the Message: The Missionary Impact on Culture* (New York, 1989).

15. Anneke Stasson, "Modern Marital Practices and the Growth of World Christianity during the Mid-Twentieth Century," *Church History* 84 (2015), 394–420. See also a searching study of "missionary feminism," Elizabeth E. Prevost, *The Communion of Women: Missions and Gender in Colonial Africa and the British Metropole* (New York, 2010). For other studies that emphasize the ways in which indigenous peoples make creative use of tools derived from missionaries, see Ryan Dunch, "Beyond Cultural Imperialism: Cultural Theory, Christian Missions, and Global Modernity," *History & Theory* 41 (2002) and several works by Ussama Makdisi, especially "Tolerance and Conversion in the Ottoman Empire: A Conversation," *Comparative Studies in Society and History* 51 (2009), and "Anti-Imperialism, Missionary Work, and the King-Crane Commission," in Ian Tyrrell and Jay Sexton, eds., *Empire's Twin: U.S. Anti-Imperialism from the Founding Era to the Age of Terrorism* (Ithaca NY, 2015), 118–134.

16. Robert D. Woodbury, "The Missionary Roots of Liberal Democracy," *American Political Science Review* 106 (2012), 244–274, offers a well-documented argument that Protestant missionaries from Western Europe and the United States functioned to modify, diminish, and ultimately undermine colonial regimes worldwide, and actually promoted democracy. See also Robert D. Woodbury, "Reclaiming the M-Word: The Legacy of Missions in Nonwestern Societies," *Review of Faith & International Affairs* 4 (2006), 3–12.

17. For a lucid articulation of this view of the American missionary project in relation to world history, see Melani McAlister, "Guess Who's Coming to Dinner: American Missionaries, Racism, and Decolonization in the Congo," *OAH Magazine of History* 26 (2012), esp. 36. See also Dunch, "Beyond Cultural Imperialism," esp. 313 and 325. John K. Fairbank pushed this perspective in his Presidential Address to the American Historical Association in 1968, declaring the missionary to be an "invisible" figure in the history of the United States, but he got little traction at the time; see John K. Fairbank, "Assignment for the 70s," *American Historical Review* 74 (1969), 861–879.

18. Minnie Vautrin's story has often been told, including in popular films. She was played by actress Mariel Hemingway in the 2007 film *Nanking*. Vautrin is the

subject of a celebratory biography by Hua-ling Hu, *American Goddess at the Rape of Nanking: The Courage of Minnie Vautrin* (Carbondale IL, 2000), which takes its title from an inscription on Vautrin's gravestone in a Michigan cemetery, "The Goddess of Nanking." Hu's book includes a foreword by Illinois senator Paul Simon (1926–2003), whose parents had been Lutheran missionaries in China prior to his birth. Simon's senatorial career (1985–1997) came too late to make him a major player in the story told in *Protestants Abroad*, but he was one of the few senators even of his generation to take a special interest in Asian affairs. When he retired he was honored by the Conference on Asian Pacific American Leadership. See Frank Wu, "Saluting Simon," *Asian Week*, September 27, 1996.

19. 1 Corinthians 14:34 (KJV).

20. Such a case was the Methodist clergywoman Julia Reed Paxton, a missionary to Latin America who found that when in the United States she was excluded from Methodist pulpits; see Dana L. Robert, *American Women in Mission: A Social History of Their Thought and Practice* (Macon GA, 1997), 417, quoting Robert's interview with Paxton on May 30, 1990. That missions provided opportunities for women that were not available at home has long been recognized by students of missions, as in Patricia Hill, *The World Their Household: The American Woman's Foreign Mission Movement and Cultural Transformation, 1870–1920* (Ann Arbor MI, 1985). But the literature on the history of American women has yet to explore in any detail the importance of missionary experience when women were often in positions of institutional leadership, especially in the 1920s and 1930s.

21. Khan, "India," 92.

22. One of the few scholarly works to present accurately the role of foreign missions in American culture during the generation prior to the 1920s is Ian Tyrrell, *Reforming the World: The Creation of America's Moral Empire* (Princeton, 2010). Tyrrell also recognizes that "a newer, more genuinely ecumenical and politically engaged style of liberal Protestantism . . . gained ascendancy by the 1930s and 1940s" (237).

23. More than 200 missionaries and about 30,000 Chinese Christians were killed in the 1905 Boxer Rebellion. The Memorial Arch became a point of contention during and after the 1960s, when large numbers of Oberlin students refused to honor Oberlin's missionary dead by walking through the arch. Whitman College in Walla Walla, Washington, named after a pioneer missionary to the local indigenous population, called its athletic teams the "missionaries" until 2016. Whitman dropped the missionary mascot because it was deemed "noninclusive and imperialistic"; see *Seattle Times*, April 23, 2016 (http://www.seattletimes.com/seattle-news/education/whitman-college-dumps-missionary-mascot/).

24. The Church of Christ of Latter Day Saints, or Mormons, although eventually allied with Protestants in several aspects of American public life, did not participate in the classic Protestant missionary project. Mormon missionaries usually went abroad for only two years, and at a young age, and were exclusively male during the period I address in this book. Hence the long-term, family-intensive immersion in foreign societies that so marks the Protestant missionary project was entirely lacking in the Mormon missionary project. The effect of the missionary experience on young Mormons may have been substantial, but it has never been of interest to Mormon scholars even down to the present. A rare exception is Hui-Tzu

Grace Chou, "Missionary Experiences and Subsequent Religiosity among Returned Missionaries in Utah," *Social Sciences and Missions* 26 (2013), 199–225. There is no treatment of this question even in the many articles about missions found in Terryl L. Givens and Philip L. Barlow, eds., *The Oxford Handbook of Mormonism* (New York, 2015). American Catholics also maintained ambitious missionary projects, but scholars find relatively little consequences for American public life. See, for example, John T. McGreevy's excellent monograph, *American Jesuits and the World: How an Embattled Religious Order Made Modern Catholicism Global* (Princeton, 2016).

25. For the emergence of "evangelical Protestantism" out of "Protestant Fundamentalism" in the 1940s, see Joel Carpenter, *Revive Us Again: The Reawakening of American Fundamentalism* (New York, 1999) and Matthew Avery Sutton, *American Apocalypse* (Cambridge MA, 2014).

26. James DeForest Murch, *Cooperation without Compromise: A History of the National Association of Evangelicals* (Grand Rapids MI, 1956).

27. The relationship between these two families of American Protestants in the twentieth century, and the rise of the second to political prominence, is a major theme of my *After Cloven Tongues of Fire* (Princeton, 2013). See also two very important recent books by Kevin Kruse, *One Nation Under God: How Corporate America Invented Christian America* (New York, 2015), and E. J. Dionne, Jr., *Why the Right Went Wrong: Conservatism from Goldwater to the Tea Party and Beyond* (New York, 2016).

28. The most striking exception appears, at first, to be Wheaton College graduate Kenneth Landon, but as I explain in chapter 8, it is not as much of an exception as it seems. Landon had privately abandoned his fundamentalist faith before he became a major figure in the OSS, the State Department, and the academic field of Area Studies. Landon's wife, Margaret Landon, the author of *Anna and the King of Siam*, was also a Wheaton graduate and is closer to being an exception, but while she remained a churchgoer throughout her life she did so in the most frequent company not of fundamentalists, but of Quakers and ecumenical Presbyterians.

29. James Campbell, *Middle Passages: African American Journeys to Africa, 1787–2005* (New York, 2005), 185–186.

30. Walter L. Williams, *Black Americans and the Evangelization of Africa, 1877–1900* (Madison WI, 1982), 9, 176. Elizabeth Engel, *Encountering Empire: African American Missionaries in Colonial Africa, 1900–1939* (Frankfurt, 2015), argues that the African American missionary endeavor undercut pan-Africanism more often than it advanced it, and in its church-intensive preoccupations contributed to the separation of black Protestants from other Protestants and from politically radical African Americans.

31. The closest to an exception was Max Yergan (1892–1975), an African-American who spent a dozen years as a YMCA missionary in South Africa before returning to the United States in 1936 and renouncing the Baptist faith for the Communist Party. Yergan later turned against the Communists, bore witness against them during the McCarthy era, and finally defended the apartheid system of South Africa. His unusual life is carefully detailed by David Henry Anthony, *Max Yergan: Race Man, Internationalist, Cold Warrior* (New York, 2006).

32. W.E.B. Du Bois, *Color and Democracy: Colonies and Peace* (New York, 1945), 23, 137–138.

33. Langdon Gilkey, *Shantung Compound: The Story of Men and Women under Pressure* (New York, 1966), 188; see also 173, 180–183. Gilkey concluded that the conservative missionaries from Europe were less narrow than their American counterparts. He described Eric Liddell, the famous Scottish missionary who was an Olympic track and field champion, as the most saintly man he had ever met (192). *Shantung Compound* is best known for Gilkey's recounting of how the experience of watching people under stress led him to question the optimistic views of human nature that were common among his companions. In his later career as a theologian, he allied himself with Reinhold Niebuhr on the "realist" as opposed to the "idealist" side of arguments within the ecumenical Protestant leadership.

34. For examples of this, see Alan Scot Willis, *All According to God's Plan: Southern Baptist Missions and Race, 1945–1970* (Lexington KY, 2005); and Mark Banker, "Of Missionaries, Multiculturalism, and Mainstream Malaise: Reflections on the 'Presbyterian Predicament,'" *Journal of Presbyterian History* 81 (Summer 2003), 77–102. One detailed study of late nineteenth- century home missions finds extensive evidence of racism, and argues that by 1900 the Baptist home missionaries, especially, had moved away from the most egalitarian aspects of Christianity, and made their peace with the hardening of anti-black racism, even with the lynch law that accompanied it; see Derek Chang, *Citizens of a Christian Nation: Evangelical Missions and the Problem of Race in the Nineteenth Century* (Philadelphia, 2010).

35. The memoirs of missionary children are filled with accounts of killings and near-killings. See, e.g., Timothy S. Harrison, *Before Oil: Memories of an American Missionary Family in the Persian Gulf, 1910–1939* (Rumford RI, 2008), 125-126. This memoir of the family of a Dutch Reformed medical missionary is a classic in the tradition of missionary stoicism, calmly recounting one trauma after another, including the author's depressed mother jumping from a ship to her death while crossing the Indian Ocean. Even those memoirs recounting relatively happy and protected childhoods refer to raids by bandits or bombs from the Japanese; see, e.g., Nancy Thomson Waller, *My Nanking Home, 1918–1937* (Cherry Valley NY, 2010), 74–75. When American officials ordered American citizens to leave war zones, missionaries often refused to comply.

36. James C. Thomson, Jr., Peter W. Stanley, and John Curtis Perry, *Sentimental Imperialists: The American Experience in East Asia* (New York, 1981), 45. The chief author of this book, Thomson, was a missionary son whose career I discuss in chapter 9.

37. Gilkey, *Shantung Compound*, esp. 179.

38. Charles T. Cross, *Born a Foreigner: A Memoir of the American Presence in Asia* (Lanham MD, 1999). Cross was a distinguished diplomat, whose postings included serving as ambassador to Singapore. His book is one of the most reflective of the autobiographies of missionary children. Carolyn N. Smith, ed., *Strangers at Home: Essays on the Effects of Living Overseas and Coming "Home" to a Strange Land* (Puna, India, 1996). Sociologist (and missionary son) Jeffrey Swanson's account of this "missionary strangerhood," as he calls it, focuses on evangelical missionaries. But this psychosocial condition applied to all varieties of missionary activity. See Swanson, *Echoes of the Call: Identity & Ideology among American Missionaries in Ecuador* (New York, 1995), esp. 19.

39. Sarah R. Mason to Anne Lockwood Romasco, May 14, 1974, in Box 5, Folder 27, Sarah Mason Papers, Archives of the Yale Divinity School, henceforth cited as Mason Papers.

40. The sociological literature on "Third Culture Kids" rarely distinguishes between missionary, business, diplomatic, and military children, and focuses heavily on the period since World War II. The concept of "third culture" in this literature refers to these children as belonging to some culture other than that of their parents, and also distinct from the society in which they grew up abroad. One of the few studies that does try to distinguish the missionary children from others is Ann Baker Cottrell, "Educational and Occupational Choices of American Adult Third Culture Kids," in Morten G. Ender, ed., *Military Brats and Other Global Nomads: Growing Up in Organization Families* (Westport CT, 2002), 229–253. Cottrell studied more than 600 children growing up abroad. She found that these people in adulthood, no matter what the occupation of their foreign-based parents, achieved dramatically higher educational levels than other Americans—81 percent of the foreign-reared graduated from college, while only 21 percent of other Americans of the same generation did so. Cottrell found, further, that the sons and daughters of missionaries were at the high end of educational attainment, and were much more likely than the others to obtain post-graduate degrees, especially in medicine.

41. James Lilly, *China Hands: Nine Decades of Adventure, Espionage, and Diplomacy in Asia* (New York, 2004), 17, describes how stiff and hypocritical some of the business children found the missionary schools to be. It is one of very few memoirs of growing up abroad written by someone who was not a missionary child. Lilly eventually served as Ambassador to the People's Republic of China. Missionary children who attended these schools comment frequently on the presence of nonmissionary children but always emphasize the enduring tightness of the bond among the missionary children themselves. See, e.g., Stephen Alter, *All the Way to Heaven: An American Boyhood in the Himalayas* (New York, 1997).

42. This was also true outside the churches. In 1935 a leading eugenicist argued the missionary children were distinctive types. Ellsworth Huntington, "The Success of Missionary Children," *Missionary Review of the World* 58 (February 1935), 75: "The missionaries are selected because of intellectual ability, religious earnestness, altruism, the spirit of adventure, moral courage, physical courage and good health," declared Huntington. In "no other profession" was selection "on both sides of the family" nearly so rigorous, with the result that the children of such couples are of "high-grade" quality. Huntington observed that "it takes the finest kind of courage to proceed quietly with one's work when a Boxer uprising or the fierce anger of savages endanger one's life."

43. Dan B. Brummitt, "The Fate of Missionaries' Children," *Missionary Review of the World* 57 (February 1934), 37–38.

44. William G. Lennex, *The Health and Turnover of Missionaries* (New York, 1933), cited by Mason, "Missionary Conscience," 3, where several other mid-1930s writings in the same mode are mentioned. A mid-1980s survey of research found that the field had been essentially created in the 1930s; see Clyde N. Austin and Billy Van Jones, "Reentry among Missionary Children: An Overview of Reentry Research from 1934–1986," *Journal of Psychology and Theology* 15 (1987), 315–321.

45. An especially ambitious example was published in 1989 by an evangelical group on the basis of a conference at which 90 papers were delivered; see Pam Echerd, et al., eds. *Understanding and Nurturing the Missionary Family* (Pasadena CA, 1989). Many of the authors insist that the children of missionaries are no more prone to suicide than other young people, but the sheer size and intensity of this volume's discussion of the special challenges faced by missionary children indicates how widespread concerns had become about the particular circumstances of growing up abroad in a missionary context.

46. Robert Goheen, interview, Princeton NJ, May 18, 2000.

47. John Hersey, *The Call* (New York, 1986). For more on this important novel, see chapter 2.

48. J. D. Stahl, "Missionary Children: where do we belong?" *Gospel Herald* (March 3, 1981), 171. Stahl was so engaged by the traumas of sons and daughters of missionaries that he conducted a survey of 35 of the Mennonite missionary children he knew, and found that nearly all of them reported serious emotional and social challenges that they believed were much worse than the normal adolescent confusions and anxieties. Although most of the daughters remained Mennonites, many of the sons did not. Stahl himself became a Quaker. J. D. Stahl, letter to me, September 22, 2000.

49. J. E. Miller, *Wilbert B. Stover: Pioneer Missionary* (Elgin IL, 1931), 59–60. For a probing discussion of the psychological costs of separations of this kind, see Ruth E. Van Reken, "Possible Long-Term Implications of Repetitive Cycles of Separation and Loss During Childhood on Adult Missionary Kids," Paper for Christian Association for Psychological Studies, February 1997.

50. Ann Lockwood Romansco to Sarah Mason, May 1, 1974, Box 5, Folder 27, Mason Papers.

51. Joan Smythe's parents served in China from the late 1920s through 1951. Her father was one of the chief witnesses to the Japanese army's Nanking Massacre of 1937–38. Young Joan and her mother had left the city shortly before the arrival of the Japanese. For Lewis Smythe's letters and other reports, see Zhang Kaiyuan, ed., *Eyewitnesses to Massacre: American Missionaries Bear Witness to Japanese Atrocities in Nanjing* (Armonk NY 2001), 252–317. David Roy and Marilyn Young have shared with me their memories of Smythe as a fellow student.

52. Joseph F. Littell, *A Lifetime in Every Moment* (Boston, 1995), 291. Although Littell wrote in an ostensibly forgiving spirit, the story his book actually tells is one of persistent and egregious parental neglect.

53. Eugene Irschick, interview, Berkeley CA, May 2, 2005.

54. Robert Goheen, interview, Princeton NJ, May 18, 2000.

55. Edwin O. Reischauer, *My Life Between Japan and America* (New York, 1986), 37.

56. As accessed November 2015.

57. James M. Landis (1899–1964) is remembered as the supreme "regulator" of the financial industry during the New Deal era, and a highly innovative dean. One of the most radical of the New Dealers, he generated controversy as the chair of the Securities and Exchange Commission. He also gained notoriety as the hearing officer who, after ten weeks of testimony in 1941, cleared the labor leader Harry Bridges of charges of being a Communist and thus, as a non-citizen, of being subject by a law then in effect to deportation to his native Australia. Landis was forced to resign as dean of

the Harvard Law School in 1946 when it became known that he was cohabiting with a woman who was not his wife. Landis was born in Japan of Presbyterian parents but showed virtually no interest in Japan after the time he left it to attend high school in the United States. He experienced a meteoric academic and political career until his ability to perform was derailed by severe alcoholism and depression. He served a brief prison term for tax evasion shortly before his death, which was widely thought to be a suicide but probably was simply the result of an alcohol-related drowning in the swimming pool of his home. Landis's personal traumas are dealt with in an excellent biography by Donald A. Ritchie, *James M. Landis: Dean of the Regulators* (Cambridge MA, 1980). Shortly before her own death, Landis's daughter published a novel based on her relationship as a teenager with her troubled father: Ann L. McLoughlin, *Amy and George* (Boston, 2013).

58. Mason, "Missionary Conscience," 400–409. Mason sent out questionnaires to 219 of the former students, and received 200 responses. She is not clear on how the 219 were selected out of the several thousand who attended Shanghai American School between the 1910s and 1949, but availability of addresses and chronological distribution across the decades appear to have been paramount. Another study, conducted by Guy Emery, found that a number of missionary sons distinguished themselves in physics. Guy Emery (e-mail of July 8, 2014, reporting a study still in progress) called my attention to Walter Sydney Adams, Craig M. Crenshaw, Harry Hepburn Hall, Stanley Sweet Hanna, Wallace Hayes, and James Albert Phillips.

59. "John Espey; Author, UCLA English Professor," *Los Angeles Times* (September 30, 2000). Beginning in the 1940s, Espey wrote many sketches of the Chinese milieu of his childhood and published them in several collections. His most complete volume of memories and reflections is one of the most skillfully written in the missionary memoir literature: John Espey, *Minor Heresies, Major Departures: A China Mission Boyhood* (Berkeley CA, 1994).

60. Edward Haskell, *Lance: A Novel about Multicultural Men* (New York, 1941), 330. While Haskell's use of "multicultural" does appear to be the earliest, the word appears from time to time in the 1950s and 1960s in the writings of other missionary-connected authors. An important example is ex-missionary Wilfred Cantwell Smith's proclamation that the world's future was "multicultural," voiced in a widely-discussed article, "Christianity's Third Great Challenge," *Christian Century* (April 27, 1960), 505.

61. Haskell, *Lance*, 321. Fitting, too, is the fact that Haskell's publishing house was John Day, which also published Margaret Landon's *Anna and the King of Siam* and most of the books of Pearl Buck.

62. Nathan Glazer, *We Are All Multiculturalists Now* (Cambridge MA, 1997).

63. Werner Sollors, "The Word 'Multicultural,'" in Greil Marcus and Werner Sollors, eds., *A New Literary History of America* (Cambridge MA, 2009), 757–761.

64. The most thorough critical study of *Lance* is Brian Flota, "Multicultural Men? The Early, Exclusionary Multicultural Vision of Edward F. Haskell's *Lance*," *EAPSU Online: A Journal* 7 (Fall 2010), 6-28.

65. The only extensive account of his life known to me is a website developed by an admirer who came to know him in his final years, http://futurepositive.synearth .net/2002/04/28/?print-friendly=true.

66. Dust jacket, *Lance*.

67. I have explored this tension in a number of other contexts. See, esp. "Ethnic Diversity, Cosmopolitanism, and the Emergence of the American Liberal Intelligentsia," *American Quarterly* 28 (1975), 133–151; "How Wide the Circle of the We: American Intellectuals and the Problem of Ethnos since World War II," *American Historical Review* 98 (1993), 317–337; *Postethnic America: Beyond Multiculturalism* (New York, 3rd edition, expanded, 2006); and *Cosmopolitanism and Solidarity* (Madison WI, 2006).

Chapter Two: To Make the Crooked Straight

1. Pearl S. Buck, *Fighting Angel: Portrait of a Soul* (New York, 1936), 54.

2. John Hersey, "Pearl S. Buck," *Proceedings of the American Academy of Arts and Letters* (New York, 1974), 102–105.

3. Pearl S. Buck, *God's Men* (New York, 1951). Buck assigns to her mendacious protagonist an abundance of personal traits and actions that are based literally on Luce's known public life.

4. Alan Brinkley, *The Publisher: Henry Luce and His American Century* (New York, 2010), 457; Robert E. Herzstein, *Henry R. Luce, Time, and the American Crusade in Asia* (Cambridge MA, 2006), 1.

5. Luce, "The American Century," as reprinted in *Diplomatic History* 23 (1999), 170–171.

6. Luce, "American Century," 170.

7. These features of Luce's life are documented by Brinkley, *Publisher*, and Herzstein, *Luce*, and by the most hostile of Luce's biographers, W. A. Swanberg, *Luce and His Empire* (New York, 1972). Swanberg was one of many to see similarities between Luce and the newspaper magnate, William Randolph Hearst, of whom Swanberg also wrote a biography, *Citizen Hearst: A Biography of William Randolph Hearst* (New York, 1961).

8. John Hersey, "Henry Luce's China Dream," *New Republic* (May 2, 1983). A slightly revised version of this essay was reprinted as "Henry Luce and the Gordian Knot," in Stephen R. MacKinnon, and Oris Friesen, eds., *China Reporting: An Oral History of American Journalism in the 1930's and 1940's* (Berkeley CA, 1987), 7–22.

9. For these remarks of Alan Grover and others, see Brinkley, *Publisher*, 291, 324, 352, and 386.

10. *Time*, June 12, 1939, referred to what had always been the Great War as "World War I," and also speculated that the world was in the process of entering "World War II."

11. Brinkley, *Publisher*, 248.

12. Luce, "American Century," 165.

13. Luce, "American Century," 170–171.

14. The popularity of Luce's vision during and after the war has been widely commented upon; see, e.g., Oliver Zunz, *Why the American Century?* (Chicago, 1998), 185.

15. Reinhold Niebuhr, "Imperialism and Responsibility," *Christianity and Crisis* (February 24, 1941), 6; *Christian Century* (March 19, 1941), 381; "Luce Thinking," *Nation* (March 1, 1942); Henry Wallace, "The Century of the Common Man," was first

delivered as an address in 1942 and then expanded into a brief book, *The Century of the Common Man* (New York, 1943). That Wallace's vision for the role of the United States in the world was much more explicitly Christian than Luce's is often forgotten.

16. Speeches of 1951 and 1961 as quoted in Michael H. Hunt, "East Asia in Henry Luce's 'American Century'," *Diplomatic History* 23 (1999), 322. Hunt is correct to see Luce's conflation of the American legal order with natural law as a sustaining foundation for the "sweeping globalism" that animated him even through his dogged defense of the Vietnam War.

17. Brinkley, *Publisher*, 438–439.

18. The story of Luce's enchantment with the China of Chiang Kai-shek has been told many times. A lively version of it can be found in James Bradley, *The China Mirage: The Hidden History of American Disaster in Asia* (Boston, 2015), esp. 112–115.

19. Hersey, "China Dream."

20. For a more extensive discussion of the China Lobby and its constituency, see chapter 7.

21. On this episode, see William Inboden, *Religion and American Foreign Policy, 1945–1960: The Soul of Containment* (New York, 2008), 74, 181.

22. Brinkley, *Publisher*, 420–421.

23. Buck's relative neglect is especially surprising in the field of American women's history. She is not among the hundreds of women listed in the indices of Sharon Block, *Major Problems in American Women's History* (5th edition, New York, 2015); Gail Collins, *America's Women: 400 Years of Dolls, Drudges, Helpmates, and Heroines* (New York, 2007); Nancy Cott, ed., *No Small Courage: A History of Women in the United States* (New York, 2004); Vicki L. Ruiz and Ellen Carol DuBois, eds., *Unequal Sisters: An Inclusive Reader in U. S. Women's History* (4th edition, New York, 2007); Rosalind Rosenberg, *Divided Lives: American Women in the Twentieth Century* (revised edition, New York, 2008), Kate Schatz, *Rad American Women A–Z: Rebels, Trailblazers, and Visionaries Who Shaped Our History* (San Francisco, 2015); and Susan Ware, *American Women's History: A Very Short Introduction* (New York, 2015).

24. James Claude Thomson Jr., "Pearl S. Buck and the American Quest for China," in Elisabeth J. Lipscomb, et al., eds., *The Several Worlds of Pearl S. Buck: Essays Presented at a Centennial Symposium* (Westport CT, 1994), 14.

25. By way of perspective, *WorldCat* credits Jack London with translations in 48 languages and Mark Twain with 45.

26. Peter Conn, *Pearl S. Buck: A Cultural Biography* (Cambridge MA, 1996), 382.

27. Hilary Spurling, *Pearl Buck in China: Journey to the Good Earth* (New York, 2010), 228–229.

28. Deborah Friedell, "Don't you just love O-lan?" *London Review of Books* (July 22, 2010), 24. Friedell's title comes from Winfrey's expression of excitement about the peasant heroine. The *Good Housekeeping* poll is cited by Conn, *Buck*, 359.

29. The reaction of Buck's neighbor and close friend, Margaret Thomson, is recalled in Thomson's daughter's memoir: "Pearl gave the manuscript to Mother to read. Mother said, 'Don't cut a word!'," Nancy Thomson Waller, *My Nanking Home, 1918–1937* (Cherry Valley NY, 2010), 45.

30. Charles Hayford, "China By the Book: China Hands and China Stories, 1848–1949," *Journal of American-East Asian Relations* 16 (2009), 296.

31. Paul Hutchinson, "Breeder of Life," *Christian Century* (May 20, 1931), 683. Hutchinson himself had served as a missionary in China for five years.

32. Will Rogers is quoted by Conn, *Buck*, 153.

33. Harold Isaacs, *Scratches on Our Mind: American Images of China & India* (New York, 1958), 155, 157. This positive image of the Chinese has been described as a variation on the "Orientalism" that Edward Said ascribed to the bulk of western writings about Asia. See, e.g., Karen J. Leong, *The China Mystique: Pearl S. Buck, Anna May Wong, Mayling Soong and the Transformation of American Orientalism* (Berkeley CA, 2005), esp. 56, where Leong attempts to balance Buck's repudiation of many stereotypes with her facilitating a new, Americo-centric vision of the Chinese people. One study that strongly emphasizes the ways in which *The Good Earth* flattered rather than challenged American feelings of superiority to the Chinese is Mari Yoshihara, *Embracing the East: White Women and American Orientalism* (New York, 2003); see 149–169, esp. 145.

34. The picture of Chinese politics found in Edgar Snow, *Red Star Over China* (New York, 1937) harder to assimilate. Snow introduced readers to a variety of historical trends in China, and offered an ambitious and sympathetic analysis of the growth of the Communist movement. Snow, a journalist who was not missionary-connected, was a close friend of T. A. Bisson and other missionaries discussed in later chapters of *Protestants Abroad*. The contrast between Buck and Edgar Snow is developed well in Michael H. Hunt, "Pearl Buck—Popular Expert on China, 1931–1949," *Modern China* 3 (1977) 56-57. Isaacs found Snow second only to Buck in the frequency of mention in the interviews Isaacs conducted.

35. These two books of Buck's are mentioned only in passing in an ambitious effort to recognize and analyze missionary fiction as a subgenre of American letters, Albert H. Tricomi, *Missionary Positions: Evangelicalism and Empire in American Fiction* (Gainsville FL, 2011), 108. Tricomi focuses on the classical canon of American literature, and treats works of Cooper, Melville, and Twain as "missionary fiction" while attending hardly at all to works flowing out of the missionary experience and engaging it in a sustained fashion. Tricomi devotes only two pages (177–178) to John Hersey's *The Call* and makes no reference to Margaret Landon's *Never Dies the Dream* or to Mischa Berlinski's *Fieldwork*. Missionary fiction awaits a more comprehensive and probing study.

36. Pearl S. Buck, *The Exile* (New York, 1936), 307.

37. Many readers have suggested that Buck, in *Fighting Angel*, had finally come in her mid-thirties to recognize in herself some of her father's traits of personality, especially his pride and imperious demeanor. See Spurling, *Buck*, 227–228 (where Spurling also praises the book's "combination of cool, sharp, scrutinizing intelligence and passionate emotion") and Grant Wacker, "Pearl Buck and the Waning of the Missionary Impulse," in Daniel H. Bays and Grant Wacker, eds., *The Foreign Missionary Enterprise at Home* (Tuscaloosa AL, 2003), 202–205.

38. Buck, *Fighting Angel*, 54.

39. For one of the few sustained analyses of Buck's two missionary volumes of 1936, see Vanessa Kunnemann, *Middlebrow Mission: Pearl S. Buck's American China* (Bielefeld, Germany, 2015), 89–131.

40. It is not known what Buck or Frost were thinking to themselves in April 1962 when the two were seated on either side of President John F. Kennedy and the First Lady at a White House celebration of American Nobel laureates.

41. Alfred Kazin, *On Native Grounds: A Study of American Prose Literature from 1890 to the Present* (New York, 1942).

42. Faulkner's comment has been widely quoted; see, e.g., Sheila Melvin, "The Resurrection of Pearl Buck," *Wilson Quarterly* (Spring 2006). A few years later, Faulkner of course accepted the Nobel Prize awarded to him.

43. Spurling, *Buck*, 239–240.

44. James D. Hart, *The Popular Book: A History of America's Literary Taste* (Berkeley CA, 1950), 253.

45. See Conn, *Buck*, 181, 278.

46. Conn, *Buck*, 241–242. Conn compares Buck's statements about sexism to the writings of Margaret Fuller of many generations earlier and to those of Margaret Atwood in *The Handmaid's Tale*.

47. Pearl S. Buck, *Of Men and Women* (New York, 1941), 116–117. Although written in a breezy, often flippant style, this book is a substantive and probing critique of sexism that invites more scrutiny as a document of feminism's history than it has received.

48. Pearl S. Buck, cited by John D'Entremont, "Pearl S. Buck and American Women's History," *Randolph-Macon Woman's College Alumnae Bulletin* (Fall 1992), 14–15. http://faculty.randolphcollege.edu/fwebb/buck/argregg/women.html

49. Mike Wallace interview with Pearl S. Buck, August 2, 1958, available at http://www.hrc.utexas.edu/multimedia/video/2008/wallace/buck_pearl_t.html.

50. Buck's intimacy with Harris was undisguised, but during the early sixties she was also involved semisecretly with the philosopher William Ernest Hocking, who had recently lost his wife, until he died in 1966. For Buck's affair with Hocking, who was nineteen years Buck's senior, see John Kaag, *American Philosophy: A Love Story* (New York, 2016), 210–218.

51. Betty Friedan, *The Feminine Mystique* (New York, 1963), 145.

52. Conn, *Buck*, 349–350.

53. *New York Times* (September 15, 1943), as cited by Conn, Buck, 257.

54. Pearl S. Buck, review of Du Bois, *New York Herald Tribune* (1945), as cited by Conn, *Buck*, 291.

55. Conn, *Buck*, 264.

56. Conn, *Buck*, 312–312.

57. Some advocates of international adoption may have exaggerated the extent of mistreatment of children fathered in Korea to American soldiers, white and black, but scholars agree that such mistreatment was common, and severe. A recent and convincing study is Arissa H. Oh, *To Save the Children of Korea: The Cold War Origins of International Adoption* (Stanford CA, 2015), esp. 22–23, 51–54. Oh distinguishes between programs of varying integrity, ranging from those rightly accused of "commodifying" babies and exploiting adoption for sectarian religious purposes, and those like Buck's that were more consistent in responding to genuine needs.

58. Conn, *Buck*, 222.

59. Pearl S. Buck, *Dragon Seed* (New York, 1941).

60. See Jonathan Spence, "The Triumph of Madame Chiang," *New York Review of Books* (February 25, 2010), for a vivid account of Mme. Chiang's visit to Washington.

61. Buck's memorandum to Eleanor Roosevelt of March 22, 1943, is summarized by Conn, *Buck*, 272.

62. Pearl S. Buck, "A Warning about China," *Life* (May 10, 1943); John K. Fairbank, *Chinabound*, 453. For Luce's concerns, see Conn, *Buck*, 273.

63. Conn, *Buck*, 273 and 325, has an efficient and well documented account of this episode.

64. Conn describes (*Buck*, 258, 263–264, 382) Buck's sensibility accurately: "She inhabited an uncomplicated, well-lit ethical world, in which self-evident principles led to straightforward conclusions about right and wrong." She often claimed to be "apolitical," but "what she actually meant was that she had neither the training nor the inclination for substantive political argument." Buck was "serenely self-confident in debates over political and social issues," hurrying "from one public question to another, offering up solutions to a whole list of national and international problems."

65. For the important case of the missionary-turned-journalist T. A. Bisson, see chapter 9.

66. Hunt, "Buck," 55.

67. Conn, *Buck*, 373.

68. Buck's childhood home in Zhenjiang, Jiangsu Province was designated a cultural heritage site by the Chinese government in 1992, and has since become the site of a research center and museum.

69. This picture of Buck's final self-presentation is based on Spurling, *Buck*, esp. 252–253. For James Thomson's reflections, see his "Pearl S. Buck and the American Quest for China," in Elizabeth P. Lipscomb, Frances E. Webb, and Peter Conn, eds., *The Several Worlds of Pearl S. Buck* (Westport CT, 1994), 7–15. For the neighborly scene in China, see the recollections of James Thomson's real aunt, Nancy Thomson Waller, *Nanking*, 45.

70. John Hersey, "Pearl Buck," *Proceedings of the American Academy of Arts and Letters and the National Institute of Arts and Letters* (November 1974), 102–105.

71. Eugene Burdick and William Lederer, *The Ugly American* (New York, 1958).

72. John Hersey, "A Mistake of Terrifically Horrible Proportions," in John Armor and Peter Wright, eds. *Manzanar: Ansel Adams' Lost Photographic Document* (New York, 1988), 1–66.

73. John Dee, "John Hersey, The Art of Fiction," interview, *Paris Review*, No. 92 (1986). http://www.theparisreview.org/interviews/2756/the-art-of-fiction-no-92-john-hersey

74. *Paris Review*, no pagination.

75. Theodore White had no missionary background and learned Chinese in order to work as a foreign correspondent. While a number of former missionaries and missionary children became writers, relatively few became "beat reporters" like White, regularly sending news stories from abroad to American newspapers and magazines. The most professionally successful of those who did was Peggy Armstrong Durdin, a daughter of missionaries to China. She wrote articles from throughout East Asia and South Asia for more than thirty years following her marriage, in 1938, to the chief *New York Times* correspondent for China, Tillman Durdin, who, like White, had no missionary background and learned Chinese in order to work as a reporter. For Hersey and Luce on China, see David Sanders, *John Hersey Revisited* (Boston, 1991), 2: the two disagreed "about virtually every Chinese question except the imperative of victory over the Japanese."

76. John Hersey, *A Bell for Adano* (New York, 1944), 47–48.

77. Hersey, *Adano*, 207.

78. Susan L. Carruthers, "'Produce More Joppolos': John Hersey's *A Bell for Adano* and the Making of the 'Good Occupation'," *Journal of American History* 100 (March 2014), 1105.

79. Carruthers, "Good Occupation," correctly identifies this tradition of writing and Hersey's role in creating it, esp. 1111–1113.

80. *Life* and the *New Yorker* "hated each other," Hersey later recalled, "but I made separate arrangements with them to do a given number of articles for each one." *Paris Review* interview.

81. Wilder had grown up in China, too, but as the son of a customs official rather than in a missionary family. The two seem not to have known each other. Thornton Wilder, *The Bridge at San Luis Rey* (New York, 1927).

82. For an extensive account of the reception of *Hiroshima*, see Paul Boyer, *By the Bomb's Early Light: American Thought and Culture at the Dawn of the Atomic Age* (New York, 1985), 203–210.

83. "Journalism's Greatest Hits," *New York Times* (March 1, 1999).

84. Jeremy Treglown, "Organs Underground," *Times Literary Supplement* (June 5, 2015), 15.

85. John Hersey, *Hiroshima* (New York, 1946), 22–23.

86. Hersey, *Hiroshima*, 29.

87. David Schmid, "The non-fiction novel," in Leonard Cassuto, ed., *The Cambridge History of the American Novel* (New York, 2011), 993, 999.

88. Michael Yavenditti, "John Hersey and the American Conscience: The Reception of 'Hiroshima'," *Pacific Historical Review* 43 (1974), 48.

89. Yavenditti, "Conscience," 48.

90. Ruth Benedict, *The Chrysanthemum and the Sword* (Boston, 1946).

91. John Hersey, *The Wall* (New York, 1950), 503, where one man says, amid a debate over whether to circumcise a newborn boy, "circumcision would be folly in the time of an anti-Jewish holocaust."

92. David Daiches, "Record and Testament," *Commentary* (April 1950).

93. For disputes over how much, or how little discussion there was of the Holocaust before the 1960s, see Peter Novick, *The Holocaust in American Life* (New York, 1999), 306; and Hasia R. Diner, *We Remember with Reverence and Love: American Jews and the Myth of Silence After the Holocaust, 1945–1962* (New York, 2009), 16, 73–74, 98–99.

94. Werner Sollors, *Ethnic Modernism* (Cambridge MA, 2008), 224.

95. *Paris Review* interview.

96. Paris Review *interview*; Sanders, *Hersey*, 43.

97. Sanders, *Hersey*, 79–82. For another account of the writing and reception of *The Algiers Motel Incident*, see one of the few critical studies of Hersey's oeuvre, Nancy L. Huse, *The Survival Tales of John Hersey* (Troy NY, 1983), 153–159. Huse wrote before Hersey had published *The Call*, which would have enabled her to strengthen her case against the complaints of Leslie Fielder, Dwight Macdonald, and other critics that Hersey was a sentimental do-gooder and a mere "middlebrow" writer. Indeed, part of the significance of *The Call* is its critique of good-doers who are too sentimental to understand the world in which they try to perform their good works. Huse, like Sanders, is a helpful guide to Hersey's many books, but Hersey awaits a scholarly, crit-

ical treatment that can distinguish his major literary contributions from his highly uneven occasional writings.

98. Hersey would almost certainly not have known Kenneth Landon, whose real-life experience of long conversations with the freethinking Alfred Eustace Haydon—which led Landon to find no meaning in religious faith—have a similar dynamic; for Landon and Haydon, see chapter 8, below.

99. John Hersey, *The Call* (New York, 1986), 637, 641, 655, 666.

100. Hersey's father appears in his own name, suddenly; Hersey, *Call*, 145.

101. Hersey, *Call*, 752.

102. For an analysis of the Landon novel, see chapter 8.

103. Hersey, *Call*, 687.

Chapter Three: To Save the Plan

1. For the Edinburgh meeting of the International Missionary Council and its place in the history of missions, see Brian Stanley, *The World Missionary Conference: Edinburgh 1910* (Grand Rapids MI, 2009); Dana L. Robert, *Christian Mission: How Christianity Became a World Religion* (Malden MA, 2009), esp. 53–60; and William R. Hutchison, *Errand to the World: American Protestant Thought and Foreign Missions* (Chicago, 1987), esp. 125–138.

2. Arthur H. Smith, *Chinese Characteristics* (New York, 1894), 137. Smith and like-minded contemporaries are quoted at length in a chapter of Paul A. Varg's still valuable *Missionaries, Chinese, and Diplomats: The American Protestant Missionary Movement in China, 1980–1952* (Princeton, 1958), 105–122.

3. Grant Wacker, "The Protestant Awaking to World Religions," in William R. Hutchison, ed., *Between the Times: The Travail of the Protestant Establishment in America, 1900–1960* (New York, 1989), 261.

4. The popularity of this motto and the functions it performed in assuring missionaries they were talking about a faith that could be separated from the particularities of American culture is addressed by Paul William Harris, *Nothing But Christ: Rufus Anderson and the Ideology of Protestant Foreign Missions* (New York, 1999). See, especially, Harris's overview, 8–9.

5. Committee on the War and the Religious Outlook, *The Missionary Outlook in the Light of the War* (New York, 1920), esp. 307, where Cavert, an official of the Federal Council of Churches, offers his own summary.

6. Dana L. Robert, "The First Globalization?: The Internationalization of the Protestant Missionary Movement Between the Wars," *International Bulletin of Missionary Research* (2002) calls attention to the effusion in 1925 of utterances that crystalize and popularize concerns that had been building up in the missionary community for a number of years. My account follows Robert's and adds additional texts of that same historical moment.

7. For Rawlinson, see the work of his son, John Lang Rawlinson, *Rawlinson, The Recorder, and China's Revolution: A Topical Biography of Frank Joseph Rawlinson* (Cultural Crossroads, no date), and Lian Xi, *The Conversion of Missionaries: Liberalism in American Protestant Missions in China, 1907–1932* (University Park PA, 1997), esp. 79.

8. Daniel J. Fleming, *Whither Bound in Missions* (New York, 1925), 41, 47, 52, 187.

9. Daniel J. Fleming, "If Buddhists Came to Our Town," *Christian Century* (February 28, 1929), 293–294. For the fame this article achieved, see Hutchison, *Errand*, 213. Critics of missionary pretentions have composed many variations of this song; see, e.g., the comments of a *New York Times* columnist in 2010 concerning a group of evangelicals who traveled to Haiti with the intention of rescuing poverty-stricken children following a flood (some called the enterprise "kidnapping for Jesus") and putting them up for adoption in Idaho with Christian families: "Imagine if a voodoo minister from Haiti had shown up in Boise after an earthquake, looking for children in poor neighborhoods and offering 'opportunities for adoption' back in Haiti." Timothy Eagan, "The Missionary Impulse," *New York Times* (February 24, 2010).

10. "The Indian Road," *Time* (April 8, 1929), compared the popularity of Jones's book to Sinclair Lewis's *Main Street*, which had sold 500,000 copies in nine years.

11. E. Stanley Jones, *The Christ of the Indian Road* (London, 1925), 11, 46, 141, 254. Surprisingly, Hutchison does not even mention Jones in his *Errand to the World*, yet Jones was a major character in the story that book tells. Hutchison focused on Congregationalists and Presbyterians, and paid virtually no attention to Methodists. This peculiarity applies to every period in Hutchison's narrative. Only in passing does he mention even Edmund D. Soper, a missionary theorist—and a Methodist—who figures largely later in this chapter and in chapter 11. Hutchinson's parents had been Presbyterian missionaries in Iran, although Hutchison was born in the United States.

12. Jones, *Indian Road*, 18, 140.

13. Frank C. Laubach, *The People of the Philippines: Their Religious Progress and Preparation for Spiritual Leadership of the Far East* (New York, 1925), 452, as cited by Dana Robert, "Internationalization."

14. A. K. Reischauer, *The Task in Japan: A Study in Modern Missionary Imperatives* (New York, 1926).

15. Mary Schauffler Platt, *A Straight Way Toward Tomorrow* (New York, 1926).

16. Howard Bliss, "The Modern Missionary" *Atlantic* (May 1920), 666. This essay is a cogent statement of the outlook of the most liberal missionaries on the eve of the contentious disputes of the 1920s and 1930s. Among Bliss's most consistent themes is the priority of "untrammeled" inquiry over inherited faiths. "Coming in contact with men who are as convinced of the truth of their own faiths as the missionary is of his," Bliss proclaimed in a key passage (667), "his appeal to them must be upon the common basis of absolute fidelity to truth. He must strive to be unflinchingly, scrupulously honest in his own intellectual processes and habits. Our students at Beirut are repeatedly reminded of Coleridge's great aphorism, applicable to all religions as well as Christianity; 'He who begins by loving Christianity better than truth will proceed by loving his own sect or church better than Christianity, and end by loving himself better than all.'" The perspective of fundamentalists of Bliss's time could not have been more different, warranted as it was by 2nd Corinthians 10:5, in which Paul the Apostle demands the condemnation of "imaginations, and every high thing that exalteth itself against the knowledge of God," and calls for the "bringing into captivity every thought to the obedience of Christ." (KJV)

17. Jonathan Spence, *To Change China: Western Advisors in China, 1620–1960* (New York, 1969), esp. 176, 181. Hume wrote one of the most readable of memoirs of the missionary life of his generation: Edward H. Hume, *Doctors East Doctors West: An American Physician's Life in China* (New York, 1946).

18. Samuel Higginbotham, *Sam Higginbotham, Farmer: An Autobiography* (New York, 1950), 102.

19. Gary R. Hess, *Sam Higginbotham of Allahabad: Pioneer of Point Four to India* (Charlottesville VA, 1967), declares (134) that Higginbotham did more to promote "the improvement of Indian agriculture" than "any other individual in the twentieth century."

20. Andrew Porter shows that the British missionaries in the Middle East rapidly and decisively opposed premillenialism in their domains, although the Americans displayed more of it and stayed with it longer; see, esp. Andrew Porter, *Religion Versus Empire? British Protestant Missionaries and Overseas Expansion, 1700-1914* (Manchester, 2004).

21. M. Searle Bates, "The Theology of American Missionaries in China, 1900-1950," in John K. Fairbank, ed., *The Missionary Enterprise in China and America* (Cambridge MA, 1974), observes (137) that many missionary societies and sent evangelists and educators who possessed "only a general, Biblical knowledge of the Christian religion." Of the several studies of American missionaries to the Middle East, see, especially, Heather J. Sharkey, *American Evangelicals in Egypt: Missionary Encounters in an Age of Empire* (Princeton, 2008), and the first three chapters of a detailed account of the teaching faculties of the Near Eastern School of Theology, George F. Sabra, *Truth and Service: A History of the Near East School of Theology* (Beirut, Lebanon, 2009).

22. James Alan Patterson, "The Loss of a Protestant Missionary Consensus: Foreign Missions and the Fundamentalist-Modernist Conflict," in Joel A. Carpenter and Wilbert R. Shenk, eds., *Earthen Vessels: American Evangelicals and Foreign Missions, 1880-1980* (Grand Rapids MI, 1990), 80.

23. Stuart had written that "the Christian religion," while "the fullest, the finest, and the final revelation," is but one of many admirable faiths and is "not different in kind from the revelation of earlier ages." In 1921 the *Princeton Theological Review* published a lengthy denunciation, "Modernism in China." It was only the first of a series of attacks on Stuart that led to his being brought to trial for heresy by his home synod in Virginia. Stuart survived, and served his church and the Harvard-connected Yenching University for nearly three more decades. E. H. Griffith Thomas, "Modernism in China," *Princeton Theological Review* 13 (1921), esp. 653-654. For a brief account of the campaign against Stuart, which lasted several years, and his final escape from its trauma, see Yu-Ming Shaw, *An American Missionary in China: John Leighton Stuart and Chinese-American Relations* (Cambridge MA, 1992), 72-72, 82-87.

24. Carpenter, "Propagating the Faith," in Carpenter and Shenk, *Vessels*, 126-127. See also Kevin Xiyi Yao, *The Fundamentalist Movement among Protestant Missionaries in China, 1920-1937* (Wheaton IL, 2003).

25. The most discerning account of Mott's career is within Tyrrell, *Reforming the World*, passim. A number of hagiographic studies do not do justice to Mott as a historical figure; see, e.g., C. Howard Hopkins, *John R. Mott: 1865-1955, A Biography* (Grand Rapids MI, 1979).

26. For a brief account of John D. Rockefeller Jr.'s religious outlook and close connections with ecumenical leaders, see the early chapters of Gerard Colby with Charlotte Dennett, *Thy Will Be Done: The Conquest of the Amazon: Nelson Rockefeller and Evangelism in the Age of Oil* (New York, 1995), esp. 19-40. The intimacy of

the missionary project with the Rockefellers is evidence of how much more central that project was to mainstream life in the United States than in any of the nations of Western Europe, despite the formal authority there of established churches. Those nations still had substantial missionary societies in the 1920s and 1930s, but the process of secularization had pushed them to the margins. This difference has not been lost on historians of European missions; see, e.g., the comments about missions and money in the United States in Andrew F. Walls, *The Missionary Movement in Christian History: Studies in the Transformation of Faith* (Maryknoll NY, 1996), 230–232.

27. William Ernest Hocking, *The Meaning of God in Human Experience* (New Haven CT, 1912). For Hocking's career as a philosopher, the best treatment remains Bruce Kuklick, *The Rise of American Philosophy: Cambridge, Massachusetts, 1860-1930* (New Haven CT, 1977). For a sympathetic treatment oriented more to Hocking's personal life, see John Kaag, *American Philosophy: A Love Story* (New York, 2016).

28. *Re-Thinking Missions: A Laymen's Inquiry After One Hundred Years*, by the Commission of Appraisal, William Ernest Hocking, Chairman (New York, 1932), x.

29. *Re-Thinking Missions*, 65, 67, 70, 77, 246, 254. Simultaneously with the publication of the *Layman's Report*, Hocking brought out a book of his own that made clear how far his own thinking had gone in the same cultural relativist directions by which Margaret Mead and other anthropologists were then making a mark. In *The Spirit of World Politics, With Special Studies of the Far East* (New York, 1932), Hocking asked rhetorically (8) if he and his readers had any right to "apply our standards of civilization to cultures other than our own?"

30. Frederick Bohn Fisher, "Re-Thinking Missions," *Christian Century* (December 14, 1932).

31. *Re-Thinking Missions*, 29, 40, 44.

32. Hutchison, *Errand*, 166–169; Grant Wacker, "The Waning of the Missionary Impulse: The Case of Pearl S. Buck," in Daniel H. Bays and Grant Wacker, eds., *The Foreign Missionary Enterprise at Home* (Tuscaloosa AL, 2003), 191–205.

33. Hutchison, *Errand*, 165, 170. Hutchison provides an extensive summary of the reactions of several leading figures, including Robert Speer, head of the Presbyterian Missionary Board and a long-time advocate of indigenization.

34. Hutchison, *Errand*, 174–175.

35. International Missionary Council, *The World Mission of Christianity: Messages and Recommendations of the Enlarged Meeting of the International Missionary Council Held at Jerusalem, March 24-Apri 8, 1928* (New York, 1928), esp. 7–9.

36. *Re-Thinking Missions*, 33.

37. "Statement Adopted by the Council: Racial Relationships," International Missionary Council, *Report of the Jerusalem Meeting of the International Missionary Council, March 24-April 8, 1928*, vol. 4, *The Christian Mission in Light of Race Conflicts* (London, 1928), 237, as cited by Michael G. Thompson, *God and Globe: Christian Internationalism in the United States between the Great War and the Cold War* (Ithaca NY, 2015), 112. Thompson observes that the delegates voted for it "with the bombardment of Peking" still in close memory.

38. International Missionary Council, *The World Mission of the Church: Findings and Recommendations of the International Missionary Council, Tamvbaram, Madras, India, December 12th to 29th, 1938* (New York, 1939). Albert Monshan Wu

explores the sharp conflict within the missionary movement between Americans, who usually wanted more rapid indigenization, and the Europeans, especially the Germans, who wanted less of it; Wu, "The Quest for an 'Indigenous Church': German Missionaries, Chinese Christians, and the Indigenization Debates of the 1920s," *American Historical Review* 122 (February 2017), 85–114.

39. For Kagawa and the extensive attention given him, see Robert Shaffer, "'A Missionary from the East to Western Pagans': Kagawa Toyohiko's 1936 U.S. Tour," *Journal of World History* 14 (2013), 577–621. See also Dana L. Robert, "Cross-Cultural Friendship in the Creation of Twentieth-Century World Christianity," *International Bulletin of Missionary Research* 35 (April 2011), 100–107.

40. Edmund Davison Soper, *The Philosophy of the World Christian Mission* (New York, 1943), 16. This volume is a revealing window on how the period's most intellectually ambitious leaders of ecumenical Protestantism connected their plans for the world with scripture. The first ninety pages are devoted to scriptural exegesis, displaying Soper's learning in biblical scholarship and his classically liberal willingness to discard some passages of the bible as based on unreliable sources. See, e.g., 45, where he explains why parts of the book of Mark are not to be taken seriously. There, too, he relies on the translation of the New Testament by the Scottish divine James Moffatt, who was known for dropping from the text a number of passages found in the King James Version and in the American Standard Version, the two English translations most in use during the first half of the twentieth century. Moffatt's translation was also the favorite of E. Stanley Jones and many other ecumenical missionaries.

41. Edmund Davison Soper, *The Religions of Mankind* (New York), 1921. This classic of comparative religion has been reprinted continually and was brought out in new editions in 2005 and 2009. Throughout the 20th century, missionaries and sons of missionaries were prominent in the study of the "Great Religions" in the seminaries. Union Theological Seminary's Robert E. Hume, a missionary son from India, was another example. Hume's *World Living Religions* (New York, 1924), was a prominent textbook, also frequently reprinted. China missionary son Huston Smith wrote what became the most popular book in the field, *The World's Religions: Our Great Wisdom Traditions* (New York, 1958). One of the twentieth century's most respected students of the comparative study of religions, Wilfred Cantwell Smith of the Harvard Divinity School, spent much of the 1940s teaching at a missionary college in India. The experience proved formative for him. Grant Wacker has pointed out that the study of non-Christian religions was developed almost exclusively by ecumenical Protestants, and not by evangelicals; see Wacker, "Second Thoughts on the Great Commission: Liberal Protestants and Foreign Missions, 1890–1940," in Joel Carpenter and Wilbert R. Shenk, eds., *Earthen Vessels: American Evangelicals and Foreign Missions, 1880–1980* (Grand Rapids MI, 1990), 300. Tomoko Masuzawa, *The Invention of World Religions, Or, How European Universalism Was Preserved in the Language of Pluralism* (Chicago, 2005), is a valuable study that makes little reference to American scholars. Missionary-connected individuals were also prominent in another of the inquiries that flourished in the seminaries, biblical archaeology. William Foxwell Albright, a son of Methodist missionaries to Chile, gained fame as one of the authenticators of the Dead Sea Scrolls.

42. Soper, *Philosophy*, 215, 225, 268.

43. Soper, *Philosophy*, 226–228, 231.

44. Soper, *Philosophy*, 299, 301.

45. Charles W. Forman, "A History of Foreign Mission Theory in America," in R. Peirce Beaver, ed., *American Missions in Bicentennial Perspective* (South Pasadena CA, 1977), 108. Forman, who had a distinguished career as a missiologist at the Yale Divinity School, was himself a missionary son from India. Soper has yet to find a biographer. Of the ecumenical Protestant intellectuals of his generation he is one of the most deserving of further study. As I explain in chapter 9, his role in the antiracism of the 1940s was just as distinctive as his leadership in the theory of missions and in the development of comparative religion as an academic field.

46. Henry P. Van Dusen, *World Christianity: Yesterday, Today, Tomorrow* (New York, 1947), 196–198.

47. Kenneth Scott Latourette, *A History of the Expansion of Christianity, Volume VII, Advance Through Storm: A. D. 1914 and After, With Concluding Generalizations* (New York, 1945), 52.

48. Latourette, *Through Storm*, 503–504.

49. Van Dusen's friend and comrade in many of the churchly struggles of the period, Edwin Lobenstine, was during these same years defending Hocking's line and confessing to doubts that Van Dusen was inclined to deny. See, e.g., Lobenstine's address of 1951, "How My Thinking about Protestantism Has Developed Over the Years," in which Lobenstine not only praises *Re-Thinking Missions*, but declares that his greatest support for the previous twenty years has been his alliance with Hocking. It is unclear, Lobenstine allowed, if the religion toward which people of his orientation are headed will still be called Protestant. The China Records Project, Personal Papers, Group 8, Box 119, Folder 18, Yale Divinity School Archives.

50. Normal Goodall, "Thinking Again About Missions," *Christian Century* (December 20, 1950), 1521–1523.

51. Harold Lindsell, *A Christian Philosophy of Missions* (Wheaton IL, 1949). For an account of evangelical discussions of missions during this period, see George M. Marsden, *Reforming Fundamentalism: Fuller Seminary and the New Evangelicalism* (Grand Rapids MI, 1987), esp. 84.

52. Keith R. Bridston, "Introduction," in Bridston, ed., *Shock and Renewal: The Christian Mission Enters a New Era* (New York, 1955), 7–12.

53. Normal Goodall, "World Mission in a New Era," in Bridston, *Shock and Renewal*, 62.

54. Bridston, "Introduction," 7–12.

55. M. Richard Shaull, *Encounter with Revolution* (New York, 1955), x, 82, 126–127.

56. Missionary son Robert Barnett, a Foreign Service officer whose career I discuss in chapter 7, marveled in retrospect at the popularity of the notion of "Christian presence," finding "almost beyond belief" what he in his secular adulthood had come to regard as "the arrogance of anyone thinking he is an example of Christianity." Robert Barnett, as interviewed by Sarah R. Mason, June 25, 1974, as quoted in Mason, "Missionary Conscience," 364.

57. Rodger C. Bassham, *Mission Theology, 1948-1975: Years of Worldwide Creative Tension* (London, 1979), 27, 39. Another study of mission theory during this period,

focusing on Presbyterians, is Sherron George, "Faithfulness Through the Storm," in Scott W. Sundquist and Caroline M. Becker, eds., *A History of Presbyterian Missions, 1944–2007* (Louisville KY, 2007), 85–109. George's analysis downplays the severity of disagreements, and does not engage Shaull's *Encounter with Revolution* even though Shaull was a Presbyterian. A more comprehensive analysis of the politics of Protestant missions during the second half of the twentieth century, found within the same volume, is Theodore A. Gill Jr., "Historical Context for Mission, 1944–2007," in Sundquist and Becker, *Presbyterian*, 13–35.

58. Henry P. Van Dusen, *One Great Ground of Hope: Christian Missions and Christian Unity* (Philadelphia, 1961). This book repeated many passages from its 1947 predecessor, *World Christianity*, and stands as an example of the eagerness of many ecumenical leaders down through the early 1960s to minimize the challenges to their tradition manifest in decolonization and secularization.

59. Bassham, *Theology*, 65. An ambitious conference of two hundred mission-involved Protestant leaders convened by the Southern Presbyterians in 1962 at Montreat, North Carolina, was yet another conclave of the period displaying deep uncertainties. The representatives from "the third world" shocked the Americans by the fervor of their attacks on the paternalism and colonialism of the traditional missionary project, even though the Americans had been exposed to complaints of this kind since the 1938 Madras convention of the IMC. Further, the fundamentalist preacher Harold Ockenga lashed into the ecumenical leadership for having downplayed the goal of conversion. This, too, was an old argument, but Ockenga made sure the liberals present at Montreat knew it had not declined in intensity. See the account by Winburn Thomas, "Consultation on World Missions," *Christian Century* (November 7, 1962), 1366–1367.

60. Ralph E. Dodge, *The Unpopular Missionary* (New York, 1964). The controversy generated by this book is discussed helpfully in Linda Gesling, *Mirror and Beacon: The History of Mission of The Methodist Church, 1939–1968* (New York, 2005), 231–233. The early 1960s conflicts between Portuguese colonial authorities and Angolan nationalists were widely noted in the American religious press. The missionaries sometimes took pride in having trained the nationalists, with whose cause they sympathized; see, for example, George Daniels, "Agony in Angola," *Christian Century* (November 15, 1961), 1364–1366.

61. James A Scherer, *Missionary Go Home! A Reappraisal of the Christian World Mission* (New York, 1964), 170.

62. Bassham, *Theology*, 69. See also Ronald K. Orchard, ed., *Witness in Six Continents* (Edinburgh, 1964).

63. Cecil Northcott, "Renewal in Mission," *Christian Century*, (August 21, 1968), 1042.

64. Goodall, quoted in Hutchison, *Errand*, 183.

65. For McGavran's intervention at the time of Uppsala, see Hutchison, *Errand*, 188–190.

66. Key texts were Harold Lindsell, *Missionary Principles and Practice* (Westwood NJ, 1955) and Donald McGavran, *The Bridges of God: A Study of the Strategy of Missions* (London, 1955). Lindsell fulminated against the classics of ecumenical missiology for failing to emphasize the agency of the Holy Spirit.

67. Lindsell, 227. For Laubach and his program of literacy reform, see chapter 10. While it is true that Laubach hoped the millions of new readers would read the bible,

his aims were much broader than this. Laubach, further, was a vehement critic of social injustices and was by no means contained within Lindsell's evangelical priorities.

68. Gordon Hedderly Smith, *The Missionary and Anthropology: An introduction to the study of primitive man for missionaries* (Chicago, 1945); for "savages," see Smith's concluding mediation on the spiritual satisfactions of missionary work, 135. Eugene A. Nida, *Customs and Cultures: Anthropology for Christian Missions* (New York, 1954).

69. Two scholars who have studied in detail the missionary discourse of the Southern Baptist Convention in the 1940s and 1950s assure me that liberal theorists were avoided like the plague; the Hocking Report was virtually never mentioned in these circles, even to be refuted; Alan Willis, e-mail of December 17, 2007, and Elizabeth Miller-Davenport, e-mail of March 14, 2013.

70. The Wheaton declaration is quoted by Bassham, *Theology*, 210–211.

71. This is the summary of the Fuller debates offered by David R. Swartz, *Moral Minority: The Evangelical Left in an Age of Conservatism* (Philadelphia, 2012), 80.

72. Gill, "Historical Context," 34.

73. For the founding of Church World Service in the context of ecumenical Protestant's political mobilization at the end of World War II, see chapter 4.

74. J. Leslie Dunstan, "The Pacific Islands," in Wilber C. Harr, ed., *Frontiers of the Christian World Mission Since 1938* (New York, 1962), 79, and in the same volume, Winburn T. Thomas, "Southeast Asia," esp. 31, 33. This volume—a Festschrift for the historian of missions, Kenneth Scott Latourette—is a representative document of the perspectives of older ecumenical missionaries about 1960. Francis Schaeffer and his followers were especially notorious for attacking ecumenical Protestants as virtually anti-Christian.

75. Sympathetic discussants of the record of evangelical missionaries often describe these steps as wise innovations, showing a greater flexibility and sophistication on the part of evangelicals, without acknowledging that the evangelicals were adopting more and more of the outlook the hated ecumenists had developed by the 1920s. Several examples of this can be found in Carpenter and Shenk, *Vessels*, especially in two essays, Charles E. Van Engen, "A Broadening Vision: Forty Years of Evangelical Theology of Mission, 1946–1986," esp. 215, 221–224, 227–228; and Orlando E. Costas, "Evangelical Theology in the in the Two–Thirds World," esp. 241 (endorsing a "contextual hermeneutics" by which scriptures are to be interpreted in relation to the contexts in which they were written and are now read), although Costas is unusual in granting (248) that "ecumenical theologians" have dealt with the problems of "oppression and alienation" in ways from which evangelicals can learn, but Costas was also a regular in WCC circles and "doubled" as an evangelical and an ecumenist. That his voice was so conspicuous in evangelical circles is actually a sign of the slowness of evangelicals to move in this direction.

76. Bassham, *Theology*, 232, 240.

77. Margaret Flory, *Moments in Time: One Woman's Ecumenical Journey* (New York, 1995), is an autobiography that is the main source of information about Flory's life and career. See also, "Legendary Mission Innovator Margaret Flory Dies at 95," https://www.pcusa.org/news/2009/10/2/legendary-mission-innovator-margaret-flory-dies-95/.

78. For an exhaustive and highly informative study of the Frontier Interns in in Missions, see Ada J. Focer, "Frontier Internship in Mission, 1961–1974: Young

Christians Abroad in a Postcolonial and Cold War World," PhD dissertation, Boston University, 2016. Focer interviewed 118 (virtually all of those still living) of the 140 American interns and provides a detailed account of their experiences abroad.

79. Carpenter, "Propagation," 131. Carpenter refers to the study by Robert T. Coote, "The Uneven Growth of Conservative Evangelical Missions," *International Bulletin of Missionary Research* 6 (July 1982), 118–123.

80. I have addressed this historical development in *After Cloven Tongues of Fire: Protestant Liberalism in Modern American History* (Princeton, 2013).

81. Even Hutchison's *Errand*, the most comprehensive and sustained interpretation of the history of American Protestant missionary theory, fails to register the long-term significance of the Hocking Report.

82. Grant Wacker, "Parliament," 268.

83. John R. Fitzmer and Randall Balmer, "A Poultice for the Bite of the Cobra: The Hocking Report and Presbyterian Missions in the Middle Decades of the Twentieth Century," in Milton J. Coalter, et al., eds., *The Diversity of Discipleship: Presbyterians and Twentieth-Century Christian Witness* (Louisville KY, 1991), 113.

84. The most ambitious of Hocking's later works was *The Coming World Civilization* (New York, 1956).

85. For Laubach's influence as a literary reformer, see chapter 10. Laubach has received very little attention from historians, but a recent and welcome exception is the discussion of Laubach in Matthew S. Hedstrom, *The Rise of Liberal Religion: Book Culture and American Spirituality in the Twentieth Century* (New York, 2012), 214–219.

86. Rawlinson's faith struggles are apparent in his last letters to his wife, September 27 and October 11, 1936, Rawlinson Family Papers, Group 8, Box 61, Folder 36, Yale Archives. See also Xi, *Conversion*, who interprets (esp. 75) Rawlinson's views near the end of his life as close to paganism.

87. Wilbert Shenk, *Changing Frontiers of Mission* (Maryknoll NY, 1999). See, esp., Shenk's chapter 5.

88. Andrew F. Walls, "Cross-cultural Encounters and the Shift to World Christianity," *Journal of Presbyterian History* 81 (Summer 2003), 112–116. This brief essay is a sharper expression of ideas Walls developed earlier in Andrew F. Walls, "The Eighteenth-Century Protestant Missionary Awakening in Its European Context," in Brian Stanley, ed., *Christian Missions and the Enlightenment* (Grand Rapids MI, 2001), esp. 22, and even earlier in Andrew F. Walls, *The Missionary Movement in Christian History: Studies in the Transmission of Faith* (Maryknoll NY, 1996). See also the work of the South African scholar David J. Bosch, *Transforming Mission: Paradigm Shifts in Theology of Missions* (Maryknoll NY, 1991), which has been influential among defenders of the global unity of the faith.

Chapter Four: The Protestant International and the Political Mobilization of Churches

1. I have not found the term "Protestant International" in any of the contemporary sources, or in the scholarly literature that has advanced our understanding of the formation to which I am applying the term. The closest approximation known to me is A. J. Muste, "The True International," *Christian Century* (May 24, 1939),

heralding the growing anti-fascist solidarity of ecumenical Protestants as a "True Scarlet International," comprised of men and women whose "robes" have been made "white in the Blood of the Lamb," and "among whom is neither Aryan, Negro, Slave, Japanese, or Maylay." Muste was invoking Revelation 7:14: "These are they which came out of great tribulation, and have washed their robes, and made them white in the blood of the Lamb" (KJV). I am grateful to Michael G. Thompson for calling my attention to this article.

2. R. Pierce Beaver, *Ecumenical Beginnings in Protestant World Mission: A History of Comity* (New York, 1962), 16.

3. For an account of Cheng's role in the Edinburgh conference and in the ecumenical movement within China, see Daniel H. Bays, *A New History of Christianity in China* (Malden MA, 2012), esp. 98. Cheng quickly emerged as a major leader of the community of Protestants in China. As a vigorous Chinese nationalist, he remained a regular interlocutor with Western missionaries throughout the 1920s and 1930s.

4. David M. Thompson, "Ecumenism," in Hugh McLeod, ed., *The Cambridge History of Christianity, Volume 9: World Christianities c. 1914–c. 2000* (Cambridge, Engl., 2006), 52–53.

5. By 1932 the YMCA claimed 54,000 members in more than thirty Chinese cities; Shirley S. Garritt, *Social Reformers in Urban China: The Chinese YMCA, 1895–1926* (Cambridge MA, 1970), 78.

6. Sherwood Eddy, "Church Union in India," *Christian Century* (March 18, 1920), 13.

7. Historians of ecumenism have long agreed on the unique importance of missions and of the Edinburgh meeting; for examples of this consensus, see Thompson, "Ecumenism," 50, and Amanda Porterfield, *The Transformation of American Religion: The Story of a Late Twentieth-Century Awakening* (New York, 2001), 33–38.

8. Eddy's presence within ecumenical Protestant circles of the 1920s and 1930s is well documented by Rick L. Nutt, *The Whole Gospel for the Whole World: Sherwood Eddy and the American Protestant Mission* (Macon GA, 1997). For a more analytic study, see Michael G. Thompson, "Sherwood Eddy, the Missionary Enterprise, and the Rise of Christian Internationalism in 1920s America," *Modern Intellectual History* 12 (2015), 65–93.

9. Michael G. Thompson, *For God and Globe: Christian Internationalism in the United States between the Great War and the Cold War* (Ithaca NY, 2015), 17.

10. These reform activities often had international dimensions, well analyzed by Ian Tyrrell, *Reforming the World* (Princeton, 2010).

11. H. Richard Niebuhr, *The Social Sources of Denominationalism* (New York, 1929), esp. 21. Niebuhr mentioned missions only briefly, endorsing the creation of indigenous churches apart from Western denominational distinctions but warning against the suborning of the gospel to the political regimes and social customs of indigenous peoples; see, esp. 271–273.

12. On this understudied part of Dulles's career, see Mark G. Toulouse, *The Transformation of John Foster Dulles* (Mercer GA, 1985).

13. The most extensive analysis of the Oxford meeting of 1937 and of its impact on Dulles is Thompson, *God and Globe*, esp. 94–99, 120–144. See also John S. Nurser, *For All Peoples and All Nations: The Ecumenical Church and Human Rights* (Washington DC, 2005), esp. 17.

14. Leiper's career is traced with reverent detail in William J. Schmidt and Edward Ouellette, *What Kind of a Man? The Life of Henry Smith Leiper* (New York, 1986). The single person generally credited with being the architect of the WCC was Joseph W. Oldham of England, a former Anglican missionary to India who served throughout the 1920s and 1930s as general secretary of the International Missionary Council and before that had been the executive secretary of the Edinburgh conference itself.

15. The close connection of missions to Church World Service is carefully explained by Harold E. Fey, *Cooperation in Compassion: The Story of Church World Service* (New York, 1966), esp. 169–175. Writing in the mid-1960s, in the wake of vigorous criticism of Church World Service from evangelicals, on the one hand, and left-wing critics on the other, Fey said (175) that the churches working together in Church World Service were "not imperialists but servants."

16. See Virginia Lieson Brereton, "United and Slighted: Women as Subordinated Insiders," in Hutchison, *Between the Times*, 163, and Susan M. Hartmann, "Expanding Feminism's Field and Focus: Activism in the National Council of Churches in the 1960s and 1970s," in Margaret Lamberts Bendroth and Virginia Lieson Brereton, eds., *Women and Twentieth-Century Protestantism* (Chicago, 2002), 49–69, which describes the struggle of women to contest patriarchy within the churches in the 1960s and 1970s.

17. This document is quoted by Nurser, *All Peoples*, 59 and 67. The letter's message was exactly that of a book published that year by the executive secretary of the Foreign Missions Conference, Luman J. Shafer, *The Christian Alternative to World Chaos* (New York, 1940); see, esp. the chapter "What is the Christian to Do?" 166–195. Shafer had been a missionary to China for twenty-three years. Yet another institutional player in this consolidation of an organized Protestant political presence was the Movement for World Christianity. Originally designed to defend the Hocking Report of 1932, this small, Chicago-based collection of high-profile Protestant leaders gradually shifted from missions to the need for a unified Protestant presence in public affairs. The group published the journal *World Christianity: A Digest*. Former missionaries were at the center of this organization, including Daniel J. Fleming, E. Stanley Jones, and the ubiquitous Sherwood Eddy. John A. Mackay, another activist in this group, had become president of Princeton Theological Seminary in 1936, following a long term of service as a Presbyterian missionary in Latin America. Mackay was a regular participant in Life and Works, and in 1947 began a ten-year term as chair of the International Missionary Council. The Movement for World Christianity was a "power elite" if there ever was one in American Protestantism.

18. For a detailed analysis of this meeting, see David A. Hollinger, *After Cloven Tongues of Fire: Protestant Liberalism in Modern American History* (Princeton, 2013), 56–81.

19. The resolutions of this conference are most easily available in *Christian Century* (March 25, 1942), 390–397. The core provisions are reprinted in Nurser, *All Peoples*, 187–189.

20. The Six Pillars manifesto is reprinted in Nurser, *All Peoples*, 191. For the manifesto's role in discussions leading to the founding of the United Nations, see Andrew Preston, *Sword of the Spirit, Shield of Faith* (New York, 2012), 394–395.

21. The most accessible summary of this conference is in *Christian Century* (January 31, 1945).

22. For Bates in 1937–38, see Zhang Kaiyuan, ed., *Eyewitness to Massacre: American Missionaries Bear Witness to Japanese Atrocities in Nanjing* (Armonk NY, 2001), 3–81.

23. John Stuart, "Empire, Mission, Ecumenism and Human Rights: 'Religious Liberty' in Egypt, 1919–1956," *Church History* 83 (2014), 124.

24. Nurser, *All Peoples* (esp. 111-118), provides a detailed and dramatic account of the meetings in San Francisco. See also Nurser's yet more extensive and well-documented telling of this story, "The 'Ecumenical Movement' Churches, 'Global Order,' and Human Rights: 1938–1948," *Human Rights Quarterly* 15 (2003), 864–875.

25. Samuel Moyn, *Christian Human Rights* (Philadelphia, 2015), 148. For a more extensive analysis of the human rights discussion in the United States leading up to the United Nations Charter, see Mark Philip Bradley, *The World Reimagined: America and Human Rights in the Twentieth Century* (New York, 2016), esp. 70–86, which places the success of the FCC lobbyists in the context of their cooperation with the American Jewish Committee and points out, further, that the US government's delegation to the San Francisco meeting was confronting for the first time credible and widely publicized accounts of Nazi death camps. Bradley also gives extensive attention to the early 1940s writings of political scientist Quincy Wright and other Americans pushing in the same direction. The latest and most comprehensive analysis of secular and religious debates of the 1940s concerning the world's political future is Or Rosenboim, *The Emergence of Globalism: Visions of World Order in Britain and the United States, 1939–1950* (Princeton, 2017).

26. The Dulles Commission's executive leadership included former missionaries Leiper, Shafer, Warnshuis, and Kenneth Scott Latourette. Hocking, too, was a member of the small executive body that planned the commission's conferences Hocking stepped in to replace Dulles as acting chair when Dulles was absent, including when Dulles was added to the American delegation to the United Nations founding meeting in 1945.

27. O. Frederick Nolde, ed., *Toward World-Wide Christianity* (New York, 146), 142.

28. *Time* (June 7, 1943), reporting (52) Willkie's address to the national assembly of the Presbyterian Church. Willkie's *One World* (New York, 1943) was widely distributed by agencies of the federal government, and is remembered by historians as the high-water mark of the tide of internationalist thinking that ended with the onset of the Cold War.

29. Robert Park, "Missions and the Modern World," *American Journal of Sociology* 50 (November 1944), 177–183. This was the last essay Park wrote before his death.

30. W.E.B. Du Bois, *Color and Democracy* (New York, 1945).

31. This step by a major, white-dominated organization has long been recognized as a watershed moment; see, for example, David W. Wills, "An Enduring Distance: Black Americans and the Establishment," in Hutchison, *Between the Times*, 168–192, esp. 172.

32. Eugene Barnett was the father of A. Doak Barnett, the China scholar whose career is discussed in chapter 9, and of Robert Barnett, an officer of the OSS and the Foreign Service dealt with briefly in chapter 7. A third son, Dewitt Barnett, was

himself an employee of the YMCA for many years and then, after having become a Quaker, of the American Friends Service Committee. Dewitt's detailed account of the Barnett family is in the Sarah Mason Papers, Yale, Box 2, Folder 11.

33. For the YMCA's accommodation with segregationist practices prior to 1946, see Nina Mjagkij, *Light in the Darkness: African Americans and the YMCA, 1852–1946* (Lexington KY, 1993).

34. By far the best treatment of the FCC's resolution and the maneuvering behind it is Gene Zubovich, "The Global Gospel" (PhD dissertation, University of California, Berkeley, 2015), esp. 86–100.

35. How these ecumenical projects of the 1940s looked to the evangelical enemies of the mainstream Protestant leaders is summarized in a polemical volume, C. Gregg Singer, *The Unholy Alliance* (New Rochelle NY, 1975). William Imboden, *Religion and American Foreign Policy, 1945–1960: The Soul of Containment* (New York, 2008), provides a more scholarly account of the evangelical attack on the ecumenical leadership throughout this period.

36. William McGuire King, "The Reform Establishment and the Ambiguities of Influence," in Hutchison, ed., *Between the Times*, 132. In addition to Nurser, *All Peoples,* the most important work to date on what I am calling "the Protestant International" is Gene Zubovich, "The Protestant Search for 'the Universal Christian Community' between Decolonization and Communism," *Religions* 8 (2017). Zubovich discusses the largely forgotten efforts of the ecumenical leadership to engage the Chinese Communists who attended the opening meeting of the World Council of Churches in 1948. T.C. Chao, one of the Chinese supporters of the revolution then in progress under Mao Zedong, was indeed elected one of the co-presidents of the WCC. Zubovich also explores the tension between a liberal wing of this leadership, led by Methodist Bishop Francis J. McConnell and the self-styled "realist" wing of that leadership, led by Reinhold Niebuhr.

37. John C. Bennett, *Christians and the State* (New York, 1958), 5–6.

38. Bennett, *Christians and the State,* 10, 187–188.

39. Soper, *World Mission,* 273–275.

40. Henry P. Van Dusen, *World Christianity: Yesterday, Today, Tomorrow* (New York, 1947), 288.

41. The long and sometimes tortuous debates of the Congregationalists and the German Reformed about merger are helpfully addressed by Margaret Bendroth, *The Last Puritans: Mainline Protestants and the Power of the Past* (Chapel Hill NC, 2015).

42. http://www.churchesunitinginchrist.org/what-you-can-do/speeches/46-blake -s-sermon-pike-s-response provides access to Blake's sermon and to supporting comments of Episcopal Bishop James A. Pike.

43. The struggles of the ecumenical Protestant churches with merger issues are described in Martin E. Marty, *Modern American Religion: Under God Indivisible, 1941–1960* (Chicago, 1996), 248–273.

44. Nevertheless, a number of small mergers did take place. The United Methodists absorbed the Evangelical United Brethren in 1968. This merger, like that of the Congregationalists and the German Reformed, was significant because it bridged the ethnic gap between predominantly English and predominantly German ancestries. German groups often united among themselves before finding themselves ready to

merge with English bodies. The Evangelical United Brethren had itself been formed in 1946 out of a merger of two smaller denominations of German origin. So, too, had the German Reformed church been formed by the integration in 1934 of two histori-cally German churches. Several Lutheran bodies also merged, bringing together some traditionally Scandinavian and German populations, although not without struggles attributable to ethnic differences. Hence the great majority of mergers in the great age of Protestant ecumenism were facilitated by common ancestries, even while what counted as "common" expanded in the course of the assimilation process. Over time, distinctions between Danes, Norwegians, Swedes, and Finns became less important.

45. The Presbyterian merger was orchestrated by a church executive who was the son of missionaries, J. Randolph Taylor.

46. For the Methodist controversies over administrative segregation and the role of missionary-connected Methodists in bringing it to a halt, see Linda Gesling, *Mirror and Beacon: The History of Missions of the Methodist Church, 1939–1968* (New York, 2005), esp. 316–319.

47. Ethnicity was an important factor in shaping the United Church of Canada, which in 1925 brought together Congregationalists, Methodists, and Presbyterians. These non-Anglican, English-lineage Protestants of Canada were concentrated in the Prairie provinces. In Canada, the many German, Ukrainian, and other ethnically-defined confessions of Canada continued to go their own way, including several Lutheran bodies. Canadian missionaries facilitated the Canadian mergers, but, un-like in the United States, foreign missions were not the most important driving force.

48. Niebuhr, *Denominationalism*, 284.

49. H. Richard Niebuhr, *The Kingdom of God in America* (New York, 1937), esp. ix.

50. Creighton Lacy, "Toward a Post-Denominational World Church," in Jackson Carroll and Wade Clark Roof, eds., *Beyond Establishment: Protestant Identity in a Post-Protestant Age* (Louisville KY, 1993), 327–342, esp. 341.

51. John Coventry Smith, *From Colonialism to World Community: The Church's Pilgrimage* (Philadelphia, 1982), esp. 31, 36, 39–40, 42, 54, 119, 131, 137.

52. Smith, *World Community*, 280.

53. The political waves made by fundamentalist activists in the 1950s and 1960s are too often ignored by a scholarship that focuses on evangelical political mobili-zation following the *Roe v. Wade* decision of the US Supreme Court in 1973. A help-ful and well-documented reminder of the strength of this earlier activism, and the problems it created for the ecumenical leadership, is Markku Ruotsila, *Fighting Fundamentalist: Carl McIntire and the Politicization of American Fundamentalism* (New York, 2015).

54. Smith, *World Community*, 228–229.

55. Smith was no theologian, but his career as an institutional leader can be instructively compared with that of Methodist John B. Cobb (1925–) as a theolog-ical leader. A missionary son, the Japan-born Cobb exemplifies the many ecumen-ical theologians who have worked outside of any preoccupation with institutional mergers. As one of the most philosophically technical of all theologians, developing a "process theology" inspired by Alfred North Whitehead, Cobb never won a pop-ular constituency. But in the 1970s he became an engaged environmentalist and participated in the ecumenical leadership's efforts to turn the world's politics toward

the preservation of the planet. For Cobb's career, see Gary Dorrien, *The Making of American Liberal Protestant Theology: Crisis, Irony, & Postmodernity, 1950-2005* (Louisville KY, 2006), esp. 208-215. Although Cobb's missionary background undoubtedly influenced some of his theological ideas, the missionary project had fewer visible consequences for theology than for churches as institutions. Dorrien's magisterial history of ecumenical theology does not mention missions in its index.

56. Jill K. Gill, "The Politics of Ecumenical Disunity: The Troubled Marriage of Church World Service and the National Council of Churches," *Religion and American Culture* 14 (2004), 189, 192.

57. For a summary of the relevant demographic studies, see Hollinger, *After Cloven Tongues*, 38, 53-54.

58. For this perspective on gender dynamics within the ecumenical Protestant churches, I am indebted to conversations with Margaret Bendroth and Dana Robert.

59. For an extended discussion of these developments, see Hollinger, *Tongues of Fire*, 18-55.

Chapter Five: Anticolonialism vs. Zionism

1. Thomas W. Lippman, *Arabian Knight: Colonel Bill Eddy USMC and the Rise of American Power in the Middle East* (Vista CA, 2008), 148. The first to compare Eddy to Lawrence was apparently Philip Baram, in his indispensable monograph, *The Department of State in the Middle East, 1919-1945* (Philadelphia, 1978), 76.

2. Robert D. Kaplan, *The Arabists: The Romance of an American Elite* (New York, 1995), 8.

3. For the very first years of this mission field, the early 1820s, see Christine Leigh Heyrman, *American Apostles: When Evangelicals Entered the World of Islam* (New York, 2015), who correctly notes (255) how early the Congregationalists and Presbyterians of this particular mission field adopted the ecumenical outlook that spread more widely in the twentieth century. For later eras of the Protestant missionary endeavor in the Middle East, see Ussama Makdisi, *Artillery of Heaven: American Missionaries and the Failed Conversion of the Middle East* (Ithaca NY, 2008); Heather J. Sharkey, *American Evangelicals in Egypt: Missionary Encounters in an Age of Empire* (Princeton, 2008); and Mehmet Ali Dogan and Heather J. Sharkey, eds., *American Missionaries and the Middle East: Foundational Encounters* (Salt Lake City, 2011).

4. Frederick Greene, *Armenian Massacres, or, The Sword of Mohammed* (Philadelphia, 1896).

5. The most recent and authoritative history of this event and of the ways in which various parties reacted to it is Ronald G. Suny, *A History of the Armenian Genocide: They Can Live in the Desert but Nowhere Else* (Princeton, 2015).

6. Barton's account of the founding of Near East Relief reveals that with very few exceptions, the instigators and supervisors of the operation were leaders of missionary organizations and their networks of philanthropic support. See Joseph L. Barton, *Story of Near East Relief (1915-1930): An Interpretation* (New York, 1930), esp. 6-7. It is a mark of how well established Near East Relief and the American Board of Commissions of Foreign Missions were in 1930 that a preface to this book was contributed by former president Calvin Coolidge. For a study of Barton's extraordinary career grounded in

a deep understanding of the contemporary culture of American Protestantism, see Kaley M. Carpenter, "A Worldly Errand: James L. Barton's American Mission to the Middle East," PhD dissertation, Princeton University, 2009.

7. Cleveland Dodge's son, Bayard Dodge, would become president of the American University in Beirut. He served from 1923 to 1948. Later, Bayard Dodge's son, David Dodge, served as president in the 1970s and was taken hostage by jihadists and held captive for a year. The best study of AUB is Betty S. Anderson, *The American University of Beirut: Arab Nationalism & Liberal Education* (Austin TX, 2011). Awareness of the historical connection between the United States and AUB was reestablished in the 2010s with the rise to pubic prominence of Steve Kerr, the politically progressive coach of the Golden State Warriors basketball team. Kerr was the son of Malcolm Kerr, another AUB president, assassinated in 1983 by jihadists. See the extensive story, "Why Steve Kerr Sees Life Beyond the Court," *New York Times* (December 25, 2016).

8. Barton, *Story*, 54.

9. Andrew Patrick, paper delivered at meeting of the Society for Historians of American Foreign Relations, June 27, 2015.

10. Joseph L. Grabill, *Protestant Diplomacy and the Near East: Missionary Influence on American Policy, 1810–1927* (Minneapolis, 1971), 288. This book remains after more than four decades a reliable guide to its topic.

11. Andrew Preston, *Sword of the Spirit, Shield of Faith: Religion in American War and Diplomacy* (New York, 2012); see, especially, Preston's summary (184): "For every missionary who wanted to force the spread of the Christian faith . . . there was a counterpart who sympathized with the plight of the subjugated. For every missionary who wanted to convert the heathen, there were many more who wanted to educate and heal the locals regardless of their faith. For every missionary who wanted to enable American empire, there were those, as in Japan-held Korea, who promoted anti-colonialism and self-determination."

12. My account of the King-Crane Commission relies heavily on Andrew Patrick, *America's Forgotten Middle Eastern Initiative: The King-Crane Commission of 1919* (New York, 2015). See also Ussama Makdisi, *Faith Misplaced: The Broken Promise of US-Arab Relations: 1820–2001* (New York, 2010), 137–143. The archives of the American University in Beirut reveal the frustration of the missionary leadership there with the conversations in Paris. AUB President Daniel Bliss was in Paris as an adviser to Wilson, and complained to his colleagues in Beirut that the European delegations were not interested in what the Arab populations might want. Bliss reported three separate conversations with Balfour himself, of no avail. Bliss left Paris discouraged about the fate of what he called the "Syrians," referring to the Arab population of what later became Lebanon and Israel as well as Syria. See Bliss's letters to Edward Nickolay of February 24 and March 17, 1919, Edward Nickolay Collection, Box 1, Folder 2.3.3.1.2, American University in Beirut.

13. The King-Crane recommendations thus reflected and resisted what historian Eric D. Weitz calls the "Paris System" of international organization, emphasizing ethnic groups as potentially national units. The special treatment of the Armenians and the Turks partook of the ethnic-centered vision for the eventual sovereignty of these peoples, but the prescription of an ethnically diverse city of Constantinople and the

refusal to separate the Jews and the Arabs registered the divided minds of the commissioners. See Eric D. Weitz, "From the Vienna to the Paris System: International Politics and the Entangled Histories of Human Rights, Forced Deportations, and Civilizing Missions," *American Historical Review* 113 (2008), 1313–1343. The commission sought borders that would diminish the likelihood of vast deportations of the sort that Weitz correctly identifies as a major consequence of the Paris System's prioritizing of ethnicity as a foundation for sovereignty.

14. Norman E. Saul, *The Life and Times of Charles R. Crane: 1858-1939* (Lantham MA, 2013).

15. Patrick, *Forgotten*, 260.

16. Baram, *State*, 83.

17. Baram, *State*, esp. 94. Yale told Baram that Hitler's antagonism toward Jews was the fault of Jews themselves.

18. Donovan's letters to Mary Gavin Eddy are in the William A. Eddy Papers, Mudd Library, Princeton University, Box 3, Folder 2. Eddy's exploits in North Africa are well described in Lippman, *Arabian Knight*, 61–97, and in Hugh Wilford, *America's Great Game: The CIA's Secret Arabists and the Shaping of the Modern Middle East* (New York, 2013), esp. 22–25. Eddy is a major character in Smith's *OSS*, the first and still-classic historical study of the OSS; see, esp., 40–58. Barry M. Katz's justly admired *Foreign Intelligence: Research and Analysis in the Office of Strategic Services, 1942-1945* (Cambridge MA, 1989), is entirely about OSS operations for Europe, and says nothing about the Near Eastern, South Asian, or East Asian operations. But even the strongly Europe-centered William L. Langer, the Harvard historian who headed the OSS's Research and Analysis branch, was highly conscious of Eddy's doings and long remembered him as "my good friend," whose contacts in the Middle East Langer and his wife used as the basis for their own travels there in the 1950s. See William L. Langer, *In and Out of the Ivory Tower: The Autobiography of William L. Langer* (New York, 1977), 200, 243.

19. Bradley F. Smith, *The Shadow Warriors: O.S.S. and the Origins of the CIA* (New York, 1983), provides a detailed and authoritative account of Eddy's activities gathering intelligence, instigating sabotage, and maintaining a secret network of French ready to turn against Vichy and support Operation Torch; see, esp., 149–154.

20. Eddy reported the king's regarding him like a son in a letter he wrote to his wife, October 27, 1947, Eddy Papers, Box 6, Folder 2. This letter was written on the occasion of Eddy's departure from official government service and his taking up his responsibilities as senior consultant to the oil industry's operations in Saudi Arabia.

21. The meeting on the *Quincy* is addressed in the literature on the diplomatic history of the 1940s. For a thorough account of it, detailing the challenges Eddy faced in arranging the meeting, see Lippman, *Arabian Knight*, 125–144. Letters Eddy and his wife wrote to family members also describe the preparations for this meeting; see Eddy Papers, Box 3, Folder 2.

22. The basic source for the exchanges between the president and the king is Eddy's own account, William A. Eddy, *F.D.R. Meets Ibn Saud* (New York, 1954), esp. 34. This is a short book published by American Friends of the Middle East, an organization revealed in 1967 to have been heavily financed by the CIA.

23. For the origins of the Balfour Declaration, focusing on British interests during World War I, see Jeremy Renton, *The Zionist Masquerade: The Birth of the Anglo-Zionist Alliance, 1914–1918* (New York, 2007).

24. The most authoritative historian of the diplomacy of the mandate system insists that "keeping the gates of Palestine open" under the British mandate was seen by European leaders of many different political stripes as "almost entirely a means of resolving Europe's 'Jewish Question.'" Susan Pederson, *The Guardians: The League of Nations and the Crisis of Empire* (New York, 2015), 357–393, esp. 358.

25. For Roosevelt's promise and how it was understood by the various parties, see Lippman, *Arabian Knight*, 141–142.

26. George Antonius, *The Arab Awakening* (London, 1938).

27. The early chapters of Wilford, *Great Game*, describe the role of Eddy and other Arab specialists in the politics of Washington in the second half of the 1940s.

28. Lippman, *Arabian Knight*, 220–222, quotes in full Eddy's memorandum to Loy Henderson, and on 223 quotes the State Department's official summary of the meeting.

29. Eddy, *F.D.R. Meets Ibn Saud*, 37.

30. The CIA memorandum is quoted in Wilford, *Great Game*, 63, and Lippman, *Arabian Knight*, 251. It was many decades until American policy-makers took seriously the Muslim Brotherhood, identified here by name.

31. The minutes of this briefing are reproduced in full in Michael J. Cohen, "William A. Eddy, the Oil Lobby, and the Palestinian Problem," *Middle Eastern Studies* 30 (1994), 169–174. Eddy mistakenly predicted here, as he did several other times during this build-up to the recognition of Israel, that the Arab forces would quickly defeat the Jewish forces in a military conflict.

32. Lippman, *Arabian Knight*, 234–235, 247–248.

33. Bayard Dodge, "Must There Be War in the Middle East?" *Reader's Digest* (April 1948). Dodge was a towering figure in the American missionary community in the 1940s. His standing was all the greater for his having lost a son in the fighting France in 1944. For a sympathetic account of Dodge's activities, see Brian VanDeMark, *American Sheikhs: Two Families, Four Generations, and the Story of American's Influence in the Middle East* (Amherst NY, 2012), 123–125. Dodge's *Reader's Digest* article was widely faulted for not treating the destruction of European Jewry by the Nazis as sufficient justification for the Zionist cause.

34. John S. Badeau, *The Middle East Remembered* (Washington DC, 1983), 113–115.

35. William A. Eddy, "The Political Temperature in the Near East Today and U.S. Strategy in the Cold War," Address delivered at the Naval War College, Newport RI, April 1, 1953, esp. 5, 17. This pamphlet is found in several archival collections. In this angry address, Eddy compares to Hitler's racism Israel's privileging of one people, invokes the egalitarianism of the missionary tradition to which Eddy was proudly an heir, and refers to his acquaintance with the Arab Christian writer, George Antonius.

36. For a detailed study of how the missionary community—the chief foundation for the pro-Arab lobby of the late 1940s and 1950s—was divided between a) awareness of the injustices being done to the Palestinians and b) a newly vibrant pro-Semitism produced by the Holocaust, see G. Daniel Cohen, "Elusive Neutrality:

Christian Humanitarianism and the Question of Palestine, 1948-1967," *Humanity* 5 (2014), 183–210. Cohen concludes (204) that after many struggles with this conflict, the missionary-influenced ecumenical Protestants "ultimately endorsed Zionist state-making over Palestinian political demands."

37. Eddy's cavalier remark at the time of the assassination of Jordan's prime minister is in "Dear Chilluns," August 30, 1960, in Eddy Papers, Box 6, Folder 7. For the successful operations of the Zionist lobby in Washington, see Wilford, *Great Game*, and John B. Judis, *Genesis: Truman, American Jews, and the Origins of the Arab/Israeli Conflict* (New York, 2014). See also Makdisi, *Faith Misplaced*. Makdisi's account (189–191) of the presentations before various forums and congressional committees by Philip Hitti and Albert Hourani is a valuable reminder that the Arab lobby had interests much beyond oil.

38. Edwin M. Wright, oral history interview, July 26, 1974, conducted by Richard D. McKinzie. https://www.trumanlibrary.org/oralhist/wright.htm Although Wright's expertise was Iran, the interviewer found him determined to talk only about Zionist influence on American foreign policy.

39. Leonard Dinnerstein, "American Immigration Policy 1945-1950," in Israel Gutman and Avital Saf, eds, *Rehabilitation and Political Struggle* (Jerusalem, 1990), 357–363.

40. Lippman, *Arabian Knight*, 294.

41. Eddy to Family, May 2, 1960, Eddy Papers, Box 6, Folder 7; Eddy's account of the 1950 incident is quoted in Lipmann, *Arabian Knight*, 293–294.

42. Eddy to Family, March 6, 1962, Eddy Papers, Box 6, Folder 7. This long, reflective letter reviews the basic history of the Protestant missionary movement in the Near East and resoundingly affirms Eddy's feeling of personal identity with it. I thank Hugh Wilford for calling my attention to this letter.

43. Eddy's 1950 speech is quoted in Lipmann, *Arabian Knight*, 277.

44. Eddy displayed this romanticism more than any of the Arabists to whom Kaplan, *Arabists*, ascribes this sensibility. Kaplan mentions Eddy, but seems not to understand his importance.

45. Eddy, *F.D.R. Meets Ibn Saud*, 42.

46. These autobiographical fragments are in Eddy Papers, Box 17, Folder 1. These quotations are from a typescript entitled "The Moors Draw Their Knives in Tangier." For the general atmosphere, see the fragment entitled "Spies and Lies in Tangier." The notion that one can walk with the devil until you get to the bridge was widely quoted after Roosevelt used it in a press conference of 1942 (http://www.presidency.ucsb.edu/ws/index.php?pid=16202), but it was an old Bulgarian proverb that Eddy would have learned growing up in the Middle East.

47. "Our Communist Allies" is in Eddy Papers, Box 17, Folder 1.

48. For an account of the Grand Mufti during and after World War II, see Michael J. Cohen, *Britain's Moment in Palestine: Retrospect and Perspectives, 1917–1948* (London, 2014), 418–441.

49. A widely discussed and impressively documented indictment of ARAMCO's labor practices is Robert Vitalis, *America's Kingdom: Mythmaking on the Saudi Oil Frontier* (Stanford CA, 2007), in which Eddy's high position in ARAMCO's councils is mentioned frequently. For Eddy's "rare exception" to the ARAMCO practice of denying the legitimacy of worker grievances, see 152–153.

50. Lippman, *Arabian Knight*, 188. Lippman's discussion of Eddy's mission to Yemen quotes extensively from Eddy's letters about the multiple features of Yemeni life offensive to civilized tastes.

51. For Eddy's assertion that the United States did not "teach social revolution nor tear off veils" in Saudi Arabia, see Vitalis, *Kingdom*, 137.

52. Wilford, *American's Game*, xxi, 276, and 288–289; see also 109, 160, 214, 243, and 298 for Wilford's development of this crucial theme. Pertinent, too, is the account of American policy in the Middle East in Makdisi, *Faith Misplaced*.

53. Baram, *State*, 75, 92.

54. Arthur served the CIA in the Middle East for 28 years; Raymond for 26. The Close brothers are featured characters in the memoir-exposé of former agent Wilbur Crane Eveland, *Ropes of Sand: America's Failure in the Middle East* (New York, 1980). Eveland, who had no missionary connections, describes (127) Arthur Close as "the workhorse of the Damascus CIA station, performing full-time cover duties as a diplomat and spending his evenings making clandestine contacts with agents." Wilford, *America's Great Game*, warns (230) that Eveland was a considerably more eager disciple of Allen Dulles's Cold War outlook than Eveland's representation of his own history acknowledges.

55. Raymond Close, "We Can't Defeat Terrorism by Bombs and Bombast," *Washington Post* (August 30, 1998); (electronic access: http://www.pbs.org/wgbh /pages/frontline/shows/binladen/bombings/close.html).

56. Kaplan, *Arabists*, treats the lot indiscriminately as romantics, unable to see reality because of their idealized image of the Arab peoples. He extends this analysis to individuals who had no missionary connections but had ostensibly been infected by missionary deficiencies. Kaplan ends (297) with a description of April Glaspie, the State Department's notoriously ineffective leader in the diplomacy with Iraq leading up to the Gulf War of 1991, as looking "every inch a missionary" even though Glaspie did not have any missionary connections at all and it is far from clear that her failings had anything to do with the missionary connections of her predecessors.

57. Interview of Ambassador William A. Stoltzfus, Jr., May 18, 1994, Foreign Affairs Oral History Project (http://www.adst.org/OH%20TOCs/Stoltzfus,%20 William%20A.%20Jr.toc.pdf), 20.

58. Interview of Ambassador Talcott W. Seelye, September 15, 1993, Foreign Affairs Oral History Project (http://www.adst.org/OH%20TOCs/Seelye,%20Talcott%20W .toc.pdf), 46, 126–127.

Chapter Six: Who Is My Brother?

1. Sidney Gulick, *The White Peril in the Far East: An Interpretation of the Significance of the Russo-Japanese War* (Chicago, 1905). In 2003 the Australian scholar, Daniel A. Metraux, brought out this book in a new edition (Canberra, 2003). Gulick positively interpreted the rise of Japan as a world power. He believed Russia's defeat in the Russo-Japanese War should result the transferal of much of Siberia from Russian to Japanese control. Gulick was part of one of the most illustrious missionary families in the South Pacific, led by Gulick's father, Luther Halsey Gulick Sr. Sidney Gulick's uncle, John Thomas Gulick, was a biologist who took an early and sympathetic

interest in Darwinian evolution. Sidney Gulick's brother, Luther Halsey Gulick Jr., was a physician and health reform crusader who founded the Campfire Girls and is often credited with helping to invent the game of basketball. Sidney Gulick, confusingly, named his own son Luther Halsey Gulick, after his brother. This Luther Halsey Gulick became a political scientist specializing in public administration. He spent most of his career at Columbia University. His own son was also named Luther Halsey Gulick Jr., not to be confused with the older man named Luther Halsey Gulick Jr.

2. Sandra C. Taylor, *Advocate of Understanding: Sidney Gulick and the Search for Peace with Japan* (Kent OH, 1984) is a thorough and sympathetic account of Gulick's life and career,

3. Missionaries Peter Parker and Samuel Wells Williams served in diplomatic capacities during the middle and late decades of the 19th century.

4. Warren I. Cohen, *America's Response to China: A History of Sino-American Relations* (5th edition, New York, 2010), 82–83. A study documenting the influence of missionaries on American foreign policy in the era prior to World War I is James Reed, *The Missionary Mind and American East Asian Foreign Policy, 1911–1915* (Cambridge MA, 1983).

5. For a discussion of Williams's later academic career, see chapter 9.

6. Two years prior to his provocatively entitled book of 1905, Gulick published *The Evolution of the Japanese: Social and Psychic*, which established him as a leading authority on Japanese culture. Gulick argued that the Japanese were a dynamic and creative people much more responsive to a diverse world than the stereotype of an isolated and aloof Japan would suggest. This volume was widely reviewed and went through many editions. A sign of Gulick's persuasive powers was that William James, who had never met Gulick, wrote to him, praising the book for enabling him to understand the Japanese as never before. James said the volume should serve as "a model for future studies in ethnic character." Sidney Gulick, *The Evolution of the Japanese: Social and Psychic* (New York, 1903). Taylor, *Advocate*, cites (47) James's letter of August 2, 1904.

7. Roger Daniels, *The Politics of Prejudice: The Anti-Japanese Movement in California and the Struggle for Japanese Exclusion* (Berkeley CA, 1962), 79. During this period Gulick wrote another important book, *The American Japanese Problem* (New York, 1914). John Higham's classic work of 1955, *Strangers in the Land: Patterns of American Nativism* (New Brunswick NJ, 1955), 285, recognized the special role of the Federal Council of Churches in denouncing the antisemitism of the movement for immigration restriction. Jennifer C. Snow concludes that "Protestant missionaries were the most consistent and vocal defenders of the rights of Asians to immigrate to the United States." See Jennifer C. Snow, *Protestant Missionaries, Asian Immigrants, and the Ideologies of Race in America, 1850–1924* (New York, 2007), xiv.

8. Robert Speer, *Of One Blood* (New York, 1924). Speer took his title from Acts 17:26 (KJV), in which the Apostle Paul declares that God "made from one blood every nation of men."

9. Popular perspectives on Asian peoples had many dimensions, and shifted somewhat from decade to decade in response to political events; for a detailed analysis, see Robert G. Lee, *Orientals: Asian Americans in Popular Culture* (Philadelphia, 1999).

10. A reliable account of the interwar activities of Fisher, Davis, and Gleason is Sarah Griffith, "'Where We Can Battle for the Lord and Japan': The Development of Liberal Protestant Antiracism before World War II," *Journal of American History* 100 (2013), 429–453. See also Eckhard Toy, "Whose Frontier? The Survey of Race Relations on the Pacific Coast in the 1920s," *Oregon Historical Quarterly* 107 (2006), 36–63, and Henry Yu, *Thinking Orientals: Migration, Contact, and Exoticism in Modern America* (New York, 2001), esp. 19–46.

11. The Institute for Pacific Relations deserves a much more extensive and probing historical study than any now in existence. The best available is Tomoko Akami, *Internationalizing the Pacific: The United States, Japan and the Institute of Pacific Relations in War and Peace, 1919–1945* (London, 2002). This book is most helpful on the interaction between IPR and various individuals and government agencies based in Japan.

12. William L. Holland, *Remembering The Institute of Pacific Relations: The Memoirs of William L. Holland*, edited and introduced by Paul F. Hooper (Tokyo, 1995), 139, 141, 218. See also the recollections of Carter, Davis, and others by John B. Condliffe in the same volume, esp. 431, 433, and 436.

13. Daniel J. Fleming, "Peace and Religion in the Pacific: The Religious Aspect of the Institute of Pacific Relations," *Missionary Review of the World*, September 1925.

14. R. H. Tawney, *Land and Labor in China* (London, 1931).

15. Akami, *Internationalizing*, 257.

16. Jon Thares Davidann, *Cultural Diplomacy in US-Japanese Relations, 1919–1941* (New York, 2007). Davidann attends throughout this book to the role of missionary-connected Americans in the nongovernmental interaction between Americans and Japanese during the decades before Pearl Harbor. Davidann (6–7) credits "John Mott, Sherwood Eddy, and Sidney Gulick" especially as "very influential informal diplomats who helped shape American policy and public opinion."

17. Owen Lattimore (1900–1989) grew up in Tianjin, China, where his American parents were employed as English teachers at a Chinese-operated university not affiliated with missionaries. Most of the other Americans and Europeans he knew in China as a child and then as an adult were missionaries. When Lattimore visited Yenan in 1937 and came to know the leaders of the Chinese Communist Party, he traveled with his close friend, the former missionary teacher turned journalist, T. A. Bisson. When Lattimore gained fame in the McCarthy era for helping to "lose China" to the Communists, it was in the context of his having advanced the same views expressed by the missionaries and missionary children who were similarly accused. Owen Lattimore was so much "the type" that he was often assumed to have been born into a missionary family, but was not.

18. Karl Wittfogel, *Oriental Despotism: A Comparative Study of Total Power* (New Haven CT, 1957). By the time Wittfogel published this work he had become an adamant anti-Communist. He had been an active Communist in Germany and was imprisoned there briefly before moving the United States. While a denizen of IPR in the 1930s, he identified himself as a Marxist.

19. E. Herbert Norman, *Japan's Emergence as a Modern State* (New York, 1940); Kenneth Perry Landon, *The Chinese in Thailand* (New York, 1941); T. A. Bisson, *America's Far Eastern Policy* (New York, 1945); T. A. Bisson, *Japan's War Economy*

(New York, 1945). Another creative scholar of this era who moved in and out of IPR circles was Tyler Dennett, who had been a staff writer for the Methodist Missionary Board in the 1910s. While in the employ of the Methodists, he wrote a book ascribing to missionaries a positive influence on democratic political movements in China, Japan, and elsewhere in the Pacific: *The Democratic Movement in Asia* (New York, 1918). Although he came to specialize more in American diplomatic history than in Asian history, Dennett was a regular commentator on Asian affairs and a consistent critic of European imperialism. He taught at Princeton and Columbia Universities, served for a short time as president of Williams College, and won the Pulitzer Prize for his biography of the American diplomat John Hay. In a 1942 IPR conference in Quebec, Dennett insisted that the American public would demand a postwar settlement in the Pacific that would entirely eliminate the European empires. See Dennett, "Security in the Pacific and the Far East," *Proceedings of Institute of Pacific Relations Quebec Conference*, 9. I thank E. Bruce Reynolds for calling my attention to this document.

20. Service and his fellow government employees did not know that one of the journalists using IPR as a base, Philip Jaffe, was a source for Soviet intelligence. The purging of Service and other "China Hands" in the postwar political environment is discussed in the next chapter.

21. Gulick was one of the exceptions. He blamed the Manchurian invasion on American failures to appreciate Japanese interests.

22. The most decisive of these was the "Hull Note" of November 26, 1941, demanding the complete withdrawal of Japanese troops from China and from French Indochina as a condition of the restoration of full economic relations with the United States.

23. Frank W. Price continued after Pearl Harbor to write on behalf of the people of China, and in 1942 co-authored a collection of essays to mark the historical moment before America's friends of China divided more sharply among themselves about the Kuomintang. Yi-fang Wu and Frank W. Price, eds., *China Rediscovers Her West: A Symposium* (London, 1942), begins with an essay by Madame Chiang but includes accounts of recent Chinese developments written by a great range of Chinese and American authors, including many progressives (e.g., missionary Andrew T. Roy and the literary and agricultural reformer, Y. C. James Yen, whose remarkable career I discuss in chapter 10).

24. Since Judd became a major figure in postwar era, I discuss him in the following chapter.

25. Jerome Greene was known as an egalitarian within the circles of the Harvard elite even through the administrations of A. Lawrence Lowell, James Conant, and Nathan Pusey. He was an outspoken opponent of Lowell's effort to limit the numbers of Jewish students. In 1958, at the age of 74, he published in the *Harvard Crimson* a dissent from President Nathan Pusey's refusal to allow the use of the university's Memorial Church for Jewish and other non-Christian weddings and funerals; "The Right of Rite," April 12, 1958. His copious correspondence with his brother, Roger Sherman Greene (Roger Sherman Greene Papers, Houghton Library, Harvard University), show him to be a more skilled diplomat and political operative than his self-righteous sibling. See also the account of Jerome Greene in Morton Keller and Phyllis Keller, *Making Harvard Modern: The Rise of America's University* (New York, 2001), esp. 3-10.

26. Evarts Boutell Greene wrote what is still one of the finest biographies ever written about an American missionary, a study of his father's life and career, *A New-Englander in Japan: Daniel Crosby Greene* (Boston, 1927).

27. Greene's letters (especially in Folders 301-313, Roger Sherman Greene Papers, Houghton Library, Harvard University), concerning these issues can be read as betraying the patrician's disdain for the *nouveaux riches*, but even in his most petulant moods Greene was defending genuine expertise against someone of whatever social position who just refuses to deal with the facts on the ground. In a characteristic letter (October 24, 1934) to his brother, Jerome, Roger Sherman Greene declared "as a medical school it is our moral duty, and one might say our Christian duty, to select only the best qualified men available, and not to require, or even inquire into, religious views." Greene admitted to a friend after he had been pushed out that he had not been "very tactful in my reaction to my treatment, never dreaming that the older men [meaning John D. Rockefeller, Jr., and Raymond Fosdick] would take the youngster so seriously as they have done." See Roger Sherman Greene to Nelson Johnson, March 1, 1934.

28. Warren I. Cohen, *The Chinese Connection: Roger S. Greene, Thomas W. Lamont, George E. Sokolsky and American-East Asian Relations* (New York, 1978), 200.

29. For a fine study of Greene's career and of his quarrels with Rockefeller leadership, see Mary Brown Bullock, *An American Transplant: The Rockefeller Foundation and the Peking Union Medical College* (Berkeley CA, 1980), 48–77.

30. Cohen, *Chinese Connection*, 3. Donald J. Friedman, *The Road from Isolation: The Campaign of the American Committee for Non-Participation in Japanese Aggression, 1938-1941* (Cambridge MA, 1968) deals extensively with Greene but also takes up in some detail the activities of the Price brothers and documents the missionary-intensive character of the committee's core group. Friedman draws on interviews with Harry Price and T. A. Bisson, as well as from contemporary documents.

31. A brief account of Moran's career in the Marine Corps is found in Roger Dingman, *Deciphering the Rising Sun: Navy and Marine Corps Codebreakers, Translators, and Interpreters in the Pacific War* (Annapolis MD, 2009), 69–75. Dingman's account depends heavily on what he was told by Moran's grandson, who has since died, but who in 2005 created a website with much valuable information: http://home.comcast.net/~drmoran/home.htm. Moran was thus more than a decade older even than William Eddy when Eddy rejoined the Marines at about the same time. The two Marine colonels never knew each other, so far as I have been able to determine.

32. Sherwood F. Moran, "Suggestions for Japanese Interpreters Based on Work in the Field," memorandum of July 17, 1943, issued by Intelligence Section, First Marine Division, United States Marine Corps, San Francisco. Available at http://mysite.verizon.net/vze6kt7j/id1.html via the MCITTA website.

33. See the website created by Moran's family, https://web.archive.org/web/20060302194147/http://home.comcast.net/~drmoran/home.htm .

34. Sherwood F. Moran, "Suggestions for Japanese Interpreters Based on Work in the Field," memorandum of July 17, 1943, issued by Intelligence Section, First Marine Division, United States Marine Corps, San Francisco. Available at http://mysite.verizon.net/vze6kt7j/id1.html via the MCITTA website.

35. Moran, "Suggestions."

36. Moran, "Suggestions." The proverb "all men are brothers" is often attributed to Confucius.

37. Prior to the dissemination of Moran's manual, Marines outside Moran's First Division floundered. As Dingman notes (*Deciphering*, 76), the Marines of the Third Division had no "Pappy Moran" around "to teach them how to interrogate prisoners or to run interference for them against senior officers."

38. Hackett told me about this in 1987 when he and I were colleagues at the University of Michigan, long before I thought about writing a book about missionaries.

39. Sherwood F. Moran, "The Psychology of the Japanese," 1. Roger Hackett gave me a photocopy of his own carbon copy of this typescript document in 1987. Hackett and I were then unable to find any reference to the document in the literature on World War II. So far as I know this document was never cited in public until 2005, when it was mentioned in the website created by Moran's family. More recently, it is cited James A. Stone, David P. Shoemaker, and Nicholas R. Dotti, *Interrogation: World War II, Vietnam, and Iraq* (Annapolis MD, 2012), 25, where its location is given as "Training Records of MITC, Camp Ritchie MD, Records of the War Department General and Special Staffs, Record Group 165, NARA College Park MD 1." Hackett said this document was given to him in the fall of 1943 when he reported to duty as a Marine Lieutenant. See also http://www.usna.edu/History/_files/documents/Honors-Program/2011/Olivas_CloseEncounters_Submission.pdf, an honors thesis filed in 2010 at Annapolis, which is the earliest cite in a scholarly work known to me.

40. Moran, "Psychology," 26–27.

41. Moran, "Psychology," esp. 21.

42. The Marine Corps Interrogator Translator Teams Association.

43. Stephen Budiansky, "Truth Extraction," *Atlantic* (June 1, 2005). Budiansky compared Moran's technique with that of a Luftwaffe interrogator of the same period who defied Nazi-style abuse of prisoners and managed to extract valuable information from American and British prisoners in late 1944 and early 1945. See also http://www.dailykos.com/story/2014/12/10/1350709/-Here-s-A-Wrecking-Ball-for-Cheney-and-The-Torture-Apologists-To-Suck-On# and Mark Benjamin, "Why the New Torture Debates Still Does Not Make Sense," *Time* (May 4, 2011), concluding that infliction of pain is "the tool of the pseudo-tough and the ignorant."

44. Yet it would a mistake to assume that all of the missionaries shared the outlook of these three men. Willis C. Lamott, a writer with nearly twenty years of experience in Japan as a Presbyterian missionary, gained wide attention with his severely negative book of *1944, Nippon: The Crime and Punishment of Japan*. Lamott lamented that the Japanese had never developed a great art form or poetry. Lamott was best known for its insistence that "the entire fabric of Japan's spiritual and ethical life" was beyond redemption and would be "torn to shreds" by an allied victory. Willis C. Lamott, *Nippon: The Crime and Punishment of Japan* (New York, 1944), 8. While Sherwood Moran took a generous view of the capabilities of the Japanese people once liberated from the military leaders who had taken them into war, Lamott, by contrast, worried that the conquering Americans would probably exaggerate the ability of the Japanese people to break with their militarist and imperialist past. Lamott did modify his outlook slightly just before the war's end, when he urged the readers of *Harper's* to "stop thinking" of the Japanese people as "warlike, cruel, cunning, unreliable, crafty,

and generally loathsome." The Japanese were not "racially subhuman devils, monkeys without tails, or something slimy that crawled from under a rock," Lamott continued. Willis C. Lamott, "What *Not* to Do with Japan," *Harper's* (June 1945), 585, cited John D. Chappell, *Before the Bomb: How America Approached the End of the Pacific War* (Lexington KY, 1996), 31.

45. John W. Dower, *War Without Mercy: Race & Power in the Pacific War* (New York, 1986); Akira Iriye, *Power and Culture: The Japanese-American War, 1941–1945* (Cambridge MA, 1981).

46. Ulrich Straus, *The Anguish of Surrender: Japanese POWs of World War II* (Seattle, 2003), 113. This extremely valuable book, based on extensive correspondence and interviews with former POWs, was written by a career officer of the Foreign Service who was born and raised in Japan as the son of Jewish migrants from Germany. His preface (ix-xvii) describes his own life first in Japan, then as a 1940 immigrant to the United States as an "enemy alien," as a then young US Army soldier, and finally as a Japan-based Foreign Service officer.

47. Cary's difficulties at Attu are described in Dingman, *Deciphering*, 114.

48. Straus, *Anguish*, 134.

49. Although Cary never wrote in any detail in English about his wartime experiences, he did edit a collection of letters exchanged during the five months following the Japanese surrender within a circle of servicemen he knew; see Otis Cary, ed., *War-Wasted Asia: Letters, 1945–46* (Tokyo, 1975).

50. Straus, *Anguish*, 113.

51. James C. McNaughton, *Nisei Linguists: Japanese Americans in the Military Intelligence during World War II* (Washington DC, 2006). 70–74.

52. John A Burden, "The Work of the Language Section," 21-page document of July 22, 1943, Burden Papers, Hoover Library, Stanford University, 8. Much has been written on Marine attitudes toward the Japanese from Guadalcanal campaign. See, e.g., Craig M. Cameron, *American Samurai: Myth and Imagination in the Conduct of Battle in the First Marine Division, 1941–1951* (New York, 1994).

53. Moran's son, Shelly Moran, did come to know Otis Cary by the war's end; correspondence between the two is included in Cary, *War-Wasted*. The stories of the trio have remained so separated that even Straus, who is attentive to the careers of Cary and Burden without connecting them, mentions Moran only in passing.

54. This practice has been described in many works on the Pacific war, including Studs Terkel's *"The Good War"*, which mentioned one Marine who carried with him the pair of testicles he had cut off a dead "Jap." In another widely quoted interview (62) one old Marine veteran confessed to Terkel: "I've seen guys shoot Japanese wounded when it really was not necessary and knock gold teeth out of their mouths. Most of them had gold teeth. I remember one time at Peleliu, I thought I'd collect gold teeth. One of my buddies carried a bunch of 'em in a sock. What you did is you took your K-bar . . . putting the tip of the blade on the tooth of the dead Japanese— I've seen guys do it on wounded ones—and hit the hilt of the knife to knock the tooth loose. . . . We were savages."

55. Burden, "Autobiography," dated July 20, 1992, 16. This document is in the Chamberlin Library, Defense Language Institute, Seaside CA. It was found for me by archivist Kurt Kuss.

56. Burden, "Language Section," esp. 6, 10. In the same unnumbered folder in the single box that constitute the Burden Papers there are undated copies of lectures to new interrogators, presumably delivered on Guadalcanal and later in Honolulu.

57. Straus, *Anguish*, 122. Straus (259) cites this report as "Summary of Prisoner of War Interrogation/Translation Conducted on Guadalcanal" under cover of Headquarters Fourth Army, Forward signed by Col. John Weckerling, published 10 November 1943, under cover of a memorandum issued by G-2 Headquarters, Fourth Army, National Archives, Entry 165, RG38, 390/35/25/5, box 769. So far as I know, Straus is the only scholar ever to cite this document.

58. Straus, *Anguish*, 116–117.

59. Burden's dairy for 1944 in in the Burden Papers.

60. It is a mark of Burden's disappearance from history that, despite his centrality to the army's interrogation program, he is not mentioned in Dingman, *Deciphering*. The most extensive account of his life known to me is posted on a website of Military Intelligence Service Veterans Club of Hawaii, http://www.javadc.org/burden.htm.

61. Following recent scholarship, I do not use the traditional word, *internment*, to describe what happened to the Japanese Americans during World War II. As Greg Robinson explains, *internment* "properly refers to the detention of enemy nationals by a government during wartime." The US government did intern enemy nationals, but most of the Japanese Americans sent to the campus were American citizens. The continued use of *internment* makes it easier to ignore the citizenship of most of the Japanese Americans who were sent to the camps. Robinson adds that *evacuation* and *relocation* were government-invented euphemisms, and that *incarceration*, now favored by many discussants, implies that the camps were penitentiaries, which they were not. See Greg Robinson, *A Tragedy of Democracy: Japanese Confinement in North America* (New York, 2009), vii.

62. See "The Pacific Coast Committee on American Principles and Fair Play," Records, Bancroft Library, University of California, Berkeley.

63. Two books by Greg Robinson describe in detail the activities of Norman Thomas and the eventual coming around of several African American groups to public opposition to the internment. Robinson also calls attention to a number of individual cases in which black Americans, conscious of the parallel between their own status and that of the Japanese Americans, offered substantial support to the internees. See Greg Robinson, *Tragedy*, esp. 106–109, and Greg Robinson, *After Camp: Portraits in Midcentury Japanese American Life and Politics* (Berkeley CA, 2012). Overall, however, organizations of African Americans, like Jewish organizations, remained aloof from the issue; see Cheryl Greenberg, "Black and Jewish Responses to Japanese Internment," *Journal of American Ethnic History* 14 (1995), 3–37.

64. *Korematsu v. United States*, 323 U. S. 214 (1944).

65. Robert Shaffer, "Cracks in the Consensus: Defending the Rights of Japanese Americans During World War II," *Radical History Review* 72 (1998), 91, 108. See also the somewhat overlapping article that has additional information and analysis, Robert Shaffer, "Opposition to Internment: Defending Japanese American Rights During World War II," *Historian* 61 (1999), 597–619. The committee Fisher headed went through several names during its years of operation, but here I shall refer to it only as the Committee for American Principles and Fair Play. See also Stephanie

Bangarth, *Voices Raised in Protest: Defending Citizens of Japanese Ancestry in North America, 1942–1949* (Vancouver BC, 2008), 94. Bangarth deals with Canada as well as the United States, but adds little to Shaffer's account of what happened in the United States. The most thorough and reliable study of the confinement is Robinson, *Tragedy.*

66. Galen Fisher, "Our Japanese Refugees," *Christian Century* (April 1, 1942), 424.

67. Harry Kingman, oral history interview, 229. http://content.cdlib.org/view?docId=kt9199p014&doc.view=entire_text

68. For a detailed account of the Fair Play Committee day-to-day operations, see the oral history interview of Ruth Kingman carried out by Rosemary Levenson; Earl Warren Oral History Project, http://content.cdlib.org/view?docId=ft1290031s;NAAN=13030&doc.view=frames&chunk.id=d0e7608&toc.depth=1&toc.id=d0e7608&brand=calisphere. For Fisher's mention of Smith, see Fisher, "Refugees, 426.

69. Ruth Kingman, oral history interview, Bancroft, 25b, has a full list of the affiliated individuals.

70. The cooperative relations the Fair Play Committee achieved with certain government officials has often been noted; see the detailed account offered by Ruth Kingman, oral history interview, Bancroft Library, e.g., 34b.

71. Nearly half of the witnesses in the San Francisco hearing voiced criticism of the policy of confinement, largely as a result of Fisher's mobilization. In Portland, Oregon, where Fisher's committee had a smaller base, only one of the sixteen witnesses before the Tolan Committee found the policy morally offense. That one witness, however, was a former missionary to Japan, Azalia Emma Peet. For the differences between the Portland hearings and those in other cities, see Ellen Eisenberg, " 'As Truly American as Your Son': Voicing Opposition to Internment in Three West Coast Cities," *Oregon Historical Quarterly* 104 (2003), 542–564. Eisenberg's title comes from the assertion of former missionary Frank Herron Smith that the Japanese American boys he knew were just as American as the sons of the members of the US Congress.

72. Galen Fisher, "Our Two Japanese Policies," *Christian Century* (August 25, 1943), 961.

73. Fisher's articles appeared in the issues of April 2, 1942; August 18, August 25, September 1, and September 8, 1943; and November 8, 1944. Fisher continued to comment on the American treatment of Japanese Americans after the war, in *Christian Century* articles of 1945 and 1946. Shaffer, "Cracks in the Consensus," 100. See also Bangarth, *Voices*, 99.

74. "Citizens or Subjects?" *Christian Century* (April 29, 1942), 551–553.

75. Henry Smith Leiper, "A Blot on Our Record," *Christianity & Crisis* (April 20, 1942), 1–2; Reinhold Niebuhr, "The Evacuation of Japanese Citizens," *Christianity & Crisis* (May 18, 1942), 2. Niebuhr himself did sign a petition circulated by Norman Thomas condemning Roosevelt's decision.

76. Charles Iglehart, "Citizens Behind Barbed Wire," *Nation* (June 6, 1942), 649–651.

77. Shaffer, "Cracks in the Consensus," 99, 103–104.

78. Carr's courage has been widely celebrated in recent years—e.g., http://www.americanthinker.com/articles/2011/12/the_lone_politician_who_stood_against_japanese_internment.html—but Greg Robinson has established that Carr largely

supported incarceration and did very little to justify the praise later heaped upon him; see Robinson, "Two Wartime Governors and Their Response to Japanese Americans," *Nichi Bei Times* (July 24, 2008).

79. The Civil Liberties Act of 1998 provided financial reparations for survivors of the wartime confinement.

80. For Nicholson's work during World War II, see Michi Weglyn and Betty E. Mitson, eds., *Valiant Odyssey: Herbert Nicholson In and Out of America's Concentration Camps* (Upland CA, 197 8). See also Herbert V. Nicholson and Margaret Wilke, *Comfort All Who Mourn: The Life Story of Herbert and Madeline Nicholson* (Fresno CA, 1982), and the entry, "Herbert Nicholson" in the Densho Encyclopedia (http://encyclopedia.densho.org/Herbert_Nicholson/)).

81. For Peppers's career, see Linda Popp Di Biase, "Neither Harmony nor Eden: Margaret Peppers and the Exile of the Japanese Americans," *Anglican and Episcopal History* 70:1 (March 2001), 101–17.

82. Anne Michele Blankenship, *Christianity, Social Justice, and the Japanese American Incarceration during World War II* (Chapel Hill, 2016), 131–132.

83. Blankenship, *Christianity*, 130.

84. Van Harvey, interview, Palo Alto, Calif., October 9, 2000.

85. Harry Kingman, interview by Rosemary Levenson, Bancroft, 108–109. http://content.cdlib.org/view?docId=kt9199p014&doc.view=entire_text

86. Orin Starn, "Engineering Internment: Anthropologists and the War Relocation Authority," *American Ethnologist* 13 (1986), 700–720, esp. 705.

87. Mary Blocher Smeltzer, "Japanese-American Resettlement Work," in Donald F. Durnbaugh, ed., *To Serve the Present Age* (Elgin IL, 1975), 126. The Smeltzers later facilitated the placing of more than 1,000 internees in jobs and housing in Chicago. On the Smeltzers' activities, see Blankenship, *Incarceration*, 182, 210.

88. Starn, "Engineering," 710.

89. Starn, "Engineering," 710. For a more generous view of Opler than Starn's, see Greg Robinson, "Morris Opler," *Densho Encyclopedia* (http://encyclopedia.densho.org/Morris_Opler/).

90. Elizabeth Colson, "Forging an Approach," *Annual Review of Anthropology* 18 (1989), 9.

Chapter Seven: Telling the Truth about the Two Chinas

1. J. Stapleton Roy, "The China Hands: Profiles in Courage and Lessons for the Future," Open Forum of the Secretary of State, December 24, 2001, found at http://www.freerepublic.com/focus/news/596512/posts. What the China Hands had said during World War II did not look so problematic after 1972, when President Richard Nixon recognized the People's Republic of China and reopened full diplomatic relations with that country. The dismissed Foreign Services officers were celebrated as prophets of a new epoch in American-Chinese relations and as victims of an unjust purge. A number of books of that era marked the new perspective; see, especially, E. J. Kahn, *The China Hands: America's Foreign Service Officers and What Befell Them* (New York, 1975), and Joseph W. Esherick, ed., *Lost Chance in China: The World War II Dispatches of John S. Service* (New York, 1974).

The historic role of the China Hands is now widely recognized in China; see, for example, "'Dixie Mission' Americans Scorned for Backing Mao are Hailed in China," *New York Times*, January 1, 2017.

2. John S. Service, "Editor's Forward," *Golden Inches: the China Memoir of Grace Service* (Berkeley, 1989), xix. Grace Service's memoir is an eloquent and moving account of day-to-day life for a missionary wife in China.

3. Unpublished "Memoir," John S. Service Papers, Bancroft Library, University of California, Berkeley, Carton 3, folder 72, pages 52–53, and folder 73, page 92. Oral history interview, Foreign Service History Association, 1977, page 70. This interview with Service is much more professional than most of those in this series, which are usually conducted by fellow officers of the Foreign Service not inclined to ask hard questions. The interview with Service resulted in a transcript of 444 pages. It was conducted by Rosemary Levenson, widow of the Berkeley historian Joseph R. Levenson, and herself well versed in modern Chinese history.

4. The best study of Service's life and career is now Lynne Joiner, *Honorable Survivor: Mao's China, McCarthy's America, and the Persecution of John S. Service* (Annapolis MD, 2009), which differs from earlier studies largely as a result of the availability of recently declassified government documents and Service's unpublished autobiography, plus Joiner's extensive interviews with Service himself, his wife, Caroline, and several acquaintances. In a review of Joiner's book, a prominent journalist declared that Service had confessed to him in a telephone interview shortly before Service's death in 1999 that he had, in fact, passed information of military significance to a friend whom he knew to be in contact with Soviet intelligence. Service wanted at last to "get it off his chest." See Jonathan Mirsky, "In Whose Service?" *Wall Street Journal* (December 20, 2009). Yet I, like many other scholars who have studied Service's life, do not find this report credible. Mirsky waited ten years before reporting what students of the China Hands would have found a sensational revelation and on which they would have wanted immediately to follow up. Moreover, many trusted friends who were close to Service during the final months of his life, and to whom he would more likely have spoken in this way if he were troubled about his conscience, insist that Service never hinted to them anything remotely like what Mirsky reports.

5. Carolle J. Carter, *Mission to Yenan: American Liaison with the Chinese Communists, 1944–1947* (Lexington KY 1997).

6. On this remarkable figure in the history of espionage and counterintelligence, see Frederic Wakeman Jr., *Spymaster: Dai Li and the Chinese Secret Service* (Berkeley, 2003). The quarrels within the OSS and the State Department about how to deal with Chiang's own intelligence operation are discussed in many works, including Yu, *OSS in China*. I adopt the spelling "Tai" instead of "Dai" since that was in use when the China Hands were dealing with him.

7. Chao moved to the United States and resumed a friendship with Service in about 1980. Her correspondence with Service after that date is in Box 2, Folders 8 and 9, of the Service Papers, Bancroft Library. Many of these letters are in Chinese, but they include a number in English addressed to both Service and his wife, Caroline, especially after Chao was married in 1986. Caroline Service's own oral history makes no mention of Val Chao, and the interviewer does not ask about her; see http://www .adst.org/OH%20TOCs/Service,%20Caroline%20S.%201987%20-%20TOC.pdf

conducted January 10, 1987 by Jewell Fenzi. Through the 1970s, John Service had been reluctant to talk about this part of his life. There is no mention of it in Kahn, *China Hands*, or other accounts of Service's career prior to Joiner's extensive discussion, *Survivor*, 50–52, on which I rely here.

8. Service dispatch of October 9, 1944, in Joseph W. Esherick, *Lost Chance in China: The World War II Dispatches of John S. Service* (New York, 1974), 249.

9. Service memorandum to Gen. Stillwell, October 10, 1944, in Esherick, *Lost Chance*, 162–165.

10. A recent study of the military activities of the Nationalist, Communist, and Japanese armies in the Sino-Japanese war that exemplifies recent scholarship's greater respect for Chiang's strategic vision is Mark Peattie, Edward J. Drea, and Hans van de Ven, *The Battle for China: Essays on the Military History of the Sino-Japanese War of 1937–1945* (Stanford, 2011). See also the important work of Rana Mitter, *China's War With Japan: The Struggle for Survival* (London, 2013). Barbara Tuchman's best-selling *Stillwell and the American Experience in China, 1911–1945* (New York, 1970), is still reliable in most respects, but uncritically accepts Stillwell's perceptions which did not always reflect an understanding of the complexity of the conditions he faced.

11. Service dispatch of September 4, 1944, in Esherick, *Lost Chance*, 194–198.

12. An example of this evasive approach to the Chinese communists was T. A. Bisson, "China's Part in a Coalition War," *Far Eastern Survey* (July 14, 1943). For a discussion of Bisson's career as a journalist and scholar, see chapter 9.

13. Joiner, *Survivor*, 78.

14. Joiner, *Survivor*, 99–100.

15. A lucid account of the fast-moving diplomatic events of 1944 and 1945 can be found in Warren I. Cohen, *America's Response to China: A History of Sino-American Relations* (5th edition, New York, 2010), esp. 154–166.

16. The successes of Gen. McArthur and Admiral Nimitz in the south and central Pacific rendered less necessary the attacking of Japan from the Chinese mainland. The core of this secret arrangement with Stalin had been agreed to at the Teheran Conference near the end of 1943. By October of 1944, well before the beginning of the Hurley fiasco in China, the American ambassador to the Soviet Union, Averill Harriman, had worked out details with Stalin and Churchill. The Soviets would enter the Pacific war several months after the defeat of Germany, and would support Chiang instead of Mao while gaining territory from a defeated Japan. This plan was more formally enacted in a secret provision of the Yalta accords in February of 1945. Even Vincent, the State Department's chief of East Asian Affairs, was not informed of this hugely important secret until July 1945, at the Potsdam Conference.

17. These events of late 1944 are well described in Joiner, *Survivor*, esp. 100–102.

18. That Mao had asked in early 1945 to meet with the president of the United States remained classified until 1972.

19. Service, dispatch of March 13, 1945, in Esherick, *Lost Chance*, 372.

20. Kahn, *China Hands*, 153. Hurley repeated this vow often, reported by many who heard it.

21. The prosecutors could not introduce their evidence that Jaffe was in touch with Soviet intelligence, since the FBI wiretaps of conversations between Jaffe and Bernstein had been illegal. The connection to the Soviets was confirmed by what

came to be called the Venona Transcripts, the Soviet intelligence cables of 1943 and 1944 that had been decoded by the United States, but their content could not be made public without signaling the Soviets that their code had been broken. The documents were released only in 1995. For Jaffe and Bernstein, see John Earl Haynes and Harvey Klehr, *Venona: Decoding Soviet Espionage in America* (New Haven, 1999), 176–177.

22. For a detailed account of this episode and of the documents in question, see Service's own exhaustive account, John S. Service, *The Amerasia Papers: Some Problems in the History of US-China Relations* (Berkeley, 1971).

23. A copy of this intense but carefully argued letter of July 31, 1945, is in the Service Papers, Box 2, Folder 15.

24. Joiner, *Survivor*, 227–228.

25. Joiner, *Survivor*, 232.

26. Davies's account of his testimony is in John Paton Davies, Jr., *China Hand* (Philadelphia, 2012), 328–329.

27. Joiner, *Survivor*, 287–288.

28. Joiner, *Survivor*, 304.

29. *Service v. Dulles*, 354 U.S. 363 (1957). Dulles was named as the defendant because he, not Acheson, was then secretary of state.

30. Foreign Service oral history, 233, 23. Service's remarks following Wilbur's death in 1997 emphasize Wilbur's abiding defense of his integrity against his detractors; see "Remembering Marty," *Chinese Studies in History* 33 (1999), 67–69.

31. Joiner, *Survivor*, 147, 344.

32. Service, "Memoir," Page 18, chapter 7, Service Papers, Carton 3, folder 82.

33. Foreign Service oral history, 429.

34. Foreign Service oral history, 432.

35. Davies, *China Hand*, 224, 232.

36. Davies, *Dragon by the Tail*, quoted in Kahn, *China Hands*, 59.

37. Davies, *China Hand*, 12–13.

38. Davies, dispatches quoted in *China Hand*, 212–214.

39. Davies, dispatch of November 7, 1944, quoted in Kahn, *China Hands*, 136–137.

40. Davies, *China Hand*, 155, 159.

41. Kahn, *China Hands*, 149.

42. Davies's perspective on the Soviet Union and its relation to China is helpfully discussed by Bruce Cummings in his epilogue to Davies's memoirs; see *China Hand*, 335–338.

43. An excellent study of Vincent's career is Gary May, *China Scapegoat: The Diplomatic Ordeal of John Carter Vincent* (Washington DC, 1979), who documents Vincent's Baptist upbringing and rapport with liberal missionaries (see, e.g., 25, 35, and 50).

44. Kahn, *China Hands*, 245–246, 251.

45. Davies, *China Hand*, 5.

46. Eric Sevareid broadcast as quoted by Kahn, *China Hands*, 30. Sevareid had told the story of Davies's heroism at greater length in his memoir of 1947, *Not So Wild a Dream* (New York, 1947), esp. 250–301.

47. For Ronning's career in Canadian politics and diplomacy, see Brian L. Evans, *The Remarkable Chester Ronning: Proud Son of China* (Edmonton, 2013), and the

memoir of Ronning's daughter, Audrey Ronning Topping, *China Mission: A Personal History from the Last Imperial Dynasty to the People's Republic* (Baton Rouge, 2013). Both of these books make clear that Ronning's missionary father was an extreme theological liberal within the Lutheran community, and a vigorous, public critic of fundamentalism. Chester Ronning's secular orientation emerged quite easily from the style of Protestantism in which he was raised, and which one of his brothers perpetuated as himself a Lutheran missionary to China. During the Vietnam era, Ronning became a secret intermediary between the American government and the North Vietnamese. The conference room in today's Canadian embassy in Beijing is named for him. For the handshake incident, which became a diplomatic legend, see Seymour Topping, *On the Front Lines of the Cold War* (Baton Rouge, 2010), 333. Hence Ronning, while he did not live his adulthood in the United States, fits the pattern of most China-born missionary sons who did.

48. Robert W. Barnett, *Wandering Knights: China Legacies, Lived and Recalled* (London, 1990), 39–53, and Robert W. Barnett, oral history, 3–4. Barnett's consistently skeptical view of the Kuomintang is registered in the memoranda he produced for the State Department, as analyzed in Mason, "Missionary Conscience," esp. 329–368.

49. For Lockwood's case, see the interview of him conducted by Sarah R. Mason, June 13, 1974, a record of which is in the Sarah R. Mason Papers, Yale University Special Collections, Box 5, folder 29.

50. For Culver Gleysteen's remarks, see his interview in *New York Times* (October 3, 1999); for William Gleysteen's remarks about China, see his Foreign Service oral history, 12.

51. Arthur Hummel, Jr., undated mid-1970s note to Sarah Mason, Box 4, Folder 26, Mason Papers.

52. Armistead Lee, "A Mishkid's Homecoming," 2. This is an undated typescript probably written in 1983 on the occasion of Lee's visit to his native China, in possession of Lee's daughter, Eleanore Lee, Berkeley, California. Armistead Lee's career was almost certainly damaged by the persisting rumors about his brother, Duncan. He eventually resigned from the Foreign Service to pursue a career in the pharmaceutical business. He continued to engage diplomatic issues; see the manuscript, Amistead M. Lee, "Pragmatism and Foreign Policy: Lectures on International Relations," 1993, in possession of Eleanore Lee, esp. 46, 59, 69, 94, and 98.

53. Rice, quoted by Kahn, *China Hands*, 115.

54. On Drumright, see Kahn, *China Hands*, esp. 38, 97, 153. Gleysteen remembered Drumright as a hard-line cold warrior who would not allow any messages sent to Washington from Taipai that were critical of Chiang's government; Gleysteen, oral history, 21.

55. John C. Brewer and Kenneth W. Rea, "John Leighton Stuart and U. S. China Policy," in Niell, *Attitudes and Policies*, 230–244, esp. 233.

56. Robert F. Smylie, "John Leighton Stuart: A Missionary Diplomat," *Presbyterian History* 53 (1975), 273.

57. Kenneth W. Rea and John C. Brewer, eds., *The Forgotten Ambassador: The Reports of John Leighton Stuart, 1946–1949* (Boulder CO, 1981). Anyone investigating Stuart's life and career should be aware that the later sections of his autobiography, *Fifty Years in China* (New York, 1954), were heavily edited by Stanley Hornbeck, who

was eager to make the text more ideological. This book displays a much harsher outlook on the Communists than was characteristic of Stuart's other writings. Stuart had been incapacitated by a stroke in 1952, and died in 1962. A more reliable guide to his life is Yu-Ming Shaw, *An American Missionary in China: John Leighton Stuart and Chinese-American Relations* (Cambridge MA, 1992). Stuart often described himself as no less Chinese than American. He had always asked that his ashes be buried in China next to the graves of his parents, which they finally were in 2008.

58. Alice Browne Frame was a strong feminist and an advocate for greater leadership for Chinese women. See Carolyn Wakeman, "Beyond Gentility: The Mission of Women Educators at Yenchng," in Arthur Lewis Rosenbaum, ed., *New Perspectives on Yenching University, 1916-1952* (Leiden, 2012), 349–377.

59. This episode is discussed by Harris, *OSS*, 268–269.

60. Jannet Conant, *A Covert Affair: Julia Child and Paul Child in the OSS* (New York, 2011), esp. 63–64.

61. Thibaut de Saint Phalle, *Saints, Sinners, and Scalawags: A Lifetime in Stories* (Brookline NH, 2003), 164. Other than her widowed husband's memoirs, the most extensive treatment of Rosamond Frame is in the lively account of OSS life by one of her co-workers, Elizabeth P. McDonald, *Undercover Girl* (New York, 1947), esp. 210–220. McDonald knew Frame well, but repeatedly describes her as an enigma. McDonald had a long postwar career in the CIA and, under the name of McIntosh, continued to write about the wartime experience of women in government service; see Elizabeth P. McIntosh, *Sisterhood of Spies: The Women of the OSS* (New York, 1996), esp. 287, 307. For my perspective on Rosamond Frame I am also indebted to her son, Pierre de Saint Phalle, e-mail, May 10, 2016.

62. For Price and Steele, see Maochun Yu, *Oss in China: Prelude to War* (Annapolis MD, 1996), esp. 78–82.

63. McDonald, *Undercover Girl*, 105.

64. McDonald, *Undercover Girl*, 102.

65. Oliver J. Caldwell, *A Secret War: Americans in China, 1944-1945* (Carbondale IL, 1972). This book is "100 per cent ego-trip," wrote Warren I. Cohen, "New Light on the China Tangle?" *Reviews in American History* 1 (1973), 293. See also Yu, *OSS*, 304.

66. Fahs's activities are described at several points in Smith, *Shadow Warriors*.

67. Mark A. Bradley, *A Very Principled Boy: The Life of Duncan Lee, Red Spy and Cold Warrior* (New York, 2014). Duncan Lee's niece, Eleanore Lee, told me that the family doggedly defended her uncle against the charges that he was a spy, and that the revelation, when it came, was devastating. Interview, Berkeley, California, July 8, 2014.

68. For Birch and the circumstances of his death, see Yu, *OSS*, 235–241, and Terry Lautz, *John Birch: A Life* (New York, 2016), which is not only an excellent study of the fabrications of the John Birch Society, but also provides a detailed and well-documented account of Birch's peculiar behavior when meeting Communist guerillas and rejecting the advice of his Nationalist army adjutant on how to deal with them (esp. 146–151).

69. After the war a number of missionary sons served in the CIA, but few have left publically available accounts of their doings. Much of the CIA's work in relation to China is still regarded as relevant to national security. One such CIA man was William Wark Tyng, who served from the time of its founding until his retirement in

1975. Another was John S. Thomson, a Washington-based CIA analyst who was so discreet that his own children could not figure out what he thought about the Vietnam War. Thomson was the brother of James C. Thomson Jr., whose academic career and opposition to the Vietnam War I discuss in a later chapter. See "John S. Thomson, 77, CIA Analyst and Canoeist," *New York Times* (August 6, 1998). See chapter 9, below, for James C. Thomson Jr. and the recollections of Thomson family members of the two brothers.

70. Joyce Mao clarifies its character succinctly: "an inconsistent conglomeration of American individuals and interest groups that advocated an overhaul of US foreign policy in favor of Chaing," neither "formalized as a political entity nor registered as such." See Joyce Mao, *Asia First: China and the Making of Modern American Conservatism* (Chicago, 2015), 44.

71. For this dynamic, see Sarah E. Ruble, *The Gospel of Freedom and Power: Protestant Missionaries in American Culture after World War II* (Chapel Hill NC, 2012), 21.

72. The ferocity of the evangelical attack on ecumenical Protestants concerning the diplomatic recognition of the People's Republic of China is detailed by William Inboden, *Religion and American Foreign Policy, 1945–1960: The Soul of Containment* (New York, 2008). Mao, *Asia First*, tells in detail the story of the China Lobby with very little mention of missionary-connected groups and individuals other than Walter Judd.

73. Interviews with former missionaries done in the 1970s show a consistently negative view of the Kuomintang and a feeling that the Communist regime, whatever its faults, came to power because of the failure of the Nationalist government to serve the Chinese people well. "China Missionaries Oral History Project," Bancroft Library, University of California, Berkeley, BANC MSS 73/185 z.

74. Unsigned commentary, "1953: Presbyterian Response to Communism," *Journal of Presbyterian History* (Summer 2003), 127–129.

75. For Rowe and his testimony against Lattimore, see Robert P. Newman, *Owen Lattimore and the "Loss" of China* (Berkeley, 1992), 385. Newman also explains that Rowe was exceptional even within the China Lobby for the degree of his sympathy for European colonialism and its legacies, and for his notion that the Kuomintang's authoritarianism was reasonable given the circumstances of China. The obituary for Rowe in *National Review* (August 12, 1985) reveals how different a character he was from most of the missionary children of his generation, and how estranged from them.

76. A helpful account of Judd's career is Tony Ladd, "Mission to Capitol Hill: A Study of the Impact of Missionary Idealism on the Congressional Career of Walter H. Judd," in Patricia Neils, ed., *United States Attitudes and Policies Toward China: The Impact of American Missionaries* (Armonk NY, 1990), 263–283. See also Lee Edwards, *Missionary for Freedom: The Life and Times of Walter Judd* (New York, 1990).

77. Among the most discerning guides to the literature on Mao and his regime is Roderick MacFarquhar; see, e.g., his "The Worst Man-Made Catastrophe, Ever," *New York Review of Books* (February 10, 2011), 26–28, and "Who Was Mao Zedong?" *New York Review of Books* (October 25, 2012), 48–51. See also Timothy Cheek, ed., *A Critical Introduction to Mao* (New York, 2010).

78. That the mistakes of American policy makers were too deeply embedded in the minds of the Kennedy and Johnson administrations to have been overcome, even had the China Hands still been in positions of influence, is made compellingly by Ernest R. May, "The China Hands in Perspective: Ethics, Diplomacy, and Statecraft," in Paul Gordon Lauren, *The China Hands' Legacy* (Boulder CO, 1987), 97–123.

79. Prominent among the books that promoted this idea in the early 1970s was the volume edited by Esherick, *Lost Chance*. Service himself developed this idea in the concluding remarks to a book of his own, John S. Service, *The Amerasia Papers: Some Problems in the History of US-China Relations* (Berkeley, 1971), esp. 191–192.

Chapter Eight: Creating America's Thailand in Diplomacy and Fiction

1. Kenneth Landon, State Department oral history project, interview conducted by Albert T. Atwood, April 1982 (http://www.adst.org/OH%20TOCs/Landon,%20Kenneth%20P.toc.pdf). This interview reveals Kenneth Landon to be a brilliant storyteller, but shows the interviewer to be an oral historian's disaster. Atwood was more interested in how Landon got into the Cosmos Club and what his experiences were there—a topic to which he returns repeatedly—than with how Landon interacted with Franklin Roosevelt and Ho Chi Minh. Landon was one of several former missionaries and missionary children to be shocked at the weakness of American military intelligence concerning Asia. When missionary son Robert Goheen reported to army intelligence in early 1942, he found that his unit's understanding of India consisted mostly of articles published in *Time* magazine. Interview, Robert Goheen, Princeton, May 18, 2000.

2. Landon, State Department interview, 32. Landon describes the friendship that he then formed with Arthur Hummel, the head of the Oriental section of the Library of Congress, a former missionary to China and the father of the later ambassador, Arthur Hummel Jr.

3. See, especially, Daniel Fineman, *A Special Relationship: The United States and Military Government in Thailand, 1947–1958* (Honolulu, 1997), and E. Bruce Reynolds, *Thailand's Secret War: The Free Thai, OSS, and SOE During World War II* (New York, 2005).

4. Landon's then-secret cable is in *Foreign Relations of the United States*, 1946, volume 8, "French Indochina," 26–27. For its place in public history, see George C. Herring, ed., *The Pentagon Papers, Abridged Edition* (New York, 1993), 4.

5. Susan Morgan, *Bombay Anna: The Real Story and Remarkable Adventures of the King and I Governess* (Berkeley, 2008), 221.

6. The Landons describe their missionary years in great detail in the Landon Chronicles, an extensive, 95-hour oral history archive created when the Landons were in their 80s by their son, Kenneth Landon Jr., housed in the Papers of Kenneth and Margaret Landon, Special Collections, Wheaton College, and online at http://www.wheaton.edu/learnres/ARCSC/collects/Sc38/LandonChroniclesSynopsis.pdf.

7. See the volume put together by family members, *The Eakin Family in Thailand* (Bangkok, 1955), and George Bradley McFarland, ed., *Historical Sketch of Protestant Missions in Siam, 1828–1928* (Bangkok, 1928).

8. Landon Chronicles, Hour 60, Clip 6.

9. The dreadful missionary lady of the novel is Grace Rutherford, introduced early in the book; Margaret Landon, *Never Dies the Dream* (New York, 1949), 4.

10. Landons to Board of Missions of the Presbyterian Church of the USA, October 9, 1940, Box 272, Folder 20, Landon Papers.

11. Landon Chronicles, Hour 70, Clip 11.

12. For this philosophical atmosphere, see Andrew Jewett, *Science, Democracy, and the American University: From the Civil War to the Cold War* (Cambridge MA, 2012), 192–195.

13. KL to ML, April 2, 1942, Box 20, Folder 32. This important letter appears to have been written over several days, and carries dates of April 8 and 10 as well as April 2. See also Kenneth's oral history references of his debates with Hayden, Landon Chronicles, Hour 72, Clip 18.

14. Kenneth Landon Jr., letter to me, May 5, 2016.

15. Kenneth to Margaret, April 2, 1942, Landon Papers, Box 10, Folder 32. See also KL to ML, October 2, 1941, Landon Papers, Box 10, Folder 22.

16. State Department interview.

17. Kenneth Perry Landon, *Siam in Transition: A Brief Survey of Cultural Trends in the Five Years since the Revolution of 1932* (Chicago, 1939). For the reference to Pridi as the book's hero, see State Department interview, 15.

18. For Landon's enjoyment of this professional meeting of philosophers, see his letter to Margaret, December 28, 1939, Box 10, Folder 18, Landon Papers.

19. Kenneth Perry Landon, *The Chinese in Thailand* (New York, 1941), 145.

20. This claim may be technically true, although there were philosophically informed courses in Chinese literature offered on several campuses by 1939.

21. Margaret describes this chain of connections in her "Author's Note" at the end of *Anna*, 357–360.

22. State Department interview, 13.

23. State Department interview, 14.

24. KL to ML, August 16, 1941, Box 10, Folder 19.

25. KL to ML, October 13, 1941, Box 10, Folder 23.

26. KL to ML, October 21, 1941, Box 10, Folder 23.

27. KL to ML, January 8, 1942, Box 10, Folder 27.

28. See, e.g., KL to ML, August 26, 1941, Box 10, Folder 20; KL to ML, September 10, 1941, Box 10, Folder 20; and KL to ML, September 29, 1941, Box 10, Folder 22.

29. KL to ML, December 17, 1941, Box 10, Folder 15.

30. Reynolds, *Secret War*, notes (19–20) that Seni's later claim to have dramatically and tearfully told Secretary Hull to his face that he would not deliver the declaration of war was a fabricated exaggeration of a less dramatic meeting with Undersecretary Adolph Berle.

31. KL to ML, December 17, 1941, Box 10, Folder 25.

32. R. Harris Smith, *OSS: The Secret History of America's First Central Intelligence Agency* (New York, 1972), 295.

33. Landon, State Department interview, 15. This story is also told in Landon Chronicles, Hour 64, Clip 8. See Smith's account of the US-Thai-British diplomacy, *OSS*, 315–317.

34. For a detailed account of the anti-Japanese operations in Thailand and of Landon's role in them, see Reynolds, *Secret War*, e.g., 191.

35. State Department interview, 15–16.

36. KL to ML, March 14, 1942, Box 10, Folder 30.

37. Anna Leonowens, *The English Governess at the Siamese Court: Being Recollections of Six Years at the Royal Palace at Bangkok* (originally 1870; available in reprint, New York, 1988), and Anna Leonowens, *The Romance of the Harem* (originally 1873; available in reprint, Charlottesville VA, 1991).

38. Landon, *Anna*, 360.

39. Landon, *Anna*, 82.

40. Alfred Habegger, *Masked: The Life of Anna Leonowens, Schoolmistress at the Court of Siam* (Madison WI, 2014), 381.

41. Landon, *Anna*, 345.

42. Morgan, *Bombay Anna*, 217.

43. For a sensitive account of the variations on the story introduced by Rogers and Hammerstein and in the later film versions, including the 1999 movie in which Jodie Foster played Anna, see Habegger, *Masked*, 382–407. Habegger argues plausibly that Yul Brynner's Broadway and Hollywood version of the king, more aggressively sexual than Rex Harrison's, did much to ensure the popularity of *The King and I*.

44. Christina Klein, *Cold War Orientalism: Asia in the Middlebrow Imagination, 1945–1961* (Berkeley, 2003), 195. Klein correctly reminds readers of the role of missionaries in the production and dissemination of popular images of Asia, but attends only in passing to the anticolonial missionary voices pushing for greater empathic identification with indigenous peoples and criticizing the Cold War policies of the US government. Although she offers an incisive analysis of *Reader's Digest* and notes that magazine's links with missionaries, Klein does not mention the *Digest*'s most extensive project in image-making about Asia, the celebration of James Yen. This missionary-sponsored Chinese reformer, whom I take up in chapter 10, complicates the "Orientalism" of *Reader's Digest*.

45. Susan Kepner, "Anna (and Margaret) and the King of Siam," *Crossroads: An Interdisciplinary Journal of Southeast Asian Studies* 10 (1996), 2.

46. Habegger, *Masked*, 4. This is a more exhaustively detailed biography of Anna Leonowens than Morgan's *Bombay Anna*, and is based on previously unexamined archival sources.

47. Habegger, *Masked*, 375, 506, documents Landon's reactions to skeptics.

48. State Department interview, 17. Landon told historian Ronald Spector in 1971 that within the State Department at the time, only the specialists in East Asia and Southeast Asia were sympathetic with Roosevelt's negative view of the French Indochina; see Ronald H. Spector, *Advice and Support: The Early Years—The US. Army in Vietnam* (Washington DC, 1985), 44.

49. Smith, *Shadow Warriors*, 326–327.

50. KL to ML, November 6, 1945, Box 10, Folder 39.

51. Landon offered a vivid account of his oral exchange with Bird in a letter to Margaret, November 12, 1945, Box 11, Folder 7. Bird asked Landon if his father might be the Landon who had written the important book about Thailand that was the

source of virtually all British knowledge about that country, and Kenneth, as he proudly describes the conversation, informed the incredulous Bird that he, himself, was the basis for Bird's own office's understanding of Thailand. Reynolds, *Secret War*, 412, is the authoritative account of this encounter.

52. State Department interview, 18. For the US-Thai alliance, see Fineman, *Special Relationship*.

53. KL to ML, January 25, 1946, Box 11, Folder 14.

54. KL Diary, January 19 and 20 and February 14, 1946, Box 38, Folder 10.

55. Landon Chronicles, Hour 72, Clip 4.

56. Smith, *Shadow Warriors*, 327.

57. State Department interview, 21.

58. Landon Chronicles, Hour 72, Clip 7.

59. State Department interview, 21.

60. Landon, Diary, February 15 through 25, 1946, Box 38, Folder 10.

61. These documents are quoted in Scott L. Bills, *Empire and Cold War: The Roots of Third-World Antagonism, 1945–47* (Basingstoke, Eng., 2010), 198.

62. The Chakri dynasty continues to occupy the throne well into the twenty-first century. For a biography of King Bhumibol Adulyadej, who became king in 1946 and whom Landon knew well, see Paul M. Handley, *The King Never Smiles* (New Haven CT, 2006).

63. Fineman, *Special Relationship*, 40–41. For a highly informative analysis of the political regimes of Southeast Asia in the years since World War II, including the military-run governments of Thailand that have operated in cooperation with the monarchy, see John T. Sidel, "The Fate of Nationalism in the New States: Southeast Asia in Comparative Historical Perspective," *Comparative Studies in Society and History* 54 (2012), 114–144.

64. See Joshua Kurlantzick, *The Tragedy of Jim Thompson and the American Way of War* (New York, 2011), and KL to ML, March 28, 1950, Box 11, Folder 20.

65. KL to ML, April 11, 1950, Box 11, Folder 22.

66. Landon Chronicles, Hour 86, Clips 1 and 2; Kenneth Landon Jr., letter to author, May 5, 2016.

67. Kenneth Landon Jr., to me, May 5, 2016.

68. KL to ML, February 17, 1947, Box 11, Folder 16.

69. Landon was abroad when McCarthy himself made dramatic headlines in 1950. Margaret wrote Kenneth frequently concerning the developing anti-Communist hysteria, which she described as "more ominous than anything I have observed in years," fomented by a man who was "a true demagogue of the Hitler-Mussolini-Stalin pattern." ML to KM, May 12, 1950, Box 11, Folder 49.

70. Landon Chronicles, Hour 67, Clip 20.

71. KL to ML, February 11, 1947, Box 11, Folder 16

72. Kenneth Perry Landon, *Southeast Asia: Crossroad of Religion* (Chicago, 1949).

73. Landon, *Crossroad*, vi.

74. Landon, *Crossroad*, 172.

75. Landon, *Crossroad*, 203.

76. Landon, *Crossroad*, 167.

77. Landon, *Crossroad*, 196–197. See also Landon's reference to Ho, 177.

78. G. William Skinner, *Chinese Society in Thailand: An Analytic History* (Ithaca NY, 1957), while more ambitious than Landon's 1941 volume on Thailand's Chinese population, was indebted to it. For Landon's account of his intellectual relationship with Skinner and other Southeast Asian academic specialists, see Landon Chronicles, Hour 73, Clip 9.

79. The Landon Chronicles devote extensive attention to Margaret's recollections of these events in the mission field; two of the clearest accounts are found in Hour 45, Clip 1 and Hour 62, Clip 1.

80. See the Landon Chronicles on this episode, and *Dream*.

81. Donn V. Hart, "Overseas Americans in Southeast Asia: Fact in Fiction," *Far Eastern Survey* 30 (1961), 1–15.

82. Jane Martin, review of *Never Dies the Dream*, *New York Times* (November 20, 1949).

83. Kenneth Landon Jr., to me, May 5, 2016. KL to KL Jr., November 14, 1963, in possession of Kenneth Landon Jr.

84. KL, Diary, February 12, 1946, Box 38, Folder 10.

85. KL to ML, February 17, 1947, in Box 11, Folder 16.

Chapter Nine: Against Orientalism

1. Box 2, Folder 1, W. Norman Brown Papers, University of Pennsylvania.

2. John Whitney Hall, "Beyond Area Studies," in Donald E. Thackerey, ed., *Research—Definitions and Reflections* (Ann Arbor MI, 1967), 48–66, esp. 53–57.

3. A partial exception was Samuel Guy Inman, a Disciples of Christ missionary to Mexico who, after a career of journalistic writings strongly critical of American policy toward Latin America as imperialist, served as a lecturer at Columbia and then, from 1937 to 1942, on the faculty of the University of Pennsylvania. But Inman was not a major influence on the development of academic studies of Latin America. For a fair-minded study of Inman's career as a diplomat and scholar, see Virginia S. Williams, *Radical Journalists, Generalist Intellectuals, and U.S.-Latin American Relations* (Lewiston NY, 2001), 46–73. Inman is also an important figure in Mary A. Renda, *Taking Haiti: Military Occupation and the Culture of U. S. Imperialism, 1915–1940* (Chapel Hill NC, 2001). Renda (232–234) emphasizes that even while Inman was opposed to American military interventions in the Caribbean, he was culturally conservative in his approach to missionary activity and preoccupied with issues in sexual morality. For the important literary side of Latin American Studies, see Rolena Adorno, "Havana and Macondo: The Humanities in US Latin American Studies, 1940–2000," in David A. Hollinger, ed., *The Humanities and the Dynamics of Inclusion Since World War II* (Baltimore, 2006), 372–404.

4. A helpful collection of essays on the development of African Studies in the United States is a special issue of *African Studies Review* 26 (1983) devoted to that topic. See, especially, Gwendolen M. Carter, "The Founding of the African Studies Association," which lists those present at the 1957 meeting when the association was

founded; missionary names are conspicuous by their absence (Carter, 7). Historically black Howard University developed a strong African Studies program beginning in the 1930s, but it was almost entirely ignored by mainstream academics. For the development of International Studies at Howard, especially but not exclusively in relation to Africa, see Robert Vitalis, *White World Order, Black Power Politics: The Birth of American International Relations* (Ithaca NY, 2015).

5. For an example of this negative assessment of Area Studies, see Masao Miyoshi and H. D. Harootunian, eds., *Learning Places: The Afterlives of Area Studies* (Durham NC, 2002). A compelling critique of this book as tendentious is Andrew Gordon, "Rethinking Area Studies, Once More," *The Journal of Japanese Studies* 30 (2004), 417-429.

6. David Szanton, "Introduction: The Origin, Nature, and Challenges of Area Studies in the United States," in David Szanton, ed., *The Politics of Knowledge: Area Studies and the Disciplines* (Berkeley, 2004), 1-3. Among the many virtues of Szanton's essay is his charting of the involvement of the various academic disciplines in Area Studies over time, noting especially that economists, very important in the early years, drop out almost entirely when their discipline becomes more uniformly committed to model-building that treats regional particularities as irrelevant.

7. That the intellectual content of the scholarship carried out under the canopy of Area Studies was much less government driven than commonly supposed is also a finding of David Engerman, "The Ironies of the Iron Curtain: The Cold War and the Rise of Russian Studies," in Hollinger, *Dynamics of Inclusion*, 314-344. Engerman calls attention to the World War II foundation for what became Area Studies even in regard to the greatest of the Cold War enemies, the Soviet Union.

8. Rosane Rocher, "W. Norman Brown, 1892-1975," *Journal of the American Oriental Society* 15 (January-March 1976), 5; Maureen L. P. Patterson, "Institutional Base for the Study of South Asia in the United States and the Role of the American Institute of Indian Studies," in Joseph W. Elder, Edward C. Dimock, Jr., and Ainslie T. Embree, eds., *India's Worlds and US Scholars, 1947-1997* (New Delhi, 1998), 22.

9. For Brown's views, see W. Norman Brown, "Carbolic Acid for India," *Nation* (July 13, 1927) 40-41, and W. Norman Brown, "Answering Miss Mayo," *Nation* (May 30, 1928), 617. Kathryn Mayo, *Mother India* (New York, 1927), while it drew to some extent on images of India that had been retailed by nineteenth-century missionaries, was a great embarrassment to American missionaries of the 1920s, who almost unanimously criticized it. Yet the mistaken impression that Mayo was a missionary, or spoke for missionaries, has been slow to disappear; see, e.g., Andrew Rotter, *Comrades at Odds: The United States and India, 1947-1965* (Ithaca NY, 2000), which offers no distinction between missionary perspectives and those of Mayo. The missionary communities' denunciation of Mayo is extensively documented in Mrinalini Sinha, *Specters of Mother India: The Global Restructuring of Empire* (Durham NC, 2006), 130-136. See also Susan Haskell, "The India Mission Field in American History, 1919-1947," PhD dissertation, University of California, Berkeley, 2006.

10. Marshall Windmiller, "A Tumultuous Time: OSS and Military Intelligence in India, 1942-1946," *International Journal, of Intelligence and Counterintelligence* 8 (Spring 1995), 113-115.

11. On the Phillips Report, see Kenton J. Clymer, *Quest for Freedom: The United States and India's Independence* (New York, 1995), 128–145. See also Rebecca Solnit, "India Lobby," http://blogs.dickinson.edu/hist-solnit/files/2011/10/Solnit-honors -thesis.pdf

12. For the support of missionary groups for Indian independence see Khan, dissertation, 250, and Gary R. Hess, *America Encounters India, 1941–1947* (Baltimore, 1971), 18–19. For the cult of Gandhi among ecumenical Protestants, see Jones, *Indian Road,* and Jones's later *Gandhi* (New York, 1948). John Haynes Holmes, a leading Unitarian minister and pacifist, had no missionary experience but traveled frequently to India and was Gandhi's most persistent and vocal champion in the United States from 1919 on through the 1940s. Holmes was a leader of the American League for India's Freedom, founded in 1932. For this organization, see Clymer, *Quest*, 22, 31, 42.

13. Harris, *OSS*, 34.

14. Richard D. Lambert did his doctorate at Penn and was for many years Brown's colleague there and eventually his successor as head of the program and a major figure in Area Studies nationally. But he was the exception. Even the missionary sons who became productive South Asian specialists did not study with Brown. Crane, Robert Frykenberg, and Eugene Irschick took history degrees at Yale, London, and Chicago, respectively. Henry Hart, born in India as the son of a YMCA official, earned a political science degree at the University of Wisconsin. Joseph Elder, whose missionary upbringing was in Iran, did his degree in sociology at Harvard. Ainslie Embree served as a missionary teacher in India for a decade before completing a history doctorate at Columbia.

15. Brown's correspondence with his Penn colleagues frequently displays tensions, often involving resentment at Brown's way of doing things. See, for example, Ernest Bender's letters to Brown over the course of a number of years, Box 1, Folder 2, Brown Papers, Penn. Brown appears to have been unperturbed if those with whom he worked found him high-handed. My impressions of Brown's collegial style are also based on conversations with Lloyd Rudolph and Susanne Rudolph.

16. W. Norman Brown, *The United States and India and Pakistan* (Cambridge MA, 1953); later editions of 1967 and 1972 were titled slightly differently.

17. The persistence of Brown's cultural determinism was noted in a respectful review by Howard Wiggins, *Political Science Quarterly* 88 (1973), 778–780. Even two decades after the first edition, Brown's account of domestic politics, the economy, and international affairs lagged behind the work of other scholars.

18. Brown, *India*, 36.

19. Nicholas B. Dirks, *Autobiography of an Archive: A Scholar's Passage to India* (New York, 2015), 270.

20. Brown Papers, Box 2, Folder 8, contains correspondence between Lattimore and Brown beginning in 1948. Crane sensed that his future in government after the war was threatened by his demonstrable left-wing associations. He left government service and entered the politically safer domain of academia. Joseph Elder was a Quaker antiwar activist for much of his life, and remains so today. Henry Hart was proud of being "progressive." He was a member of the Communist Party for several years in the 1930s and suffered career challenges as a result. For Hart, see his oral history, http://minds.wisconsin.edu/handle/1793/65036.

21. Charlotte Viall Wiser and William H. Wiser, *Behind Mud Walls* (New York, 1930).

22. The most widely influential of Wiser's later works was William Hendricks Wiser, *The Hindu Jamani System* (Lucknow, 1936). This study of patron-client relationships detailed the precise services and rights of twenty caste groups as revealed in their interactions with one another.

23. Susan Snow Wadley, "William and Charlotte Vaill Wiser: Missionaries as Scholars and Development Officers," in Leonard Ploticov, Paula Brown, and Vinson Sutlive, eds., *Anthropology's Debt to Missionaries* (Pittsburgh, 2007), 100. A recent overview mentions the Wisers as edited and updated by Wadley and Peter Berger, "Theory and Ethnology in the Modern Anthropology of India," *Journal of Ethnographic Theory* 2 (2012), 337.

24. Dirks notes (*Archive*, 276) that many social scientists relied on English translations and on Anglophone informants.

25. Of the several studies of the history of Japanese Area Studies, the best is Andrew Barshay, "What Is Japan to Us?" in Hollinger, ed., *Dynamics of Inclusion*, 345–371. See also Alan Tansman, "Japanese Studies: The Intangible Act of Translation," in David Szanton, *The Politics of Knowledge* (Berkeley, 2004), 184–216. Tansman is careless about the missionary matrix of Japanese Studies. He speaks (186) of "the second generation of American Japanese scholars" who were trained in language school during World War II, and asserts that "many" were "missionary children." He names four (Marius Jansen, Donald Keene, Edward Seidensticker, and Howard Hibbert), but none of these were, in fact, missionary children or were importantly connected to missionary families. Keene, moreover, was already fluent in Japanese before he entered government service in 1942. The mistake at least reveals how widespread is the impression that missionary-connected individuals entirely dominated the early academic study of Japan.

26. J. C. Hepburn, *A Japanese and English Dictionary* (London, 1867). Hepburn was a Disciples of Christ medical missionary who resided in Japan from 1859 to 1892. Hepburn's contemporary, the art connoisseur Ernest Fenollosa, who popularized Japanese art in the United States, was not a missionary. For his career, see Lawrence W. Chisolm, *Fenollosa: The Far East and American Culture* (New Haven CT, 1963).

27. Yasaka Takagi, *Japanese Studies in the Universities and Colleges of the United States* (Honolulu, 1935), as quoted by Marius Jansen, "History: General Survey," in the Japan Foundation, *Japanese Studies in the United States* (1988), 18. Another important source for the development of Japanese Studies is Peter X. Zhou, *Collecting Asia: East Asian Libraries in North America, 1868–2008* (Austin TX, 2010).

28. Fluency in Japanese was so rare that as late as 1941, the US Navy could find only fifty-six individuals in the entire country between the ages of twenty and thirty-five who knew enough of the language to justify possible training in the interests of national defense. Most of the fifty-six had lived or studied in Japan or China, the majority of whom—apparently excluding the ethnic Japanese, who were suspect for defense-related work—were from missionary families. See Robert Matthew, *Language and Area Studies in the Armed Services: Their Future Significance* (Washington DC, 1947), 15. This inquiry was commissioned by the American Council on Education. Some young Americans of that era who had resided in Japan or China had done so with commercial or diplomatic families (the novelist Thornton Wilder, for example,

was the son of a diplomat long stationed in China), but the majority were missionary-connected. Matthew does not clarify whether this number fifty-six included Japanese Americans. He does refer (21) to "first- or second-generation Japanese-Americans" who did teaching in Navy language schools, but he allows that "many Nisei could not qualify even though they had an excellent command of colloquial spoken Japanese, for anyone who could not handle reading and writing . . . was unsuited for the task."

29. John K. Fairbank and Edwin Reischauer, *East Asia: Tradition and Transformation* (Boston, 1973).

30. See the *Festschrift* presented to Reischauer on the occasion of his 60th birthday: Albert H. Craig and Donald H. Shively, eds., *Personality in Japanese History* (Berkeley, 1970), which contains articles by fourteen of Reischauer's doctoral students. In keeping with the norms of the period, most of Reischauer's doctoral students were male, but several were female, including Mary Elizabeth Berry, Dorothy Borg, and Helen McCullough.

31. Reischauer, *My Life*, 18, 20.

32. Helen Oldfather Reischauer's father, Jeremiah Oldfather, was a leader of Presbyterian missions in Persia for many years. Her brother, William Abbott Oldfather (1880–1945), became a distinguished professor of classics at the University of Illinois. The classicist's biographer found that this uncle of Edwin Reischauer joined virtually every liberal organization known to him. He was, reports Winton U. Solberg, "a member of the American Association of University Professors, the American Civil Liberties Union, the American Friends of Greece, the American Committee for Democracy and Intellectual Freedom, the Committee to Defend America by Aid the Allies, the American League Against War and Fascism, the American Friends of Spanish Democracy, the League for Industrial Democracy, and the Tom Mooney Defense Committee." See Winton U. Solberg, "William Abbott Oldfather: Making the Classics Relevant to Modern Life," unpublished paper, 2003.

33. A. K. Reischauer, *The Task in Japan: A Study in Modern Missionary Imperatives* (New York, 1926). See also A. K. Reischauer, *Studies in Japanese Buddhism* (New York, 1917), and the account of A. K. Reischauer offered by George R. Packard, *Edwin O. Reischauer and the American Discovery of Japan* (New York, 2010), esp. 14. For the controversy over *The Layman's Report*, see chapter 3.

34. Edwin O. Reischauer, "Life with Father (and also Mother)," in *The Life of Dr. A. K. Reischauer* (Tokyo, 1961), 51.

35. Reischauer, *My Life*, 6–7.

36. Reischauer, *My Life*, 17.

37. Reischauer's translation of the monk's diary was not published until 1955; Edwin O. Reischauer, *Ennin's Travels in T'ang China* (New York, 1955).

38. Reischauer's autobiography speaks extensively about his relationship with his brother, but a yet fuller and more candid version is found in a private letter: Edwin O. Reischauer to George Akita, September 1, 1978, Reischauer Papers, Harvard, esp. 6. I owe my awareness of this important and revealing document to Mary Elizabeth Berry.

39. Resichauer's pique at Americans who found fault with Japanese imperialism but had no objection to British, Dutch, and French imperialism follows in the tradition of Sidney Gulick, as noted in chapter 6.

40. This document is quoted and summarized in Rieschauer, *My Life*, 87–88.

41. Reischauer, *My Life*, 87–88; Packard, *Reischauer*, 64.

42. On Hornbeck, see Packard, *Reischauer*, 65–66.

43. Packard, *Reischauer*, 64.

44. Reischauer, *My Life*, 100–101.

45. Packard, *Reischauer*, 71, 79.

46. Edwin O. Reischauer, *Japan: Pasts and Present* (New York, 1946), and later editions of 1951, 1954, 1966, 1970, and 1974; Barshay, "Japan," 353. Reischauer's confidence in the Japanese liberals was consistent with the views Sherwood Moran pressed upon his fellow Marines as noted in chapter 6.

47. Thomson said this in a private letter quoted by Packard, *Reischauer*, 94.

48. Of the many accounts of this conference, one that helpfully connects the political to the scholarly controversies is Victor Koschmann, "Modernization and Democratic Values: The 'Japanese Model' in the 1960s," in David C. Engerman, et al., *Staging Growth: Modernization, Development, and the Global Cold War* (Amherst MA, 2003), 225–249. For Hall's major work, see *Government and Local Power in Japan, 500 to 1700* (Princeton, 1960). See also Barshay and Packard. For the modernization debates as a whole, the standard work is Nils Gilman, *Mandarins of the Future: Modernization Theory in Cold War America* (Baltimore, 2003). For Reischauer's own construction of this conference, see his letter to Akita, 1978, 225.

49. E. H. Norman, *Japan's Emergence as a Modern State* (New York, 1940), and E. H. Norman, *Soldier and Peasant in Japan* (New York, 1943). The first of these was brought out in a 60th anniversary edition, edited by Lawrence T. Woods (Vancouver BC, 2000), with analytic essays by ten historians.

50. For Dower's intervention, see his 1975 introduction to his volume *Origins of the Modern Japanese State: Selected Writings of E. H. Norman* (New York, 1975). For Reischauer's reaction to Dower's critique, see Edwin O. Reischauer, "Herb Norman: The Perspective of a Lifelong Friend," in Roger W. Bowen, ed., *E. H. Norman: His Life and Scholarship* (Toronto, 1984), 3–13, esp. 10–12, an essay contributed to a volume of appreciations of Norman. A perspicacious review of Dower's commentary on Norman and Reischauer is Marius Jansen, review of Dower, *Writings of E.H. Norman*, in *American Political Science Review* 72 (1978), 307–309.

51. For a detailed, hour-by-hour account of Norman's conduct and communications in the days before his suicide, see Roger Bowen, *Innocence Is Not Enough: The Life and Death of Herbert Norman* (Vancouver, 1986), 290–320. For an argument I find unpersuasive that Norman, despite the lack of any "smoking gun" evidence of actual espionage, used his position to advance Soviet aims see James Barros, *No Sense of Evil* (Toronto, 1986).

52. Reischauer, *My Life*, 126.

53. See, for example, George Akita, "An Examination of E. H. Norman's Scholarship," *Journal of Japanese Studies* 3 (1977), 375–419, a strongly pro-Reischauer reading.

54. Missionary son John W. Hall did advance the modernization-centered interpretation of his mentor, and Borton's major book of 1955, *Japan's Modern Century*, could be so construed even though Borton never pushed the point and his ideas were not major points of contention; see Hugh Borton, *Japan's Modern Century* (New York, 1955).

55. Cyril Powles, "E. H. Norman and Japan," in Bowen, *Life and Scholarship*, 14; Reischauer in Bowen, *Life and Scholarship*, 4.

56. Ruth Benedict, *The Chrysanthemum and the Sword* (New York, 1946). Benedict's achievement was all the more impressive since she did not read Japanese and had never visited Japan.

57. Missionary son John Hersey's *Hiroshima* is also remembered as a profoundly anti-exceptionalist document, and noted in chapter 2, above.

58. Packard, *Reischauer*, 221. Packard's extended treatment of Reischauer's relation to the Vietnam War is Packard's strongest contribution. Reischauer's own discussion of this part of his life in his autobiography is mildly apologetic but still evasive; see *My Life*, 284-304.

59. Reischauer, *Asian Policy*, 256. Another prominent feature of this book of 1955 was Reischauer's systematic refutation of the arguments against the diplomatic recognition of the People's Republic of China.

60. Reischauer, *My Life*, 285.

61. Packard, *Reischauer*, 141-143.

62. Reischauer, *My Life*, 317. Edwin O. Reischauer, *Beyond Vietnam: The United States and Asia* (New York, 1967). In a 1979 addition to his letter to Akita, Reischauer described Vietnam as "an awful mistake" on the part of the United States "from beginning to end" (32). Like Kenneth Landon, Reischauer in private expressed stronger criticisms of the Vietnam War than he ever did in public.

63. These included Howard Hibbett, Marius Jansen, Edward Seidensticker, and Thomas C. Smith.

64. The driving force for the study of Japan at Columbia before Borton was missionary son Evarts B. Greene—brother of Roger Sherman Greene and Jerome Greene—who, despite being a professor of US rather than Japanese history, served as director of the tiny Institute of Japanese Studies. Japanese-born Tsunoda taught Japanese language and literature, but it was first Greene, and then Borton, who provided institutional leadership. See the recollections of Donald Keene, http://www.columbia.edu/cu/lweb/news/libraries/2008/2008-06-26.tsunoda.html. Donald Keene reports (e-mail to me, July 9, 2008) that by the time he started as a student at Columbia in 1940 Greene must have withdrawn because Borton was already very much in charge. For Borton's reflections, see Hugh Borton, *Spanning Japan's Modern Century: The Memoirs of Hugh Borton* (Lanham MD, 2002). This volume was published under the supervision of Borton's colleague James W. Morley.

65. John K. Fairbank, *Chinabound: A Fifty-Year Memoir* (New York, 1982), 376.

66. Fairbank promoted the study of missionaries in many contexts. His most important publication about missionaries was John K. Fairbank, ed., *The Missionary Enterprise in China and America* (Cambridge MA, 1974).

67. Latourette was the first Asian history specialist to be elected president of the American Historical Association. Fairbank was the second. For the two presidential addresses, see Kenneth Scott Latourettte, "The Christian Understanding of History," *American Historical Review* 54 (1949), 259-276 and John K. Fairbank, "Assignment for the '70s," *American Historical Review* 74 (1969), 877. In later years, two other China scholars were elected to the AHA presidency, Frederic Wakeman and Jonathan Spence.

68. Latourette, *American Historical Review,* 1921 and 1930. Latourette continued to write overviews of the field for many years; see his last one, "Far Eastern Studies in the United States: Retrospect and Prospect," *Far Eastern Quarterly* 15 (November 1955), 3-11.

69. For the appointment of the committee, and its membership, see ACLS, *Bulletin* # 10 (April 1929), 64.

70. The oldest of the affiliated societies was the American Academy of Arts and Sciences, dating from 1780, and concerned with all branches of learning.

71. ACLS, *Bulletin* # 9 (December 1928), 46-47. Pages 33 to 52 offer a summary transcript of the meeting at the Harvard Club, and conclude with a list of all of the participants.

72. Late in life Latourette published a brief autobiography, *Beyond the Ranges: An Autobiography* (Grand Rapids MI, 1967). For his awareness that many historians found his religious apologetics troubling, see 115.

73. Kenneth Scott Latourette, *The Chinese: their History and Culture,* 2 vols. (New York, 1934).

74. M. S. Bates, review of Latourette, *American Historical Review* 39 (1934), 709-711.

75. Kenneth Scott Latourette, *A History of the Expansion of Christianity,* 7 vols. (New York, 1937-1945).

76. Norman Kutcher, "'The Benign Bachelor': Kenneth Scott Latourette between China and the United States," *Journal of American-East Asian Relations* 2 (Winter 1993), 399-424, is the best study of Latourette's career. Kutcher shows how Latourette's religious ideas were a foundation for his scholarly work.

77. At Chicago, Harley F. McNair, who had taught at a missionary college in Shanghai for nearly two decades, focused on the history of international relations. At Berkeley, Edward Thomas Williams, a former missionary discussed earlier in this book in the context of his diplomatic service, also moved away from the study of Christianity. Yale was much more important than Chicago or Berkeley on account of its long tradition of extensive involvement in China, presenting Latourette with an opportunity that many colleagues elsewhere wished he had exploited more energetically. Latourette's failure to exploit his opportunities at Yale is discussed by Robert McCaughey, *International Studies and Academic Enterprise: A Chapter in the Enclosure of American Learning* (New York, 1984), 88.

78. Lewis Hodus, another of the six missionary-connected scholars who had been members of that original ACLS Committee, was a professor of missions at Hartford Theological Seminary.

79. Samuel Wells Williams, *The Middle Kingdom,* 2 vols. (New York, 1948). This work went through several editions, including one published shortly before his death in 1883 and prepared in cooperation with his son, Frederick Wells Williams, himself a Yale professor of missions. Samuel Wells Williams, as with so many missionaries of the nineteenth and early twentieth centuries, also served as a diplomat. He was head of the American legation in the imperial court of China during much of the 1850s and 1860s. Samuel Wells Williams is a major character in the illuminating study by John R. Haddad, *America's First Adventure in China* (Philadelphia, 2013). Beach wrote a number of books, including *Dawn in the Hills of the T'ang* (New York, 1898).

80. Edward Thomas Williams, *China Yesterday and Today* (New York, 1923), 315.

81. Dimitri D. Lazo, "The Making of a Multicultural Man: The Missionary Experiences of E. T. Williams," *Pacific Historical Review* 51 (1982), 361. It is a sign of how little attention scholars have paid to the impact of missionary experience on American life that when I wrote to Lazo in 2015 about this valuable article, he told me I was the first person to mention it to him in the then thirty-three years since he had published it.

82. Fairbank, *Chinabound*, 134–135.

83. Kenneth Scott Latourette, *Christianity in a Revolutionary Age: A History of Christianity in the 19th and 20th Centuries*, 5 vols. (New York, 1958–1962).

84. Wilber C. Harr, ed., *Frontiers of the Christian World Mission* (New York, 1962).

85. For the history of Yenching University, including an account of its connection to Harvard, see Philip West, *Yenching University and Sino-Western Relations, 1916–1952* (Cambridge MA, 1976), esp. 187–194.

86. Paul M. Evans, *John Fairbank and the American Understanding of Modern China* (New York, 1988), 180.

87. Of these, Rawlinson, Roy, and Thomson were missionary children. A number of Fairbank's students presented Fairbank with a *Festschrift* on his 60th birthday; Albert Feuerwerker, Rhoads Murphy, and Mary C. Wright, eds., *Approaches to Modern Chinese History* (Berkeley, 1967).

88. David Shambaugh, ed., *American Studies of Contemporary China* (Washington DC, 1993).

89. Fairbank, *Chinabound*, 136.

90. Fairbank, *Chinabound*, 5, 40–41, 60.

91. Edgar Snow, *Red Star Over China* (New York, 1937).

92. Fairbank's accounts of his contact with these individuals are highly readable; *Chinabound*, 66–77 (Smedley) and 78–84 (Isaacs).

93. Fairbank, *Chinabound*, 111–113. For other examples of Fairbank's appreciative reliance upon missionaries during this early 1930s residency in China, see *Chinabound*, 30, 36, 39, 43, 48, 58, 81, 91-91, 95, 106–107, 116, and 164.

94. Fairbank, *Chinabound*, 229, 232, 248, 256. During these 1940s residencies in China, Fairbank was also working for the Library of Congress, charged with collecting Chinese language materials of his choice. Fairbank took this public role seriously, but it was also a cover for his work on behalf of the OSS.

95. Fairbank's experiences in the McCarthy era are extensively discussed in Evans, *Fairbank*, 134–164. Fairbank details his experiences with various investigations and charges in *Chinabound*, 331–351. Taylor, who led the Asian Studies group at the University of Washington, was one of very few China scholars to give any legitimacy to government investigations of Area Studies scholars during the 1950s. Another was Japan specialist Kenneth Colgrove of Northwestern University, who attacked Reischauer as well as Fairbank for being in the "pro-Communist" rather than the "pro-American" camp. The only missionary son to speak this way was David N. Rowe of Yale. For Rowe's high standing among political conservatives, see his obituary in *National Review* (July 12, 1985).

96. John K. Fairbank, "Our Chances in China," *The Atlantic* (September 1946).

97. John K. Fairbank, *The United States and China* (Cambridge MA, 1948). Later editions of this work appeared in 1958, 1971, and 1979.

98. Evans, *Fairbank*, 105.

99. There was no secret about Chalmers Johnson's affiliation with the CIA between 1967 and 1973; see "Chalmers Johnson Dies at 79," *New York Times* (November 24, 2010). Johnson later changed his mind about the role of the United States in world politics and became a strident critic of American imperialism. Frederic Wakeman recalled (interview, September 21, 2000) hearing Johnson brag about this CIA connection when Wakeman was a student and then junior faculty member at Berkeley. David Szanton was a senior staff officer at the Social Science Research Council and recalls the CIA name tags. See also "John S. Thomson. 77, CIA Analyst and Canoeist," *New York Times* (August 6, 1998).

100. Shambaugh, *China*, 176-195.

101. For this transition, see Charles Hayford, "China by the Book: China Hands and China Stories, 1848-1948," *Journal of American-East Asian Relations* 16 (2009), 285-311.

102. T. A. Bisson, autobiographical sketch, Box 1, Folder 2, T. A. Bisson Papers, University of Maine. I thank Elizabeth Russell for finding this document for me.

103. Bisson's career has attracted very little scholarly attention, but is the subject of an excellent chapter in Howard B. Schonberger, *Aftermath of War: Americans and the Remaking of Japan, 1945-1952* (Kent OH, 1989), 90-110, here quoting from page 92. Schonberger made use of the T. A. Bisson Papers at the University of Maine, and interviewed Bisson and his wife shortly before their deaths.

104. John Gunther, *Inside Asia* (New York, 1939), e.g. 235. Gunther was a conscientious and discerning journalist, whose writings, sometimes patronized by scholars, were usually well-informed.

105. T. A. Bisson, *Japan in China* (New York, 1938); T. A. Bisson, *Yenan in June 1937: Talks with the Communist Leaders* (Berkeley, 1973). Bisson said he had lost track of the Yenan journal for many years. Bisson's son, Thomas N. Bisson, has informed me that T. A. Bisson had forgotten about the 1937 documents until he rediscovered them in a box of his possessions that he had left with friends from 1952 to 1967.

106. Buck's article of 1943 is discussed above, in chapter 2.

107. T. A. Bisson, "China's Part in a Coalition War," *Far Eastern Survey* (July 14, 1943).

108. T. A. Bisson, *America's Far Eastern Policy* (New York, 1945).

109. T. A. Bisson, *Prospects for Democracy in Japan* (New York, 1949).

110. Schonberger, *Aftermath*, 92-93. *China Today* was published by the American Friends of the Chinese People, an organization closely tied to the Communist Party of the United States.

111. Schonberger *Aftermath*, 109.

112. T. A. Bisson, "Why the United States Should Not Be in Vietnam," *Public Affairs Pamphlet No. 391* (New York, 1966), 15-30.

113. T. A. Bisson, *Zaibatsu Dissolution in Japan* (Berkeley, 1954).

114. See, e.g., John Earl Haynes and Harvey Klehr, *In Denial: Historians, Communism, and Espionage* (New York, 2005), 108.

115. Venona Transcripts, Dispatch of June 16, 1943, New York to Moscow: https://www.cia.gov/library/center-for-the-study-of-intelligence/csi-publications/books-and-monographs/venona-soviet-espionage-and-the-american-response-1939-1957/b12.gif/image.gif.

116. Bates' dispatches from Nanking are printed, along with the reports of other missionaries, in Zhang Kaiyuan, ed., *Eyewitness to Massacre: American Missionaries Bear Witness to Japanese Atrocities in Nanjing* (Amonk NY, 2001), 3–81.

117. John H. M. Linbeck's *Understanding China* (New York, 1971) was the Ford Foundation's survey of resources in the United States for the study of China. Linbeck was the brother of the Yale theologian George Lindbeck, a leader in Lutheran ecumenical activities described in chapter 4.

118. A. Doak Barnett was the brother of Foreign Service officer Robert Barnett, whose escape from the purging of the China Hands I described in chapter 7. The two were the sons of Eugene Barnett, a YMCA missionary to China whom I discuss in chapter 11 in relation to his work on behalf of civil rights for African Americans.

119. For a careful analysis of Pye's career, see Nils Gilman, *Mandarins of the Future: Modernization Theory in Cold War America* (Baltimore, 2003), esp. 167–172.

120. Mills published very little as a scholar, but was well known for her relatively sympathetic view of the Chinese Communists, even having been their prisoner for four years after she had signed, under duress, a confession of committing espionage. Five years after her release, she published "Thought Reform: Ideological Remolding in China," *The Atlantic* (December 1959), 71–77. She never repudiated her confession, and continued in years after to display a positive attitude toward the conditions of her imprisonment. See, e.g., her comments to Sarah R. Mason, in Mason, "Missionary Conscience," 69–71, and Mason Papers, 5–32. See also her obituary, "Harriet Mills, Scholar Accused of Spying, 95," *New York Times* (March 29, 2016).

121. Kennedy was known to be an alcoholic and was only marginally functional for a number of years before his death in 1960, at the age of 59.

122. A widely discussed article of 1972 by the then left-wing writer David Horowitz (later more famous as a right wing critical of leftists) pushed these accusations especially hard; see David Horowitz, "The China Scholars and U. S. Intelligence," *Ramparts* (February 1972), 31–39. For a helpful overview of these debates, see Richard Madsen, "The Academic China Specialists," in Shambaugh, *China*, 168–171.

123. Evans, *Fairbank*, 265. While Evans's biography is overwhelmingly sympathetic, he is clearly disappointed that Fairbank temporized for so long on the Vietnam question.

124. For the Barnett family's divisions over the war, see the interviews conducted by Sarah Mason in the mid-1970s; especially the long interview of October 16, 1976, with DeWitt Barnett, Mason Papers, Box 2, Folder 11.

125. A prominent example was the US history specialist Howard Zinn, who famously struggled with Fairbank over a microphone at the December 1968 meeting of the American Historical Association when Fairbank, as president, concluded that Zinn had violated the rules by holding the floor for too long a time. Marilyn Young recalls Fairbank's generous and even-handed approach to those of his students who differed from him on the war; Young interview, New York, February 27, 2015.

126. A good account of Thomson's maneuverings in the administrations of Kennedy and Johnson is found in Packard, *Reischauer*, 134–141.

127. James C. Thomson Jr., "How Could Vietnam Happen? An Autopsy," *The Atlantic* (April 1968). His revised doctoral dissertation was James C. Thomson Jr., *When China Faced West: American Reformers in Nationalist China, 1928-1937* (Cambridge MA, 1969).

128. Christopher Thomson, letter to me, February 18, 2015. My understanding of the Thompson family dynamic also depends on Alison Brown, letter to me, February 17, 2015.

129. Lucian Pye, interview, Cambridge, Massachusetts, May 28, 2003. Pye's opinion that there was no missionary school of Chinese Studies is shared by many others whom I have asked about this, including Frederic Wakeman, interview, September 21, 2000, and Samuel C. Chu, interview, August 8, 2003. Historian Richard Madsen has offered a more culturally focused analysis of the missionary/nonmissionary distinction. "The missionaries or children of missionaries" tended to write in "more of a moral tone" than the others, Madsen observed ("Academic," 171) without providing convincing documentation. I find no evidence for this claim, even in the Vietnam debates, where moral intensity and realistic detachment were both widely distributed.

130. The historians among the missionary sons, for example, worked in very different directions. Crane focused on the development of Indian nationalism. Robert Frykenberg began by studying British imperial administration, then wrote chiefly about the history of Christianity in India. Eugene Irschick worked in the Orientalist mode of Brown until midcareer, when he became engaged by the theoretical works of Michel Foucault and Mikhail Bakhtin and wrote in a vigorously anti-Orientalist manner.

131. There had been a small program at Cornell since the 1930s, but by the time the field expanded in the 1960s it was able to recruit persons with military and diplomatic rather than missionary experience. The timing and character of Southeast Asian Studies was also affected by the sheer presence of the European empires. British, Dutch, and French scholars working in relation to their own nations' empires developed sophisticated literatures on which American academics could draw. For the slow development of Southeast Asian Studies, see John Bowen, "Southeast Asian Studies," in Szanton, *Knowledge*, 386–425.

132. McCune died in 1948 just as he was winning plaudits for his energetic development of Korean Studies at Berkeley; see his In Memoriam entry, University of California, Berkeley.

133. The most thorough study of the development of Area Studies for the Middle East is Zachary Lockman, *Field Notes: The Making of Middle East Studies in the United States* (Stanford, 2016). Another helpful account is Timothy Mitchell, "The Middle East in the Past and Future of Social Science," in Szanton, *Knowledge*, 74–118.

134. First published in 1926, Berlin-trained James Henry Breasted's *The Conquest of Civilization* was brought out by the Literary Guild in a lavishly illustrated edition of 1938.

135. There was a missionary connection of sorts in Hitti's appointment, since he was recruited from the American University in Beirut, the missionary college where he had been educated by American Presbyterians. A quarter century after Hitti's

recruitment at Princeton, Columbia in 1951 hired Charles Issawi, an Arab Christian born in Egypt who had been teaching at the American University in Beirut. The role AUB played in educating several generations of civic, business, and academic leaders in the Arab world has been widely recognized; see, e.g., Betty S. Anderson, *The American University of Beirut: Arab Nationalism & Liberal Education* (Austin TX 2011).

136. For Leonard Binder's leadership, see Leonard Binder, ed., *The Study of the Middle East: Research and Scholarship in the Humanities and Social Sciences* (New York, 1976), esp. Binder's "Area Studies: A Critical Reassessment," 1–28, introducing this volume of ten discipline-specific essays. Binder, writing before Edward Said, offers a critique of "Orientalism" that is less sweeping than Said's but equally pointed.

137. The leading student of the history of Middle Eastern Studies, Zachary Lockman, explains that Lybyer's interpretation of the Ottoman state was long acclaimed "as a major scholarly advance" because of an erroneous assumption that "the Ottoman sources were of little real value." Once that assumption was rejected, Lybyer's work ceased to find its place in the footnotes of scholars. Albert Howe Lybyer, *The Government of The Ottoman Empire in the Time of Suleiman the Magnificent* (Cambridge MA, 1913). Zachary Lockman, *Contending Visions of the Middle East: The History and Politics of Orientalism* (New York, 2010), 104–105.

Chapter Ten: Toward the Peace Corps

1. Paul A. Rodell, "John S. Noffsinger & and the Global Impact of the Thomasite Experience," http://peacecorpsworldwide.org/john-s-noffsinger-and-the-global-impact-of-the-thomasite-experience/.

2. Arthur F. Raper, "Some Ruminations about Technical Aid," unpublished memorandum of August 1956, in Arthur R. Raper Papers, Southern Historical Collection, Wilson Library, University of North Carolina at Chapel Hill, Box 16, Folder 720, italics in original. I owe my awareness of this document to Daniel Immerwahr. For a brief account of Raper's career, see Daniel Immerwahr, *Thinking Small: The United States and the Lure of Community Development* (Cambridge MA, 2015), 54–55. In Raper's prewar career as a rural sociologist, he had published widely discussed studies of tenant farming and lynching in his native North Carolina and elsewhere in the American South.

3. In the extensive literature on these larger-scale development endeavors, see especially David Ekbladh, *The Great American Mission: Modernization & the Construction of an American World Order* (Princeton, 2010) and Nils Gilman, *Mandarins of the Future: Modernization Theory in Cold War America* (Baltimore, 2007).

4. Arthur F. Raper, "The Role of Pilot and Demonstration Problems in Community Development Work," *Community Development Bulletin* (September 1956), 31–32, italics in original. Another of the US government's leading technical aid officials recognized the same aspects of missionary service, altogether independently of Raper. The engineer-architect Albert Mayer identified the village-centered work of Charlotte and William Wiser—discussed in the previous chapter—as the appropriate model for development programs in India. Mayer consulted repeatedly with the Wisers during his own extensive career as a development expert during the postwar years.

5. Laubach's letter of 1930 is quoted by Peter G. Gowing, "The Legacy of Frank Charles Laubach," *International Bulletin of Missionary Research* (April 1983), 59–60.

6. The English translation from the Portuguese of Freire's 1968 volume, *Pedagogy of the Oppressed* (New York, 1970), included a forward by the American missionary Richard Shaull, whom I discuss in several earlier chapters. Freire, a Christian socialist, was promoted by the ecumenical missionary community and served as an adviser to the World Council of Churches.

7. Laubach's role in the history of the advancement of literacy is recognized routinely in histories of literacy campaigns; see, e.g., Mary Hamilton, et al., eds., *Literacy as Numbers* (New York, 2015); Andrew J. Kirkendall, *Paulo Freire and the Cold War Politics of Literacy* (Chapel Hill NC, 2010), and Barbara J. Guzzetti, ed., *Literacy for the New Millenium* (Westport CT, 2007).

8. Laubach's dissertation was published as *Why There Are Vagrants* (New York, 1916).

9. Laubach's 1930 letter; cited here by Gowing, "Legacy," 59–60.

10. Frank Charles Laubach, *The People of the Philippines: Their Religious Progress and Preparation for Spiritual Leadership in the Far East* (New York, 1925), xi–xii, 444.

11. Frank Charles Laubach, *Seven Thousand Emeralds* (New York, 1929), 141–142.

12. Laubach voiced complaints about corporate profiteering and exploitation of Filipino peasants in *Missionary Herald* 132 (1926), 309, cited by Gowing, "Legacy," 60.

13. Luke 23:34; John 19:30 (KJV).

14. Frank C. Laubach, *Rizal: Man and Martyr* (Manila, 1936), vii, 402–403. Historian Paul Kramer treats Rizal as an emblem for the deepest strain of anti-imperialist feeling within the political culture of the Philippines; see Paul A. Kramer, *The Blood of Government: Race, Empire, the United States & the Philippines* (Chapel Hill NC, 2006), 433–434.

15. Kenton J. Klymer, *Quest for Freedom: The United States and India's Independence* (New York, 1995), 26.

16. Frank C. Laubach, *Towards a Literate World* (New York, 1938).

17. Among Laubach's most literacy-focused volumes were *Teaching the World to Read: A Handbook for Literacy Campaigns* (New York, 1947), and *Forty Years with the Silent Billion* (Old Tappan NJ, 1970). His *Channels of Spiritual Power* (Westwood NJ, 1954) was typical of his devotional writing. See also his *Letters by a Modern Mystic* (New York, 1937), a volume published by the Student Volunteer Movement. Some of his books presented the literacy campaign, however religion-neutral its methods, as religiously functional; see, e.g., his *How to Teach One and Win One for Christ* (Grand Rapids MI, 1964).

18. Frank C. Laubach, *Wake Up or Blow Up: America, Lift the World or Lose It!* (New York, 1951), 12.

19. Matthew Hedstrom, *The Rise of Liberal Religion: Book Culture and American Spirituality in the Twentieth Century* (New York, 2013), 216–217.

20. An overview of Laubach's career presenting him as a lifelong witness for Christianity is Gowing, "Legacy." Celebratory biographies in this spirit include Helen M. Roberts, *Champion of the Silent Billion* (St. Paul MN, 1961), and David E. Mason, *Frank C. Laubach, Teacher of Millions* (Minneapolis, 1967). These studies contain information about their subject, but they are significant chiefly as manifestations of the magnitude and intensity of Laubach's following. Laubach has yet to attract a scholarly biographer.

21. The only detailed study of Yen's career is Charles W. Hayford, *To the People: James Yen and Village China* (New York, 1990). For Yen's work in the Philippines, see Jose V. Abueva, *Focus on the Barrio: The Story Behind the Birth of the Phillipine Community Development Program under President Ramon Magsaysay* (Manila, 1959).

22. On the list, too, were the Nobel Prize winning scientists Thomas Hunt Morgan and E. O. Lawrence, representing biology and physics, respectively, and W. M. Stanley, a chemist who would get his own Nobel a few years later. The other honoree was Igor I. Sikorsky, then a legend in technology circles for his development of the helicopter and the sea-landing "Clipper" aircraft. Yen was the only one of the ten who was not an American citizen, and the only one who was nonwhite. For Yen's selection as a Copernican giant, see Stacy Bieler, *"Patriots or Traitors": A History of American-Educated Chinese Students* (New York, 2004), 259. The committee charged with selecting the ten was chaired by Yale University President James R. Angell. President Franklin Roosevelt sent a message to be read on the occasion of the presentation of the citations at Carnegie Hall in New York.

23. Butterfield, who had served as president of what became Michigan State University and the University of Massachusetts at Amherst, was close to the missionary leadership and had been an adviser to the International Missionary Council's Jerusalem meeting of 1928.

24. George Shepherd, "Tinghsien's Challenge to the Church Today," *Chinese Recorder* 64 (1933), 391–392.

25. He contributed an essay to the missionary-intensive volume of 1942 coedited by Yi-Fan Wu and Frank W. Price, eds., *China Rediscovers Her West* (London, 1942), esp. 78–85.

26. Pearl Buck, *Tell the People: Talks with James Yen about the Mass Education Movement* (New York, 1945).

27. The board was chaired by General Electric President Gerald Swope, and included the department store magnate Marshall Field, Montgomery Ward president Sewell Avery, advertising titan Bruce Barton, and labor leader Walter Reuther.

28. Hayford, *Yen*, 141, 186. Indusco was first organized at the outset of the war by the writer Edgar Snow, who had been impressed by Yen's work.

29. http://www.nytimes.com/1987/12/28/obituaries/rewi-alley-expatriate-in-china.html

30. For Pruitt's tortured life and convoluted political career, see Marjorie King, *China's American Daughter: Ida Pruitt (1888–1985)* (Hong Kong, 2006). For Pruitt's work on behalf of Rewi Alley, see esp. 140–154. Pruitt liberated herself from the missionary milieu at a fairly early age, and remained hostile to the missionary project throughout her adulthood. King recognizes this theme but underplays its severity, which is evident in Pruitt's private writings. "I hate my parents," she wrote in one meditation of the 1930s. More generally, Pruitt condemned a number of specific missionary effects on China, including "the injection into Chinese culture of the Western sense of sin in sex." Pruitt Papers, Schlesinger library; Box 9, Folder 146 and Box 36, Folder 929.

31. Alley was widely assumed to be homosexual and after his death was celebrated as such in a 1998 opera, *Alley*, by the New Zealand composer and gay activist, Jack Body. See Anne-Marie Brady, *Friend of China: The Myth of Rewi Alley* (London, 2002).

32. Hayford, *Yen*, 65.

33. Hayford, *Yen*, 213.

34. Immwahr, *Thinking Small*, 124. For skepticism about the scope and character of the CIA's involvement in the Philippines during Yen's time there, see James R Prescott, "Ramón Magsaysay—the Myth and the Man," *Journal of American-East Asian Relations* 23 (2016), 7–32.

35. The sponsorship of Toyohiki Kagawa's lecture tours in the United States was another. The bringing of the Arab scholar Philip Hitti from the American University in Beirut to Princeton in 1927 was yet another. The celebrations of Gandhi and Chiang are additional cases, although pursued at a distance and in relation to more sharply defined political agendas. Yen, like Kagawa and Hitti but with a much larger popular following, was a physical presence in the United States and turned up repeatedly in the councils of men and women of power. The Chinese intellectual Hu Shih, a secularist and a disciple of John Dewey, was also extensively promoted in the United States by Protestant groups.

36. The most thorough account of the origins of IVS is Paul Rodell, "International Voluntary Services in Vietnam: War and the Birth of Activism, 1958-1967," *Peace and Change* 27 (2002), 225–244. See also Galen Beery, "A Brief History of International Voluntary Services, Inc.," typescript found on the Southeast Asian Images and Texts website, http://digicoll.library.wisc.edu/cgi-bin/SEAiT/SEAiT-idx?type=turn&entity=SEAiT.IVSMiscMemos.p0069&id=SEAiT.IVSMiscMemos&isize=M.

37. Dale D. Clark, interview for the Foreign Affairs Oral History Collection, 15–16. Clark was interviewed by Robert Zigler on October 14, 1998.

38. Autobiographical sketches of IVS volunteers emphasize this close-to-the-ground feature of their experience, living often in small and poorly appointed housing and being paid sixty dollars a month; for dozens of such accounts, see Thierry J. Sagnier, *The Fortunate Few: IVS Volunteers From Asia to the Andes* (Portland OR, 2015). The continuity between the social service practices of the ecumenical missionaries, IVS, and the Peace Corps is recognized by Jonathan Zimmerman, *Innocents Abroad: American Teachers in the American Century* (Cambridge MA, 2002), esp. 201.

39. Winburn T. Thomas, *The Vietnam Story of International Voluntary Service* (Washington DC, 1972), 31, quotes this comment of 1960 attributed to IVS staff member Daniel Russell. Thomas was one of the *Christian Century*'s regular commentators on the state of the missionary project throughout the 1940s, 1950s, and 1960s.

40. Franklin E. Huffman, State Department oral history interview, January 30, 2006, 15. http://www.adst.org/OH%20TOCs/Huffman,%20Franklin%20E.toc.pdf Later in life Huffman was himself a Foreign Service officer. Huffman describes his IVS experience in more detail in his memoir, *Monks and Motorcycles: From Laos to London by the Seat of My Pants, 1956-1958* (New York, 2004).

41. Ekbladh, *American Mission*, 177.

42. Immerwahr, *Thinking Small*, 140. See also the eyewitness account of Nofsinger's interaction with Shriver and other officials by Galen Beery, in Sagnier, *Fortunate Few*, 57–60. That the Peace Corps continued a missionary tradition of service became a point of great pride for many writers and memoirists in the missionary contingent. An example is Edward Bliss Jr., *Beyond the Stone Arches: An American*

Missionary Doctor in China, 1892-1932 (New York, 2001), viii, describing the memorialist's father as "a predecessor to those in Peace Corps" who "healed, farmed, delivered babies, and bred cattle for the glory of God and dignity of man." The most ambitious scholarly book on the missionary project, William R. Hutchison's *Errand to the World: American Protestant Thought and Foreign Missions* (Chicago, 1987), treats the project's legacy for the Peace Corps as one of its most important claims to historical significance, see esp. 60, 177, and 203-204.

43. Thomas, *Vietnam Story*, 17.

44. This point is emphasized by Jessica Elkind in what is the most thorough treatment of IVS's involvement in Vietnam, *Aid Under Fire: Nation Building and the Vietnam War* (Lexington KY, 2016), 209. Elkind concludes (216) that IVS's critical feedback to the US government about its wrongheaded approach to Vietnam was essentially sound, and that had officials in Washington followed IVS advice the calamity of the Vietnam War might have been avoided.

45. Rodell, "Birth of Activism," 239. See also Don Luce and John Sommer, *Vietnam: The Unheard Voices* (Ithaca NY, 1969), 315-321, which includes the full text of the letter of September 17, 1967. The thunderous disillusion with the US government experienced by IVS volunteers in Vietnam and Laos is a major theme in the autobiographical sketches collected in Sagnier, *Fortunate Few*.

46. Edwards's case is treated as representative by Ekbladh, *American Mission*, 26-28.

47. Eugene Burdick and William Lederer, *The Ugly American* (New York, 1958).

Chapter Eleven: Of One Blood

1. Edmund Davidson Soper, quoted in *Time* (November 8, 1926). Soper spoke as the founding dean of the Duke Divinity School. Although it was unusual for a churchman in a Jim Crow state to speak so forthrightly, northerners did so more often.

2. Historians have rightly focused on US government concerns about the impact of domestic racism abroad, but have been almost entirely unaware of the identical development within Protestant churches, going back many decades, and evident in even the most cursory examination of the record. See, e.g., the otherwise excellent work of Mary Dudziak, *Cold War Civil Rights* (Princeton, 2002). For a cogent account of the sharpening of this concern among churches in the late 1950s and early 1960s, see David L. Chappell, *A Stone of Hope: Prophetic Religion and the Death of Jim Crow* (Chapel Hill NC, 2004), 147-150.

3. The plea was endorsed by the denomination's Mission Board but shunted aside by leaders of the denomination as a whole. Ernest Trice Thompson, *Presbyterians in the South: Volume Three, 1890-1972* (Richmond VA, 1973), 442. I rely also on the recollections of former missionary to Africa Lamar Wilkinson, who recalls (e-mail to me, May 26, 2008) that segregationists in control of the Southern Presbyterian governing body not only kept the petition from reaching the floor of the assembly, but insisted on holding the assembly's annual meeting in a segregated church in Memphis despite the protest of the missionary constituency that the site be changed. See also Joel L. Alvis, Jr., *Religion & Race: Southern Presbyterians, 1946-1983* (Tuscaloosa AL, 1994), who notes (72-73) the frequency with which the missionaries warned that

their efforts "were adversely affected by the continued practice of segregation in the United States."

4. "In Christ There is No East or West" was composed by the English poet and clergyman John Oxenham for the 1908 meeting of the London Missionary Society and quickly became the standard missionary hymn throughout the English speaking world. It replaced among ecumenical Protestants a much older hymn, "From Greenland's Icy Mountains," that was more aggressively evangelical and disparaged non-Christian religions as "heathen":

> From Greenland's icy mountains, from India's coral strand . . .
>
> They call us to deliver their land from error's chain . . .
>
> The heathen in his blindness bows down to wood and stone.

5. For Soper's work as a mission theorist, see chapter 3.

6. Soper was then a professor at Garrett Seminary in Evanston, Illinois. After leaving Duke, he had served in the 1930s as president of Oho Wesleyan University.

7. Edwin Soper Papers, Garrett, Box 8, Folders 21 and 22, contain documents for this series of seminars and the conference. Among the participants in the conference were the African American scholar Rayford Logan of Howard University, University of Chicago anthropologist Robert Redfield, YMCA Executive Secretary Eugene Barnett, and representatives of the Rosenwald Foundation and the *Christian Century*. For an account of Soper's seminars and conference, and Methodist Missionary Board Executive Director Ralph Diffendorfer's encouragement and funding of them, see Gene Zubovich, "The Global Gospel," PhD dissertation, University of California, Berkeley, 2015, 110–111.

8. Edmund Davison Soper, *Racism: A World Issue* (New York, 1947), 295; Revelation 7:9-12.

9. Soper, *Racism*, 272.

10. Soper, *Racism*, 175, 229, 244–245.

11. Soper, *Racism*, 9, 285. Soper's list of eight readers of his entire manuscript included the missionary theorist Daniel J. Fleming in addition to L. S. Albright and J. W. Becker of the International Missionary Council, Wynn C. Fairfield of the Foreign Missions Conference of North America, E. C. Lobenstine of the National Christian Council of China, R. E. Diffendorfer of the Methodist Mission Board, and Charles T. Inglehart, a 35-year missionary in Japan. The eighth was John C. Bennett of Union Theological Seminary, whose connections with the missionary project were less direct. For other assistance, Soper thanked a multitude of missionary-connected individuals, including Thelma Stevens of the Methodist Women's Missionary Board and Kenneth Scott Latourette of Yale, the leading historian of missions discussed in chapter 9. The missionary context for *Racism: A World Issue* has rarely been noticed by historians. Thomas Borstelmann, *Cold War and Color Line: American Race Relations in the Global Arena* (Cambridge MA, 2001), 286, does understand the book's importance but not its origins.

12. Mobley's speech is quoted in Will D. Campbell, *The Stem of Jesse: The Costs of Community at a 1960s Southern School* (Mercer GA, 1994), 69–70. Goerner saw himself as an antiracist force among Southern Baptists. See his *America Must be Christian* (Louisville KY, 1947), esp. 133–137.

13. The fight over Oni's admission to Mercer University is well told in Willis, *God's Plan*, 170–172.

14. Campbell, *Stem of Jesse*, 71.

15. For the power achieved by the women's missionary boards and the efforts of male church leaders to rein them in, see Dana L. Robert, *American Women in Mission: A Social History of Their Thought and Practice* (Macon GA, 1997), 313–316. See also Catherine B. Allen, "Shifting Sands for Southern Baptist Women in Missions," in Dana L. Robert, ed., *Gospel Bearers, Gender Barriers* (Maryknoll NY, 2002), 113–126.

16. For Matson's career, and the support he received from female missionaries and the women's missionary board, especially, see Willis, *God's Plan*, 14–25.

17. Linda Gesling, *Mirror and Beacon: The History of Mission of the Methodist Church, 1939–1968* (New York, 2005, 4: "Much of the leadership for change in racial attitudes and practices came from the Woman's Division."

18. Gesling, *Mirror and Beacon*, 304–309. The quarrel over the segregated governance structure is the main theme of Peter C. Murray, *Methodists and the Crucible of Race, 1930–1975* (Columbia MO, 2004), which also documents the leadership of the Woman's Division in trying to end this and other discriminatory practices (see esp. 64–65). The final, successful push to eliminate the Central Jurisdiction was led by a man, a former missionary, Tracy Jones.

19. Tilly was one of two women to serve on this committee; for her career, see Andrew Manis, "'City Mothers': Dorothy Tilly, the Georgia Methodist Women, and Black Civil Rights," in Glenn Fledman, ed., *Before Brown: Civil Rights and White Backlash in the Modern South* (Tuscalosa AL, 2004), 116–143.

20. Sara M. Evans, "Introduction," in Sara M. Evans, Ed., *Journeys that Opened Up the World: Women, Student Christian Movements, and Social Justice, 1955–1975* (New Brunswick NJ, 2003), 5–6. *New York Times*, December 31, 1955, 6. The *Times* gave extensive coverage to the conference of 1955; see also the stories of December 29, 1955 (4) and December 30 (12).

21. The collaboration of Flory and Harris in organizing the SVM Quadrennials of 1955 and 1959 is ably discussed in Ada Focer, "Internship in Mission, 1961–1974: Young Christians Abroad in a Post-Colonial and Cold War World," PhD dissertation, Boston University, 2015. Focer rightly emphasizes the radical nature of Flory's decision to feature Shaull at both of these conferences. Although Flory's personality was less forceful and inspiring than Harris', Flory's antiracist commitments made a deep impression on many of the young people with whom she worked, and Flory, too, is an example of missionary-connected individuals pushing conspicuously for racial equality. See Tamela Hultman, "Tamela Hultman," in Evans, *Journeys*, 148–150.

22. Charlotte Bunch, "Charlotte Bunch," in Evans, *Journeys*, 126.

23. See Gary May, *The Informant: The FBI, The Ku Klux Klan, and the Murder of Viola Liuzzo* (New Haven CT, 2005). Harris's own account of this experience is in Ruth Harris, "Ruth Harris," in Evans, *Journeys*, 40–41.

24. Rebecca Owen, "Rebecca Owen," in Evans, *Journeys*, 73.

25. Evans, Introduction, *Journeys*, 9.

26. Harris, "Harris," in *Journeys*, 42–43.

27. Harris, "Harris," in Evans, *Journeys*, 20–21.

28. Harris, "Harris," in Evans, *Journeys*, 21–23, and Ruth Harris to "My dear friends," letter of January 1, 1948, sent to friends in the United States, in Pat Patterson's possession.

29. Interview with Pat Patterson, Claremont, California, December 26, 2013. Patterson served in Japan, 1957–1961 and 1965–1972.

30. For a helpful analysis of the different social settings for "Boston marriages," their changing meaning over time, and the challenges they present for historical study, see Estelle B. Freedman, ""The Burning of Letters Continues': Elusive Identities and the Historical Construction of Sexuality," *Journal of Women's History* 9 (1998), 181–200.

31. Patterson, interview.

32. This unpublished poem, "Inner Harbor," was shared with me by Patterson herself. Patterson's other verse has been published in *Autumn Leaves: A Book of Poetry* (Shelbyville KY, 2013).

33. Students of the career of Bayard Rustin have long speculated about the relationship between his gay identity and his work as an activist, different—as is the case of any African American male—from the cases of white women. Rustin's arrest in 1953 for homosexual acts led the leader of FOR, A. J. Muste, to push him out of the official leadership, although Muste and others continued to work with him. See Dimilio, *Lost Prophet*, and Leilah Claire Danielson, *American Gandhi: A. J. Muste* (Philadelphia, 2014).

34. The best source for Thelma Stevens is an oral history interview conducted on February 13, 1972, available at http://docsouth.unc.edu/sohp/G-0058/menu.html.

35. Billings was terminated by the Methodist Church in 1992, and given a "severance package" that outraged conservative Methodists; see, e.g., Allen O. Morris, "The Church in Bondage," http://cmpage.org/bondage/appendixj.html. For a brief account of Billings's life, including a description of the household she shared with a woman companion, see http://www.ithacajournal.com/story/news/2016/02/02/peggy-billings-missionary-justice-worker-poet/79711308/. For an example of conservative Methodist antagonism toward Billings in the years leading up to her resignation, see http://www.ucmpage.org/articles/msum_history.html.

36. Jeanne Audrey Powers, "Jeanne Audrey Powers," in Evans, *Journeys*, 65.

37. For Flory's account of her own career, which mentions no relationships with men even in her youth, see Margaret Flory, *Moments in Time: One Woman's Ecumenical Journey* (New York, 1995). Margaret Shannon's name appears in *Moments in Time* only in the caption for a photograph (facing page 53) of Shannon speaking at an event in Flory's honor. For a detailed and sympathetic analysis of Flory's career, focusing on her role in recruiting young missionaries but also detailing her having worked closely with Harris in organizing conferences of ecumenical youth, see Focer, dissertation.

38. Loveland, *Lillian Smith*, 39. Smith's fame as a writer followed from her 1944 novel, *Strange Fruit*, and her 1949 collection of essays and memoirs, *Killers of the Dream*. The novel's depiction of black-white sexual intimacy as an acceptable form of love was welcomed by many antiracists. The novel was banned as pornographic in many locales, including the cities of Boston and Detroit, and banned from mailing by the US Postal Service until President Franklin Roosevelt overturned the ruling at

the insistence of First Lady Eleanor Roosevelt. Smith's sister, Bertha Smith Barnett, married the YMCA leader Eugene Barnett discussed in chapter 4.

39. Margaret Rose Gladney, "Personalizing the Political, Politicizing the Personal: Reflections on Editing the Letters of Lillian Smith," in John Howard, ed., *Carryin' On in the Lesbian and Gay South* (New York, 1997).

40. Harris, in Evans, *Journeys*, 18, and Patterson, interview, and letter, Ruth Harris to "Dear Pat," February 17, 1995, in Pat Patterson's possession. In this letter to her partner, which is in fact a lengthy autobiography, Harris describes a respectful relationship with her psychiatrist, about whose efforts to move her toward heterosexual relationships she speaks generously.

41. Rosemary Skinner Keller, *Georgia Harkness: For Such a Time as This* (Nashville, 1992), describes the relationship between Harkness and Miller in detail, esp. 231–235, and notes that the relationship appears to have ended a period of depression that Harkness had been experiencing. Keller reports (162–163) an oral tradition at the Yale Divinity School to the effect that Harkness had a brief romance with Kenneth Scott Latourette in the late 1920s, but neither Harkness nor the lifelong bachelor Latourette, who is discussed in several other chapters of this book, ever acknowledged it.

42. For this information I am indebted to Pat Patterson.

43. Bunch, "Bunch," in Evans, *Journeys*, 130. Bunch became an outspoken lesbian within her own generation's feminist movement, and left the Methodist church on account of its homophobia. On Bunch's role as an editor of *motive* and the demise of that gay-friendly Methodist periodical in 1970, see Hollinger, *After Cloven Tongues*, 39–40.

44. Hutchins has attracted more attention as an episode in lesbian history than as a Communist. See Janet Lee, *Comrades and Partners: The Shared Lives of Grace Hutchins and Anna Rochester* (New York, 2000); and Julia M. Allen, *Passionate Commitments: The Lives of Anna Rochester & Grace Hutchins* (Albany NY, 2013).

45. A number of missionary-connected individuals were sufficiently sympathetic with the party in the 1930s and 1940s to join organizations affiliated with it, but very few joined the party itself. Maude Russell was a longtime member of the party but exercised no leadership within it. Max Yergan was an active Communist for a shorter time and not in a leadership role. E. H. Norman was a member for a brief time in the late 1930s and later tried to conceal it. Duncan Lee, although he worked briefly as a spy, was never a member of the party.

46. Cited by Allen, *Passionate Commitments*, 66.

47. Grace Hutchins and Anna Rochester, *Jesus Christ and the World Today* (New York, 1922), v. Hutchins and Rochester recommend (esp. 145–149) the latest and most progressive of the modernist writings of the period, including the books and articles by Shailer Mathews, Harry F. Ward, and Kirby Page. The book is designed for use by "Church Study Groups" and proposes a series of questions for churchgoers to consider.

48. Grace Hutchins, *Labor and Silk* (New York, 1929).

49. Hutchins's documented willingness to characterize Chambers as a "homosexual pervert" has caused puzzlement and discomfort among her recent admirers. It is the chief concern of Robin Hackett in a foreword to Allen's *Passionate Commitments*. Hackett finds Hutchins's behavior so counterintuitive as to be an enduring

enigma (see xi–xii). Allen herself ponders the matter at length, finally speculating (243) plausibly that Hutchins probably felt that Chambers's apparently promiscuous "relations with men did not constitute partnerships" like her own with Rochester, but were "rather anonymous encounters, not always welcomed by the other party." Lee is more direct, and suggests sensibly (217) that Hutchins "reflected general CPUSA discomfort with homosexuality" and, knowing the government to be eager to link Communism with homosexuality, wanted to "distance herself as much as possible from this issue."

50. Grace Hutchins, *Women Who Work* (New York, 1934). This book was brought again in 1952 by its publisher, the Communist Party house, International Publishers. Another representative example of Hutchins's writings of this period is her *Children under Capitalism* (New York, 1933), a pamphlet in the Labor Re search Association series published by International Publishers. Here, Hutchins offered a series of affecting stories of poverty-stricken children, including the especially desperate situation of "Negro Worker's Children" (13–15). See also Grace Hutchins, *Youth in Industry* (New York, 1931); and Grace Hutchins, *The Truth about the Liberty League* (New York, 1936).

51. Grace Hutchins, *Japan's Drive for Conquest* (New York, 1935), 29.

52. For a thoughtful analysis of the life and career of Bloor, see Kathleen A. Brown, "The 'Savagely Fathered and Un-Mothered World' of The Communist Party, USA: Feminism, Maternalism, and Mother Bloor," *Feminist Studies* 20 (1999), 537–570. Just as some churchwomen found that remaining single provided more opportunities for leadership, so did some women in the Communist Party find that remaining unmarried had certain advantages. Bloor had risen to the top of the party as a married woman, but she was an exception, and by moving from one husband to another did not fit the standard model of a married woman. Elizabeth Gurley Flynn, another labor organizer, had been divorced for fifteen years before she joined the party in 1936 and eventually became its national chair.

53. Whittaker Chambers, *Witness* (New York, 1952), 49–50, offers a recognizable portrait of Hutchins in the early 1930s, "sitting among the handsome old pieces in her Greenwich Village apartment, describing in her cultivated voice how difficult" underground work was among the Japanese students she was trying to recruit for "Communist work in Japan." Chambers said he met Hutchins again in the late 1930s "on other underground business," and that she always displayed a "grand manner" that was joked about in "the more proletarian levels of the Communist Party."

54. Sam Tanenhaus, *Whittaker Chambers*, 342, describes these events and notes that the Hiss attorney to whom Hutchins spoke about Chambers's sexual orientation later left the Hiss team when he became convinced that Hiss was guilty and was lying to him. Another account can be found in Allen Weinstein, *Perjury: The Hiss-Chambers Case* (New York, 1978), 315–316, 380–381. Hutchins's later admission that the party did indeed send her to visit Shemitz is in a document of 1963, "Recent Comment by Grace Hutchins on Whittaker Chambers and his book, *Witness*, pp. 48–51," in Hutchins Papers, University of Oregon Special Collections. I owe my awareness of this document to Julia Allen.

55. Allen, *Passionate Commitments*, 265–281.

56. Houser's role in the founding of CORE is recognized on the CORE website, http://www.congressofracialequality.org/george-houser.html. See also the extensive

account of Houser's leadership in August Meier and Elliott Rudwick *CORE: A Study in the Civil Rights Movement* (New York, 1973), esp. 19–21.

57. Joseph Kip Kosek, *Acts of Conscience: Christian Nonviolence and Modern American Democracy* (New York, 2009). See also the lengthy obituary, "George Houser, Freedom Rides Pioneer and a Founder of CORE," *New York Times*, August 20, 2015, and the treatment of Houser in Leilah Danielson, *American Gandhi: A. J. Muste and the History of Radicalism in the Twentieth Century* (Philadelphia, 2014).

58. Houser, interview, accessible at http://www.noeasyvictories.org/interviews /int02_houser.php

59. Thomas J. Sugrue, *Sweet Land of Liberty: The Forgotten Struggle for Civil Rights in the North* (New York, 2008), 146.

60. For detailed accounts of this event, see Kosek, *Acts*, 204–208, and John Dimilio, *Lost Prophet*. Rustin served three weeks on a North Carolina chain gang upon his conviction for violating the North Carolina statute that had been ruled unconstitutional by the US Supreme Court. See also Raymond Arsenault, *Freedom Riders: 1961 and the Struggle for Racial Justice* (New York, 2011), 27–29.

61. Kosek, *Acts*, 203.

62. This development has been widely discussed; a prominent example is Carol Anderson, *Eyes Off the Prize: The United Nations and the African American Struggle for Human Rights, 1944–1954* (New York, 2003).

63. Penny M. Von Eschen, *Race against Empire: Black Americans and Anticolonialism, 1937–1957* (Ithaca NY, 1997), 143. Von Eschen laments Houser's willingness to work within an anti-Communist frame, and misleadingly implies reluctance on the part of Houser to work with black leaders. Houser's work for ACOA is discussed briefly by Carol Anderson, *Bourgeois Radicals: The NAACP and the Struggle for Colonial Liberation* (New York, 2014), 324–326.

64. George M. Houser, *No One Can Stop the Rain: Glimpses of Africa's Liberation Struggle* (New York, 1989).

65. Buell G. Gallagher, *Color and Conscience: The Irrepressible Conflict* (New York, 1946), 57, 214.

66. Gallagher, *Conscience*, esp. 174.

67. Gallagher, *Conscience*, 188.

68. Gallagher, *Conscience*, 175.

69. Gallagher, *Conscience*, 214–220, esp. 215.

70. Gallagher, *Conscience*, 73, 95. Gallagher was an attentive reader of Du Bois and corresponded with him during the 1930s. Long before Du Bois's paragraph on "double-consciousness" from *The Souls of Black Folk* became foundational for thinking about the place of African Americans in modern life, Gallagher quoted it (32).

71. For my understanding of Gallagher's career after he wrote *Color and Conscience*, I am indebted to Gene Zubovich. Two of Gallagher's allies among Congregationalists were Galen Weaver and Albert Palmer, both of whom had extensive experience in the missionary community of Hawaii. The missions in Hawaii were usually administered as part of "home missions" after the annexation of Hawaii in 1898, but long retained a "foreign" feel and endowed Weaver and Palmer, stalwarts of the progressive social service projects of the Congregationalists, with the authority of service abroad.

72. Buell G. Gallagher, "The Honor of a Certain Aim," *Christian Century* (December 22, 1948), 1393–1394, described his experience of the campaign.

73. For this event at the City College of New York and its place in the race-related conflicts of the era, see David E. Lavin et al., *Right Versus Privilege: The Open-Admissions Experiment at the City University of New York* (New York, 1981), and David E. Lavin and David Hyllegard, *Changing the Odds: Open Admissions and the Life Chances of the Disadvantaged* (New Haven CT, 1996).

74. Buell G. Gallagher, *Campus in Crisis* (New York, 1974).

75. It is a mark of how fully the books by Gallagher and Soper have been forgotten that neither is discussed even in so comprehensive a study as Sugrue's *Sweet Land of Liberty*, which mentions Gallagher only as the author of brief article of 1957 and says nothing about Soper.

76. Reeb's life and death was recounted immediately after his death by Duncan Howlett, *No Greater Love: The James Reeb Story* (New York, 1966).

77. Gallagher, *Conscience*, 55–56.

Chapter Twelve: Conclusion

1. Buell G. Gallagher, *Color and Conscience*, 66. Gallagher invoked Genesis 4:9: "The Lord asked Cain, 'Where is your brother, Abel?' 'I don't know,' Cain responded. 'Am I my brother's keeper?'" (KJV)

2. Recent scholarship demonstrates that American critics of the old European empires often welcomed the decolonization process on terms that benefited Americans and enhanced the political and military influence of the United States. A fine example of this scholarship is Ian Tyrrell and Jay Sexton, eds., *Empire's Twin: U. S. Anti-Imperialism From the Founding Era to the Age of Terrorism* (Ithaca NY, 2015). See, esp., Tyrrell and Sexton's summary (12) of this analysis.

3. "Washington footed much of the bill," historian Fredrik Logevall summarizes what historians have long understood, "supplied most of the weaponry, and pressed Paris leaders to hang tough when their will faltered." Logevall observes that Ho Chi Minh himself long "clung to the hope that the United States *was* different, a new kind of world power that had been born out of an anticolonial reaction and was an advocate of self-determination for all nations, large and small." Fredrik Logevall, *Embers of War: The Fall of an Empire and the Making of America's Vietnam* (New York, 2012), xxi–xxii.

4. Andrew Preston, *Sword of the Spirit, Shield of the Faith: Religion in American War and Diplomacy* (New York, 2012), 175–197.

5. Edward Said, *Orientalism* (New York, 1978). Said had remarkably little to say about missionaries, even those whose writings would lend support to his critique of Western prejudices. By not taking more seriously the writings of missionaries, Said greatly limited the scope of his inquiry, missing some deep tensions within Western discourse about the East.

6. See, e.g., Robert Irwin, *For Lust of Knowing: The Orientalists and Their Enemies* (London, 2006); Daniel Martin Varisco, *Reading Orientalism: Said and the Unsaid* (Seattle, 2007); Bernard Porter, *The Absent-Minded Imperialists: Empire, Society, and Culture in Britain* (New York, 2006); and Suzanne I. Marchand, *German*

Orientalism in the Age of Empire: Religion, Race, and Scholarship (New York, 2010), esp. xxv.

7. R. Pierce Beaver's *American Protestant Women in World Mission: A History of the First Feminist Movement in North America* (Grand Rapids MI, 1960) describes the emergence in the nineteenth century of ecumenical missionary activity by women, and is consistent with the opening of opportunities for women in the mission field. In fact, missionary women were not prominent in movements today's scholars recognize as feminist. Beaver's title leaves a false impression.

8. Dana L. Robert, *American Women in Mission: A Social History of Their Thought and Practice* (Macon GA, 1997), esp. 314–316. Robert suggests that a missionary tendency toward self-abnegation may have played a role in the passivity of missionary-connected women within and beyond the churches.

9. These included Bella Abzug, Vivian Gornick, Gloria Steinem, Robin Morgan, Shulamith Firestone, Meredith Tax, Letty Cottin Pogebrin, Betty Freidan, Florence Howe, Ellen Willis, Alix Kates Schulman, Andrea Dworkin, and Gerda Lerner. Secular Jewish women were overrepresented demographically in the leadership of second-wave feminism by several thousand percentage points. Even Kate Millett and Catherine MacKinnon, who had grown up Catholic, were not the products of a Protestant culture.

10. Ruth Harris to "Dear Pat," February 17, 1995, in Pat Patterson's possession.

11. "Molly Yard, Advocate for Liberal Causes, Dies at 93," *New York Times* (September 25, 2005); "NOW Chief Molly Yard Was 'Born a Feminist,'" *Los Angeles Times* (July 21, 1987).

12. As a result of this protest, Swarthmore put into effect a ban on sororities that stood for eighty years. Swarthmore itself celebrates these events, as illustrated in a brief sketch in one of the college's own publications, Molly Yard, "Getting Out the Vote," in *The Meaning of Swarthmore* (Swarthmore PA, 2004), 15–17.

13. Robert Cohen, *When the Old Left Was Young: Student Radicals and America's First Mass Student Movement, 1929–1941* (New York, 1993), esp. 393.

14. Yard was a key staff member of the 1950 congressional campaign of Helen Gehegan Douglas, remembered because of the success with which Douglas's opponent, Richard Nixon, depicted her as sympathetic with Communists. Much later, Yard served for a decade on the national staff of the National Organization of Women before she was asked, to her great surprise and pleasure, to become its president, a role in which she was highly effective in increasing membership and raising money.

15. "Therefore as the church is subject unto Christ, so let the wives be to their own husbands in everything" (Ephesians 5:24, KJV). For this incident, see Keller, *Harkness*, 251.

16. 1 Corinthians 11:3 and 14:34–36; Ephesians 5:22–24; Colossians 3:18; 1 Timothy 2:11–15; Titus 2:4–5, and 1 Peter 3:1. That the Christian scriptures were an obstacle to equality for women was recognized by the most important feminist ever nurtured by Protestantism, Elizabeth Cady Stanton. Her *Woman's Bible* (New York, 1895) boldly threw out passages that the freethinking Stanton deemed prejudicial toward women.

17. For an argument that classic secularization theory works reasonably well for the history of the United States, if carefully formulated and used to explain religious

liberalization as well as the appeal of more fully secular world-views, see David A. Hollinger, "Christianity and Its American Fate: Where History Interrogates Secularization Theory," in Joel Isaac, et al., *The Worlds of American Intellectual History* (New York, 2016), 280–303.

18. This liberalization is evident throughout the writings of missionary-connected Americans but is rarely studied statistically. One survey done in 1969 of 130 American and Canadian missionary children who had attended the Canadian School of West China found that two-thirds regarded themselves as less religious than their parents, and that those who continued to profess the Christian faith had adopted markedly more liberal theological views than those of their parents. See Donald Wilmott, "Canadian Schoolers," *Canadian School in West China* (Canadian School Alumni Association, 1974), cited by Mason, "Missionary Conscience," 5.

19. I emphasize the Jewish component in the immigrant transformation of the United States because Jews were not even Christians, and, more importantly, they achieved strong class position more rapidly. Jews were visible in the professions, the arts and sciences, and the corporate world. Their prominence was reinforced in the World War II era by a numerically small but culturally formidable wave of émigré intellectuals. Empowered Anglo-Protestants were obliged to contend with Jews more often than with Catholics. Both Jews and Catholics suffered discrimination, but many Anglo-Protestants who became accustomed to dealing with Jews continued until the early 1960s to regard Catholics as ignorant pawns of Rome, no more suitable partners in running the country than the much-patronized and even scorned evangelicals.

20. Charles Peirce, "The Fixation of Belief," Christian W. Kloesel, et. al., eds., *Writings of Charles Peirce: A Chronological Edition, Volume 3, 1872–1878* (Bloomington, 1986), 250, 252, originally published in *Popular Science Monthly* 12 (November 1877). Peirce was defending the cosmopolitanism of science, according to which the widest possible range of experiences is taken into account in the making of a judgment about what is true.

21. Allport's family had long been involved in missions. Three of his brothers were named after missionaries. For Allport's life and career, see Katherine Pandora, *Rebels within the Ranks: Psychologists' Critique of Scientific Authority and Democratic Realities in New Deal America* (New York, 1997). A narrower study, focusing on the development of Allport's theory of human personality through the 1930s, contains a more detailed account of his year as a missionary teacher: Ian A. M. Nicholson, *Inventing Personality: Gordon Allport and the Science of Selfhood* (Washington, 2003). Nicholson finds (58) that Allport was not interested in the religious conversion of the Turks, but was fully part of the affirmation at Robert College of "world peace, tolerance, general education, science, and social service."

22. Gordon W. Allport, *The Nature of Prejudice* (New York, 1954), esp. 261–281. Allport's hypothesis gained new popularity in recent years regarding sexual orientation and religion. Individuals and entire families who had earlier felt contempt for same-sex intimacy were changed upon learning that a respected friend or a member of their own family was gay. Robert Putnam and David Campbell establish that tolerance for religious difference increases dramatically when adherents of one religion experienced sustained contact with persons of another faith with the same class position. Putnam and Campbell, *American Grace: How Religion Divides and Unites*

Us (New York, 2010). Putnam provides one of the most lucid of recent social scientific discussions of "contact theory" in his "*E Pluribus Unum*: Diversity and Community in the Twenty-first Century: The 2006 Johan Skytte Prize Lecture," *Scandinavian Political Studies* 30 (2007). Contact theory's credibility has also been enhanced by the relative success with which black Americans with strong class position—notably, immigrants from Africa and the Caribbean—have been able to navigate the barriers created by white racism. The election of the son of a black immigrant as president of the United States in 2008 is an emblem for this development.

23. I have reflected at greater length about "the problem of solidarity" in "From Identity to Solidarity," *Daedalus* (Fall 2006), 23–31.

INDEX

A NOTE ON THE TYPE

THIS BOOK has been composed in Miller, a Scotch Roman typeface designed by Matthew Carter and first released by Font Bureau in 1997. It resembles Monticello, the typeface developed for The Papers of Thomas Jefferson in the 1940s by C. H. Griffith and P. J. Conkwright and reinterpreted in digital form by Carter in 2003.

Pleasant Jefferson ("P. J.") Conkwright (1905–1986) was Typographer at Princeton University Press from 1939 to 1970. He was an acclaimed book designer and AIGA Medalist.

The ornament used throughout this book was designed by Pierre Simon Fournier (1712–1768) and was a favorite of Conkwright's, used in his design of the *Princeton University Library Chronicle*.